TEACH YOURSELF BOOKS

latin

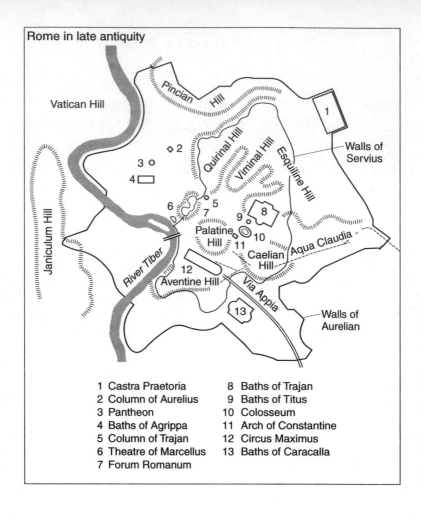

Rome in late antiquity

Vatican Hill

Pincian Hill

Janiculum Hill

Quirinal Hill

Viminal Hill

Esquiline Hill

Walls of Servius

River Tiber

Palatine Hill

Caelian Hill

Aqua Claudia

Aventine Hill

Via Appia

Walls of Aurelian

1 Castra Praetoria
2 Column of Aurelius
3 Pantheon
4 Baths of Agrippa
5 Column of Trajan
6 Theatre of Marcellus
7 Forum Romanum

8 Baths of Trajan
9 Baths of Titus
10 Colosseum
11 Arch of Constantine
12 Circus Maximus
13 Baths of Caracalla

latin

Gavin Betts

TEACH YOURSELF BOOKS

The author wishes to acknowledge the help of A.S. Henry and
L. Newnham in the detection of errors; of D.R. Blackman, G.A.
Scott, and J. Hinde in compiling the main vocabulary, and of Anne
Abersteiner and Lea Swanson in preparing the manuscript.

For UK order queries: please contact Bookpoint Ltd, 78 Milton Park, Abingdon, Oxon
OX14 4TD. Telephone: (44) 01235 400414, Fax: (44) 01235 400454. Lines are open from
9.00–6.00, Monday to Saturday, with a 24 hour message answering service.
Email address: orders@bookpoint.co.uk

For U.S.A. & Canada order queries: please contact NTC/Contemporary Publishing,
4255 West Touhy Avenue, Lincolnwood, Illinois 60646–1975, U.S.A.
Telephone: (847) 679 5500, Fax: (847) 679 2494.

Long renowned as the authoritative source for self-guided learning – with more than
30 million copies sold worldwide – the *Teach Yourself* series includes over 200 titles in
the fields of languages, crafts, hobbies, business and education.

A catalogue record for this title is available from The British Library.

Library of Congress Catalog Card Number: On file

First published in UK 2000 by Hodder Headline Plc, 338 Euston Road, London, NW1 3BH.

First published in US 2000 by NTC/Contemporary Publishing, 4255 West Touhy Avenue,
Lincolnwood (Chicago), Illinois 60646–1975 U.S.A.

The 'Teach Yourself' name and logo are registered trade marks of Hodder & Stoughton Ltd.

Copyright © 2000 Gavin Betts

Typeset by Transet Limited, Coventry, England.
Printed in Great Britain for Hodder & Stoughton Educational, a division of Hodder
Headline Plc, 338 Euston Road, London NW1 3BH by Cox & Wyman Ltd, Reading,
Berkshire.

Impression number   10 9 8 7 6 5 4 3 2
Year   2005 2004 2003 2002 2001 2000

CONTENTS

INTRODUCTION

How to use this book

Tuccia, a Roman lady who was a priestess of the goddess Vesta and who, as such, was obliged to maintain her virgin state, was on one occasion accused of unchastity. She vindicated herself by carrying water in a sieve from the Tiber to the temple of Vesta. There is, unfortunately, no similar clear-cut method for testing an ability to learn Latin, but to approach the subject in a wrong way will automatically put you at a disadvantage. If you are working on your own, your first step should be to make yourself completely familiar with the arrangement of this book, what material it contains, and how this material is presented.

The section on pronunciation, which follows in the Introduction, contains a large amount of detailed information which is meant more for future reference than for initial comprehension. It would, in fact, be somewhat unprofitable to try to master every point of Latin pronunciation without reference to whole sentences in Latin. A better plan is to skim through the information provided and to study it fully after the first five units; in this way you will be able to check the pronunciation of the words you have learnt against the rules given there. More important for a beginner than pronunciation is a knowledge of the grammatical terms given in the next section (**Glossary of grammatical terms**), as these are used at every stage to explain the structure of Latin. As much of this as possible should be absorbed before starting on Unit 1. It is important to remember the terms themselves, but it is vital to understand the concepts behind them. If full comprehension eludes you at first (as well it may, if you have no previous experience in such things), be sure to refer back to this list whenever uncertain of the meaning of a particular term.

The body of the book consists of thirty-one units, which slowly increase in size to match the increasing familiarity of the reader with the subject. Each unit consists of either two or, more often, three sections. The first section is devoted to grammar, the second contains sentences and passages in Latin for reading (together with the necessary vocabulary in the first nine units), while the third is either an excursus on a subject of interest for Latin studies or a longer Latin passage for additional reading. A key for all Latin reading exercises will be found on pp. 299–342. For those experienced in the Internet, extra reading for each unit after Unit 1 and revision exercises covering the whole book can be accessed at the website http://tylatin.org .

The sections headed .1 are carefully graded over the course of the book so that the basic (and many not so basic) features of the grammatical structure of Latin are presented in a systematic and digestible way. Each should be mastered before tackling the next as more often than not a particular section cannot be understood without a proper knowledge of its predecessors. Grammar as a whole can be divided into two parts, one which involves the forms of words, which can often be arranged in lists (as of the various forms which a first declension noun can take, p. 1), and one which deals with how these forms are used in phrases and sentences (as how we express *time when* and *time how long*, p. 40). Obviously the former must be learnt by heart, but the latter, which is called syntax, can only be fully understood by learning a general rule and by seeing actual examples of that rule. For this reason the examples quoted as illustrations are nearly always original Latin. They include famous sayings as well as sentences from ancient poets and prose writers, and every effort should be made to understand them in their entirety. By reading them carefully every time you revise a unit, you will not only better understand the grammatical point involved but also extend your vocabulary.

The reading in the .2 (and .3) sections should not be attempted with one finger on the appropriate page of the key, though full use should be made of any notes provided. A full translation of the entire exercise should be written down before the key is consulted at all. It is only by learning to analyse the forms of Latin words and patiently working out the construction of clauses and sentences that progress can be made. When you have completed your version, compare it with the key. If you have made mistakes, chase up the point of grammar involved and be sure you understand exactly why and how you went wrong. Next, read over the Latin, preferably aloud, until you are able to translate it without referring to your own version, the vocabulary, or anything else. In this way you will familiarise yourself with the constructions used and with new words.

In any language work, the acquisition of an adequate vocabulary is a problem. If you can learn words in lists, so much the better. Few, however, are able to do this to any degree, and it is generally more effective to learn a new word within the context of a sentence. To memorise some of the many short poems given in the reading exercises will be found both rewarding and enjoyable. Further, an enormous number of English words are related to Latin, and this can be a help in learning Latin vocabulary. On p. 25 a short account is given of the form this relationship can take. Often an English word differs somewhat in meaning from its Latin relative, but the very fact that there is a connection can help fix the latter in one's mind. English dictionaries which give details on the origins of words can be a treasure trove for the student of Latin.

The tables of verbs given at pp. 280–96 and the vocabulary which follows should be used from the earliest stage possible. The arrangement of both conforms to the normal pattern used in Latin reference works and will provide an easy transition to further study. The index on p. 386 is for easy and quick reference to all points of grammar in the .1 sections.

The pronunciation of Latin

By using a wide range of evidence, scholars have been able to gain a fairly complete idea of how Latin was spoken, and their findings have, to a large degree, been adopted in teaching the language. However, as Latin is no longer used as a vehicle of oral communication, we do not need to devote as much attention to its pronunciation as we would with a modern language. Some known features (e.g. hidden quantities – see below) are of interest only for historical linguistics and can be ignored for present purposes.

Latin was, to a very large degree, phonetically written, and, unlike English, nearly every letter has a consistent value. The Latin alphabet, which is the basis of our own, was made up of twenty-three letters:

A B C D E F G H I K L M N O P Q R S T V X Y Z

Today Latin is printed in both upper- and lower-case, although this distinction was not made by the Romans, who used capitals (sometimes slightly modified) exclusively. The letter **K** is a doublet of **C** and only occurs (as an alternative for it) in a very few words. **Y** and **Z** were only used in borrowed Greek words. **I** and **V** were each given two values, one as a consonant, the other as a vowel. **J**, **U** and **W** are additions in the English alphabet, and of these **U** is used in this book for the vocalic **V**, while **V** itself is used for the consonant. Up to a century ago **J** was used for consonantal **I**, but this has now been universally abandoned.

Consonants

Of the Latin consonants, **d**, **f**, **h**, **l**, **m**, **n**, **p**, **q** (which, as in English, occurs only in the combination **qu**), **r**, and **z** should be pronounced in the same way as they are when occurring by themselves in English (*dad, fad, had,* etc.; on **qu** see below). **h** is never silent as in the English *honour*; the Latin **honor**, **hōra** have the same initial sound as the English *honey*. The pronunciation of the other consonants is as follows:

b   as in English except before **s** and **t** where it is pronounced *p*: **bōs**, **brevis**, **urbs** (urps).

c   (and **k**) always as in *come*, *call* (**never** as in *city*, *civil*) except that the combination **ch** is pronounced as an emphasised **c**: **Cicerō** (kikerō), **cēna** (keyna; on the pronunciation of vowels see next subsection), **pulcher** (pulKer)

g   always as in *game*, *go* (**never** as in *gesture*, *ginger*): **gignō**, **ingrātus**.

i   (consonantal) always as *y* in *yes*, *yellow* (never as *j* in *jam*): **iam** (yam), **iungō** (yungō). On the doubling of consonantal **i** when occurring between vowels, see below, note 3.

s   always as in *sun*, *sing* (**never** as in *is*, *was*): **sum**, **fīlius**.

t   always as in *table*, *tangle* (**never** as *t* in *nation*; the Latin **nātiō** is pronounced as three syllables **nā-ti-ō**).

v   always as *w* in *wish*, *want* (**never** as a normal English *v*): **vīs** (wees), **verbum** (werbum).

x always as in *exceed* (**never** as in *example* where *x* is pronounced as *gs*): **rex, lex**.

Ideally, repeated consonants, as in **pellō** (pel-lō), **reddō** (red-dō), should both be pronounced, but this is difficult for us as it only occurs in English in compounds such as *book-keeper*.

In addition to **ch** (see above), four other consonant groups are pronounced together: **ph, th, gu** (when preceded by **n**), **qu**. Of these, **ph** and **th** are normally (but unhistorically) given their English sounds of *f* (*philosophy*) and *th* (*theory*); **gu** (preceded by **n**) and **qu** are pronounced as *gw* and *kw* respectively, e.g. **sanguis** (sangwis) but **gustus** (gus-tus), **quod** (kwod). **Su** is similarly pronounced in all the forms (and compounds and derivatives) of the two verbs **suādeō** (swādeō) and **suescō** (sweskō), in the adjective **suāvis** (swāwis), and the proper noun **Suēbī** (sweybee); elsewhere **su** always has a vocal **u** (i.e. is pronounced *su*): **suī** (su-ee), **suus** (su-us).

Vowels

As we shall see, Latin words have a stress accent as in English. In many modern European languages, including English, a stressed vowel tends to be lengthened and an unstressed one to be shortened, e.g. *extínction, accentuátion, ingenúity*. In Latin, however, each vowel, irrespective of where the accent fell, received a lengthened or shortened pronunciation, and vowels are classified accordingly as either long or short.

In dictionaries and works of reference, long vowels (usually with the exception of hidden quantities—see below) are indicated by a macron (⁻) placed above them, and short vowels are left unmarked. The technical term for the lengthened or shortened pronunciation of vowels is vowel quantity. The pronunciation of Latin vowels is as follows:

ā as in *father*: **fātum, fāma**.

a (short) a shortened version of **ā**, like *u* in *but*; not as *a* in *cat* (this sound did not exist in Latin): **amīcus, apis**.

ē as *ey* in *they*: **tē** (tey), **frētus** (freytus).

e (short) as in *net*: **enim, iter**.

ī as *ee* in *keep*: **īra** (eera), **perīculum** (pereekulum).

i   (short) as in *pit*: **inde**, **it**.
ō   as in *note*: **mōs**, **amō**.
o   (short) as in *not*: **domus**, **locus**.
ū   as *oo* in *food*: **ūnus** (oonus), **fūnus** (foonus).
u   (short) as in *put*: **bonus**, **cum**.
y   which only occurs in Greek words, should be pronounced as a long
     or short version of the French *u* or German *ü* but is normally
     assimilated to **i**.

When, in a particular word, a vowel is followed by only one consonant
or by no consonant at all, we know its quantity in that word (i.e.
whether it is long or short) from Latin poetry, which is constructed on
an entirely different principle from that of English verse (24.1/1). We
cannot, however, learn in this way the quantity of nearly all vowels
followed by two or more consonants (usually called hidden quantities,
because whether such vowels are long or short is of no consequence
for the structure of Latin verse). For this reason long vowels followed
by two or more consonants are not marked here. Many (but not all)
such cases have been determined by examining the internal structure
of Latin and the derivatives of Latin words in the Romance languages
(see 1.3), but they are usually ignored when reading Latin aloud.
Elsewhere, however, vowel quantity is important and should be learnt
with each Latin word.

Diphthongs

A diphthong is a combination of two vowels (as *oi* in *noise*), and in
Latin the more common are:

ae, pronounced as *i* in *pile* (which is really a diphthong and not a long
       i; we may represent it by I): **caelum** (kIlum), **praeda** (prIda).
au, pronounced as *ow* in *cow* (**never** as *au* in *cause*): **aurum** (owrum),
       causa (kowsa).
oe, pronounced as *oi* in *soil*: **proelium** (proi-li-um), **moenia** (moi-ni-a).

Of these combinations, **ae** is always to be read as a diphthong. The
other two very occasionally must be pronounced as two separate
vowels: **aēr** (a-eyr), **coēgī** (ko-ey-gee). This information is given in the
vocabulary. The less common Latin diphthongs are:

ei,   pronounced as *ei* in *reign* but only occurring in **heia**. Elsewhere **ei**
         is used in two ways:
         (*a*) when followed by a consonant (except in certain compounds
         of the verb **iaciō** – see below, note 4) or at the end of a word, each
         vowel is pronounced separately: **eīs** (e-ees), **meī** (me-ee);
         (*b*) when followed by a vowel, the **i** is pronounced as *y* or *yy* (see
         below, note 3).

eu,   which only occurs in **ceu, heu, neu, neuter, seu**, and in Greek proper
         names such as **Orpheus**. Its pronunciation is that of *you* but with
         the lips held closer to the mouth and with loss of the initial *y*.

ui,   which also does not have an English equivalent but is made by
         combining **u** (as in *put*) with **i**. It occurs in **huic** (**<hic**, 8.1/2), **cui**
         (**<quī**, 10.1/1*f*) and compounds of the latter. Elsewhere **ui** is not a
         diphthong and is used in two ways:
         (*a*) when preceded by **q**, the **u** is pronounced as *w* (see above): **quid**
         (kwid), **aliquis** (alikwis), **quia** (kwia);
         (*b*) when followed by a vowel and not preceded by **q** the **i** is
         pronounced *yy* (see below, note 3): **cuius** (kuy-yus).

Notes on the pronunciation of consonants and vowels

1   Combinations of vowels other than those given above do not form
    diphthongs and must be pronounced separately: **creō** (kre-ō),
    creātus (kre-ā-tus), **diū** (di-oo), **audiī** (ow-di-ee), **audiēbam** (ow-di-
    ey-bam).

2   For the Latin words included in this book, both intervocalic **i** and
    initial **i** followed by a vowel are consonantal except in **heia, Iūlus** (i-
    oo-lus), and **Trōius** (trō-i-us). When at the end of a word, or not
    intervocalic, **i** is a vowel, except when first letter of the second part
    of a compound: **bellī** (bel-lee), **clārior** (klā-ri-or), but **coniūrō** (kon-
    yoo-rō) and other words beginning with **coniu-** (these are all
    compounds with **con-**). When followed by a consonant at the
    beginning of a word **i** is always a vowel: **idem** (i-dem).

3   Intervocalic **i** is pronounced as a double consonant: **maior** (may-
    yor), **Troia** (troy-ya), **huius** (huy-yus). This does not apply when a
    word beginning with **i** is used as the second element of a
    compound: **trāiēcī** (trā-yey-kee, **<trā + iēcī**).

4 In compounds of **iaciō** *throw*, **ic** is to be pronounced as *yik*: **trāiciō** (trā-yi-ki-ō). This shorthand writing of **i** for **ii** does not occur elsewhere. In **ēiciō** (<**ē** + **iaciō**) **ēi** is a combination of **ē** with **i** used in this way.

Syllable division

A word contains as many syllables as it does vowels and diphthongs. A syllable consists of one vowel or one diphthong, either alone or with adjoining consonants: **a-rō**, **fau-cēs**. The rules for dividing words into syllables are:

(*a*) A single consonant between vowels or diphthongs is taken with the second: **a-vā-rus**, **ē-mē-ti-or**.

(b) An initial consonant (or consonants) belongs to the first syllable, a final consonant (or consonants) to the last: **ge-li-dus**, **strī-dor**, **a-mant**.

(*c*) Where two or more consonants occur between two vowels or diphthongs, the syllable division is immediately before the last consonant: **ē-mer-gō**, **in-for-tū-ni-um**. An exception to this is that **h** is disregarded (**e-le-phan-tus**), as are **r** and **l** when either is the second consonant of a group of two (**pa-tris**; for a different treatment in verse see 24.1/1).

Quantity of syllables

Just as with vowels, individual syllables in Latin words are classified as long or short. A long syllable either:

(*a*) contains a long vowel or diphthong,

or (*b*) ends with two consonants,

or (*c*) ends with a consonant and is followed by a syllable which begins with one.[1]

All other syllables are short and must contain a short vowel, which

---

[1] **x** (= **c** + **s**) and **z** (= **d** + **s**) were regarded as double consonants; consequently the syllable division in a word such as **axis** was taken as **ac-sis**, making the first syllable long. However **qu** only counts as one consonant and is therefore not divided: **se-quor**.

can only be followed by a consonant (within its syllable) if it is at the end of a word. A long syllable does not necessarily contain a long vowel or diphthong. With either (*b*) or (*c*) we may have a short vowel, and this vowel remains short although it is part of a long syllable.

If the rules in the last two subsections seem rather complicated at this stage, the following rule of thumb may help:

> **A syllable is long if it contains a long vowel or diphthong, or a vowel followed by two (or more) consonants, of which the second is not *r* or *l* (*h* is not to be counted, and *x* and *z* are double consonants). All other syllables are short.**

It is important to know the length of the syllables in a Latin word because this determines its accent.

Word accent

Each Latin word of more than one syllable (except disyllabic prepositions, which are unaccented) has a stress accent, which appears to have been similar to that in English. An acute (´) is used when the accent needs to be marked in works of reference, but in normal printed Latin it is never shown. The position of this accent is determined by the quantity of the last syllable but one, and the rule involved is called the law of the penultimate (i.e. last but one):

> **If the penultimate syllable of a word is long, it takes the accent, but, if it is short, the accent falls on the preceding syllable.**

Words of two syllables are accented on their first syllable, whether long or short; a few apparent exceptions have lost their final syllable (**illíc, illúc** and the few others that occur are marked in the vocabulary).

The effect of this rule is that the accent of a Latin word can be automatically determined. As vowel lengths are given in words and examples quoted in each unit and in the main and subsidiary vocabularies, the correct accent of each word can be seen at a glance. As a further help, it is marked in subsidiary vocabularies and most paradigms.

Latin has three monosyllabic words, **-que**, **-ve** (3.1/5) and **-ne** (3.1/8), which are attached to an immediately preceding word but which cannot be used independently: **Brūtúsque, praemióve, Áfricámne**. As these monosyllables are pronounced together with the preceding word, the accent of the latter is affected as indicated; without them these words would be accented: **Brūtus, praémiō, Áfricam**. The forms of a Latin word can also vary in accent according to the ending involved: **puélla** but **puellárum** (1.1/2); **ámō** but **amámus** (2.1/2). In every case the quantity of the penultimate syllable is the determining factor.

GLOSSARY OF GRAMMATICAL TERMS

Listed below are the most important general terms in traditional English grammar, which is the framework we will use in approaching Latin. If you are not familiar with this terminology you should study this list carefully. Start with the **parts of speech**, viz **adjective, adverb, conjunction, interjection, noun, preposition, pronoun, verb**. These are the categories into which words are classified for grammatical purposes and are the same for Latin as for English, except that Latin does not have any **article**, either **definite** (English *the*) or **indefinite** (*a, an*).

Adjective An adjective is a word which qualifies (i.e. tells us of some quality of) a noun or pronoun: *a **red** car*; *a **short** Roman*; *Cleopatra was **sensitive***; *she is **tall***.

Adverb Adverbs qualify verbs, adjectives or other adverbs: *he walks **quickly***, an ***excessively** large Gaul, my chariot was going **very slowly***. Certain adverbs can qualify nouns and pronouns: ***even** I can do that*. They may even qualify a whole clause: *we went to Greece last year; we **also** visited Istanbul*. In English many adverbs end in *-ly*.

Apposition A noun (or noun phrase) is in apposition to another noun or pronoun when it follows by way of explanation and is exactly parallel in its relation to the rest of the sentence: *we, **the rightful owners**, were evicted from our home; I, **the undersigned**, have the pleasure of telling you . . .* Occasionally clauses function in the same way (cf. note on 31.2, 4).

Attributive *Attributive* and *predicative* are the terms applied to the two ways in which adjectives can be used. An adjective used attributively forms a phrase with the noun it qualifies, and in English always comes immediately before it: ***ancient** Rome, a **high** building,* *the **famous** poet*. An adjective used predicatively tells us what is predicated of, or asserted about, a person or thing. A verb is always involved in this use, and in English a predicative adjective always, in prose, follows the noun or pronoun which it qualifies, generally with the verb coming between them: *men are **mortal**, Caesar was **bald***. This use frequently involves the verb *to be*, but there are other possibilities: *he was thought **odd**, we consider Cicero **eloquent***. All adjectives can be used in either way, with the exception of some possessive adjectives in English (4.1/4).

Auxiliary verb   Many tenses in English are formed with the present or past participle of a verb together with some part of *have* or *be* (or both); when so used the latter are called auxiliary verbs: *he **was** running when I saw him*; *I **have** read the introduction five times*; *we **have been** working for the past week*. These combinations (*was running, have read*, etc.) are called composite tenses. Other auxiliary verbs in English are *shall, will, should, would*. Latin has a much smaller number of composite tenses and a single auxiliary (**sum**) is used (cf. 14.1/2; on **īrī** as an auxiliary see 14.1/3).

Case   In any type of expression where it occurs, a noun (or pronoun) stands in a certain relationship to the other words, and this relationship is determined by the meaning we want to convey. The two sentences *my brothers bite dogs* and *dogs bite my brothers* contain exactly the same words but have opposite meanings, which are shown by the relationship in each sentence of the nouns *brothers* and *dogs* to the verb *bite*; here (as is normal in English) this relationship is indicated by word order. In Latin, where word order is used differently, it is indicated by particular case endings applied to nouns. If a noun is the subject of a verb (i.e. precedes it in a simple English sentence such as the above), it must, in Latin, be put into the nominative case with the appropriate ending; if it is the object of a verb (i.e. follows it in English), Latin puts it into the accusative case. In English we still have this system with pronouns; we say *I saw her today*, we cannot say *me saw her* because *I* is the nominative case, required here to show the subject of the verb, whereas *me* is the accusative case. With nouns in English we only have one case which can be indicated by an ending and this is the genitive: *girl's, boy's*. In Latin we have seven cases, **nominative**, **vocative**, **accusative**, **genitive**, **dative**, **ablative** and **locative** (the use of the last is very restricted).

Clause A clause is a group of words forming a sense unit and containing one finite verb, e.g. *the Gauls **feared** Caesar, I **am** sick of orgies at Baiae* (the finite verb is in bold type). We can have either **main clauses**, which can stand on their own, or **subordinating clauses**, which cannot. In the sentence *Nero bought a lion which had eaten three Christians*, the first four words constitute the main clause and this forms a complete sense unit; if, however, you were to say to a friend *which had eaten three Christians* you would risk being thought odd because as a subordinate clause it cannot be used by itself. Subordinate clauses are further divided into **adverbial**, which function as adverbs, **adjectival**, which function as adjectives, and **noun** clauses, which function as nouns.

Comparison (of adjectives and adverbs)   See **Inflexion**.

Conjugation See **Inflexion**.

Conjunction Conjunctions are joining words and do not vary in form. Some conjunctions can join clauses, phrases or individual words (e.g. *and, or*) but most have a more restricted use. Those that are used to join clauses are divided into co-ordinating conjunctions (*and, or, but*), which join a main clause to a preceding one (*I went to the theatre **but** you were not there*), and subordinating conjunctions, which subordinate one clause to another (*the doctor came **because** I was sick*).

Declension See **Inflexion**.

Finite This term is applied to those forms of verbs which can function as the verbal element of a clause. The only non-finite forms of a verb in English are participles and infinitives. We can say *Caesar defeated the Britons* because *defeated* is a finite form of the verb *to defeat*. We cannot say *Caesar to have defeated the Gauls* because *to have defeated* is an infinitive and therefore non-finite, nor can we say (as a full sentence) *Caesar having defeated the Gauls* because *having defeated* is a participle. In Latin several other parts of a verb are non-finite, viz supine, gerund and gerundive.

Gender In English we only observe natural gender (apart from such eccentricities as supposing ships feminine). If we are talking about a man we refer to him by the masculine pronoun *he*, but we refer to a woman by the feminine pronoun *she*, and we refer to a thing, such as a table or sword, by the neuter pronoun *it*. Latin, however, observes natural gender with living beings (generally), but other nouns, which may denote things, qualities and so on, are not necessarily neuter. For example, **mensa** *table* is feminine, **gladius** *sword* is masculine. This has important grammatical consequences, but the gender of individual nouns is not difficult to learn as, in most cases, it is shown by the ending.

Imperative   See **Mood**.

Indicative   See **Mood**.

Infinitive   Infinitives are those parts of a verb which in English are normally preceded by *to*, e.g. *to eat, to be eaten, to have eaten, to have been eaten*. These are, respectively, the present active, present passive, past active and past passive infinitives of the verb *eat*. As in English, a Latin verb has active and passive infinitives, and infinitives exist in different tenses. A Latin infinitive is not preceded by anything corresponding to the English *to*.

Inflexion   The form of adjectives, adverbs, nouns, pronouns and verbs changes in English and in Latin (but much more so) according to the requirements of meaning and grammar. Inflexion is the overall term for such changes and covers **conjugation**, which applies only to verbs (2.1/1), **declension**, which applies to nouns, pronouns and adjectives (which include participles) (1.1/1, 8.1/1, etc., 4.1/1, etc.), and **comparison**, which applies to adjectives and adverbs (19.1/1 & 2). The term **conjugation** is also used for the categories into which verbs are classified, and the term **declension** is similarly used for those of nouns and adjectives.

Interjection   Interjections are words used to express one's emotions. They do not form part of sentences and have only one form (i.e. are not subject to inflexion). Examples are: **euge!** *bravo!* **heu!** *alas!*

Intransitive   This is a term applied to verbs which cannot, because of their meaning, take a normal object, e.g. *come, die, go*. The opposite term is **transitive**; transitive verbs can take an object, *make, hit, repair*. *He hit the man* is a perfectly possible sentence but *he dies the man* is nonsense. Sometimes in English we have a pair of verbs, one transitive and the other intransitive, which are obviously connected in sense and etymology, as *to fall* and *to fell*. We can say *John is falling from the tree* but *John is falling the tree* is without sense. If we mean *John is causing the tree to fall*, we can say *John is felling the tree*; hence *to fall* is intransitive, *to fell* is transitive. Some verbs are transitive in English but intransitive in Latin and vice versa. There are also a number of verbs in English which can be either transitive or intransitive, while their Latin equivalents are exclusively one or the other, e.g. *Caesar **burned** the camp of the Gauls* (transitive); *Nero fiddled while Rome **burned*** (intransitive). The Latin **ūrō** *burn*, however, can only be used transitively.

Mood   Mood is a term applied to verbs. Every finite form of a verb is in one of three moods, which are:

> **Indicative**, to express a fact: *the doctor **operated** on me yesterday*.
> **Subjunctive**, to express something that might happen, might be happening, or might have happened: *if I **were** you, I **would do** this* (in Latin both verbs would be in the subjunctive).
> **Imperative**, to give an order: ***do** this immediately!*

There is also a fourth, the infinitive mood, which is solely taken up by infinitives. The other parts of the Latin verbs (participles, etc.) are not considered to be in any mood.

Noun   A noun is a naming word: *book, river, truth, Cicero, Rome*. Proper nouns are those we write with a capital letter, all others are common nouns.

Number   A noun, or pronoun, or verb is either singular or plural in Latin just as in English.

Object   A noun or pronoun which is the object of an active verb suffers or receives the action of that verb: *Vergil wrote an **epic**; Claudius executed many **senators**; Augustus rebuilt **Rome***. By definition we cannot have an object of this sort after intransitive verbs or (normally) verbs in the passive voice. It is sometimes called a **direct object** to distinguish it from an **indirect object** which we get after verbs of saying and giving: *he told a story to **the child***. In English we can express this slightly differently: *he told **the child** a story*; but *child* is still the indirect object because the direct object is *story*.

Participle   Participles are those forms of a verb which function as adjectives: *the **running** horses, a **fallen** tree*.

Person There are three persons, **first, second** and **third. First person** is the person(s) speaking, i.e. *I* or *we*; **second person** is the person(s) spoken to, i.e. *you*; and **third person** is the person(s) or thing(s) spoken about, i.e. *he, she, it, they.* The term **person** has reference to pronouns and also to verbs because finite verbs must agree with their subject in **number** and **person**. Naturally when we have a noun as subject of a verb, e.g. *the dog ran across the forum*, the verb is in the third person.

Phrase A phrase is an intelligible group of words which does not have a finite verb: *into the woods, Hannibal's five tired elephants.* A phrase can only be used by itself in certain circumstances, as in answer to a question.

Predicative See **Attributive**.

Preposition Prepositions are invariable words which govern a noun or pronoun and show the relationship of the noun or pronoun to the rest of the sentence: *Horace went **to** Greece; we live **in** Athens; I saw Julia **with** him.*

Pronoun Pronouns stand in place of nouns. The English personal pronouns are: *I, you, he, she, it, we, they.* Other words such as *this, that* can function as pronouns (*I do not like **that**!*) or as adjectives (*I do not like **that** habit!*); for convenience we shall call them demonstrative pronouns. For the reflexive pronoun see 9.1/4 and for the relative pronoun see 10.1/2.

Sentence A sentence is a unit of speech which normally contains at least one main clause. It may be either a statement, question or command. In English and in Latin we mark the end of a sentence with a full-stop, a question mark or an exclamation mark.

Stem The stem is the form of a word before endings are applied. In Latin, nouns have only one stem, which sometimes cannot be deduced from the nominative singular. With verbs in Latin we have different stems for some, but not all, tenses. English verbs such as *to break* are comparable; *break-* is the present stem and to it the ending of the third person singular is added (giving *breaks*); *brok-* is the past stem, giving us *brok-en* for the past participle.

Subject The subject of a clause is the noun or pronoun which governs its verb. In English and Latin a finite verb's person and number are determined by the subject. We cannot say *I is* because *I* is the first person pronoun and *is* is third person; we must use the first person (singular) form *am*. Likewise we must say *we are* and not *we am* because *we* is plural. An easy way to find the subject is to put *who* or *what* in front of the verb; with the sentence *the ship was hit by a submerged rock*, we ask the question *what was hit by a submerged rock?* and the answer, *the ship*, is the subject of the clause.

Subjunctive   See **Mood**.

Tense   Tense is a term applied to verbs. Every finite form of a verb, as well as participles and infinitives, indicates that the action or state expressed takes place in a particular time. The verb in *I am sick* refers to the present, in *I will be sick* to the future. These temporal states are called tenses, and in Latin we have six: **future, future perfect, present, imperfect, perfect** and **pluperfect**.

Transitive   See **Intransitive**.

Verb   A verb, when finite, is the **doing** or **being** word of its clause. It must agree with the subject of the clause in **person** and **number**, and it will also show the time in which the clause is set (**tense**). For non-finite forms of verbs see **Finite**. A finite verb varies according to **person, number, tense, mood** and **voice**.

Voice   This term is applied to verbs, whether finite or non-finite. There are two voices, **active** and **passive**. The subject of an active verb is the doer of the action: *the centurion **lifted** his shield*. With a passive verb the subject suffers or receives the action: *the shield **was lifted** by the centurion*.

ABBREVIATIONS

a. *or* acc.	accusative	lit.	literally
abl.	ablative	*ll.*	lines
act.	active	m. *or* m	masculine
adj.	adjective	n. *or* n	neuter
adv.	adverb	n. *or* nom.	nominative
c.	**circā**, about	n.o.p.	no other parts
cf.	**confer**, compare	pass.	passive
compar.	comparative	perf.	perfect
conj.	conjunction	pers.	person
dat.	dative	pl.	plural
exclam.	exclamatory	plpf.	pluperfect
f. *or* f	feminine	pple.	participle
f.	following	prep.	preposition
fut.	future	pres.	present
gen.	genitive	pron.	pronoun
imp.	imperative	reflex.	reflexive
impf.	imperfect	s.	singular
ind.	indicative	subj.	subjunctive
indecl.	indeclinable	sup.	supine
inf.	infinitive	supl.	superlative
interr.	interrogative	tr.	transitive *or*
interj.	interjection		translate
intr.	intransitive	v. *or* voc.	vocative
l.	line	viz	that is to say

Round brackets ( ) contain explanatory material, supplementary words or a literal translation; in the vocabulary round brackets are also used to indicate alternative forms. Square brackets [ ] are used in translations for words which are required by English idiom but have no equivalent in the Latin original; not all such words are marked in this way. Square brackets are also used to supply missing words.

+ means *in conjunction with, compounded with,* or *followed by.*

< means *is derived from.*

> means *produces.*

UNIT 1

1.1 Grammar

1.1/1 Nouns in Latin

In English the gender of a noun is determined by its meaning; *man* is masculine, *girl* is feminine, *car* is neuter, and when referring to these we would say *he, she, it* respectively. In Latin, however, the gender of a noun is often arbitrary and does not necessarily indicate anything about what it denotes. While, for example, **puella** *girl* is feminine and **vir** *man* is masculine, **insula** *island* is feminine, and **mūrus** *wall* is masculine, though **bellum** *war* is, understandably, neuter. More often than not we cannot see why a particular noun is a particular gender. It is, however, generally possible to tell the gender of a noun by its ending in the nominative and genitive singular, and it is also according to these endings that Latin nouns are grouped into five classes, which are called declensions. Each declension has a distinctive set of endings which indicate both case and number (see **Glossary of grammatical terms**), just as in English we have *child, child's, children, children's*, though Latin distinguishes more cases. To go through the list of all possible forms of a noun is to *decline* it.

1.1/2 First declension

All nouns in the first declension end in **-a** and (with very few exceptions) have the same set of endings. In the table below **puella** *girl* is declined. Notice that the endings are added to the stem **puell-**, which is invariable.

	SINGULAR		PLURAL	
Nominative	**puéll-a**	*a (the) girl*	**puéll-ae**	*(the) girls*
Vocative	**puéll-a**	*O girl*	**puéll-ae**	*O girls*
Accusative	**puéll-am**	*a (the) girl*	**puéll-ās**	*(the) girls*
Genitive	**puéll-ae**	*of a (the) girl*	**puell-árum**	*of (the) girls*
Dative	**puéll-ae**	*to or for a (the) girl*	**puéll-īs**	*to or for (the) girls*
Ablative	**puéll-ā**	*(by, with or from) a (the) girl*	**puéll-īs**	*(by, with or from) (the) girls*

Notes

1 Latin does not have either a definite or an indefinite article (in English *the* and *a/an*). **Puella** can mean either *a girl* or *the girl* according to the context.
2 Some endings (**-a, -ae, -īs**) have more than one function. The context will always show which function is involved.
3 Most nouns of the first declension are feminine. The few masculines are almost always terms involving male occupations, e.g. **nauta** *sailor*, **agricola** *farmer*.

1.1/3 Basic uses of cases

In English the only case ending in nouns is that of the genitive (as in *boy's*, *men's*, etc.). Elsewhere the function of a noun is shown by its position in a clause (the difference in meaning between *the policeman hit the demonstrator* and *the demonstrator hit the policeman* depends solely on word order) or by a preposition: *the demonstrator was hit by a car* (here the part played by the car is indicated by the preposition *by*). In Latin each of the six cases has its own particular functions, which are:

(*a*) The subject of a clause must be put in the **nominative**.
(*b*) When we address a person the **vocative** is used; this is often preceded by **Ō** and always followed by a mark of punctuation.
(*c*) The direct object of a verb must be put in the **accusative**; this case is also used after certain prepositions.
(*d*) The **genitive** expresses possession: *Caesar's chariot* (in English we can also say *the chariot of Caesar*).
(*e*) The **dative** expresses the indirect object after verbs of giving and saying. In *Calpurnia gave a new toga to Caesar* the direct object is

toga (answering the question *gave what?*), and the indirect object is *Caesar* (*gave to whom?*). Note that in English we can also say, with the same meaning, *Calpurnia gave Caesar a new toga.* In either case the Latin would be the same, with *toga* in the accusative and *Caesar* in the dative. As we will see, the dative has other uses as well. They can nearly always be translated by *to* or *for.*

(*f*) The uses of the **ablative** vary according to the noun involved and its context. With living beings such as **puella** it is used in conjunction with certain prepositions (**ā puellā** *by a* (*the*) *girl*, **cum puellīs** *with* (*the*) *girls*) and in two constructions we shall meet subsequently (12.1/1 and 20.1/1).

1.1/4 Word order

This subsection is given here because it is relevant to the exercise which follows. As, however, it deals with some classes of Latin words which are the subject of subsequent units, it should be re-studied after further progress has been made.

Because of case endings, word order in Latin is far more flexible than in English. In a simple sentence containing subject, verb, object, such as *Julia loves Portia*, the standard word order in Latin would be subject, object, verb: **Iūlia Portiam amat**. This places no emphasis on any particular word. If we vary this we add emphasis to the word or words which are no longer in their normal position. **Portiam Iūlia amat** would imply *it is Portia that Julia loves*. The beginning and end of a clause are emphatic positions for words that do not normally belong there, and so in **amat Portiam Iūlia** we would be emphasising both **amat** and **Iūlia**. The normal position for adverbs and adverbial phrases is immediately before the word they qualify: **Iūlia Portiam minus amat** *Julia loves Portia less*; this applies particularly to negatives: **Iūlia Portiam nōn amat** *Julia does not love Portia*. Adjectives when used attributively generally come after their noun: **Iūlia pulchra** *the beautiful Julia*. The same applies to genitives: **fīlia Iūliae** *Julia's daughter*; except that when a noun has with it both an adjective and noun in the genitive we normally have **pulchra Iūliae fīlia** *Julia's beautiful daughter*. As in English, prepositions come before the word they govern: **Iūlia in īnsulā cum Portiā est** *Julia is on the island with Portia.*

Word order in Latin poetry is somewhat freer than in prose. As many sentences and passages in this book have been taken from Latin poets, an order of words will often be found which varies from the prose norm. The following advice is applicable everywhere:

(*a*) Punctuation is meant to help you understand what a sentence means, and will often indicate where a clause or phrase begins and ends.

(*b*) Every word should be parsed (grammatically defined). This, taken in combination with the basic meaning of the word, must give at least a clue to its meaning in a particular context.

(*c*) The order given above for negatives and prepositions is almost never varied, that for adverbs seldom.

1.2 Latin reading

This section will contain Latin sentences and, later, passages which you should study carefully and translate, preferably in writing, before consulting the key at the end of the book. 6–10 below are phrases and would not occur on their own except in answer to questions. Note that long vowels, which are marked in grammatical sections, are not indicated in sentences and passages for reading; this is normal practice in editions of Latin texts. You must, therefore, decide on ambiguous cases from the context; e.g. in 2 we could have **taberna** *(nominative or vocative) or* **tabernā** *(ablative), but as the word comes after the preposition* **in** *which can govern (i.e. be followed by) the ablative, we must have* **tabernā***.*

1 Ubi sunt nautae?
2 Nautae in taberna sunt.
3 In tabernis puellae non sunt.
4 Ubi est Roma?
5 Roma in Italia est.
6 Aqua vitae.
7 Insula agricolarum.
8 Incolis Hispaniae et Italiae.
9 Victoriarum Romae.
10 In tabernis nautarum.

1.2/1 Vocabulary

Each .2/1 subsection (up to Unit 9) contains the new vocabulary for the preceding Latin sentences or passages, apart from words discussed in the section on grammar.

It is normal practice in Latin dictionaries and lists of Latin words to give the nominative singular of a noun, its genitive (generally in abbreviated form), and its gender. Hence **amīcitia, -ae** *(f)* friendship *means that the nominative singular of this noun is* **amīcitia,** *its genitive singular is* **amīcitiae,** *and it is feminine; this information places a noun in its correct grammatical pigeonhole as only first declension nouns have a nominative singular in* -a *and genitive singular in* -ae.

Verbs are listed separately at the end of each vocabulary.

Section A
　agrícola, -ae (m) *farmer*
　áqua, -ae (f) *water*
　et (conj.) *and*
　Hispánia, -ae (f) *Spain*
　in (prep. + abl.) *in, on*
　íncola, -ae (m *or* f) *inhabitant*
　ínsula, -ae (f) *island*
　Itália, -ae (f) *Italy*
　naúta, -ae (m) *sailor*
　nōn (adv.) *no, not*

　Rŏma, -ae (f) *Rome*
　tabérna, -ae (f) *tavern*
　úbi . . .? (interrogative adv.) *where . . .?*
　victória, -ae (f) *victory*
　vīta, -ae (f) *life*

Section B
　est *is, there is*
　sunt *are, there are*

When **est** and **sunt** are used to mean *there is, there are,* the noun which in English would immediately follow *is/are* must be in the nominative (cf. 2.1/4): **in insulā tabernae sunt** *there are taverns on the island* (depending on the context, this can also mean *the taverns are on the island*).

1.3 Excursus

Latin and its varieties

Although some languages, such as Basque or that of the Etruscans, stand in complete isolation, most can, on the basis of vocabulary and grammar, be classified into families within which two members may be as parent to child, sibling to sibling, or may have a more distant relationship. The family group to which Latin and English belong is called Indo-European; and what is for us the more interesting part of its family tree (five smaller branches have been omitted) can be represented as follows:

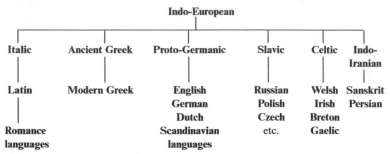

Indo-European

Italic	Ancient Greek	Proto-Germanic	Slavic	Celtic	Indo-Iranian
Latin	Modern Greek	English	Russian	Welsh	Sanskrit
		German	Polish	Irish	Persian
		Dutch	Czech	Breton	
Romance		Scandinavian	etc.	Gaelic	
languages		languages			

The original Indo-Europeans, who lived in what is now western Russia, were illiterate. It was not until long after migration, which seems to have started soon after 3000 BC, that their various descendants learnt the art of writing. The oldest Roman record, in the form of an inscription on stone, dates from the sixth century BC, although other branches in the Indo-European family attained literacy earlier. Latin literature, however, begins for us at the end of the third century BC with the comedian Plautus (other authors of the same date or earlier survive only in quotations), and we call the language of this period **Early Latin**. **Classical Latin**[1] was the language of poetry and formal prose writings (speeches, philosophical treatises, etc.) which developed with Cicero (17.3) and his contemporaries in the first half of the first century BC. Although styles changed, this became the literary norm and was used with little variation by all subsequent authors who wrote in the Roman tradition. The language of writers of the first century AD and later is sometimes called **Silver Latin** to distinguish it from that of the previous century, the Golden Age, but the difference is more a stylistic than a linguistic one. Classical Latin is the standard against which varieties of Latin are judged. These include:

---

[1]This term is sometimes restricted solely to the language of Cicero and some other authors of the first century BC.

(a) *Vulgar Latin*

We know that even Cicero himself did not habitually use formal literary Latin in everyday speech. The uneducated stratum of Roman society would have understood it to a degree but would have spoken a much simpler variety of Latin, one less bound by rules and very receptive of new elements. This language is called Vulgar Latin (from **vulgus** *mob*); it was this, not Classical Latin, that subsequently developed into the Romance languages (French, Spanish, Italian, Portuguese, Romanian) because, despite all the prestige of the latter, the former was the genuine spoken language. The most important piece of literature in Vulgar Latin is St Jerome's translation of the Bible (the **Vulgate**). His choice of language was deliberate; he wanted to reach the common man. The variety of Vulgar Latin used in many Christian writings is sometimes called **Christian Latin**.

(b) *Medieval Latin*

This was the common language for the intelligentsia of the Middle Ages in those parts of Europe where western Christianity, which was centred on Rome, had been established. This included some countries, such as Britain, where a Romance language was not spoken. It was intimately connected with religion and what remained of Roman culture, particularly law. Medieval Latin was an artificial language inasmuch as it was learnt at school as a second language after whatever vernacular a person had been exposed to from birth, although the tradition between it and Classical Latin was unbroken. The two differ in some points of grammar; the vocabulary of Medieval Latin was considerably enlarged by new formations and words taken from the vernacular languages.

(c) *Renaissance Latin*

The scholars of the Renaissance had little respect for the intellectual achievements of the Middle Ages and they regarded Medieval Latin as degenerate. They strove to get back to classical standards and many took Cicero (17.3) as the model for their prose style (almost all scholarly works were written in Latin). Classical Latin, so re-created, remained the general language of scholarship until the eighteenth century, even being used for scientific works, as e.g. Newton's *Principia Mathematica*; a small part, botanical Latin, is still with us.

(d) *Church Latin*

The tradition of Latin within the Roman Catholic Church was very strong up to comparatively recent years. Church Latin has always had a strong medieval flavour in its grammar and vocabulary and is given an Italian pronunciation.

UNIT 2

For this and all subsequent units extra reading will be found at the Internet website http://tylatin.org .

2.1 Grammar

2.1/1 Verbs in Latin

Auxiliary verbs (*shall/will, have, be*, etc.) are used to form most tenses of an English verb (*I shall teach, he has taught, we will be taught*), but in Latin this is confined to certain passive tenses and a special type of future. Elsewhere, the person, number, tense, voice (and also mood – see 13.1/1 and 21.1/1) are shown by the stem and ending. For example, we can tell by the stem and ending that **amábant** is third person plural, imperfect indicative active of the verb **amō** *I love*, and therefore means *they were loving* or *used to love*. It is superfluous to add the Latin for *they* (unless for emphasis), as this is part of the information conveyed by the ending.

In Latin, verbs, like nouns, are classified into different groups, called conjugations, and of these there are four. This classification is determined by the final letter of the present stem, which is **a** in the first conjugation, **e** in the second, a consonant in the third,[1] and **i** in the fourth. This stem, which is used for all parts of the present tense, is given a suffix to form the imperfect stem. Latin verbs are always quoted by the first person singular present indicative and the present infinitive. The following table shows how we form the present and imperfect stems from these:

---

[1]A small number of third conjugation verbs have a stem ending in **u**, e.g. **ruō** *rush*. For **-iō** verbs of the third conjugation see 7.1/3.

	PRESENT ACTIVE INDICATIVE	PRESENT ACTIVE INFINITIVE	PRESENT STEM	IMPERFECT STEM
I	ámō *I love*	amáre *to love*	ama-	amā-ba-
II	monéō *I warn*	monére *to warn*	mone-	monē-ba-
III	régō *I rule*	régere *to rule*	reg-	reg-ēba-
IV	audío *I hear*	audíre *to hear*	audi-	audi-ēba-

The underlined forms do not fit the overall pattern. We would expect **amaō** and not **amō** (the latter is, in fact, contracted from **amaō**) and **regre** not **regere** (**regre** was apparently thought difficult to pronounce and a vowel was inserted between the **g** and **r** on the analogy of the other infinitives). The identification of second and fourth conjugation verbs is simple; the former always end in **-eō** in the first person singular present, the latter in **-iō**. To distinguish, however, between first and third conjugation verbs we must know the infinitive.

2.1/2 Present indicative active

For the meaning of **indicative** *and* **active** *look up* **Mood** *and* **Voice** *in the* **Glossary of grammatical terms**.

To form this tense we take the present stem and, for the first, second and fourth conjugations, add the endings **-ō, -s, -t, -mus, -tis, -nt** with slight modifications in **ámō** (see above) and **aúdiunt**, which should be carefully noted.

SINGULAR   PLURAL
   I
1 **ámō** *I love, am loving, do love*   **amā́-mus** *we love,* etc.
2 **ámā-s** *you* (s.) *love,* etc.   **amā́-tis** *you* (pl.) *love,* etc.
3 **áma-t** *he, she, it loves,* etc.   **áma-nt** *they love,* etc.
   II
1 **móne-ō** *I warn, am warning, do warn*   **moné-mus** *we warn,* etc.
2 **móné-s** *you* (s.) *warn,* etc.   **moné-tis** *you* (pl.) *warn,* etc.
3 **móne-t** *he, she, it warns,* etc.   **móne-nt** *they warn,* etc.
   IV
1 **aúdi-ō** *I hear, am hearing, do hear*   **audí-mus** *we hear,* etc.
2 **aúdī-s** *you* (s.) *hear,* etc.   **audí-tis** *you* (pl.) *hear,* etc.
3 **aúdi-t** *he, she, it hears,* etc.   **aúdi-unt** *they hear,* etc.

In the third conjugation we have an obvious difficulty. Adding the above endings we would get awkward combinations of consonants in five out of the six forms, and in these cases a vowel is inserted, as in the present infinitive active:

1	**rég-ō** *I rule, am ruling, do rule*	**rég-imus** *we rule,* etc.
2	**rég-is** *you* (s.) *rule,* etc.	**rég-itis** *you* (pl.) *rule,* etc.
3	**rég-it** *he, she, it rules,* etc.	**rég-unt** *they rule,* etc.

Notes

1 In English we have different forms of the present tense, *I love, I am loving, I do love* and so on. There are distinctions in usage between these forms, but as Latin has only one we must decide from the context which English form we should use to translate a Latin verb in the present tense. In one context **mónent** might mean *they warn*, in another *they are warning* or *are they warning*, in another *they do warn* or *do they warn*.

2 The Latin second person singular, **ámās, mónēs**, etc. is always used when addressing one person; the plural, **amātis, monētis**, etc. when addressing more than one person. Latin has a distinction here which we do not have in English. Latin does not, however, have separate familiar and polite forms of the second person as we find in French, German and other languages.

3 The vowel of the stem in the first, second and fourth conjugations is sometimes short, sometimes long, according to a regular pattern. The inserted **i** in the third conjugation is always short.

4 In vocabularies and dictionaries the part of a Latin verb which is listed alphabetically (the lemma) is the first person singular present indicative (followed by the present infinitive), and it is by this form that we refer to a verb. In English, however, our practice is different. Verbs are listed and quoted by the present infinitive; it is under *be* that the forms *am, is, are,* etc. are to be found in an English dictionary. These two conventions are combined in Latin–English dictionaries. **Amō** is what we look up and it is explained as *to love* or *love*, although the meaning of the actual form is *I love*.

2.1/3 Imperfect indicative active

This tense would be more aptly called the **past imperfect**. It has two main uses:

(*a*) to express continuous action in the past, when it is translated *I was loving*, etc.

(*b*) to express habitual action in the past, when it is translated *I used to love*, etc.

The context of a passage shows which meaning we should choose. In isolated sentences it may often be translated either way.

As we have seen above (2.1/1), the stem for the imperfect indicative is formed by taking the present stem and, for the first and second conjugations, adding **-ba-**, for the third and fourth, adding **-ēba-**. To this stem we add endings identical with those for the present active indicative of first and second conjugation verbs, except for the first person singular.

		I	II	III	IV
SINGULAR	1	amābam	monēbam	regēbam	audiēbam
		I was loving, used to love	*I was warning, used to warn*	*I was ruling, used to rule*	*I was hearing, used to hear*
	2	amābās	monēbās	regēbās	audiēbās
	3	amābat	monēbat	regēbat	audiēbat
PLURAL	1	amābāmus	monēbāmus	regēbāmus	audiēbāmus
	2	amābātis	monēbātis	regēbātis	audiēbātis
	3	amābant	monēbant	regēbant	audiēbant

Note: A third but not so common meaning is *began to* (*I began to love*, etc.) (**inceptive imperfect**).

2.1/4 Present and imperfect indicative of *sum* (I am)

The verb *to be* is irregular in English, as is its equivalent in many other languages, including Latin. The present indicative of **sum** is conjugated:

SINGULAR	PLURAL
1 **sum** *I am*	**súmus** *we are*
2 **es** *you* (s.) *are*	**éstis** *you* (pl.) *are*
3 **est** *he, she, it is*	**sunt** *they are*

INFINITIVE **ésse** *to be*

The imperfect indicative has the same endings as other verbs but the stem is **era-**: **éram, érās, érat, erā́mus, erā́tis, érant**. The meaning is *I was, you* (s.) *were*, etc. (see also 4.1/6).

The finite forms of **sum** are always followed by the nominative because it does not express an action inflicted by the subject on an object. **Sum** equates what follows with what precedes: **nauta sum** *I am a sailor* (i.e. *I = sailor*); **Iūlia puella erat** *Julia was a girl.* See also 15.1/3.

2.1/5 Agreement of verb and subject

We have already seen how a pronoun, if the subject of a verb, need not be expressed, except for emphasis (2.1/1). **Regēbant** means *they were ruling*, **monēmus** *we warn.*[1] When we have a subject expressed, the verb must agree with it in *person* and *number*. In **nauta puellam amat** *the sailor loves the girl,* we must have **amat** (third person singular) because **nauta** is singular and third person (if we were referring to the sailor by a pronoun we would use the third person pronoun *he*). To say **nauta puellam amant** would be as ungrammatical in Latin as to say in English *the sailor love the girl.* **Amat**, in addition to being third singular, is also present tense, active voice, and indicative mood.

2.2 Latin reading

As the sentences below are more difficult than those in Unit 1 and do not fall so readily into English, it is necessary to approach them in a logical and systematic way. The following steps are suggested:

(*a*) Examine each word with reference to its meaning and ending (if it has one) and parse it fully.
(*b*) Mark all finite verbs. This will indicate the number of clauses.
(*c*) By observing the punctuation, the position of the finite verbs (which normally come last in their clauses) and conjunctions, define where each clause begins and ends.
(*d*) Taking each clause separately, see how each word relates to the finite verb in its clause.
(*e*) See from the conjunctions how the clauses are related to each other, and work out the overall meaning of the sentence.

---

[1]For how Latin expresses *he/she/it* see 8.1/2.

In the sentence **Barca incolas Hispaniae concitat** we would apply these steps as follows:

(*a*) **Barca**: a proper noun, which could be either **Barca** nominative singular, or **Barcā** ablative singular (vowel quantities are not marked in the reading exercises; see note at the beginning of 1.2); it cannot be vocative because it is neither preceded by **Ō** nor followed by a mark of punctuation. As, however, nouns denoting living beings are not used in the ablative without a preposition (1.1/3*f*; the other two possibilities we may disregard at this stage) we must have the nominative here, and therefore **Barca** must be the subject of the sentence, or at least part of it.

incolās: we know from 1.2/1 that we have a noun of the first declension **incola** *inhabitant*. Can **incolās** be a form of this noun? From 1.1/2 we see that it is, in fact, the accusative plural.

Hispāniae could be either genitive singular, dative singular or nominative plural of **Hispānia**, which is also a first declension word (it cannot be vocative plural for same reasons as given for **Barca**); we must suspend judgement until we have completed the clause.

concitat: 2.2/1 gives us a verb **concitō, -āre** *stir up*, and the table of the first conjugation (2.1/2) shows that **concitat** must be third person singular, present indicative active of this verb.

(*b*) and (*c*) **Concitat** is the only finite verb and therefore we have only one clause.

(*d*) and (*e*) **Concitat** means *he/she/it stirs up* according to the context if we do not have a subject expressed. We have, however, already decided that **Barca** is nominative singular and therefore must be the subject (we note in passing that the verb is singular to agree with the singular subject). **Barca concitat** means *Barca stirs up*. **Incolās** is accusative and, as it is not preceded by a preposition, it can only be the object of the verb, **concitat**.

Hispāniae as nominative plural can be ruled out as we already have a subject and the verb is singular; as genitive it would mean *of Spain*, as dative *to* or *for Spain*. The sense indicates *of Spain*, as a dative would require a verb with a different meaning (*give, say,* etc.).

The meaning of the whole is *Barca stirs up the inhabitants of Spain.*

In the sentence **ubi appropinquabant, pecuniam nautis dabamus** our steps would be:

(*a*) **Ubi** conjunction meaning *when* (*where* . . . ? is ruled out because we have no question mark at the end of the sentence); **appropinquābant** third person plural imperfect indicative active of **appropinquō, -āre** *approach*; **pecūniam** accusative singular of **pecūnia, -ae** *money*; **nautīs** dative or ablative plural of **nauta, -ae** *sailor*; **dabāmus** first person plural imperfect indicative active of **dō, dare** *give*.

(*b*) There are two finite verbs, **appropinquābant** and **dabāmus**, and, therefore, we have two clauses.

(*c*) We have a comma after **appropinquābant** and it is preceded by a conjunction **ubi**; it is reasonable to suppose that these two words constitute one clause and that the following words form the second.

(*d*) In the first clause we do not have a subject expressed and so the verb must mean *they were approaching* or *they used to approach*; **ubi** introduces the clause. In the second clause **pecūniam** is accusative and therefore must be the object of **dabāmus**. Together the two words must mean *we were giving money* or *we used to give money*. **Nautīs** denotes living beings and is not used with a preposition and therefore must be dative, not ablative; its meaning is *to* or *for the sailors*, but the verb **dabāmus** obviously indicates the former (*give to the sailors*). Therefore the meaning of the second clause is *we used to give money to the sailors* or *we were giving money to the sailors*.

(*e*) The first clause is introduced by a subordinating conjunction **ubi** *when* and so the second clause is the main clause. The meaning of the sentence, therefore, is *when they were approaching we were giving money to the sailors* or *when they used to approach* (or simply *when they approached*) *we used to give money to the sailors*. The first version would imply that the subject of *were approaching* was a group other than the sailors. This might be appropriate in a particular context, but when we have the sentence in isolation we would more naturally suppose that it was the sailors who were approaching. Consequently the second version is preferable.

In sentences 3 and 6 below, the object of the second verb is the same as that of the first and so need not be repeated; in English we must supply a pronoun. In sentence 4 **Sicilia** is in apposition to **insula** (cf. *the river Nile*) but English idiom requires the insertion of *of*.

1 Primo amicitiam incolarum rogabat.
2 Feminas Galliae non monebatis et nunc in viis ambulant.
3 Italiam semper amabam, et nunc amo.
4 In insula Sicilia pugnabamus sed incolae amicitiam negabant.
5 Cur agricolas Graeciae superas?
6 Amicitiam puellarum sperabatis, O nautae, sed non impetratis.
7 Feminae Graeciae cum agricolis Italiae erant sed amicitiam negabant et pecuniam semper rogabant.
8 Feminae fabulam de Graecia narramus.
9 Agricola poetis viam non monstrat.
10 In viis Romae ambulant et poetas semper audiunt.
11 Cum nautis Galliae ambulatis, O feminae.
12 In taberna nautas monebamus sed semper pugnabant.
13 Ubi feminae Graeciae in Italia habitabant, cum agricolis Hispaniae pugnabam.
14 Poetae agricolas saepe concitant ubi fabulas de feminis Galliae narrant.

2.2/1 Vocabulary

Section A

amīcítia, -ae (f) *friendship*
Bárca, -ae (m) *Barca, a Carthaginian general*
cum (prep. + abl.) *together with, with*
cūr . . . ? (interrogative adv.) *why . . .?*
dē (prep. + abl.) *about*
fábula, -ae (f) *story*
fémina, -ae (f) *woman, female*
Gállia, -ae (f) *Gaul*
Graécia, -ae (f) *Greece*

nunc (adv.) *now*
pecūnia, -ae (f) *money*
poéta, -ae (m; 3 syllables) *poet*
prīmō (adv.) *at first*
saépe (adv.) *often*
sed (conj.) *but*
sémper (adv.) *always*
Sicília, -ae (f) *Sicily*
úbi (conj.) *when* introducing an adverbial clause (as well as *where . . .?*)
vía, -ae (f) *road, street*

Section B

ámbulō, -ā́re *walk*	**nárrō, -ā́re** *narrate, tell*
appropínquō, -ā́re *approach*	**négō, -ā́re** *deny, refuse*
cóncitō, -ā́re *stir up*	**púgnō, -ā́re** *fight*
dō, dáre *give*	**rógō, -ā́re** (+ acc.) *ask for*
hábitō, -ā́re *dwell*	**spḗrō, -ā́re** (+ acc.) *hope for*
impétrō, -ā́re *obtain by request*	**súperō, -ā́re** *overcome*
mónstrō, -ā́re *show, point out*	

Where the infinitive ending is accented (as in **ámbulō, -ā́re**), the infinitive is so accented (**ambulā́re**). If the infinitive ending has no accent, e.g. **régō, -ere**, the infinitive is accented in the same place as the preceding form (**régere**).

In the conjugation of **dō** we have a short **a** everywhere except for **dās** (and **dā** 21.1/1). Hence we have **dámus, dátis** in the present indicative, **dábam**, etc. in the imperfect, and **dábō** in the future (4.1/5); in these forms **amō** (and every other first conjugation verb) has a long **ā**: **amā́mus, amā́tis, amā́bam, amā́bō**, etc.

UNIT 3

For this and every third subsequent unit a revision exercise will be found at the Internet website http://tylatin.org .

3.1 Grammar

3.1/1 Second declension

The second declension is divided into two main groups: nouns whose nominative singular ends in **-us**, which, with a few exceptions, are masculine, and those whose nominative singular ends in **-um**, which are all neuter. Both groups have identical endings except for the nominative, vocative and accusative. For these cases second declension neuter nouns observe the rule which holds for all neuters of whatever declension:

The vocative and accusative of all neuter nouns are the same as the nominative, both in the singular and in the plural. In the plural the nominative, vocative and accusative of all neuter nouns end in -a.

	mūrus (m)	*wall*	**bellum** (n)	*war*
	SINGULAR	PLURAL	SINGULAR	PLURAL
Nom.	mū́rus	mū́rī	béllum	bélla
Voc.	mū́re	mū́rī	béllum	bélla
Acc.	mū́rum	mū́rōs	béllum	bélla
Gen.	mū́rī	mūrṓrum	béllī	bellṓrum
Dat.	mū́rō	mū́rīs	béllō	béllīs
Abl.	mū́rō	mū́rīs	béllō	béllīs

What has been said in Unit 1 about the meanings and uses of the cases applies here and to the other declensions. Both first and second declensions have the same ending (**-īs**) for the dative and ablative plural. These cases of the plural also coincide in the other declensions, though with a different ending (**-bus**).

3.1/2 Second declension nouns in *-r* and *-ius*

Masculine nouns of the second declension which originally ended in **-rus** in the nominative singular lost the ending of this case at a period before our written records begin, and so we have **ager** *field*, **puer** *boy* (originally **agrus** and **puerus**), etc. In these nouns, when the resulting final **-r** was preceded by a consonant, an **e** was inserted between the two, but this was not carried through to the other cases, e.g. **ager**, gen. **agrī**. The few nouns which originally had **e** before what became the final **-r** of the nominative singular keep this **e** through their declension, e.g. **puer**, gen. **puerī** (to this class also belongs **vir** *man, male,* gen. **virī**). To know whether the **e** is retained in the stem it is necessary to learn both nominative and genitive singular. We shall see that the same applies to many other Latin nouns.

Unlike second declension nouns in **-us**, the vocative singular of nouns in **-r** is the same as the nominative. **Ager** and **puer** are declined as follows:

	SINGULAR	PLURAL	SINGULAR	PLURAL
N. & V.	áger	ágrī	púer	púerī
Acc.	ágrum	ágrōs	púerum	púerōs
Gen.	ágrī	agrórum	púerī	puerórum
Dat.	ágrō	ágrīs	púerō	púerīs
Abl.	ágrō	ágrīs	púerō	púerīs

Nouns ending in **-ius** are irregular in the vocative singular: **fīlius** *son,* voc. **fīlī**. In the genitive singular and nominative plural the two **i**'s are sometimes contracted so that in both cases we may have **fīlī**; this also applies to the genitive singular of neuters in **-ium**, as **ingénium** *talent,* gen. **ingéniī** or **ingénī**.

3.1/3 Anomalies of the first and second declensions

(*a*) In both declensions an older form of the genitive plural in **-um** (which coincides with the accusative singular in the second declension) is occasionally found, particularly in poetry: **genus agricolum** (= **agricolārum**) *the race of farmers*, **domitor equum** (= **equōrum**) *tamer of horses*.

(b) **Deus** *god* uses the nominative singular for the vocative singular, and in the plural has **dī, dīs** more often than the regular **deī, deīs**; in the genitive plural the older form **deum** frequently occurs.

(c) **Fīlia** *daughter* and **dea** *goddess* have irregular dative and ablative plurals: **fīliābus, deābus**. This is to avoid confusion with the corresponding forms of **fīlius** *son* and **deus** *god*.

3.1/4 Prepositions

Prepositions in Latin perform the same function as in English. They define the relationship between the word they govern and the rest of the clause in which they are used. Prepositions must always govern a noun or pronoun, e.g. *over the road, in the garden, about her*. In English the noun or pronoun is in the accusative case, though it is only with pronouns that there is any difference in form (we cannot say *about she*). In Latin most prepositions take the accusative (i.e. the word which they govern must be in this case), a few the ablative. Prepositions come before the word they govern (see 8.1/1 note 5 and 9.1/4 for the only consistent exceptions).

Prepositions with the accusative

ad *to, towards, at*	**iuxtā** *next to, beside*
ante *before, in front of*	**per** *through, for the duration of*
apud *at, near*	**post** *after, behind*
circā *about*	**praeter** *except*
circum *around*	**prope** *near*
contrā *against*	**propter** *on account of*
inter *between, among, amid*	**trans** *across*

Apud can also mean *at the house* (or *shop*) *of* (cf. French *chez*) and *in the works of*: **apud Iūliam maneō** *I am staying at Julia's house*; **apud Vergilium hoc legimus** *we read this* (**hoc**) *in the works of Vergil*.

Prepositions with the ablative

ā or **ab** *by* or *from* (**ab** always before a vowel, sometimes before a consonant)	**ē** or **ex** *out of* (**ex** always before vowel, sometimes before a consonant)
cum *with*	**prō** *before; on behalf of*
dē *down from; concerning*	**sine** *without*

Two common prepositions, **in** and **sub**, take either the accusative or ablative, according to sense required. With the accusative they mean *into* (or simply *to*) and *up to* respectively, and are used in clauses containing a verb expressing motion, e.g. *he came into the country house* (**in villam**); *they approached up to the walls* (**sub mūrōs**). With the ablative they indicate *place where* and mean *in* and *under*, e.g. *we will live in a country house* (**in villā**); *she was sitting under the walls* (**sub mūrīs**).

3.1/5 Words for *and, both, or, either, even, also*

Latin has four words meaning *and*: **ac**, **atque**, **et**, **-que**. All may join words, phrases and clauses. The first two (the second is only a variant of the first) are emphatic and may sometimes be translated *and indeed, and in fact,* etc., especially when introducing a clause. **Caesar atque Brūtus** could be translated *Caesar, and Brutus as well* but would normally be translated by *Caesar and Brutus*. **Et** means simply *and*, e.g. **Caesar et Brūtus**, but **et Caesar et Brūtus** means *both Caesar and Brutus*; Latin does not have a separate word for *both*. **-que** *and*, which is even less emphatic than **et**, is placed after, and joined to, the second of the two words it connects, e.g. **Caesar Brūtusque**, which, as we have only one *and* in English, must be translated *Caesar and Brutus*; (for the pronunciation of **Brūtusque**, see p. xvii). When connecting clauses, **-que** is attached to the first word of the second clause, and the same applies to phrases, except that when a phrase begins with a monosyllabic preposition, as **in forō** *in the forum*, **-que** is normally attached to the noun, not the preposition, giving us **in forōque** *and in the forum*. Combinations of **ac** (**atque**), **et**, **-que** (such as **-que . . . et** *both . . . and*) are possible.

Aut and **vel** mean *or*, or when repeated at an interval, *either . . . or*. There is a distinction in meaning. **Aut** is used for mutually exclusive alternatives, e.g. **aut Caesar aut nihil** *either Caesar or nothing*; **vel** on the other hand is used for alternatives that are not mutually exclusive or where this is not emphasised, e.g. **servī in prātō vel in hortō sunt** *the slaves are in the meadow or the garden*. **-ve,** which functions in the same way as **-que**, has the same meaning as **vel** but is less emphatic, e.g. **puer puellave** *a boy or girl*.

Also and *even* have several Latin equivalents, the most important being:

et, used adverbially and to be translated *even, too*: **et tū, Brūte!** *you too, Brutus!*

etiam, to be translated *even, also, indeed* according to the context: **etiam mensās consūmimus?** *are we eating even the tables?*

nē . . . quidem (with the word qualified coming between) *not even* (**etiam** is *not* used with negatives): **Brūtus nē verbum quidem dīcit** *Brutus is not saying even a word* (lit. *is saying not even a word*).

quoque *also, too*, which differs from **etiam** and **et** in that it must follow the word it qualifies: **amābat nōs quoque Daphnis** *Daphnis used to love us* (**nōs**) *too.*

A common idiom is **nōn sōlum . . . sed etiam** *not only . . . but also*: **nōn sōlum Brūtus sed etiam Portia in forō erat** *not only was Brutus in the forum; Portia was there as well* (lit. *not only Brutus but also Portia was . . .*).

3.1/6 *nec/neque*

Nec . . . nec (or **neque . . . neque**; there is no distinction in meaning between the two) mean *neither . . . nor*: **neque Gallī neque Germānī Rōmānōs superant** *neither the Gauls nor the Germans defeat the Romans.*

Occurring singly, **nec/neque** will usually be translated *and not* or *and . . . not.* Latin always uses **nec/neque** and *never* **et nōn** or **et . . . nōn**: **contrā Gallōs locum mūniunt neque iūmenta solvunt** *they fortify the place against the Gauls and do not untie the beasts of burden* (**iūmenta**).

3.1/7 Omission of *sum*

For brevity the verb **sum** is often omitted, especially in main clauses. It is always obvious from the context which part of **sum** is missing:

> **Et in Arcadiā ego.** *I* (**ego**) *am even in Arcadia* (**sum** is omitted).
> **Sīc nōtus Ulixēs?** *Is thus* (**sīc**) *Ulysses known?* (**est** is omitted).

3.1/8 Direct questions (1)

Direct questions are those which are directly asked of someone else. In Latin, as in English, they are, when appropriate, introduced by a particular word: **cūr . . .?** *why . . . ?* **quis . . .?** *who . . . ?* Where we have no question word and English simply inverts the word order (*are you*

coming to see me?), Latin attaches **-ne** to the first word (or later, as
with **-que**): **sumne infēlix?** *am I unhappy?* **ad Āfricamne nāvigās?** *are
you sailing to Africa?* (on the pronunciation of the word to which **-ne**
is joined see p. xvii). Sometimes, however, the inflexion of the voice
(*you are coming to see me?*) is sufficient for this type of question:
infēlix est Fabricius quod agrum suum fodit? *is Fabricius unhappy
because* (**quod**) *he digs his own field?* Latin does not have any word
order corresponding to the inversion of verb and subject in English.
For other varieties of direct questions see 23.1/1.

3.2 Latin reading

An analysis of sentence 9 will be found in the key.

1 Ambulantne pueri cum magistro in foro?
2 Et Brutus et Cassius in Curia sedebant atque verba Pompeii
   audiebant.
3 Ego in Gallia cum Gallis pugnabam, sed tu vel in Graeciam vel in
   Asiam navigabas.
4 Cur dona aut filiis aut filiabus Cassii non datis?
5 Hodie non solum ante templa sed etiam trans forum ambulo.
6 In via Appia ambulabam et titulos sepulchrorum videbam.
7 Sub terra animae mortuorum inter tenebras habitant.
8 Trans fluvium vado quia inimici per agros sunt.
9 O di deaeque, Romanos relinquitis ubi contra Poenos pugnant?
10 Apud amicos eram et fabulam de initio Romae pueris narrabam.
11 Propter periculum feminae ante templa deorum stant et dona
    dant.
12 Apud Vergilium de excidio Troiae legimus.
13 In caelo stellas circum lunam videmus.
14 Ne ante templum quidem flammae in ara!

A Roman nose
I5 Tongilianus habet nasum; scio, non nego: sed iam
    nil praeter nasum Tongilianus habet.   Martial

Martial, who lived in the second half of the first century AD, wrote a
large collection of short poems (called **Epigrammata** *epigrams*), many
of which satirise his contemporaries. Tongilianus, of whom we have
no knowledge from other sources, was apparently a person with social

pretensions who turned up his large nose at people to indicate his imagined superiority. When the grounds for this superiority disappeared he was left with nothing but his nose! **Sed iam,** literally *but now,* could be translated *but these days.* For present purposes Latin poetry should be translated into normal English prose.

3.2/1 Vocabulary

*Latin proper nouns (***Brūtus, Asia,** *etc.) are only given in the vocabularies when they have a different form in English or require explanation.*

Section A

amícus, -ī (m) *friend*

ánima, -ae (f) *soul, spirit*

Áppia see **via Appia**

ára, -ae (f) *altar*

auxílium, -ī (n) *help*

caélum, -ī (n) *sky, heaven*

Cúria, -ae (f) *Senate-house*

dónum, -ī (n) *gift*

égo (pronoun) *I* (where emphasis is required)

excídium, -ī (n) *destruction*

flámma, -ae (f) *flame*

flúvius, -ī (m) *river*

fórum, -ī (n) *public square in the centre of a town; usually the* **Forum Rōmānum,** *the oldest forum of Rome*

Gállus, -ī (m) *inhabitant of Gaul*

hódiē (adv.) *today*

iam (adv.; 1 syllable) *already, now*

inimícus, -ī (m) *(personal) enemy*

inítium, -ī (n) *beginning*

lúna, -ae (f) *moon*

magíster, magístrī (m) *schoolmaster*

mórtuus, -ī (m) *dead man*

nãsus, -ī (m) *nose*

nīl or níhil (indecl. noun) *nothing*

perículum, -ī (n) *danger*

Poénus, -ī (m) *inhabitant of Carthage, Carthaginian*

Pompéïus, (m; 3 syllables) -ī, *Pompey*

quía (conj.) *because*

Rōmánus, -ī (m) *Roman*

sepúlchrum, -ī (n) *tomb*

stélla, -ae (f) *star*

témplum, -ī (n) *temple*

ténebrae, -árum (f) (only used in plural but to be translated by a singular in English) *darkness*

térra, -ae (f) *land*

títulus, -ī (m) *inscription*

Tróia, -ae (f; 2 syllables) *Troy*

tū (pronoun) *you* (singular; used when emphasis is required)

vérbum, -ī (n) *word*

Vergílius, -ī (m) *the Roman poet Vergil (70–19BC)*

vía Áppia *Appian Way, the road from Rome to southern Italy*

Where the genitive ending is accented (as **ténebrae, -árum**) the genitive is so accented (**tenebrárum**).

Section B
hábeō, -ére *have*   **scíō, -íre** *know*
légō, -ere *read*   **sédeō, -ére** *sit*
nāvigō, -áre *sail*   **stō, -áre** *stand*
pétō, -ere (+acc.) *seek, look for* **vádō, -ere** *go*
relínquō, -ere *leave, abandon*   **vídeō, -ére** (+acc.) *see, look at*

3.3 Excursus

Latin and English

We saw in 1.3 that Latin is connected with English in what may roughly be called a cousin relationship. It is not surprising, therefore, to find that there are some words that existed in the original Indo-European language and have come down in both Latin and English. It may require something of an act of faith to believe that *father* is the same word as **pater**, *mother* as **māter**, and *fish* as **piscis**, until we realise that not only are their meanings identical but also the same patterns of sound change can be perceived over a wider sample. Thus in an initial position English *f* corresponds to a Latin **p**, intervocalic *th* to **t**, and final **r** is unchanged. Often, however, an original Indo-European word has undergone such change in both Latin and English that other evidence has to be taken into account to establish a connection. *Cow* and **bōs**, for example, have only one common sound but they are, in fact, related. This element in our vocabulary includes many very basic words such as those denoting family relationships and domestic animals.

The Romans annexed most of Britain after the invasion of the Emperor Claudius in AD 43. The cultural and material differences between the relatively backward Celtic inhabitants and their conquerors were enormous, and the many innovations made by the Romans would naturally have had Latin names even in areas where Celtic was maintained as a language (this is attested by the numerous Latin words in modern Welsh). After the last Roman legion left Britain in AD 410 to defend Rome itself against barbarian hordes and the country lay open to marauding Germanic tribes, the relics of Roman civilisation were not renamed even in those parts subsequently occupied by the Angles and Saxons; the Latin terms were taken over into what was to become English, and hence we have *port* (**portus** *harbour*), *chest* (**cista**), *candle* (**candēla**). The most striking linguistic relic of this sort is probably *c(h)ester/caster* in English place names (*Manchester, Gloucester, Chester, Lancaster*, etc.), which is derived from **castra** (*military*) *camp*, and indicates that a Roman military establishment existed in the localities where it occurs.

The Germanic invaders themselves had come under Roman influence long before arriving in Britain. The Roman occupation of western Europe had extended up to, and in some parts gone beyond, the Rhine. This area included a number of German tribes, but Roman exports and reports of Roman civilisation spread beyond the boundaries to places such as those inhabited by the tribes who subsequently invaded Britain. In this way their language absorbed such words as *wine* (< **vīnum**), *street* (< **strāta** [**via**], lit. *paved way*), *cheese* (< **cāseus**), and *wall* (< **vallum**).

These two sources of Latin words in English, both predating the Roman withdrawal from Britain, were augmented in subsequent centuries when the Anglo-Saxons, now firmly in control of the area we call England, were converted to western Christianity, which was based in Rome and had Latin as its official language. Many of the words introduced were of an ecclesiastical nature or were connected with the scholarly pursuits of ecclesiastical life; examples are: *altar* (<**altāria**), *temple* (<**templum**), *paper* (<**papȳrus**).

The sum total of the above is about 650 Latin words in Old English, most of which still survive; but the conquest of England by the Normans in 1066 had much greater linguistic consequences. The Normans spoke a dialect of French, which is a Romance language directly descended from Latin, and Norman French became the official medium of communication. When, after two centuries, English regained its former position, it was permeated with foreign words, nearly all of Latin origin. Because these words have passed through the crucible of French they differ in form, often considerably, from their Latin original, e.g. *emperor* (<**imperātor** *commander*), *prince* (<**princeps** *leading man*), *sir* (<**senior** *older man*).

The next way in which Latin words came into English was by direct borrowing from the fifteenth century on. The civilisation of the Greeks and Romans was idolised in the Renaissance, and their cultural and intellectual achievements were taken both as models and as starting points for future progress. English was flooded with new words from Greek and Latin to cope with ever-widening intellectual horizons. As these were learned borrowings (i.e. deliberate borrowings made by scholars), they are very close in both form and meaning to the original. Latin examples are *magnitude* from **magnitūdō**, *document* from **documentum**. Sometimes the Latin word was taken over with some change in meaning but none in form: *stimulus, genius, agitator, series* (see also 20.3). The process continues today, though at a slower pace, and has given us both *radio* and *television* (the latter a Greco-Latin hybrid).

There are, of course, many English words that are not connected with anything in Latin, but if there is a connection it will fall into one of five categories:

(*a*) The English and Latin words are cognate, i.e. each has an independent derivation from the parent Indo-European language.

(*b*) The English word is a relic left over from the Roman occupation of Western Europe.

(*c*) The English word is derived from a Latin term taken into Old English (i.e. before the eleventh century).

(*d*) The English word is derived from Latin by way of Norman French.

(*e*) The English word is a direct borrowing made either during or since the Renaissance.

UNIT 4

4.1 Grammar

4.1/1 First and second declension adjectives

In English only the adjectives *this* and *that* vary according to whether the noun they qualify (i.e. go with and describe) is singular or plural: we say *this man* but *these men*. In Latin an adjective must agree with the noun it qualifies in case and gender as well as number, and this means that adjectives in Latin are declined.[1] Examples are: **vir bonus** (*the good man*), **fēmina bona** (*the good woman*), **bonās puellās** (*the good girls*, accusative), **puerōrum malōrum** (*of the bad boys*).[2] On the position of adjectives see 1.1/4.

While, as we shall see, there are five declensions of nouns in Latin, there are only two groups of adjectives. Adjectives of one group are declined wholly within the third declension, but those of the other group form their feminine in the first declension, their masculine and neuter in the second declension. They are called first and second declension adjectives. The normal method of citation is **malus, -a, -um** *bad* (first the masculine form in the nominative singular, then the corresponding feminine and neuter endings). The declension of **malus** is:

---

[1] A very few Latin adjectives (principally numerals) are indeclinable.

[2] The meanings of these phrases are given with the definite article, but here (and in subsequent examples) the definite or the indefinite article (*a good man, a good woman, good girls, of bad boys*) would be equally correct.

	SINGULAR			PLURAL		
	M.	F.	N.	M.	F.	N.
Nom.	málus	mála	málum	málī	málae	mála
Voc.	mále	mála	málum	málī	málae	mála
Acc.	málum	málam	málum	málōs	málās	mála
Gen.	málī	málae	málī	malṓrum	malā́rum	malṓrum
Dat.	málō	málae	málō	málīs	málīs	málīs
Abl.	málō	málā	málō	málīs	málīs	málīs

The majority of first and second declension adjectives follow the same pattern. The only exceptions are adjectives whose masculine form in the nominative and vocative singular ends in **-er**. Just as with second declension nouns in **-er** (see 3.1/2), most adjectives of this type do not retain the **e** in the other cases. An example is **pulcher** *beautiful*:

	SINGULAR			PLURAL		
	M.	F.	N.	M.	F.	N.
N. V.	púlcher	púlchra	púlchrum	púlchrī	púlchrae	púlchra
Acc.	púlchrum	púlchram	púlchrum	púlchrōs	púlchrās	púlchra
Gen.	púlchrī	púlchrae	púlchrī	pulchrṓrum	pulchrā́rum	pulchrṓrum
Dat.	púlchrō	púlchrae	púlchrō	púlchrīs	púlchrīs	púlchrīs
Abl.	púlchrō	púlchrā	púlchrō	púlchrīs	púlchrīs	púlchrīs

Of the few adjectives that retain **e** the most important are: **līber** *free*, **miser** *miserable*, **prosper** *prosperous*, **asper** *rough*, and **tener** *tender*. As an example we may take the last:

	SINGULAR			PLURAL		
	M.	F.	N.	M.	F.	N.
N. V.	téner	ténera	ténerum	ténerī	ténerae	ténera
Acc.	ténerum	téneram	ténerum	ténerōs	ténerās	ténera
Gen.	ténerī	ténerae	ténerī	tenerṓrum	tenerā́rum	tenerṓrum
Dat.	ténerō	ténerae	ténerō	ténerīs	ténerīs	ténerīs
Abl.	ténerō	ténerā	ténerō	ténerīs	ténerīs	ténerīs

4.1/2 Agreement of adjectives

An adjective, when not itself used as a noun (see next subsection), will always be qualifying a noun or pronoun, and must agree with this noun or pronoun in number, gender and case. No distinction is made between the attributive use of an adjective (*the good boy*, **puer bonus**) and the predicative use (*the boy is good,* **puer bonus est**). An adjective used attributively can either precede or follow its noun (**puer bonus, bonus puer**) but more often follows it (1.1/4); if preceding, it gains in emphasis.

Agreement of adjectives does not necessarily mean that an adjective will have the same ending as its noun, although this frequently happens. We do have some masculine nouns in the first declension and an adjective qualifying such a noun must be masculine, e.g. **agricola malus** *the bad farmer*, **nauta tener** *the tender sailor*. Likewise, we shall see that a large group of adjectives belongs to the third declension (9.1/1 & 2); but when these adjectives are used with nouns from other declensions they retain the forms of their own declension, e.g. **fēmina ingens** *the large woman*.

4.1/3 Adjectives used as nouns

In English we do sometimes use adjectives by themselves as nouns: *only the good die young*; *a word to the wise is sufficient*. In Latin this use is considerably broader and more common; and, because of case endings, Latin can make distinctions which are impossible in English. Hence **malī** used by itself in the nominative means (*the*) *evil men*, but the feminine, **malae**, and the neuter, **mala**, can also stand without a noun and mean (*the*) *evil women* and (*the*) *evil things* respectively. Likewise, we may have an adjective so used in the singular, e.g. **sapiens** *a wise man*. Some words, such as **amīcus** (*friendly* or *friend*), **vīcīnus** (*living near* or *neighbour*), were originally adjectives but were used so frequently as nouns that they are normally regarded as both.

The use of the neuter plural of adjectives in this way often makes for very concise expressions which need some change to be rendered into idiomatic English:

> **Multa et magna spērābat.** *His hopes were many and great* (lit. *he was hoping for many and great things*).
> **Multa cōgitat.** *He has many thoughts* (lit. *he thinks many things*).

Neuter adjectives are also used in place of abstract nouns. Both **vērum** (*a true thing*) and **vēra** (*true things*) can be translated by *truth*. Latin does have abstract nouns (as **vēritās** *truth*) but these are not used so often as in English.

4.1/4 Possessive adjectives

Possessive adjectives are of two types in English, attributive (*my, our, your, his, her, its, their*) and predicative (*mine, ours, yours, hers, theirs*; *his* is the same in both uses and *its* has no predicative form). Latin has similar possessive adjectives for the first and second persons only, but these can be used either attributively or predicatively (for the translation of *his, her(s), its* and *their(s)* see 8.1/2 and 9.1/5):

> **meus** *my*, **tuus** *your* (when referring to one person); these are declined like **malus**, except that the masculine vocative singular of **meus** is **mī** (**tuus** has no vocative).
>
> **noster** *our*, **vester** *your* (when referring to two or more persons); these are declined like **pulcher**.

Examples of the attributive and predicative uses are:

> **Liber meus apud Iūliam est.** *My book is at Julia's house* (attributive).
> **Hic liber meus est.** *This* (**hic**) *book is mine* (predicative).

Possessive adjectives in Latin are not normally used when they would refer to the subject of a clause, e.g. **fīliae pecūniam dedī** *I gave money to my daughter*; it is assumed that if someone else's daughter had been meant this would have been stated.

These adjectives can also be used as nouns: **meī** *my people* (generally = *my family*); **nostrī** *our men* (an expression frequently used by Roman historians when referring to Roman soldiers).

4.1/5 Future indicative active

This tense indicates that an action is going to take place in the future and covers both the English future simple tense (*I shall love*) and the English future continuous (*I shall be loving*). It is formed in one way in the first and second conjugations and in another in the third and fourth. For the first and second conjugations the future stem is made by adding **b** to the present stem and to this are attached the endings **-ō, -is, -it, -imus, -itis, -unt**. For the third and fourth conjugations there is no special future stem; instead we take the present stem and add the endings **-am, -ēs, -et, -ēmus, -ētis, -ent**. The result is:

		I	II	III	IV
SINGULAR	1	amáb-ō	monéb-ō	rég-am	aúdi-am
		I shall love,	*I shall warn,*	*I shall rule,*	*I shall hear,*
		shall be loving	*shall be warning*	*shall be ruling*	*shall be hearing*
	2	amáb-is	monéb-is	rég-ēs	aúdi-ēs
	3	amáb-it	monéb-it	rég-et	aúdi-et
PLURAL	1	amáb-imus	monéb-imus	reg-émus	audi-émus
	2	amáb-itis	monéb-itis	reg-étis	audi-étis
	3	amáb-unt	monéb-unt	rég-ent	aúdi-ent

The future stem of **sum** is **er-**, giving us **érō, éris, érit, érimus, éritis, érunt** (*I shall be, you will be*, etc.).

4.1/6 Perfect indicative active

The name of this Latin tense indicates only one of its two meanings. The first form given below can mean *I have loved* (as one would expect from the term *perfect tense*), but it can also mean *I loved* (or *I did love*), which is the English past simple tense. The context of a passage will tell us which tense is intended but in isolated sentences either translation can be possible.

		I	II	III	IV
SINGULAR	1	amáv-ī	mónu-ī	réx-ī	audív-ī
		I loved,	*I warned,*	*I ruled,*	*I heard,*
		have loved	*have warned*	*have ruled*	*have heard*
	2	amāv-ístī	monu-ístī	rex-ístī	audīv-ístī
	3	amáv-it	mónu-it	réx-it	audív-it
PLURAL	1	amáv-imus	monú-imus	réx-imus	audív-imus
	2	amāv-ístis	monu-ístis	rex-ístis	audīv-ístis
	3	amāv-érunt	monu-érunt	rex-érunt	audīv-érunt

The perfect stem of **sum** is **fu-**, giving us: **fúī, fuístī, fúit, fúimus, fuístis, fuérunt**. In most contexts there is not much difference between the imperfect and perfect of **sum**; strictly, **eram** means *I used to be* or *I was being*, and **fuī** *I have been* or *I was*, but more often than not we shall translate even **eram** by *I was*.

The endings for this tense are the same for all conjugations but the stem presents complications. In the first and fourth conjugations it is

formed by adding **v** to the present stem (**amā-v-, audī-v-**) and in the
second the **e** of the present stem is replaced by **u** (**mone- >monu-**). In
the third conjugation, however, there is no standard way of forming
the perfect stem, although most of its verbs fall into one of five
groups (see **Appendix 5**). It is, therefore, necessary to learn the
principal parts of all third conjugation verbs and of the few irregular
verbs which belong to other conjugations. A normal Latin verb has
four principal parts and from these all possible forms can be deduced.
These parts are:

> first person singular present indicative active (**ámō, móneō,**
>   **régō, aúdiō**);
> present infinitive active (**amáre, monére, régere, audíre**);
> first person singular perfect indicative active (**amávī, mónuī,**
>   **réxī, audívī**);
> supine (**amátum, mónitum, réctum, audítum**).

The supine is a verbal noun (*the act of loving, warning, ruling, hearing*
are the meanings of the above four); its use will be explained later
(12.1/3). In verbs with regular principal parts it is formed by adding
-tum to the present stem, with the modification of **e** to **i** in the second
conjugation (**mone- > moni-**). In the third conjugation and in irregular
verbs elsewhere we sometimes have a supine in **-sum**, e.g. **suāsum** (<
suādeō *advise*).

From this point all principal parts of verbs with an irregularity will be
given. For regular verbs only the first two principal parts will be listed
as the second two follow automatically.

Of verbs already given in vocabularies the following have irregular
principal parts:

dō, -áre, dédī, dátum *give*	**sédeō, -ére, sédī, séssum** *sit*
légō, -ere, légī, léctum *read*	**stō, -áre, stétī, státum** *stand*
pétō, -ere, petívī, petítum *seek, look for*	**vádō, -ere, vásī** (no supine) *go*
relínquō, -ere, relíquī, relíctum *leave*	**vídeō, -ére, vídī, vísum** *see*

Many verbs with irregular principal parts have a short vowel in the
present stem and a long vowel in the perfect (as **legō, sedeō**).

Notes

1 An alternative (and archaic) ending for the third person plural, perfect active indicative, **-ēre**, is very common in poetry (**amāvḗre, monuḗre**, etc.).

2 Most fourth conjugation verbs have a shorter perfect stem which is identical with that of the present (**audi-** <**audiō**), but this is not used in the second person singular or plural. We can, therefore, have: **aúdiī** (= **audḗvī**), **aúdiit** (= **audḗvit**), **audíimus** (= **audḗvimus**), **audiḗrunt** (= **audḗvērunt**). For shorter second person forms see 23.1/4.

3 Some verbs (including **sum**) have no supine.

4.2 Latin reading

The modern convention in printing Latin is to use a capital to start a paragraph, but to start later sentences in the same paragraph with a small letter (examples in 5, 9, 16, 17 below).

An analysis of sentence 15 will be found in the key.

1 Arduus equus intra muros Troiae stetit et viros fudit.
2 Quando Asiam relinquam et patriam rursus videbo?
3 O puellae pulchrae, in oppido vestro sunt nautae mali, et per cunctas vias ambulant.
4 Filius meus aedificia antiqua vidit ubi in Aegypto erat.
5 Cur, O Fortuna, caeca es? divitias saepe das non bonis sed malis.
6 Longa est via ad Corinthum sed multas et pulchras statuas ibi invenies.
7 O amici, quando ad forum Romanum venietis et monumenta Romae antiquae videbitis?
8 Poetae nostri sub umbra cupressi sederunt neque laboraverunt.
9 Sine cibo ad cenam venistis, O amici. poma et vinum solum habeo.
10 Pauci per ardua ad astra perveniunt.
11 Ignari quondam malorum, nunc miseri sumus quia publicanus in oppidum venit.
12 In Graeciam quoque vadam et servos doctos emam.
13 In Italia etiam pueri parvi vinum bibebant.
14 Prope templum Dianae magnas cupressos videbis.
15 Ubi in horto agricolae multum vinum bibebas, stulta dixisti.
16 Vera non dixisti, O Brute. hodie in Curia non eras.

Two pigs dine together
17 Non cenat sine apro noster, Tite, Caecilianus.
      bellum convivam Caecilianus habet.   Martial

> **áper, áprī** (m) *wild boar*, a favourite dish with wealthy Romans;
> **béllus, -a, -um** *nice*, a colloquial word, here used sarcastically;
> **convíva, -ae** (m) *guest at a meal*, the implication is that Caecilianus
> ate very lavishly and by himself.

4.2/1 Vocabulary

Section A

aedifícium, -ī (n) *building*
Aegýptus, -ī (f) *Egypt*
antíquus, -a, -um *ancient*
árduus, -a, -um *tall, lofty, difficult*
ástrum, -ī (n) *star*
caécus, -a, -um *blind*
céna, -ae (f) *dinner*
cíbus, -ī (m) *food*
Corínthus, -ī (f) *Corinth*
cúnctus, -a, -um *all*
cupréssus, -ī (f) *cypress*
dīvítiae, -árum (f. pl.) *riches*
dóctus, -a, -um *learned*
équus, -ī (m) *horse*
fortūna, -ae (f) *fortune*
hórtus, -ī (m) *garden*
íbi (adv.) *there, in that place*
ignārus, -a, -um (+ gen.) *ignorant of, unacquainted with*
íntrā (prep. + acc.) *inside*
lóngus, -a, -um *long*
mágnus, -a, -um *great, large*
míser, mísera, míserum *unhappy*

monuméntum, -ī (n) *monument*
múltus, -a, um *much*, in plural *many*; when **multus** and another adjective qualify a single noun **et** is normally inserted between them; see sentence 6 above
óppidum, -ī (n) *town*
párvus, -a, -um *small*
pátria, -ae (f) *native land*
paúcī, -ae, -a (generally plural) *few*
pōmum, -ī (n) *fruit*
pūblicānus, -ī (m) *tax collector*
quándō . . .? (interrogative adv.) *when . . .?*
quóndam (adv.) *once*
rúrsus (adv.) *again*
sérvus, -ī (m) *slave*
sōlum (adv.) *only*
státua, -ae (f) *statue*
stúltus, -a, -um *stupid*
úmbra, -ae (f) *shade*
vérus, -a, -um *true*
vīnum, -ī (n) *wine*

A few second declension nouns in **-us** (as **Aegyptus, Corinthus, cupressus** above) are not masculine; see 25.1/4*a*.

Section B

With verbs of the first, second and fourth conjugations principal parts are not given if regular. The principal parts of a compound verb (as **in-veniō**, **per-veniō***) nearly always follow those of the simple verb.*

bíbō, -ere, bíbī (no supine) *drink*

cénō, -áre *dine*

dícō, -ere, díxī, díctum *say, speak*

émō, -ere, émī, émptum *buy*

fúndō, -ere, fúdī, fúsum *pour, pour out*

invéniō, -íre, invénī, invéntum *find*

labórō, -áre *toil, work*

pervéniō, -íre, pervénī, pervéntum *arrive*

véniō, -íre, vénī, véntum *come*

With **bibō** and other verbs where the present and perfect stems coincide, the third singular (**bibit**) and the first plural (**bibimus**) are the same for both tenses.

UNIT 5

5.1 Grammar

5.1/1 Pluperfect and future perfect indicative active

The pluperfect tense in English always contains the auxiliary verb *had* and expresses an action or state two stages back in the past. In the sentence *when I called at his house he had already left*, the verb in the main clause *had left* refers to something that happened before *I called*; *I called* is itself in the past and is the reference point by which the time of *had left* is defined. In other words, if we regard *called* as occurring one stage in the past, *had left* must be an additional stage back.

In English the future perfect always contains two auxiliaries *shall/will have*, e.g. *When you call at nine o'clock tomorrow I shall have left for work*. Like the pluperfect, it indicates that one action happens before another, but here both actions are to take place in the future. *You call* refers to a future event but *shall have left*, though also future, is something that is going to happen before *you call*.

If we represent time as a line starting in the past and stretching into the future and these tenses as points upon it, then we have:

pluperfect	perfect	present	future perfect	future
|	|	|	|	|

The perfect tense here is to be understood only in its function of indicating a simple past act (*he saw me* not *he has seen me*).

Both these tenses are formed from the perfect stem (4.1/6) and their endings are the same for all conjugations. It is useful to remember that the pluperfect endings are the same as the actual forms of the imperfect of the verb **sum** (2.1/4), and that those of the future perfect coincide with the forms of the future of **sum** (4.1/5), except for the third person plural. For **amō** these tenses are:

Pluperfect Indicative	Future Perfect Indicative
amā́v-eram *I had loved*	amā́v-erō *I shall have loved*
amā́v-erās *you* (s.) *had loved*	amā́v-eris *you* (s.) *will have loved*
amā́v-erat *he/she/it had loved*	amā́v-erit *he/she/it will have loved*
amā́v-erāmus *we had loved*	amā́v-érimus *we shall have loved*
amā́v-erātis *you* (pl.) *had loved*	amā́v-éritis *you* (pl.) *will have loved*
amā́v-erant *they had loved*	amā́v-erint *they will have loved*

For **sum** (which is also regular) and for examples of the other conjugations, see the tables of verbs (pp. 280–96).

5.1/2 Adverbial clauses with the indicative

An adverbial clause is a subordinate clause performing the function of an adverb (see **Glossary of grammatical terms**, p. xix) and is introduced by a subordinating conjunction. Below are given some subordinating conjunctions which are followed by a verb in the indicative mood. We shall deal later with adverbial clauses whose verb must be put into the subjunctive mood (see **Mood** in **Glossary of grammatical terms**). Some subordinating conjunctions (e.g. **quod**) can be followed by either indicative or subjunctive, but there is a difference in sense (see unit 29).

quod, quia, quoniam all mean *because* or *since* (but not in a temporal sense). When followed by the indicative they introduce a clause which gives what the writer sees as a true reason or explanation.

quamquam *although*

simulac *as soon as*

ubi *when* or (less frequently) *where*. We have also had the interrogative **ubi** (**ubi est toga mea?** *where is my toga?*).

postquam *after*. Note carefully that the English *after* can be either a subordinating conjunction, *after he came I felt sick* (**postquam** would be used here), or a preposition, *after the war, after death*, where in Latin we use **post** with the accusative (**post bellum, post mortem**—3.1/4). *After* in English can also be used as an adverb (= *afterwards*): *we went into the water and soon after the jellyfish*

	attacked. The Latin adverb is **posteā**.
antequam	*before.* There is the same possibility of confusion with *before* as with *after*; the Latin preposition meaning *before* is **ante** (with the accusative), the adverb is **anteā**.
ut	*as, when.* This conjunction has a different meaning with the subjunctive (13.1/5, 16.1/1).
si	*if.* Also used with the subjunctive (22.1/2).

When **simulac, ubi** (in the sense of *when*), **postquam, antequam** and **ut** (with the indicative) are used in past narrative to introduce a clause describing an event anterior to that of the main clause, they are followed by the perfect indicative, *not* the pluperfect as we might have expected on logical grounds. We normally use the same idiom in English.

> **Caesar, postquam in Galliam pervēnit, oppidum mūnīvit.** *After he arrived in Gaul, Caesar fortified the town.*
> **Simulac forum vīdī, epistulam ad amīcōs mīsī.** *As soon as I saw the forum, I sent a letter to my friends.*

In English we could also say *after he had arrived . . ., as soon as I had seen . . . .*

The pluperfect is used with **quod, quia** and **quoniam** where appropriate: **amīcum in Graeciā nōn vīdī quod in Asiam nāvigāverat** *I did not see my friend in Greece because he had sailed to Asia.*

Sī with the pluperfect indicative also describes a prior action in the past and may be translated *if* or *whenever* (example in 5.2, 8).

5.1/3 Use of the future perfect in adverbial clauses

$\left. \begin{array}{l} If \\ When \end{array} \right\}$ *we arm the inhabitants we shall conquer the Romans.*

In each of these adverbial clauses normal English idiom is to use the present indicative *arm*, although the action will take place in the future, and, moreover, before the main verb *shall conquer*. Latin here, rather more logically, uses the future perfect in the adverbial clause: **sī/ubi incolās armāverimus, Rōmānōs superābimus** (lit. *if/when we shall have armed . . .*).

When, however, the adverbial clause expresses an action or state which will be taking place at the same time as the main verb, the future is used: **sī/ubi in Hispāniā eris, Atlanticum Ōceanum vidēbis** *if/when you are in Spain you will see the Atlantic Ocean.* Here too English can, and normally does, use the present tense in the adverbial clause.

5.1/4 Phrases expressing time (1)

Most, but not all, temporal phrases in English contain a preposition, e.g. *for three days, on Tuesday, within two months* (but in cases like *I will go this afternoon* we have only an adjective and noun). In three types of these phrases Latin simply uses a particular case, provided the noun involved signifies some period, point or division of time (*hour, night, summer, daybreak*, etc.):

(*a*) **Time how long** is expressed by the accusative, though **per** *for the duration of* with the accusative (3.1/4) may be used if emphasis is required: **decem annōs in Graeciā eram** *I was in Greece ten years.* With **per decem annōs** we would be emphasising the time involved; this could be translated: *for ten years I was in Greece.*

(*b*) **Time when** is expressed by the ablative: **autumnō folia rubra vidēmus** *in autumn we see red leaves.*

(*c*) **Time within which** is also expressed by the ablative: **bīduō ad Āfricam nāvigāvit** *within a period of two days* (**bīduum**) *he sailed to Africa.*

With nouns not indicating a period, point or division of time a preposition is normally used, **in bellō** *in* (*time of*) *war.* For further types of temporal phrases see 13.1/6.

5.2 Latin reading

An analysis of sentence 15 will be found in the key.

1 Quod Graeci Troiam deleverant, Troiani multos annos erraverunt.
2 Postquam aurum invenerunt, equos conscenderunt et ad silvam properaverunt.
3 Ubi nostros viderunt, Galli intra muros oppidi cucurrerunt.
4 Nostri, simulac in arido constiterunt, oppidum oppugnaverunt.

5 In Graecia multos annos habitavit quoniam Poeni in Italiam cum elephantis venerant.

6 Filiam tuam autumno exspectabimus ubi Romam reliquerit.

7 Si de muro cecidero, cras poenas dabis, O Dave.

8 Cassius saepe iratus erat si aspera dixeram.

9 Ubi et Gallos et Germanos vicisti, magna erat gloria tua.

10 Per decem annos bellum cum Poenis gessimus neque vicimus.

11 Antequam epistulam tuam vidi, in Graecia diu habitare dubitabam.

12 Quamquam multa Hispanorum apparebant arma, ad pugnam cucurrerunt.

13 Suspiravit et lacrimavit ut cruenta amici arma vidit.

14 Non veniam antequam libros Vergili emero.

15 Heri, ut servi mali solent, amici Davi in taberna multas horas sederunt et vinum multum biberunt.

5.2/1 Vocabulary

Section A

ánnus, -ī (m) *year*

áridus, -a, -um *dry* (in n. *dry land*)

árma, -ṓrum (n. pl.) *arms, weapons*

ásper, áspera, ásperum *rough, harsh*

aúrum, -ī (n) *gold*

autúmnus, -ī (m) *autumn*

crās (adv.) *tomorrow*

cruéntus, -a, -um *blood-stained*

Dắvus, -ī (m) *common name for a male slave*

décem (indecl. adj.) *ten*

díū (adv.) *for a long time*

elephántus, -ī (m) *elephant*

epístula, -ae (f) *letter*

Germắnus, -ī (m) *inhabitant of Germany, German*

glṓria, -ae (f) *glory*

Graécus, -ī (m) *inhabitant of Greece, Greek*

héri (adv.) *yesterday*

Hispắnus, -ī (m) *inhabitant of Spain, Spaniard*

hṓra, -ae (f) *hour*

īrắtus, -a, -um *angry*

líber, líbrī (m) *book*

poéna, -ae (f) *punishment*

poénās dō *pay the penalty, be punished*

púgna, -ae (f) *fight, battle*

sílva, -ae (f) *forest*

Troiắnus, -ī (m) *Trojan*

Section B

appā́reō, -ḗre *appear, be visible*

cā́dō, -ere, cécidī, cā́sum *fall*

conscéndō, -ere, conscéndī, conscḗnsum *climb up, mount*

cónstō, -ā́re, cónstitī (no supine) *stand together, take up a position*

cúrrō, -ere, cucúrrī, cúrsum *run*

dḗleō, -ḗre, dēlḗvī, dēlḗtum *destroy*

dúbitō, -ā́re *doubt, be hesitant*

érrō, -ā́re *wander*

exspéctō, -ā́re *wait for*

gérō, -ere, géssī, géstum *carry; bring; wage; do*

lácrimō, -ā́re *cry, weep*

oppúgnō, -ā́re *attack*

próperō, -ā́re *hurry*

sóleō, -ḗre (25.1/5e) *be accustomed*

suspī́rō, -ā́re *sigh*

víncō, -ere, vī́cī, víctum *conquer*

UNIT 6

6.1 Grammar

6.1/1 Third declension nouns – general remarks

The third declension contains nouns of all three genders. They are divided into two classes, depending on whether their stem ends in a consonant or the vowel **i**. Within each class masculine and feminine nouns have the same endings. Neuter nouns always follow the rule previously given (3.1/1). The gender of a third declension noun is only sometimes predictable from its form in the nominative singular. The main differences between the two classes are:

(*a*) In the genitive plural, consonant stems have **-um**, **i**-stems **-ium**.
(*b*) In the nominative, vocative and accusative plural, neuter consonant stems have **-a,** neuter **i**-stems **-ia**.
(*c*) In the ablative singular, neuter **i**-stems have **-ī**, elsewhere the ending is normally **-e**.

6.1/2 Third declension nouns – consonant stems

By subtracting the ending **-is** from the genitive singular we get the stem (e.g. **rex** *king*, gen. **rēgis**, stem **rēg-**) and to this stem case endings are added. As the stem is modified, sometimes beyond recognition, in the nominative singular (**l**-stems and one group of **r**-stems are exceptions – see below), both nominative and genitive singular must be learnt. Nouns are arranged according to the final consonant of their stem and within these groups we see certain patterns. The generic term for the final consonants of each group is given in brackets. The term 'liquid' refers to the sound of the consonants it describes, while the others relate to the place in the mouth where articulation occurs.

(*a*) Stems where masculine and feminine nouns (but not neuters) add
s in the nominative singular:

	c, g (palatals)	**t, d** (dentals)	**p, b** (labials)
	rex (m) *king*	**pēs** (m) *foot*	**princeps** (m) *chief, chief man*
stem	**rēg-**	**ped-**	**princip-**
SINGULAR			
N. & V.	**rex** (g+s>x)	**pēs** (ped+s)	**prínceps**
Acc.	**rḗgem**	**pédem**	**príncipem**
Gen.	**rḗgis**	**pédis**	**príncipis**
Dat.	**rḗgī**	**pédī**	**príncipī**
Abl.	**rḗge**	**péde**	**príncipe**
PLURAL			
N. & V.	**rḗgēs**	**pédēs**	**príncipēs**
Acc.	**rḗgēs**	**pédēs**	**príncipēs**
Gen.	**rḗgum**	**pédum**	**príncipum**
Dat.	**rḗgibus**	**pédibus**	**princípibus**
Abl.	**rḗgibus**	**pédibus**	**princípibus**

Caput *head*, stem **capit-**, is an example of a neuter:

	SINGULAR	PLURAL
N. V. A.	**cáput**	**cápita**
Gen.	**cápitis**	**cápitum**
Dat.	**cápitī**	**capítibus**
Abl.	**cápite**	**capítibus**

(*b*) Stems without **s** in the nominative singular (these can be any gender):

	l, r (liquids)	**n** (nasals)		
	consul (m) *consul*	**amor** (m) *love*	**leō** (m) *lion*	**nōmen** (n) *name*
stem	**consul-**	**amōr-**	**leōn-**	**nōmin-**
SINGULAR				
N. & V.	**cónsul**	**ámor**	**léō**	**nṓmen**
Acc.	**cónsulem**	**amṓrem**	**leṓnem**	**ͺnṓmen**
Gen.	**cónsulis**	**amṓris**	**leṓnis**	**nṓminis**
Dat.	**cónsulī**	**amṓrī**	**leṓnī**	**nṓminī**
Abl.	**cónsule**	**amṓre**	**leṓne**	**nṓmine**

PLURAL

N. & V.	cónsulēs	amṓrēs	leṓnēs	nṓmina
Acc.	cónsulēs	amṓrēs	leṓnēs	nṓmina
Gen.	cónsulum	amṓrum	leṓnum	nṓminum
Dat.	consúlibus	amṓribus	leṓnibus	nōmínibus
Abl.	consúlibus	amṓribus	leṓnibus	nōmínibus

Páter, pátris (m) *father*, **māter, mātris** (f) *mother* and **frāter, frātris** (m) *brother* belong here but have a vowel before the final **r** of the stem only in the nominative and vocative singular.

(*c*) **r**-stems where the nominative singular ends in **s** in all genders (most nouns in this class are neuter):

	flōs (m) *flower*	**opus** (n) *work*	**tempus** (n) *time*
stem	flōr-	oper-	tempor-

SINGULAR

N. & V.	flōs	ópus	témpus
Acc.	flórem	ópus	témpus
Gen.	flóris	óperis	témporis
Dat.	flórī	óperī	témporī
Abl.	flóre	ópere	témpore

PLURAL

N. & V.	flórēs	ópera	témpora
Acc.	flórēs	ópera	témpora
Gen.	flórum	óperum	témporum
Dat.	flóribus	opéribus	tempóribus
Abl.	flóribus	opéribus	tempóribus

Notes

1 The final short vowel of certain stems (**princip-, capit-, nōmin-**) changes in the nominative singular.

2 Monosyllabic nouns ending in two consonants (e.g. **mons, montis** (m) *mountain*; **ars, artis** (f) *skill*) belong to the **i**-stems (7.1/1).

3 Some masculine and feminine nasal stems end in **-in**, not **-ōn**: **hómō, hóminis** (m) *human being* (stem **homin-**), **vírgō, vírginis** (f) *girl* (stem **virgin-**).

4 There are several large groups of words which fall into one or other of the above subdivisions. Each group is distinguished by a

particular suffix and all nouns within a group have the same gender. Examples are:

-or, gen. **-ōris**, masculine: **dólor** (gen. **dolóris**) *grief*, **imperātor** *general*, **ōrātor** *speaker* (group b liquids).

-tās, gen. **-tātis**, feminine: **cívitās** (gen. **cīvitátis**) *state*, **cupiditās** *desire*, **calamitās** *disaster* (group a dentals).

-tiō, gen. **-tiōnis**, feminine: **nátiō** (gen. **nātiónis**) *tribe*, **ratiō** *reason, method*, **mentiō** *mention* (group b nasals).

-tūdō, gen. **-tūdinis**, feminine: **pulchritū́dō** (gen. **pulchritū́dinis**) *beauty*, **fortitūdō** *courage*, **magnitūdō** *size* (group b nasals).

-men, gen. **-minis**, neuter: **cármen** (gen. **cárminis**) *song*, **ōmen** *omen* (group b nasals).

-us, gen. **-eris**, neuter: **génus** (gen. **géneris**) *race*, **opus** *work* (group c).

-us, gen. **-oris**, neuter: **córpus** (gen. **córporis**) *body*, **tempus**, *time* (group c).

Care must be taken to distinguish nouns in the last two groups both from each other and from nouns in **-us** of the second declension and fourth declension (9.1/3) .

5 The following deserve special attention:
híems, híemis (f) *winter* is the only **m** stem.
íter, itíneris (n) *road, journey*.
Iúppiter, Ióvis (m) *Jupiter* (note difference in spelling!), the chief Roman god. The nominative and vocative, **Iuppiter**, contain a weakened form of **pater** *father*, and were originally a form of address meaning *Father Ius* which was used in prayers. The other cases are all from the stem **Iov-** (as in the English *by Jove*).
os, óssis (n) *bone* and **ōs, ṓris** (n) *mouth* can cause confusion.
Vénus, Véneris (f) *the goddess of love*, is the only noun in **-us**, gen. **-eris** which is not neuter.

6.1/3 Genitive and ablative of quality (or description)

In English we can say *a man of great wisdom*, and Latin has the same construction, **vir magnae sapientiae**. This is called a genitive of quality (or description). In Latin the word in the genitive must always be accompanied by an adjective, and consequently the equivalent of *a man of wisdom* is not **vir sapientiae** (which would be bad Latin) but simply **vir sapiens** lit. *a wise man* (**sapiens** *wise*). The genitive of quality is normally used to express internal or inherent qualities and characteristics: **magnī formīca labōris** *the much-toiling ant* (lit. *ant of much labour*). For external characteristics we use the ablative of quality, e.g. **est candidō capite** *he is white-headed* (lit. *with a white head*); here too we must have an adjective. The distinction between the genitive and ablative of quality is not always observed, and even in Cicero (17.3) we meet **vir magnī ingenī summāque prūdentiā** (*a man of great talent and the highest foresight*); we might have expected two genitives as both qualities are internal.

6.1/4 Genitive of characteristic

Where in English we say *it is the part of, the duty of, the mark of, the habit of,* or, more generally, *the characteristic of someone to do something*, in Latin we use the third person singular of **sum** with the genitive. Latin does not require a word meaning *part, duty*, etc. and we must deduce from the context what word we will supply in our translation.

> **Hominis est errāre**. *It is characteristic of a human being to err.*
> **Est imperātōris superāre hostēs**. *It is the duty of a general to overcome the enemy.*

6.2 Latin reading

1 Est barbarorum corpora pingere.
2 Regina Britannorum, magnae mulier fortitudinis, cum Romanis pugnabat.
3 Hieme Romani non navigabant quod tempestates timebant.
4 'Belua multorum es capitum' dixit Horatius.
5 Cicero non multi cibi hospes sed multi ioci erat.
6 Lex videt iratum, iratus legem non videt.
7 Est stulti in errore perseverare.
8 Bonorum virorum est dolorem tolerare.
9 Magnum Iovis templum in Capitolio erat et ibi Romani regi deorum sacrificabant.
10 Postquam iter finivimus, fanum Veneris intravimus et pro salute grates egimus.
11 Quoniam proximo anno cum patre in Sicilia eram, nomina consulum non scio.

12 Si Galli nostrum oppidum deleverint, in Italia ducem
    Romanorum cum militibus exspectabimus.

Hadrian's farewell to his soul
13   Animula vagula blandula,
      hospes comesque corporis,
      quae nunc abibis in loca,
      pallidula, rigida, nudula,
      nec, ut soles, dabis iocos?

The Emperor Hadrian lived from AD 76 to 138. Of his writings only a
few short poems and fragments survive.

The three words of line 1 and also **pallidula** and **nūdula** (*l.*4) are
diminutives formed by adding **-ulus** to the stems of nouns and
adjectives (cf. *booklet* from *book*): **animula** is from **anima** *soul*; **vagula**
from **vagus, -a, -um** *wandering*; **blandula** from **blandus, -a, um**
charming, sweet; **pallidula** from **pallidus, -a, -um** *pale*; **nūdula** from
nūdus, -a, -um *naked*. Diminutives were common in spoken Latin and
were sometimes used in poetry, as here, for a pathetic effect and
without any idea of smallness. As our use of diminutives in English is
restricted to nouns and the diminutives themselves do not have the
same connotations as in Latin, we should have to translate the first
line by something like *poor wandering sweet soul*; **pallidula** and **nūdula**
we must simply render by *pale* and *naked*. *l.*2 Because reciprocal
entertainment was an old Roman practice, **hospes, hospitis** (m or f)
can mean either *guest* or *host*; here it means the former; **comes, comitis**
(m or f) *companion*. *l.*3 **quae ... in loca** *to what places ...?* **abībis** *will
you depart* (**ab** + **eō** 15.1/6).

6.2/1 Vocabulary

Section A

bárbarus, -ī (m) *barbarian*
  (*i.e. neither Roman nor Greek*)
bēlua, -ae (f) *monster*
Británnus, -ī (m) *Briton*
Capitólium, -ī (n) *the Capitol,
  a hill on the south-west side of
  the Forum Romanum*

Cícerō, Cicerónis *Cicero,
  Roman statesman and author
  (106–43BC)*
córpus, córporis (n) *body*
dólor, dolóris (m) *pain*
dux, dúcis (m) *leader*
érror, erróris (m) *error*

fấnum, -ī (n) *shrine*
fortitū́dō, fortitū́dinis (f) *bravery*
grấtēs ágō (+ dat.) *give thanks to, thank*
híems, híemis (f) *winter*
Horấtius, -ī *Horace, Roman poet (65–8BC)*
hóspes, hóspitis (m *or* f) *host, guest* (see note to 13)

iócus, -ī (m) *joke, jest*
lex, légis (f) *law*
múlier, mulíeris (f) *woman, wife*
próximus, -a, -um *nearest, last*
rēgína, -ae (f) *queen*
rígidus, -a, -um *stiff, numb*
sálūs, salútis (f) *safety*
tempéstās, tempestấtis (f) *storm*

Section B
ágō, -ere, ḗgī, áctum *do, manage*
fīniō, -īre *finish*
íntrō, -ấre *enter*
persevḗrō, -ấre *persist*
píngō, -ere, pínxī, píctum *paint*

sacríficō, -ấre *sacrifice*
tímeō, -ḗre, tímuī (no supine; + acc.) *fear, be afraid of*
tólerō, -ấre (+ acc.) *put up with, bear*

6.3 Excursus

Roman personal names

A male Roman normally had three names, as **Marcus Tullius Cicerō, Publius Ovidius Nāsō**. These were called **praenōmen, nōmen** and **cognōmen** respectively. The **praenōmen** was a given name but was only used within the family. It is abbreviated when all three names are given (**M. Tullius Cicerō, P. Ovidius Nāsō**). As the number of **praenōmina** in normal use was restricted to about twenty they were not sufficiently distinctive to be used among acquaintances, and instead either the **nōmen** or **cognōmen** was used. In formal contexts the **praenōmen** was joined with either the **nōmen** or **cognōmen**. The **nōmen** (**nōmen** is also the general word for *name*) was the family name and usually ended in **-ius**, e.g. **Cornēlius, Claudius, Iūlius. Cognōmina** were originally additional given names and often refer to personal characteristics: **Cicerō** means *the man with a wart as large as a pea* (**cicer**), **Nāsō** the person *with the large nose* (**nāsus**). In time **cognōmina** came to be hereditary and to be used to distinguish one branch of a **gens** ([*extended*] *family*, i.e. all those with the same **nōmen**); we can compare the use of hyphenated surnames in English.

Women had a **nōmen** only, which was their family name in the feminine, e.g. **Cornēlia, Claudia, Iūlia**. If there were two daughters in a family the first was called **Maior** *Elder*, the second **Minor** *Younger* (for these comparative adjectives see 19.1/1). Further daughters were distinguished by the names **Tertia, Quarta** (*Third, Fourth*) etc.

The Romans had no formal titles corresponding to our *Mr, Mrs, Ms* or *Miss*.

In English we refer to Romans either by their **nōmen** (*Lucretius, Propertius*) or by their **cognōmen** (*Cicero, Tibullus*). Many better-known names have been abridged or changed in some way, e.g. *Vergil* or *Virgil* (**Vergilius**), *Horace* (**Horātius**), *Ovid* (**Ovidius**). Occasionally two names are used, e.g. *Julius Caesar, Mark Antony* (**Marcus Antōnius**).

UNIT 7

7.1 Grammar

7.1/1 Third declension nouns – masculine and feminine *i*-stems

The **i** in which the stem of these nouns ends is only clearly evident in certain forms, e.g. **cīvi-um**. In some forms it disappears before another vowel, e.g. **cīve, nūbe**. This causes no difficulty as nearly all **i**-stems fall into easily recognisable classes. With the exceptions mentioned below, masculine and feminine **i**-stems consist of:

(*a*) nouns ending in **-is** and **-ēs** in the nominative singular;
(*b*) monosyllabic nouns ending in two consonants (and even a few ending in one consonant as **nox, noctis** (f) *night*).

	cīvis (m or f) *citizen*	**nūbēs** (m) *cloud*	**mons** (m) *mountain*
SINGULAR			
N. & V.	cīvis	nūbēs	mons
Acc.	cīvem	nūbem	móntem
Gen.	cīvis	nūbis	móntis
Dat.	cīvī	nūbī	móntī
Abl.	cīve	nūbe	mónte
PLURAL			
N. & V.	cīvēs	nūbēs	móntēs
Acc.	cīvēs, -īs	nūbēs, -īs	móntēs, -īs
Gen.	cīvium	nūbium	móntium
Dat.	cīvibus	nūbibus	móntibus
Abl.	cīvibus	nūbibus	móntibus

Notes

1   The alternative ending for the accusative plural is older and still
    occurs in Classical Latin, particularly in verse. Some nouns in -**is** also
    have an accusative singular in -**im** and an ablative singular in -**ī**.
2   Two nouns ending in -**er** are declined as above: **ímber, ímbris** (m)
    rain, **vénter, véntris** (m) *stomach* (but **pater, māter, frāter, iter** are
    consonantal stems – 6.1/2).
3   **Vīs** (f) is irregular. In the singular it means *force, violence*, and in
    Classical Latin only occurs in the nominative **vīs**, accusative **vim**,
    and ablative **vī**. The plural means *strength* (for similar plurals see
    8.1/4): nom. and acc. **vírēs**, gen. **vírium**, dat. and abl. **víribus**.
4   I-stems with a nominative singular in -**is** or -**ēs** are mostly feminine.
    The most common exceptions are: **amnis** *river*, **collis** *hill*, **crīnis** *hair*,
    fīnis *end*, **ignis** *fire*, **pānis** *bread*, **piscis** *fish* (all masculine); **canis** *dog*,
    cīvis (both masculine or feminine); **iuvenis** *young man* is
    occasionally feminine in the sense *young woman*.
5   A few third declension words ending in -**is** or -**ēs** are not **i**-stems, as
    is obvious from their genitive singular, e.g. **cínis, cíneris** (m) *ash*
    (stem **ciner**-), **quíēs, quiḗtis** (f) *rest* (stem **quiēt**-). Also, all fifth
    declension nouns end in -**ēs** (11.1/1).
6   **Canis** and **iuvenis** are declined like **cīvis** but have -**um** not -**ium** in the
    genitive plural.

7.1/2 Third declension nouns—neuter *i*-stems

Neuter **i**-stems end in -**e**, -**al** or -**ar**, in the nominative singular. They
always have -**ī** in the ablative singular and -**ia** in the first three cases of
the plural as well as -**ium** in the genitive plural.

	sedīle (n)	**animal** (n) *living*	**exemplar** (n)
	seat	*being, animal*	*pattern*
SINGULAR			
N. & V.	**sedíle**	**ánimal**	**exémplar**
Acc.	**sedíle**	**ánimal**	**exémplar**
Gen.	**sedílis**	**animális**	**exemplāris**
Dat.	**sedílī**	**animálī**	**exemplārī**
Abl.	**sedílī**	**animálī**	**exemplārī**

PLURAL

N. & V.	sedília	animália	exemplária
Acc.	sedília	animália	exemplária
Gen.	sedílium	animálium	exemplárium
Dat.	sedílibus	animálibus	exempláribus
Abl.	sedílibus	animálibus	exempláribus

All nouns in **-e, -al** and **-ar** belong here except **sal, sális** (m) *salt*, **lar, láris** (m) *household god*, and the cognomen **Caésar, Caésaris**, which are consonant stems. Note the short final vowel of the first three cases of the singular of nouns in **-al** or **-ar**.

7.1/3 -iō verbs of the third conjugation (mixed conjugation)

A few verbs ending in **-iō** are a mixture of the third and fourth conjugations but are classified in the former because their present infinitive ends in **-ere**, not **-īre**. The present indicative active of one such verb **capiō** *take* is as follows:

	SINGULAR	PLURAL
1	cápiō	cápimus
2	cápis	cápitis
3	cápit	cápiunt
	INFINITIVE cápere	

Note particularly that the second vowel of **cápis, cápimus, cápitis** is short, whereas that of **aúdīs, audímus, audítis** is long; this affects the accent of the latter two. The future indicative active (**cápiam, cápiēs**, etc.) is exactly the same as in the fourth conjugation, and likewise the imperfect indicative active (**capiébam, capiébās**, etc.). These verbs form their perfect, pluperfect and future perfect with the same endings as every other Latin verb. The most common verbs of this type are:

cápiō, cápere, cēpī, cáptum *take*
cúpiō, cúpere, cupívī (or **cúpiī**), **cupítum** *desire*
fáciō, fácere, fēcī, fáctum *make*
fúgiō, fúgere, fūgī (no supine) *flee*
iáciō, iácere, iēcī, iáctum *throw*
rápiō, rápere, rápuī, ráptum *seize*

We shall subsequently refer to these verbs as *mixed conjugation*. For the full conjugation of **capiō** see p. 290.

7.1/4 Ablative of instrument and ablative of cause

An instrument is the tool with which an action is done. It is generally something inanimate. In Latin it is expressed by the plain ablative, in English generally by *by* or *with*:

> **Sagittā Cupīdō cor meum transfixit.** *Cupid* (**Cupīdō**) *pierced my heart with an arrow* (**sagittā**).
>
> **Ariovistus nōn virtūte sed consiliō vīcit.** *Ariovistus conquered not by courage but by strategy.*

The term *instrumental ablative* is also used to cover such cases as:

> **Britannī lacte et carne vīvunt.** *The Britons live on* (by means of) *milk and meat.*
>
> **Viā Appiā ad villam tuam vēnī.** *I came to your country house by the Appian Way.*

Closely related is the *ablative of cause*:

> **Lacrimō gaudiō.** *I am crying from joy* (**gaudium**).
>
> **Timōre ad montēs fūgērunt.** *Through fear they fled to the mountains.*

7.1/5 Ablative of price and genitive of value

The ablative of price is really another form of the instrumental ablative. Money is the *instrument* of a business transaction.

> **Eriphȳla aurō virī vītam vendidit.** *Eriphyle*[1] *sold the life of her husband* (**vir**) *for gold.*
>
> **Ēmī virginem trīgintā minīs.** *I bought the girl for thirty minae.*

Where in English verbs of valuing and assessing are used with an adverb (*I value your friendship highly*), in Latin we have an adjective in the genitive agreeing with **pretiī** (**pretium, -ī** (n) *price, value*), which is often omitted: **amīcitiam tuam magnī aestimō**. This construction can also be used after the verb *to be* and verbs meaning *buy* and *sell*: **hoc parvī ēmī** *I bought this cheaply* (**parvī** *at a small* [*price*]).

---

[1]In English we keep the original Greek form of this lady's name. In such cases Latin sometimes changes the ending – see 25.1/4*e*.

7.2 Latin reading

1   Iuvenalis, poeta Romanus, mentem sanam in corpore sano desiderabat.
2   Divina natura hominibus dedit agros, ars humana urbes aedificavit.
3   Populus Romae, principis urbium, Horatium magnum poetam putavit.
4   Hostes scalis vallum ascendere coeperunt.
5   Quod leo Davum devoraverat, de necessitate virtutem feci et novum servum emi.
6   Romani, quoniam uxores non habebant, virgines Sabinorum rapuerunt.
7   Postquam secunda proelia fecit, aliquot urbes hostium vi cepit.
8   Quoniam Galli fortasse venient, urbem vallo fossaque muniverunt.
9   Nostri celeriter arma ceperunt vallumque ascenderunt.
10 Proximo itinere in Galliam cum quinque legionibus properavit.
11 Ars est celare artem.
12 Nox erat et per cunctas terras animalia somnus habebat.
13 Cives Romani, quod magno in periculo erant, servos liberaverunt et e crinibus mulierum tormenta fecerunt.
14 Consul oppidum delevit et bona incolarum multo argento vendidit.

A Roman graffito
15 Balnea, vina, Venus corrumpunt corpora nostra,
        sed vitam faciunt balnea, vina, Venus.

Like their modern counterparts, certain sections of Roman society were keen writers of graffiti. The above, more literate than most, is one of the thousands found in Pompeii, the Roman town south of Naples which was destroyed by an eruption of Vesuvius in AD 79.

balneum, -ī (n) *public baths*; these were the entertainment centres of Roman towns and cities, and, apart from different types of baths, provided sports grounds and other facilities; **vīna** should be translated by the singular, *wine*; **Venus** the divinity's name is used for what she personifies, sexual love (9.3); **corrumpunt** *harm*.

7.2/1 Vocabulary

Section A
áliquot (indecl. adj.) *several*
argéntum, -ī (n) *silver*
ars, ártis (f) *skill*
bóna, -órum (n. pl.) *goods,*
  possessions
celériter (adv.) *quickly*
dīvīnus, -a, -um *divine*
fortásse (adv.) *perhaps*
fóssa, -ae (f) *ditch*
hóstis, -is (m) *enemy* (Latin
  often uses the plural where in
  English we would have the
  singular)
hūmānus, -a, -um *human*
légiō, legiónis (f) *largest unit in*
  the Roman army, legion
mens, méntis (f) *mind*
nātūra, -ae (f) *nature*

necéssitās, necessitátis (f)
  necessity
pópulus, -ī (m) *people*
proélium, -ī (n) *battle*
quínque (indecl. adj.) *five*
Sabīnī, -órum (m. pl.) *the*
  Sabines (a people living near
  Rome)
sānus, -a, -um *healthy*
scālae, -árum (f. pl.; cf. 8.1/4)
  ladder (originally *steps*)
secúndus, -a, -um *favourable,*
  successful
sómnus, -ī (m) *sleep*
torméntum, -ī (n) *catapult*
urbs, úrbis (f) *city*
úxor, uxóris (f) *wife*
vállum, -ī (n) *rampart*
vírtūs, virtūtis (f) *virtue*

Section B
aedíficō, -áre *build*
ascéndō, -ere, ascéndī, ascénsum
  climb
cēlō, -áre *hide*
dēsīderō, -áre (+ acc.) *desire,*
  long for
dévorō, -áre *devour*
incípiō, -ere, coépī, coéptum (the
  perfect and supine come from

a different stem and do not
have a prefixed **in-**; 25.1/5*a,* ii)
  begin
līberō, -áre *free, set free*
mūniō, -īre *fortify*
pútō, -áre *think*
véndō, -ere, véndidī, vénditum
  sell

7.3 Excursus

Topography of ancient Rome

One of the delights of modern Rome is the number of monuments
and buildings which survive from antiquity, some almost wholly

intact. The map below and that opposite the title page give the location of those described here. The famous seven hills of Rome are the Aventine, Caelian, Capitoline, Esquiline, Palatine, Quirinal, Viminal.

Aqua Claudia: one of the several aqueducts which brought water to Rome from the surrounding countryside.

Arches of Titus, Severus and Constantine: built by the emperors, after whom they are named, to commemorate military victories.

Arx: the citadel of Rome. It and the Capitol are the two peaks of the Capitoline Hill.

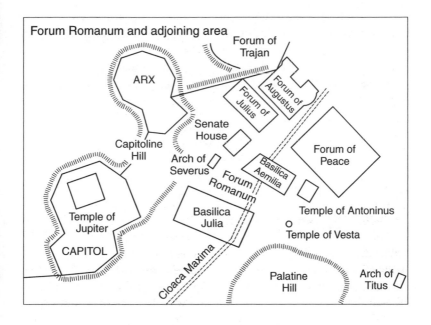

Forum Romanum and adjoining area

Baths of Agrippa, Caracalla, and Trajan: three of the largest such buildings in Rome, which served as centres of social life as well as for bathing.

Castra Praetoria: the camp of the praetorian guard, an elite body of soldiers whose main function was to protect the emperor and his immediate interests.

Circus Maximus: the largest of the tracks for chariot-racing at Rome. In its final form it could accommodate over 300,000 spectators.

Cloaca Maxima: the sewerage tunnel running under the Forum Romanum and flowing into the Tiber where its mouth is four metres wide. It is still in use.

Colosseum: an amphitheatre completed in AD 80. It was used for gladiatorial combats and other types of fighting. It could seat 50,000 spectators and was equipped with an awning to provide shade.

Columns of Aurelius and Trajan: large free-standing columns on which military exploits of each are depicted in low-relief panels.

Forum Romanum: the original public square of Rome. By imperial times it had become so cluttered with buildings and monuments that other fora were constructed to the north.

Pantheon: a large round temple with portico of the first century AD which has survived virtually intact. Its dome, of over forty metres in diameter, has an open skylight of nine metres to illuminate the interior.

Temple of Jupiter: on the Capitol, the holiest of Roman temples, where various state functions were conducted.

Theatre of Marcellus: a semi-circular, open-air theatre completed by the Emperor Augustus in 13 BC. Its tiered seats held 20,000 people.

Walls of Servius: the original walls of Rome, popularly assigned to the sixth king of Rome but in actual fact built in the fourth century BC. Only a short section survives.

Walls of Aurelian: erected by the Emperor Aurelian in AD 271–5 when barbarian invasions were feared and Rome had long since expanded beyond the older walls. These walls are mostly in good condition.

UNIT 8

8.1 Grammar

8.1/1 First and second person pronouns

Latin, just as English, has first and second person pronouns, which are declined as follows:

	FIRST PERSON		SECOND PERSON	
SINGULAR				
Nom.	**égo**	*I*	**tū** (also voc.)	*you* (s.)
Acc.	**mē**	*me*	**tē**	*you*
Gen.	**méī**	*of me*	**túī**	*of you*
Dat.	**míhi**	*to* or *for me*	**tíbi**	*to* or *for you*
Abl.	**mē**	(*by, with* or *from*) *me*	**tē**	(*by, with* or *from*) *you*
PLURAL				
Nom.	**nōs**	*we*	**vōs** (also voc.)	*you* (pl.)
Acc.	**nōs**	*us*	**vōs**	*you*
Gen.	**nóstrum** **nóstrī**	*of us*	**véstrum** **véstrī**	*of you*
Dat.	**nṓbīs**	*to* or *for us*	**vṓbīs**	*to* or *for you*
Abl.	**nṓbīs**	(*by, with* or *from*) *us*	**vṓbīs**	(*by, with* or *from*) *you*

Notes

1 The nominative forms are only used when emphasis is required, **ego hoc fēcī** *I did this.*
2 The second person singular pronoun is used when only one person is addressed (2.1/2 note 2).

3 **Nostrum/vestrum** and **nostrī/vestrī** have separate uses. The forms in
   -um are used in expressions such as **ūnus vestrum** *one of you*, where,
   as in English, the genitive is used for a group from which one or
   more are taken (partitive genitive, 27.1/4*k*). The forms in -**ī** are used
   to express an objective genitive, i.e. a genitive which stands in the
   same relation to a noun or adjective as a grammatical object does
   to a transitive verb; **memor nostrī es** literally means *you are mindful
   of us* but, because the adjective **memor** when used with the verb *to
   be* means exactly the same as *remember*, we can say that **nostrī** (and
   us in the translation) is the logical object. As **memor** (and the
   English *mindful*) is followed by the genitive, this is called an
   objective genitive (27.1/4*i*). Only **nōs** and **vōs** have two genitives;
   elsewhere both uses are covered by the one form.
4 **Meī** and **tuī** are both disyllabic and should be pronounced as such,
   mé-ī, tú-ī.
5 The ablatives of these pronouns precede, not follow, the
   preposition **cum** and are written together with it: **mēcum, tēcum,
   nōbīscum, vōbīscum** (*with me, with you*, etc.).

8.1/2 Demonstrative pronouns

The Latin demonstratives draw our attention to persons and things
(**dēmonstrō, -āre** *point out*) and are used not only as third person
pronouns but also as adjectives. The English *this* and *that* have similar
functions although their use as pronouns is restricted; *this* in *this book*
is an adjective, *that* in *I do not like that* is a pronoun. There are four
demonstratives in Latin, each with a special shade of meaning. Their
basic differences when used as adjectives are:

hic   *this near me* (the speaker); generally to be translated *this*;
iste *that near you* (the person spoken to); generally to be
          translated *that*;
ille *that over there*, away from both speaker and person spoken to;
          generally to be translated *that*;
is   *this* or *that*. Used when greater precision is either not possible
          or not desirable.

When used as pronouns **hic** will literally mean *this man near me*, **iste**
that man near you, **ille** *that man over there*; **is, ea, id** are the normal
words for *he, she, it*. **Hic, ille, iste**, when used as pronouns, may also

be translated by *he* (and the feminine by *she*, etc.) or by *this man* (**hic**), *that man* (**ille** or **iste**). The distinction between **ille** and **iste** is not one that we can make in English with single-word equivalents, and consequently both can be translated simply by *that*. **Iste vir** may be rendered by *that man*, but in a particular context it might be better translated by *that man near you* or *that man of yours* if greater precision is required. The demonstrative pronouns are declined as follows:

	SINGULAR			PLURAL		
	M.	F.	N.	M.	F.	N.
Nom.	is	éa	id	íī (éī, ī)	éae	éa
Acc.	éum	éam	id	éōs	éās	éa
Gen.	éius	éius	éius	eórum	eárum	eórum
Dat.	éī	éī	éī	éīs, íīs	éīs, íīs	éīs, íīs
Abl.	éō	éā	éō	éīs, íīs	éīs, íīs	éīs, íīs
Nom.	hic	haec	hoc	hī	hae	haec
Acc.	hunc	hanc	hoc	hōs	hās	haec
Gen.	húius	húius	húius	hórum	hárum	hórum
Dat.	huic	huic	huic	hīs	hīs	hīs
Abl.	hōc	hāc	hōc	hīs	hīs	hīs
Nom.	ílle	ílla	íllud	íllī	íllae	ílla
Acc.	íllum	íllam	íllud	íllōs	íllās	ílla
Gen.	illíus	illíus	illíus	illórum	illárum	illórum
Dat.	íllī	íllī	íllī	íllīs	íllīs	íllīs
Abl.	íllō	íllā	íllō	íllīs	íllīs	íllīs

The bracketed alternatives are less common. **Iste** is declined in exactly the same way as **ille**.

Notes

1 This is called the ***pronominal declension*** and it is followed by all pronouns except **ego, tū, nōs, vōs**; further examples are given at 10.1/1. Apart from the eccentricities of some individual pronouns, the differences between the pronominal declension and first and second declension adjectives are:
   (i) the genitive singular of all genders ends in **-ius** (the **i** is consonantal when preceded by a vowel but vocalic when

preceded by a consonant);
(ii) the dative singular of all genders ends in **-ī**;
(iii) the neuter singular nominative and accusative generally end
in **-d**.
2 Some endings of **hic** have been obscured by an added **c**, e.g. **hui-c** (one syllable).
3 In **eius** and **huius** the consonantal **i** is pronounced as a double consonant (see p. xv).
4 **Hic . . . ille** can mean *the latter . . . the former.*
5 When used adjectivally, demonstratives normally precede the noun which they qualify: **hic vir** *this man*; **illa mulier** *that woman.*

8.1/3 Motion and position

In phrases denoting motion or position (*from Italy, to Greece, in Spain*) Latin normally uses a preposition (3.1/4), except with the names of cities, towns and small islands (i.e. all Mediterranean islands except Sicily and Sardinia; usage with Cyprus and Crete varies). With these, motion towards and motion away from are expressed by the accusative and ablative respectively without any preposition.

> **Mense Augustō Rōmā abscēdam et Karthāginem cum Fabiō veniam.**
> *In the month [of] August I shall go from Rome and come to Carthage with Fabius.*
> **Caesar Brundisiō ad Āfricam nāvigāvit.** *Caesar sailed from Brundisium to Africa.*

In phrases expressing position (where we would otherwise have **in** with the ablative) the names of cities, towns and small islands are put into the locative case without any preposition. This case, which was close to extinction even in Classical Latin, is identical with the ablative, except in the singular of the first and second declensions, where it coincides with the genitive; in the third declension singular we may have either **-e** or **-ī**. Examples are **Rōmae** *at/in Rome*, **Karthāgine** (or **Karthāginī**) *at/in Carthage.*

The above constructions without prepositions are also used for the common nouns **domus** (f) *house* (loc. **domī**, 9.1/3 note 3) and **rūs, rūris** (n) *country* (as opposed to town; loc. **rūre** or **rūrī**). The locatives of **bellum, -ī** (n) *war,* **mīlitia, -ae** (f) *military service* and **humus, -ī** (f) *ground* also occur, but the first two have a temporal sense: **bellī** *in* (*time* *of*) *war*, **mīlitiae** *on military service*. In poetry the plain ablative is often used to express position, and this occurs with certain words and expressions even in prose: **terrā marīque** *on land and sea*.

8.1/4 Plural place names and special plural common nouns

For some reason now lost to us, some names of towns and cities in the ancient world were plural in form, as **Athēnae** *Athens*, **Thēbae** *Thebes*, **Fidēnae, Formiae, Cūmae** (three towns in Italy). These names must always be treated as plural and be followed by a plural verb if the subject of a clause: **Athēnae in Atticā sunt** *Athens is in Attica*.

Similar to these are common nouns which are only used in the plural (cf. English *scales, scissors, trousers*). We have already met **arma, dīvitiae, scālae, tenebrae**. Listed below are others, together with five nouns which can change their meaning in the plural (cf. **vīs, vīrēs** 7.1/1 note 3):

aédēs, -is (f)	*temple*; the plural can mean *house*.
cástra, -órum (n)	*military camp*. The singular **castrum** (*fortified post*) is very rare.
cópia, -ae (f)	*abundance* (as in **cornū cōpiae** *horn of plenty*). The plural can mean either *supplies, provisions* or *forces, troops*.
fínis, -is (m)	*end*; the plural can mean *boundary*.
insídiae, -árum (f)	*ambush*; no singular.
líttera, -ae (f)	*letter of the alphabet*. The plural can mean a letter that today you would put in a postbox.
mánēs, -ium (m)	*shades of the dead*, but can also be used of only one dead person. No singular.
mōs, móris (m)	*custom*. The plural can mean *habits, character*.

When **aedēs** is used in the plural, how can we distinguish between the possible meanings of *temples, house, houses*? The same confusion is possible with **fīnis** and **littera**. As this ambiguity existed just as much for a Roman as for us, a writer had to make clear from the context which he meant. The problem disappears if numbers are involved because a special series is employed with these nouns when used in the plural with a meaning different from that of their singular (see 12.1/4c).

8.1/5 Dative of possessor

The dative is used with **sum** to indicate the owner or possessor, especially when what is owned or possessed is mentioned for the first time:

> **Est mihi plēnus Albānī cadus.** *I have a full jar of Alban* [*wine*].
> (lit. *there is to me . . .*)
> **Cornēliae fuērunt duo fīliī.** *Cornelia had two sons.*

Est meus plēnus Albānī cadus would mean *the full jar of Alban* [*wine*] (i.e. the one already mentioned) *is mine.*

8.2 Latin reading

1 Is primus Romam quattuor elephantos duxit.
2 Sunt mihi etiam fundi et aedes.
3 Gracchus, ubi incolae cuncta ex agris in urbem vexerunt et intra muros erant, Cumas castra movit.
4 Cum his copiis Hannibal Karthagine manebat Romanosque exspectabat.
5 Magnae Graecorum copiae Athenas convenerunt et Rhodum navigaverunt.
6 Caesar, quamquam Germani quiescebant, ad fines eorum processit.
7 Si domi sum, foris est animus, sin foris sum, animus est domi.
8 Multa Romae militiaeque male fecisti.
9 Si Roma Brundisium mecum veneris, ad Graeciam nave traiciemus.

Vergiliana

Publius Vergilius Maro (known in English as Vergil or Virgil), the greatest Roman poet, lived from 70 to 19 BC. His three works are: the *Eclogues*, which consist of ten pastoral poems; the *Georgics*, a long poem on farming; and the *Aeneid*, an epic which tells how Aeneas and a band of fellow Trojans escaped from Troy after the Greek sack and, in the face of many adversities, finally established themselves in Italy to found the Roman race. The references for the lines from Vergil given below will be found with their translations.

10 Mactavit taurum Neptuno, taurum tibi, pulcher Apollo.
11 Troius Aeneas tua nos ad limina misit.

12 O Meliboee, deus nobis haec otia fecit,
    namque erit ille mihi semper deus, illius aram
    saepe tener nostris ab ovilibus imbuet agnus.
13 Hunc tu olim caelo spoliis Orientis onustum accipies.
14 Tu quoque litoribus nostris, Aeneia nutrix,
    aeternam moriens famam, Caieta, dedisti.

Notes

10 For Neptune (**Neptūnus**) and Apollo see 9.3.
11 Take **tua** with **līmina** and translate by a singular noun *your threshold* (the use of the plural for the singular is a common figure of speech in Latin poetry); **Aenēās** nom. sing.; **Trōïus** (3 syllables) *Trojan*.
12 **Meliboeus, -ī** shepherd's name; translate **ōtia** by a singular, *leisure*; **nostrīs** = **meīs**.
13 **Oriens, -entis** *the East.*
14 **Aenēïus** (4 syllables), **-a, -um** *of* or *belonging to Aeneas*; **Caiēta** was Aeneas's nurse and the place where she died was named after her; **moriens** (present participle) *dying.*

8.2/1 Vocabulary

Section A

aetérnus, -a, -um *eternal*
ágnus, -ī (m) *lamb*
ánimus, -ī *mind*
ắra, -ae (f) *altar*
fắma, -ae (f) *fame*
fórīs (adv.) *outside, out of doors*
fúndus, -ī (m) *farm*
līmen, līminis (n) *threshold*
lītus, lītoris (n) *shore*
mále (adv.) *badly*
námque or **nam** (conj.) *for* (introducing a clause)

nắvis, -is (f) *ship*
nūtrix, nūtrīcis (f) *nurse*
ólim (adv.) *once, at some time in the past, at some future time*
onústus, -a, -um *laden*
ovíle, -is (n) *sheepfold*
prīmus, -a, -um *first*
quáttuor (indecl. adj.) *four*
Rhódus, -ī (f) *Rhodes*
sīn (conj.) *but if*
spólium, -ī (n) *spoils, plunder*
taúrus, -ī (m) *bull*

Section B

accípiō, accípere, accḗpī,
  accéptum *receive, accept*
convéniō, -íre, convḗnī,
  convéntum *come together,*
  assemble
dū́cō, -ere, dúxī, dúctum *lead*
ímbuō, imbúere, ímbuī, imbū́tum
  stain
máctō, -ā́re *sacrifice*
máneō, -ḗre, mánsī, mánsum
  stay, remain

míttō, -ere, mī́sī, míssum *send*
móveō, -ḗre, mṓvī, mṓtum *move*
párō, -ā́re *prepare*
prōcḗdō, -ere, prōcéssī,
  prōcéssum *go forward*
quiéscō, -ere, quiḗvī, quiḗtum
  be quiet
trāíciō (pronounced trāíiciō,
  see p.xvi), -ere, trāiḗcī,
  trāiéctum *cross*
véhō, -ere, véxī, véctum *carry*

UNIT 9

9.1 Grammar

9.1/1 Third declension adjectives – *i*-stems

Third declension adjectives, like third declension nouns, are divided into consonant stems and **i**-stems, but the latter are far more numerous. **I**-stem adjectives have -**ī** in the ablative singular of all genders (but see also note 3), -**ia** in the first three cases of the neuter plural, and -**ium** in the genitive plural. They are divided into three classes according to the number of terminations (i.e. endings) used in the nominative singular to distinguish gender. With the first and third classes the genitive (as well as the nominative) singular must be learnt in order to discover the stem.

One-termination *i*-stems have one form for all genders in the nominative singular. The neuter shows differences elsewhere, but the masculine and feminine coincide completely in all forms. With this group it is necessary to know the stem as well as the nominative singular; an example is **ingens** *huge* (gen. s. **ingentis**, therefore the stem is **ingent-**):

	SINGULAR		PLURAL	
	M. & F.	N.	M. & F.	N.
N. & V.	íngens	íngens	ingéntēs	ingéntia
Acc.	ingéntem	íngens	ingéntēs, -īs	ingéntia
Gen.	ingéntis	ingéntis	ingéntium	ingéntium
Dat.	ingéntī	ingéntī	ingéntibus	ingéntibus
Abl.	ingéntī	ingéntī	ingéntibus	ingéntibus

Two-termination *i*-stems have the same nominative singular form for the masculine and feminine (always ending in -**is**) but a different one for the neuter (always ending in -e). This is a very large class. An example is **tristis** *sad*:

	SINGULAR		PLURAL	
	M. & F.	N.	M. & F.	N.
N. & V.	trístis	tríste	trístēs	trístia
Acc.	trístem	tríste	trístēs, -īs	trístia
Gen.	trístis	trístis	trístium	trístium
Dat.	trístī	trístī	trístibus	trístibus
Abl.	trístī	trístī	trístibus	trístibus

Three-termination *i*-stems have a masculine in **-er**, feminine in **-ris**, and neuter in **-re** in the nominative singular. Their total number is small and they represent the development of those adjectives of the previous class with a stem ending in **-ri-**. **Ācer** *keen* is declined as follows:

	SINGULAR			PLURAL	
	M.	F.	N.	M. & F.	N.
N. & V.	ā́cer	ā́cris	ā́cre	ā́crēs	ā́cria
Acc.	ā́crem	ā́crem	ā́cre	ā́crēs, -īs	ā́cria
Gen.	ā́cris	ā́cris	ā́cris	ā́crium	ā́crium
Dat.	ā́crī	ā́crī	ā́crī	ā́cribus	ā́cribus
Abl.	ā́crī	ā́crī	ā́crī	ā́cribus	ā́cribus

Notes

1 One-termination adjectives include the present participle (which ends in **-ns**) of all verbs (11.1/2). Among the few words in this class not ending in **-ns** in the nominative singular are: **aúdax** gen. **audā́cis** *bold*, **fḗlix** gen. **fēlī́cis** *happy, lucky* (and other adjectives ending in **-x**), **pār** gen. **páris** *like, equal*.

2 One common three-termination adjective keeps **e** throughout its declension, **céler**, fem. **céleris**, neut. **célere** *swift* (irregular gen. pl. **célerum**).

3 I-stem adjectives usually have an ablative singular in **-e** when used as nouns; from **adulescens** *young* we could say either **ab adulescentī homine** or **ab adulescente** with the same meaning *by a young person*.

4 As with **i**-stem masculine and feminine nouns, there is an alternative ending in **-īs** for the accusative plural of the masculine and feminine forms of **i**-stem adjectives.

9.1/2 Third declension adjectives – consonant stems

Except for comparatives (19.1/1), this is a very small class, which, however, includes some very common words. In the ablative singular, consonant stems take **-e**, in the first three cases of the neuter plural **-a**, and in the genitive plural **-um**. Like one-termination **i**-stems they have only one form for the nominative and vocative singular of the three genders; and the stem is found by subtracting **-is** from the genitive singular. **Vétus** *old* is declined as follows:

	SINGULAR		PLURAL	
	M. & F.	N.	M. & F.	N.
N. & V.	vétus	vétus	véterēs	vétera
Acc.	véterem	vétus	véterēs	vétera
Gen.	véteris	véteris	véterum	véterum
Dat.	véterī	véterī	vetéribus	vetéribus
Abl.	vétere	vétere	vetéribus	vetéribus

Other adjectives in this class are: **caélebs, caélibis** *unmarried*, **ínops, ínopis** *poor*, **mémor, mémoris** *mindful* (the last two normally have -ī in the ablative singular), **paúper, paúperis** *poor*. **Dīves, dívitis** *rich* belongs here but has a contracted form **dīs, dítis**, which is declined like a one-termination **i**-stem and which is the more common form in the plural.

9.1/3 Fourth declension

Fourth declension nouns end in **-us** or **-ū** in the nominative singular. Those in **-us** are nearly all masculine, those in **-ū** are all neuter. The former must be distinguished from nouns in **-us** of the second declension and neuters in **-us** of the third declension. There are no adjectives. **Exercitus** (m) *army* and **cornū** (n) *horn* are declined thus:

	SINGULAR	PLURAL	SINGULAR	PLURAL
N. & V.	exércitus	exércitūs	córnū	córnua
Acc.	exércitum	exércitūs	córnū	córnua
Gen.	exércitūs	exercítuum	córnūs	córnuum
Dat.	exercítuī	exercítibus	córnū	córnibus
Abl.	exércitū	exercítibus	córnū	córnibus

Notes

1 The most common feminine nouns of the fourth declension are **domus** *house, home* (see below) and **manus** *hand*.
2 Note particularly that the dative singular of nouns in -**us** ends in -**uī** (two syllables) but that of neuters ends in -**ū**.
3 **Domus** (f) *house, home* is irregular as some of its forms come from the second declension:

	SINGULAR	PLURAL
N. & V.	**dómus**	**dómūs**
Acc.	**dómum**	**dómūs** *or* **dómōs**
Gen.	**dómūs**	**dómuum** *or* **domṓrum**
Dat.	**dómuī**	**dómibus**
Abl.	**dómō**	**dómibus**

The locative singular is **dómī** *at home* (8.1/3).

9.1/4 Reflexive pronouns

A reflexive pronoun is one that refers back to the subject of a clause, e.g. **Cleopatra sē interfēcit** *Cleopatra killed herself*. In English all reflexive pronouns end in -*self* (*myself, yourself,* etc.; but note that these should be carefully distinguished from emphatic pronouns of the same form in English—see 10.1/1b). Latin does not have a separate reflexive pronoun for the first and second persons but uses the normal personal pronouns: **in speculō mē videō** *I see myself in the mirror.* For the third person we have **sē**, which is declined: *acc.* **sē** (or **sḗsē**), *gen.* **súī**, *dat.* **síbi**, *abl.* **sē** (or **sḗsē**) .

All these forms of **sē** can be either singular or plural, and masculine, feminine or neuter. We must tell from the context whether the reflexive pronoun means *himself, herself, itself,* or *themselves,* and we do this by examining the subject of its clause. There is no nominative because the reflexive can never be the subject of a finite verb. When **sē** is used with **cum** *with*, we get **sēcum** (cf. **mēcum**, etc. 8.1/1 note 5). Examples of the reflexive are:

> **Dē mūrō sē iēcit** *He threw himself from the wall.*
> **Hominem sibi cārum audīvit.** *He heard a person dear to himself.*

According to the above **sē interfēcērunt** must mean *they killed themselves*, i.e. *A killed himself, B killed himself,* etc. How then do we say *they killed each other*? The Latin idiom involves a special use of **inter** *between, among*: **inter sē interfēcērunt**. *We love each other* would be **inter nōs amāmus**.

9.1/5 Reflexive possessive adjective

Connected with **sē** is the reflexive possessive adjective **suus** (declined like **malus**) *his, her, its, their*. It is normally only used when it refers to the subject of its clause, and even then is often dropped when there is no ambiguity or when no special emphasis is required. We can say **puella mātrem suam amat** *the girl loves her mother*; but **puella mātrem amat** would be sufficient because, if it had been someone else's mother, this would have been stated (cf. 4.1/4). Latin does not, however, have a third person possessive adjective which is not reflexive; instead we must use the genitive of a pronoun (normally **is**—8.1/2). *The girl loves their mother* is, therefore, **puella mātrem eōrum amat** (lit. *the mother of them*). With the singular **eius** there is always a possible ambiguity which must be resolved from the general context; **fīliam eius amō** can mean *I love his daughter* or *I love her daughter*. For first and second person possessive adjectives see 4.1/4.

9.2 Latin reading

1 Parvi sunt foris arma nisi est consilium domi.
2 Caesar, postquam hostes superavit, litteras ad senatum de se misit 'Veni, vidi, vici.'
3 Prima luce equitatus magnam Poenorum manum fugavit.
4 Dux Romanorum omnibus copiis impetum in hostem cum caede multorum fecit.
5 Cato se manu sua interfecit.
6 Alexander, post mortem Cliti, vix a se manus abstinuit.
7 Demetrius filios apud Gnidium, hospitem suum, cum magno auri pondere commendaverat.
8 Ut Seneca philosophus dixit, ira brevis insania et impotens sui est.

Latin proverbs

The prestige which Latin enjoyed in educated circles in the Middle Ages and the Renaissance resulted in the accumulation of an enormous number of proverbs in common use. The most famous published collection was the *Adagia* (*Proverbs*) of Erasmus (1466–1536). Examples of these and of proverbial expressions from Latin authors are given below and in other reading exercises.

9 In vino veritas.
10 Pares cum paribus.
11 Felix opportunitate mortis.
12 Caeca est invidia.
13 Audaces fortuna iuvat.
14 Ars longa, vita brevis.
15 Aquae furtivae suaves sunt.
16 Naturalia non sunt turpia.
17 O vita, misero longa, felici brevis.
18 Acta deos numquam mortalia fallunt.
19 Aut insanit homo aut versus facit.
20 Heredis fletus sub persona risus est.
21 Contra felicem vix deus vires habet.
22 (*On a sundial*) Horas non numero, nisi serenas.
23 Homo doctus in se semper divitias habet.
24 Ubi solitudinem faciunt pacem appellant.
25 Felicium multi cognati.
26 De mortuis nil nisi bonum.

Notes

1 **parvī** see 7.1/5.
5 **Catō** a contemporary of Julius Caesar.
In 9 and 14 **est** must be supplied, in 10 a verb meaning *congregate*.
11 and 17 are phrases.
17 **miserō . . . fēlīcī** lit. *for a miserable man . . .for a happy man.*
19 **versūs** here acc. pl.
25 Supply **sunt**
26 A verb meaning *you must say* is to be supplied.

9.2/1 Vocabulary

Section A

áctum, -ī (n) *act, deed*
brévis, -is, -e *short*
caédēs, -is (f) *slaughter*
cognátus, -ī (m) *relative*
consílium, -ī (n) *plan, ability to plan, wisdom*
equitátus, -ūs (m) *cavalry*
flētus, -ūs (m) *(act of) weeping*
furtívus, -a, -um *stolen*
hérēs, -édis (m *or* f) *heir*
ímpetus, -ūs (m) *attack*
ímpotens, -éntis (+ gen.) *with no control over*
insánia, -ae (f) *madness*
invídia, -ae (f) *envy*
íra, -ae (f) *anger*
lux, lúcis (f) *light*
mánus, -ūs (f) *hand; band of men*
mors, mórtis (f) *death*
mortális, -is, -e *mortal, of or concerning human beings*

nātūrális, -is, -e *natural*
nísi (conj.) *unless, except*
númquam (adv.) *never*
ómnis, -is, -e *all*
opportúnitās, -tátis (f) *opportuneness, timeliness*
pax, pácis (f) *peace*
persóna, -ae (f) *mask*
philósophus, -ī (m) *philosopher*
póndus, -deris (n) *weight, quantity*
rísus, -ūs (m) *laughter*
serénus, -a, -um *cloudless, clear, cheerful*
sōlitúdō, -dinis (f) *solitude, wilderness*
suávis, -is, -e *sweet*
túrpis, -is, -e *disgraceful*
véritās, -tátis (f) *truth*
vérsus, -ūs (m) *verse*
vix (adv.) *scarcely, with difficulty*

Section B

abstíneō, -ére, abstínuī, abstántum (compound of **téneō** *hold*) *restrain*
appéllō, -áre *name, call*
comméndō, -áre *entrust*
fállō, -ere, feféllī, fálsum *deceive*
fúgō, -áre (distinguish from

fúgiō) *put to flight, rout*
insániō, -íre *be insane*
interfíciō, -ere, interfécī, interféctum *kill*
iúvō, -áre, iúvī, iútum *help*
númerō, -áre *count*

9.3 Excursus

Roman religion

In primitive societies, where the world is seen as controlled by as many supernatural powers as there are unexplained influences and forces, people easily come to believe in many gods. When a society reaches a higher level of sophistication, the beliefs inherited from earlier generations can hardly be expected to present a harmonious theological system, but the conservatism inherent in religion is usually strong enough to resist major changes. So it was with the Romans. They had always been polytheistic, and their beliefs – the accumulation of centuries, if not millennia, without even a veil of consistency and logic – resembled the store-room of a badly kept museum. Their religion was an integral part of the state and, as such, was official; but this did not result in the rejection of non-Roman gods. On the contrary, there were several occasions when a foreign divinity was officially adopted in order to gain his or her support in time of need. Such an elastic attitude made it hard for the Romans of the first centuries of our era to understand the mentality of the Jews and Christians with their claims to exclusive possession of religious truth. No Roman divinity was endowed with the mind-reading ability of the Judaeo-Christian god, and consequently it did not matter what private beliefs an individual might hold. What did matter were the age-old rituals which had proved effective in the past in winning divine favour and which might be expected to do so in the future. These consisted of prayers, festivals and sacrifices; but, whether conducted by an individual or the whole state, they were based on the principle of **dō ut dēs** *I give [to you] so that you may give [to me]*. As, however, it would have been idle to suppose that the gods were always susceptible to human bribery, the Romans also concerned themselves with trying to foretell the future, or at least to see if a particular course of action had divine approval. The least bizarre of their methods was to observe the flight of birds (**auspicium** <**avis** *bird* + **speciō** *watch*). Another method was the **haruspicium**, which involved examining the stomach of some unfortunate beast in whose entrails the gods were supposed to have recorded their decisions for the future. The fact that these primitive crudities were maintained up to the end of paganism illustrates the caution and conservatism of the Roman mentality.

The principal Roman divinities were:

Jupiter (**Iúppiter, Ióvis**, see 6.1/2 note 5): king of the gods and men, **hominum deumque rex**, and often referred to as **Iuppiter optimus maximus** *Jupiter best [and] greatest*. His main temple was on the Capitol, but, because he had been assimilated by poets to his Greek counterpart, Zeus, he was normally conceived in poetry as dwelling on Mt Olympus in north-eastern Greece.

Juno (**Iū́nō, Iūnṓnis**): wife and sister of Jupiter, with whom she was often at variance. She was the goddess of marriage and childbirth.

Neptune (**Neptū́nus, -ī**): brother of Jupiter and lord of the sea.

Pluto (**Plū́tō, -ṓnis**, also called **Dīs, Dī́tis**): brother of Jupiter and lord of the Underworld, to which the souls of the dead (the **Mānḗs**) went, irrespective of the lives they had led. His wife was Proserpine (**Prṓscrpina**, also called Persephone), the queen of the dead.

Saturn (**Sātúrnus, -ī**): father of all the above and ruler of the gods before Jupiter, by whom he was dethroned. In his reign the world had been just and humans had lived simple lives in perfect happiness.

Venus (**Vénus, Véneris**): goddess of procreation and sexual love. She was married to Vulcan, but, as befitted her office, she indulged in promiscuity. As a result of one affair with a mortal, Anchises, she gave birth to Aeneas.

Minerva (**Minérva, -ae**): daughter of Jupiter and patron of handicrafts. Her favourite sport was warfare. She, Diana, and Vesta were virgin goddesses.

Apollo (**Apóllō, Apóllinis**): son of Jupiter and patron of poetry and music. He had shrines in Greece at Delos and Delphi; in the latter place he presided over the most famous oracle of the ancient world.

Diana (**Diā́na, -ae**): sister of Apollo and goddess of the hunt and wild beasts. She was also the moon goddess and, because of the association of the moon with witches, was equated with Hecate, the goddess of the black arts.

Mars (**Mars, Mártis**): son of Jupiter and god of warfare.

Mercury (**Mercúrius, -ī**): son of Jupiter and messenger of the gods.

Vulcan (**Vulcánus, -ī**): the divine blacksmith. His forge was under the volcano of Mt Etna in Sicily or some of the volcanic islands to the north-west.

Bacchus (**Bácchus, -ī**): son of Jupiter and god of wine. Also called Dionysus.

Vesta (**Vésta, -ae**): goddess of the hearth. She had a temple in the forum where a constantly burning fire was attended by her priestesses, the Vestal Virgins.

We may also mention the **Lárēs** and **Penátēs**, spirits without individual names who presided over the welfare of a Roman household. Their statuettes were placed in a cupboard (the **larārium**) where they received daily worship. The Lares were the guardians of the hearth (**focus**) and home (**domus**), the Penates saw to the food supply.

UNIT 10

10.1 Grammar

10.1/1 Pronominal declension

We have already seen how the demonstrative pronouns follow the pronominal declension, which is very similar to that of first and second declension adjectives. Its characteristics are given at 8.1/2 note 1. A number of other pronouns belong here, some of which show minor variations. Except for slight complications with the interrogative, the indefinite, and some of their compounds, all forms of these pronouns can function as adjectives. The pronominal declension does not include the first and second person pronouns (8.1/1).

(a) **īdem** *the same* is a compound of **is**, which is declined (with modifications), and an indeclinable suffix **-dem: īdem omnīs simul ardor habet** *the same enthusiasm grips* (lit. *holds*) *them all at the same time.*

	SINGULAR			PLURAL		
	M.	F.	N.	M.	F.	N.
Nom.	īdem	éadem	ídem	ídem *or* eīdem	eaédem	éadem
Acc.	eúndem	eándem	ídem	eōsdem	eāsdem	éadem
Gen.	eiúsdem	eiúsdem	eiúsdem	eōrúndem	eārúndem	eōrúndem
Dat.	eīdem	eīdem	eīdem		īsdem *or* eīsdem	
Abl.	eōdem	eādem	eōdem		īsdem *or* eīsdem	

(b) **Ipse** means *self*: Latin has no separate emphatic pronouns for *myself, yourself, himself*, etc. Instead, it uses the relevant pronoun with the appropriate part of **ipse: ā nōbīs ipsīs** *by us ourselves*, **ea ipsa** *she herself*. It may also agree with an understood subject, e.g. **ipse lacrimāvī** *I myself cried*; **ipsa vēnit** *she came herself* (the ending of **vēnit** tells us that the subject is third singular, that of **ipsa** tells us that it is feminine. The Latin for *she came* is **ea vēnit** unless it is obvious from the context that a woman is involved; in this case **vēnit** would suffice). The English pronouns ending in *-self* can be either emphatic or reflexive; Latin has only one emphatic pronoun, **ipse**, which is never used as a reflexive (for Latin reflexive pronouns see 9.1/4).

	SINGULAR			PLURAL		
	M.	F.	N.	M.	F.	N.
Nom.	ípse	ípsa	ípsum	ípsī	ípsae	ípsa
Acc.	ípsum	ípsam	ípsum	ipsōs	ipsās	ípsa
Gen.	ipsíus	ipsíus	ipsíus	ipsórum	ipsárum	ipsórum
Dat.	ípsī	ípsī	ípsī	ípsīs	ípsīs	ípsīs
Abl.	ípsō	ípsā	ípsō	ípsīs	ípsīs	ípsīs

(*c*) **Alius** is the word for *other* where more than two persons or things are involved.

	SINGULAR			PLURAL		
	M.	F.	N.	M.	F.	N.
Nom.	álius	ália	áliud	áliī	áliae	ália
Acc.	álium	áliam	áliud	áliōs	áliās	ália
Gen.	alíus	alíus	alíus	aliórum	aliárum	aliórum
Dat.	áliī	áliī	áliī	áliīs	áliīs	áliīs
Abl.	áliō	áliā	áliō	áliīs	áliīs	áliīs

The genitive singular of **alter** (see below) can be used for **alīus** (genitive) to avoid confusion with the nominative singular. Idiomatic uses of **alius** are: **aliī alia dīcunt** *different people say different things*; **aliī hoc dīcunt, aliī illud** *some say this, others that*.

(*d*) **Alter** *other of two* must be used where only two persons or things are involved. This is not a distinction used in English. An old Latin proverb runs **Quid est amīcus? Alter ego.** *What is a friend? [He is] another I* (i.e. a duplicate of oneself).

	SINGULAR			PLURAL		
	M.	F.	N.	M.	F.	N.
Nom.	álter	áltera	álterum	álterī	álterae	áltera
Acc.	álterum	álteram	álterum	álterōs	álterās	áltera
Gen.	alterī́us	alterī́us	alterī́us	alterṓrum	alterā́rum	alterṓrum
Dat.	álterī	álterī	álterī	álterīs	álterīs	álterīs
Abl.	álterō	álterā	álterō	álterīs	álterīs	álterīs

Declined like **alter** (except that they do not elsewhere keep the **e** of the nominative singular masculine) are **uter, utra, utrum** *which of two?* together with its compound **uterque, utraque, utrumque** *each of two, either* (the indeclinable **-que** is simply added to each form), and **neuter** (2 syllables), **neutra, neutrum** *neither of two.* An example of **uterque** is: **sortī pater aequus utrīque est** [*my*] *father is equal to either fate.*

(*e*) **Sṓlus** *alone* is declined:

	SINGULAR			PLURAL		
	M.	F.	N.	M.	F.	N.
Nom.	sṓlus	sṓla	sṓlum	sṓlī	sṓlae	sṓla
Acc.	sṓlum	sṓlam	sṓlum	sṓlōs	sṓlās	sṓla
Gen.	sōlī́us	sōlī́us	sōlī́us	sōlṓrum	sōlā́rum	sōlṓrum
Dat.	sṓlī	sṓlī	sṓlī	sṓlīs	sṓlīs	sṓlīs
Abl.	sṓlō	sṓlā	sṓlō	sṓlīs	sṓlīs	sṓlīs

Like **sōlus** are declined **tōtus** *all,* **ūnus** *one,* **ullus** *any,* **nullus** *none.*

(*f*) **Quī** is the relative pronoun or adjective. For its use see the next subsection.

	SINGULAR			PLURAL		
	M.	F.	N.	M.	F.	N.
Nom.	quī	quae	quod	quī	quae	quae
Acc.	quem	quam	quod	quōs	quās	quae
Gen.	cúius	cúius	cúius	quṓrum	quā́rum	quṓrum
Dat.	cui	cui	cui	quíbus	quíbus	quíbus
Abl.	quō	quā	quō	quíbus	quíbus	quíbus

For the pronunciation of **cuius** and **cui** see p. xv; all other singular forms are monosyllabic. A variant of **quibus** found in verse is **quīs** (note long **ī**).

(*g*) The *interrogative pronoun* has the same forms as the relative, except for the masculine and feminine nominative singular **quis** and the neuter nominative and accusative singular **quid**. Examples of its use are: **quis tē, Palinūre, deōrum ēripuit nōbīs?** *which of the gods, Palinurus, snatched you from us?*; **quid fēcī?** *what have I done?* The neuter **quid** is often used adverbially in the sense of *why* (27.1/3*e*): **Galle, quid insānīs?** *Gallus, why are you raging?*

(*h*) The *interrogative adjective* is declined in exactly the same way as the relative: **quī ventī, quae fāta cursum tibi dedērunt?** *what winds, what fates gave you your course?*

(*i*) The *indefinite pronoun* **quis, qua, quid** *anyone, anything* and the *indefinite adjective* **quī, quae, quod** *any* also follow the relative in their declension in the same way as the interrogatives except:

(i) The feminine nominative singular of the pronoun is **qua** (or **quae** – see below).

(ii) The neuter plural nominative and accusative of both is **quae** or **qua**.

Their use is mainly restricted to certain types of clauses, in particular, conditional clauses introduced by **sī** *if* and **nisi** *if not, unless* (22.1/2): **sī qua bella inciderint, vōbīs auxilium feram** *if any wars occur I shall bring you help.*

These pronouns and adjectives beginning with **qu-** only differ from each other (and then not always) in the nominative and accusative; in the other cases they are always the same. With the interrogative and indefinite pronouns and adjectives the distinctions between the nominative singular of the pronominal and adjectival forms (masculine and feminine) are not always observed (this also applies to **aliquis/aliquī** – see next subsection). The distinction, however, between the neuters **quid** (pronoun) and **quod** (adjective) is kept up in both groups (and in some compounds). The following table gives all possible forms of these cases:

	Relative pronoun (and adjective) (*The man* who hears . . .)			**Interrogative pronoun** (Who *is that?*)			**Interrogative adjective** (What *chariot do you like?*)		
SINGULAR	M.	F.	N.	M.	F.	N.	M.	F.	N.
Nom.	quī	quae	quod	quis quī	quis quae } quid		quī quis	quae quis } quod	
Acc.	quem	quam	quod	quem	quam	quid	quem	quam	quod
PLURAL									
Nom.	quī	quae	quae	quī	quae	quae	quī	quae	quae
Acc.	quōs	quās	quae	quōs	quās	quae	quōs	quās	quae

	Indefinite pronoun (*If* anyone *goes . . .*)			**Indefinite adjective** (*If* any *wars occur . . .*)		
SINGULAR	M.	F.	N.	M.	F.	N.
Nom.	quis quī	qua quae } quid		quī quis	quae qua } quod	
Acc.	quem	quam	quid	quem	quam	quod
PLURAL						
Nom.	quī	quae	quae *or* qua	quī	quae	quae *or* qua
Acc.	quōs	quās	quae *or* qua	quōs	quās	quae *or* qua

(j) Compounds of *quis/qui*

These can function as either pronouns or adjectives, with the reservation mentioned above on forms containing **quid/quod** where they are given below; elsewhere (**quodcumque, quidquam**) there is only one form of the neuter singular nominative/accusative and no distinction is made. Except for **aliquis**, these compounds have **quis/quī** as their first element (**quī-dam, quis-que, quis-quam, quī-cumque**). The second element (**-dam, -que, -quam, -cumque**) does not change, and **quis/quī** is declined as above, except that with **quīdam** the final **m** of **quem, quam, quōrum, quārum** becomes **n** and we get **quendam, quandam**, etc. (cf. **īdem**).

M.	F.	N.	
áliquis, áliquī	áliqua	áliquid, áliquod	*someone, something*
quídam	quaédam	quíddam, quóddam	*a certain person or thing*
quísque	quaéque	quídque, quódque	*each*
quísquam	quísquam	quídquam (*or* quícquam)	*anyone/anything at all*
quīcúmque	quaecúmque	quodcúmque	*whoever, whatever*

The last is a relative and will be explained in the next subsection. The others do not suffer any restrictions in use similar to that of the indefinite **quis/quī** (see above). Examples are:

> **Cuncta Graecia parvum quendam locum Eurōpae tenet.** *The whole of Greece* (lit. *all Greece*) *occupies a certain small part* (lit. *place*) *of Europe.*
>
> **Dīcet aliquis 'quid ergō in hōc Verrem reprehendis?'** *Someone will say, 'Well, why do you blame Verres in this [matter]?'*
>
> **Ille Rutulōs increpat omnēs et nōmine quemque vocat.** *He upbraids all the Rutulians and calls each by name.*
>
> **Quisquam nūmen Iūnōnis adōrat?** *Does anyone at all worship the divinity of Juno?*
>
> **Amat mulier quaedam quendam.** *A certain woman loves a certain man.*

10.1/2 Adjectival clauses

Adjectival (or relative) clauses qualify nouns or pronouns and so perform the same function as adjectives. They are normally introduced by a relative pronoun,[1] in English *who, which, that,* etc.

> *Curse the man **who** burnt the Temple of Diana at Ephesus!*
> *The forum, **which** lies at the foot of the Capitol, was the centre of Roman life.*
> *The fish **that** you bought yesterday at Ostia is definitely shark.*

In English *who* and *which* can also be interrogatives (***Who** are you?* ***Which** piece of shark would you prefer?*). *That* can introduce other types of subordinate clauses (*I am certain **that** this is not mullet*—here *that* introduces a noun clause—26.1/2). It is, however, easy to see when these words are introducing an adjectival clause because there will nearly always be a noun or pronoun to which the clause refers and which it qualifies. This noun or pronoun is called the **antecedent**. The antecedents in the above examples are *man, forum, fish,* and, as we cannot say *the man which* or *the forum who*, it is obvious that the antecedent influences the form of the relative. The same applies in

---

[1] In Latin we also have adjectival clauses introduced by the relative adjective, which is the same in form as the relative pronoun (see note on 22.3). The relative adjective is also used to join sentences (see note on 17.3).

Latin, where the rule is: *a relative pronoun takes its number and gender from its antecedent but its case from its function in its own clause*. Its case is *not* determined by the antecedent but by its relationship to its clause. In *the man whom I saw will be ninety-three tomorrow*, the antecedent of the adjectival clause *whom I saw* is *man*, and *man* is the subject of the clause *the man will be ninety-three tomorrow*. *Whom*, however, is not the subject of the clause *whom I saw*; it is in fact the object (the subject is *I*), and because of this we have the accusative form *whom* (English use here can be careless and we sometimes have the nominative form *who*; this is impossible in Latin). Likewise, in *the consul whose toga I splashed was furious*, *consul* is the subject of *the consul was furious*, but *whose* is genitive because the meaning is *the toga of whom*. In Latin this will run **consul cuius togam aspersī, perīrātus erat**. One important difference between English and Latin usage is that in English we can, in certain contexts, omit the relative (*the fish I had at Baiae was infinitely better*). It is *never* omitted in Latin. Also, although the term antecedent means *coming before* (**ante + cēdō**), in Latin it sometimes follows the adjectival clause which qualifies it. We can even have an adjectival clause qualifying the unexpressed subject of a verb or serving as the object of a verb; this occurs occasionally in English: *What I need is a holiday at Baiae*; *he ignores what I think*.

The following examples illustrate these various uses:

> **Arma virumque canō, Troiae quī prīmus ab ōrīs . . . vēnit.** *I sing of arms and of the man who first came from the shores of Troy.*
>
> **Suffēnus iste, quem vidēs, homo urbānus est.** *That Suffenus, whom you see, is a refined person.*
>
> **Fīnēs Cassivellaunī ā maritimīs cīvitātibus flūmen dīvīdit quod Tamesim appellant.** *A river which they call the Thames* (**Tamesis**) *divides the boundaries of Cassivellaunus from the communities by the sea.*
>
> **Dī patriī quōrum semper sub nūmine Troia est . . .** *Ancestral gods, under whose protection* (lit. *divinity*) *Troy always is . . .*
>
> **Quod est ante pedēs nēmō spectat.** *No one sees what* (i.e. *the thing which*) *is before his feet.*
>
> **Casta est quam nēmō rogāvit.** *She is chaste whom no one has asked.*

Tribūnōs mīlitum, cum quibus[1] ad primam aciem prōcurrerat, īre ad equitēs iussit. *He ordered the tribunes of the soldiers, with whom he had run out to the first line of battle, to go to the cavalrymen.* **Quae dē legiōnibus scrībis, ea vēra sunt.** *The things which you write about the legions are true.*

Quīcumque (10.1/1*j*) is the generalising relative pronoun and functions exactly as its English equivalent *whoever*: **Iuppiter aut quīcumque oculīs haec aspicit aequīs** . . . *Jupiter or whoever views these things with just eyes . . .*

10.2 Latin reading

Starting with this unit no separate vocabularies will be given and you should look up all unfamiliar words in the vocabulary at the end of the book. Nearly all subsequent reading material will be original Latin.

1 Caelum, non animum, mutant qui trans mare currunt.
2 Quisque est faber suae fortunae.
3 Numquam aliud natura, aliud sapientia dixit.
4 Qui amoris vulnus facit, idem sanat.
5 Assidua ei sunt tormenta qui se ipsum timet.
6 Male secum agit aeger, medicum qui heredem facit.
7 Quod cibus est aliis, aliis est venenum.
8 Etiam capillus unus habet umbram suam.
9 Quemcumque quaerit, calamitas facile invenit.
10 Qui iterum naufragium facit, improbe Neptunum improbat.
11 Nullis amor est medicabilis herbis.

Epigrams from Martial
12 Thais habet nigros, niveos Laecania dentes.
        quae ratio est? emptos haec habet, illa suos.
13 Difficilis, facilis, iucundus, acerbus es idem:
        nec tecum possum vivere nec sine te.
14 Quod tam grande 'sophos' clamat tibi turba togata,
        non tu, Pomponi, cena diserta tua est.

---

[1]This could also be **quibuscum**; **cum** *with* may be placed before or after the relative pronoun (cf. 8.1/1 note 5).

15   Quem recitas, meus est, o Fidentine, libellus,
        sed, male cum recitas, incipit esse tuus.

Notes

 1   The understood subject of the main clause *they* is the antecedent
     of the relative clause.
 6   The relative pronoun (here **quī**) is not always the first word in its
     clause. This very common idiom cannot be reproduced in
     English.
12   **Thāis** and **Laecānia** (both nom. sing.) are Greek female names;
     haec *this one, the latter*; **ille**, *that one, the former*; **emptōs** *bought*
     (past participle passive – 11.1/2).
13   **īdem** is in apposition (see **Glossary of grammatical terms**) to the
     understood subject of **es** *you*; the meaning is *you, the same person*;
     possum *I can, am able* (15.1/1) is followed by an infinitive.
14   **Quod** *as to the fact that*; here virtually *when*; **sophōs**, which is
     really a Greek adverb meaning *cleverly* [*said*], was an exclamation
     of applause used by a Roman audience at recitations by authors
     of their works (*clever! bravo!*). Here it is qualified by a neuter
     adjective **grande**; **togāta** *togaed, with togas*; the toga, a large
     semicircular piece of white woollen material elaborately draped
     around the body, was the formal dress of an adult Roman male.
15   **cum** *when* 16.1/3 (a different word from **cum** *with*); subordinating
     conjunctions, like the relative pronoun (above 6), need not come
     as the first word in their clause.

UNIT 11

11.1 Grammar

11.1/1 Fifth declension

Nouns of the fifth declension (there are no adjectives) end in **-ēs** and are feminine, except for **diēs** *day* and its compound **merīdiēs** *midday*, which are generally masculine. **Diēs** and **rēs** *thing* are declined:

	SINGULAR		PLURAL	
N. & V.	**diēs**	**rēs**	**diēs**	**rēs**
Acc.	**diem**	**rem**	**diēs**	**rēs**
Gen.	**diéī**	**réī**	**diérum**	**rérum**
Dat.	**diéī**	**réī**	**diébus**	**rébus**
Abl.	**díē**	**rē**	**diébus**	**rébus**

Notes

1 **Di-ē-ī** is trisyllabic, **re-ī** disyllabic. The genitive singular and dative singular in **-eī** (not **-eī**) only occur after **i**.
2 **Rēs** is used in a variety of expressions where it would not be translated into idiomatic English by *thing*, e.g.
   rēs rustica (*the farming thing*) *agriculture*
   rēs secundae (*favourable things*) *success*
   rēs gestae (*things done*) *acts, deeds, events, history*
   rēs in angustiīs erat (*the thing was in narrow straits*) *the situation was desperate*
   rem acū tetigistī (*you have touched the thing with a needle*) *you have got to the heart of the matter, you have hit the nail on the head.*
3 **Rēs pūblica**, sometimes written together as **rēspūblica**, literally means *the public thing* but is used in the sense of *the body politic, the state* (**not** *republic*, which is **lībera rēspublica**, lit. *free state*).

Whether it is written as one word or two, both elements must be declined, **rēs pūblica, rem pūblicam, reī pūblicae**, etc.

11.1/2 Participles

Participles are those parts of verbs which function as adjectives. They have tense (*taking* is present, *having taken* is past) and voice (*taking* is active, *being taken* is passive). Theoretically, therefore, we might expect to have six participles, viz active and passive participles for present, past and future (leaving aside the possibility of having separate participles for each of the past tenses, which, fortunately, does not arise in either English or Latin). These six exist in English (although only two are single-word forms), but a normal Latin verb has only the present active, future active, and perfect (i.e. past) passive. When we might have wanted to use the others we are obliged to turn to different types of expression (see next subsection).

The present participle is formed by adding **-ns** to the present stem of the first and second conjugations, and **-ens** to that of the third and fourth. All present participles have a stem in **-nt-** and are declined like **ingens** (9.1/1). Examples are:

> **áma-ns**, gen. **amántis** *loving*
> **móne-ns**, gen. **monéntis** *warning*
> **rég-ens**, gen. **regéntis** *ruling*
> **aúdi-ens**, gen. **audiéntis** *hearing*

The perfect participle is formed by subtracting **-um** from the supine and adding **-us**; the result is declined exactly as a first and second declension adjective (4.1/1).

> **amắt-us, -a, -um** *loved* or *having been loved*
> **mónit-us, -a, -um** *warned* or *having been warned*
> **réct-us, -a, -um** *ruled* or *having been ruled*
> **audīt-us, -a, -um** *heard* or *having been heard*

The future participle is formed by taking the same supine stem and adding **-ūrus**. This also is declined as a first and second declension adjective.

> **amāt-ū́rus, -ū́ra, -ū́rum** *going to love, about to love*
> **monit-ū́rus, -ū́ra, -ū́rum** *going to warn, about to warn*

rect-ū́rus, -ū́ra, -ū́rum *going to rule, about to rule*
audīt-ū́rus, -ū́ra, -ū́rum *going to hear, about to hear*

The active participles (present and future) of transitive verbs can take an object in the same way as a finite active form (see example in note 2 below).

Notes

1 Care must be taken with English words ending in *-ing*, as this ending is used to form not only the present active participle but also the verbal noun. In *fighting is something to be avoided*, the word *fighting* is functioning as a noun, not as an adjective, and therefore is a noun, not a participle; but it is a participle in *he died while fighting*. An easy way to distinguish between the two uses is to insert *the act of* before the word ending in *-ing*; if there is virtually no difference in meaning then a verbal noun is involved, but if nonsense results we have a participle (*he died while the act of fighting* is gibberish and therefore *fighting* in the original sentence is a participle). For the treatment of verbal nouns in Latin see 18.1/1.

2 Present participles have an ablative singular in **-ī** when they are used as simple attributive adjectives (cf. 9.1/1 note 3); when they are used as nouns or when they have a verbal force the ablative singular is usually in **-e**: **ab amantī fīliā** *by a loving daughter* (attributive adjective); **ā dīcente** *by a speaker* (nominal use).

   Hoc ā patre Stōicōs irrīdente audīvī. *I heard this from my father (when he was) mocking the Stoics* (the participle has a verbal force because it governs **Stōicōs**).

3 **Sum** does not have a present or perfect participle. Its future participle is **futūrus** *about to be, going to be*.

4 Two common verbs have **-itūrus** in their future participle where we would expect **-tūrus**: **ruitū́rus** (<**ruō, -ere** *rush*) and **moritū́rus** (<**morior, -ī** *die*).

11.1/3 Use of participles

It is essential to remember that Latin does not have a future passive, present passive, or perfect active participle.[1] Latin makes up for this deficiency by employing expressions different from English. **Caesar captam urbem incendit** (lit. *Caesar burnt the having-been-captured city*) could be translated by *Caesar burnt the city, which he had captured* or *Caesar, having captured the city, burnt it.* It might be objected that the Latin does not specifically say that Caesar himself was the agent who captured the city, only that he burnt it. A point of idiom is involved. A Roman would assume that Caesar, because he is the subject of the clause, had done the capturing as well unless the contrary were stated or at least implied. We should also note that we have the perfect participle **captam** because the capture preceded the arson. The rule is: *a participle's tense does not depend on whether the action expressed by it is in the past, present or future; but on whether that action takes place before, at the same time as, or after the action of the finite verb in its clause.* English has basically the same rule but we do not apply it so rigorously. Also, English often puts words like *while*, *when*, etc. before a participle; this never happens in Latin, where such words only function as conjunctions to introduce clauses.

> **Oppugnātūrus urbem Caesar mīlitibus novōs gladiōs dedit.** *Caesar, when about to attack the city, gave his soldiers new swords.*
> **Platō scrībens clāmōrem audīvit.** *While writing Plato heard a shout.*

The above examples involve participles which agree with nouns, and this is what we would expect as participles function as adjectives. Adjectives in Latin, however, can be used as nouns (4.1/3) and the same applies to participles, as we have already seen in the previous subsection. English does not normally use participles in this way; we must often translate a Latin participle so used by an ordinary noun, or a noun and adjective, or a noun and adjectival clause.

> **Caesar captōs interfēcit.** *Caesar killed the captives* (or *the captured men*, or *the men he had captured* depending on the context).
> **Ea pariter cum caelō vīdit amantem.** *She saw her lover and the sky at the same time* (lit. *together with the sky*).

---

[1]A special class of verbs called deponents is an exception as their perfect participles are active in sense – see 14.1/4.

11.1/4 Ablative of agent

An agent is a living being, an instrument is almost always something inanimate. These terms are used to distinguish between phrases such as *by Brutus* and *with a dagger* in the sentence *Caesar was killed by Brutus with a dagger*. To express the agent we use **ā/ab** with the ablative (3.1/4), but the instrument is expressed by the plain ablative without a preposition (7.1/4). Consequently *by Brutus* would be **ā Brūtō**, while *with a dagger* would be simply **pūgiōne** (**pūgiō, pūgiōnis** m).

11.1/5 Numerals (1)

Numerals of the type *one, two, three*, etc. are called cardinals, and are in Latin, with one exception, adjectives which normally precede the noun they qualify. They will be found listed with other types of numerals on p. 298. Cardinal numerals are indeclinable except for:

(*a*) **ūnus** *one* (for its declension see 10.1/1*e*);
(*b*) **duo** *two*:

	M.	F.	N.
Nom.	dúo	dúae	dúo
Acc.	dúōs *or* dúo	dúās	dúo
Gen.	duórum	duárum	duórum
Dat.	duóbus	duábus	duóbus
Abl.	duóbus	duábus	duóbus

(*c*) **trēs** *three*:

	M. & F.	N.
Nom.	trēs	tría
Acc.	trēs	tría
Gen.	tríum	tríum
Dat.	tríbus	tríbus
Abl.	tríbus	tríbus

(*d*) the words for 200, 300, 400, 500, 600, 700, 800, 900, which are first and second declension adjectives;

(*e*) **mīlia**

Although **mille** *thousand* is an indeclinable adjective, its plural **mīlia** is declined as a third declension neuter **i**-stem (**mīlia, mīlia, mīlium, mīlibus, mīlibus**) and is the only cardinal number which is a noun. Because of this it must be followed by the genitive (cf. *a dozen eggs* but *dozens of eggs*). *A thousand soldiers* is **mille mīlitēs** but *two thousand soldiers* is **duo mīlia mīlitum** (lit. *two thousands of soldiers*).

In the compound numbers 21 to 99 the smaller number is put first and joined to the larger by **et**; the other order is possible but without **et**, e.g. **ūnus et vīgintī** or **vīgintī ūnus** (*21*), **sex et sexāgintā** or **sexāgintā sex** (*66*). In this range, however, compounds involving 8 and 9 are normally of the form *two from* (**dē**) *thirty* **duodētrīgintā** (*28*), *one from thirty* **undētrīgintā** (*29*), the three words being combined. In compound numbers above 100 the elements are generally arranged in descending order of magnitude without any joining word, **centum quadrāgintā quinque** (*145*).

11.2 Latin reading

1 Ducentos septuaginta tres milites vidi; mille nautae; octo milia nautarum.
2 A tribus milibus Romanorum; de sescentis quadraginta uno Gallis; centum Graecae.
3 Petilius ferocibus verbis milites incendebat, nullam moram facturus.
4 Mox nox, in rem!
5 Amantium irae amoris integratio est.
6 Incidis in Scyllam, cupiens vitare Charybdim.
7 Eis litteris commotus, Caesar duas legiones in Gallia conscripsit.
8 Iuppiter ex alto periuria ridet amantum.
9 Multitudo medicorum certa mors est aegrotantium.
10 Timeo Danaos et dona ferentes.
11 De ea re grammatici certant et adhuc sub iudice lis est.
12 Brevi arcem aut relictam ab hostibus aut cum ipsis hostibus capiemus.
13 Unus Pellaeo iuveni non sufficit orbis.
14 Quis custodiet ipsos custodes?
15 Salus reipublicae suprema lex.

Catulliana

> **Gaius Valerius Catullus** (about 84–34 BC) is the only lyric poet from the generation before Vergil whose works survive. Catullus's formal poetry, which includes a short epic (an epyllion), is eclipsed by his love poetry and occasional poems. His love poetry is addressed to Lesbia, a Roman lady whose real name was Clodia, and who left him after a brief but passionate affair.

B. Y. O.

16 Cenabis bene, mi Fabulle, apud me
paucis, si tibi di favent, diebus,
si tecum attuleris bonam atque magnam   3
cenam, non sine candida puella
et vino et sale et omnibus cachinnis.

17 Otium, Catulle, tibi molestum est:
otio exsultas nimiumque gestis.
otium et reges prius et beatas
perdidit urbes.

Lesbia's sparrow

18 Passer, deliciae meae puellae,
quocum ludere, quem in sinu tenere,
cui primum digitum dare appetenti   3
et acres solet incitare morsus . . .
tecum ludere, sicut ipsa, possem
et tristes animi levare curas!

Notes

4 A verb must be supplied before and after the comma.

5 Because the subject **īrae** is plural we would have expected **sunt**, not **est**. Here, and in 9 and 15 (where supply **est**), only the sense can tell us what is the subject and what the subject is said to be, i.e. what is predicated of it; **īrae** pl., i.e. *manifestations of anger, quarrels.*

6 **incidis** <**incidō** *fall into.*

8 **amantum** poetical for **amantium**.

10 **Danaōs** = **Graecōs**; **et** *even.*

12 **brevī [tempore].**

13 **Pellaeus** *of Pella*, the birthplace of Alexander the Great, who is referred to here.

16 *l.*1 **mī** 4.1/4. *l.*2 **faveō** + dative *be favourable to*. *l.*3 **attuleris**
    compound of **ad** and **ferō, ferre, tulī, lātum** (see 15.1/4) *bring*. *l.*5
    omnibus cachinnīs *all manner of laughter*.
18 *l.*1 **dēliciae** plural with singular meaning *darling*; **meae** to be taken
    with **puellae** (gen. s.). *ll.*2–4 **quōcum** = **cum quō**, cf. 8.1/1 note 5;
    prīmum digitum *the first part of* [*her*] *finger*, i.e. *the tip of her finger*
    (21.1/3); **solet** must be understood with **lūdere, tenēre** (*l.*2) and
    dare. *l.*5 **possem** *I wish I could* (optative subjunctive, 22.1/1*a*).

11.3 Excursus

Roman numerals

Only tradition and the occasional need for something distinctively
different (as on clock dials) have kept Roman numerals in use up to
the present day. The Roman system is clumsy in the extreme when
compared with the Arabic (originally Indian), which was adopted by
Europe in the Middle Ages. It has no single symbols for 2, 3, 4, 6, 7,
8 and 9; its lack of nought, 0, has serious consequences in the
expression of large numbers. The symbols which it employs are:

I	*one*	C	*hundred*
V	*five*	IↃ or D	*five hundred*
X	*ten*	CIↃ or M	*thousand*
L	*fifty*		

Other numbers are made up by the repetition, combination, or both,
of these basic elements according to the following rules:

(*a*) Repeated digits are added together (III = 3; CCCC = 400), with
       the exceptions noted in (*c*).
(*b*) A smaller digit is added to a preceding larger digit (DC = 600;
       LXXVI = 76) but subtracted from a larger number which follows
       (IX = 9). The latter procedure takes precedence within one number,
       e.g. CCCXXIV (324) = CCCXX + IV (**not** CCCXXI + V).
(*c*) Ↄ to right of IↃ multiplies it by 10 (IↃↃↃ = 50,000); by putting
       C in front of I for as many times as Ↄ follows we multiply the right-
       hand number by 2 (CCCIↃↃↃ 100,000).
(*d*) A line above multiplies by 1,000 (V̄I = 6000).

Further examples will be found in the table of numbers at p. 298.

UNIT 12

12.1 Grammar

12.1/1 Ablative absolute

This construction (*absolute* here means *independent*), in its simplest form, involves a noun or pronoun and a participle which are both in the ablative case and which stand apart from (i.e. are grammatically independent of) the rest of the sentence; naturally there is a connection in sense as otherwise there would be no point in putting the two together. We have an absolute construction (the nominative absolute) in English. Although it is a little clumsy, we can say: *the enemy having been conquered, Hannibal arrived at Carthage.* In Latin this becomes: **hoste victō Hannibal Karthāginem advēnit.**

It is important that the subject of the ablative absolute (here **hoste**) is not referred to in the rest of the sentence. We should not say: **hoste victō Hannibal eum interfēcit** (lit. *the enemy having been conquered Hannibal killed him* – i.e. someone else) if we mean that Hannibal both conquered and killed his enemy (i.e. if **hoste** and **eum** refer to the same person); the ablative absolute would not be truly absolute and grammatically detached from the rest of the sentence. We express this as: **Hannibal hostem victum interfēcit** (lit. *Hannibal killed the conquered enemy*).

The ablative absolute has the same rules about tenses and implied agents (with a perfect participle) as other uses of participles (11.1/3).

An ablative absolute can be expanded with words that qualify its subject or participle, but the two basic elements (noun/pronoun + participle) are always present, except in one particular type: **iuvenis eram consule Plancō** *I was a young man, Plancus [being] consul*, i.e. *when Plancus was consul.*

Latin does not have a present participle of the verb **sum**. Consequently when we want an ablative absolute of the type *Darius being king* (i.e. *when Darius was, is* or *will be king*, according to the tense of the finite verb) we simply put **Dārīus** and **rex** into the ablative, viz **Dārīō rēge**. The second element can also be an adjective: **tranquillō marī, ā Graeciā domum veniēmus** *the sea* [*being*] *calm*, (i.e. *when the sea is calm*), *we shall come home from Greece*.

12.1/2 Use of participles instead of abstract nouns

An abstract noun followed by a concrete noun in the genitive is a normal expression in English, e.g. *the capture of the city, the burning of the Capitol, the murder of Caesar*. Latin can form phrases of this sort but they are much less common than in English. Instead, Latin qualifies the concrete noun (*city, Capitol, Caesar*) with a participle which expresses the sense of the English abstract noun: **urbs capta, Capitōlium incensum, Caesar occīsus.** But should not these phrases mean *the city having been captured, the Capitol having been burnt, Caesar having been murdered*? The answer is that **Caesar occīsus** can mean either *the murder of Caesar* or *Caesar having been murdered* (and similarly with the other phrases), but it will always be clear in a particular context which meaning is intended. In **Caesar occīsus humum cecidit** *Caesar, having been murdered, fell to the ground*, the logical, and grammatical, subject is **Caesar** (*who or what fell to the ground?*). In **Caesar occīsus cīvēs terruit** (lit. *Caesar having been murdered terrified the citizens*) the grammatical subject is still **Caesar** but, as the answer to the question *who or what terrified the citizens?* is not *Caesar* but the fact that he had been murdered, the latter is the logical subject. We must therefore translate *the murder of Caesar terrified the citizens*. This construction can occur in other grammatical cases. It is most common with the perfect participle. Other examples are:

> **Rēs pūblica per mē dēfensa eōrum benevolentiam nōbīs conciliāvit.**
> *My defence of the state* (lit. *the state defended by me*) *won their friendship for us.*
> **Annō ante nātum Ennium.** *In the year before the birth of Ennius* (lit. *before Ennius having been born*).
> **Ab urbe conditā**. *From the foundation of the city* (lit. *from the city having been founded*. This phrase, often abbreviated to A.U.C.,

was used in dates calculated from the traditional foundation of
Rome in 753 BC).

Memorābilem pugnam fēcit Hasdrubal captus. *The capture of
Hasdrubal made the battle memorable.*

12.1/3 Uses of the supine

The supine (4.1/6) is a verbal noun belonging to the fourth declension,
but it only exists in two forms, the accusative singular, which is the
form quoted in principal parts of verbs, and the ablative singular.

The supine in **-um** (i.e. the accusative singular) is used to express
purpose after verbs of motion or verbs implying motion:

Lēgātōs ad Caesarem mittunt auxilium rogātum. *They send envoys
to Caesar to ask for help.*
Gladiātōrēs in arēnam pugnātum vocāvit. *He called gladiators into
the arena to fight.*

In this construction English normally uses an infinitive but in Latin
the infinitive is only used in this way in poetry. On how to express
purpose by a clause (which also could be used in the above examples)
see 13.1/5. For the only other use of the supine in **-um** see 14.1/3.

The supine in **-ū** (i.e. the ablative singular) is only found after certain
adjectives (used either adjectivally or as nouns), and **fās** *right*, **nefās**
wrong (25.1/4*d*), where in English we would have a present active (or
sometimes passive) infinitive. It occurs in a limited number of verbs,
mostly those indicating saying or perceiving, e.g. **mīrābile dictū**
wonderful to relate; **rēs audītū crūdēlis, vīsū nefāria** *a thing cruel to
hear, evil to see*; **fās audītū** *right to hear*.

12.1/4 Numerals (2)

There are three other types of numerals in addition to cardinals
(11.1/5). Full tables will be found on p. 298.

(*a*) *Ordinals* are the set of numerals which arrange in order, viz *first,
second, third*, etc. Latin ordinals are all first and second
declension adjectives, except for **prior** (19.1/1 note 5) and **alter**
(10.1/1*d*) which are used instead of **prīmus** *first* and **secundus**
second when a series of two only is described.

(b) *Numeral adverbs* are: **semel** *once,* **bis** *twice,* **ter** *three times,* **quater** *four times,* etc.

(c) *Distributive* numerals have no one-word equivalents in English. Their primary meaning is *one each, two each,* etc. They are all first and second declension adjectives.

> **Legiōnēs singulās posuit Brundisī, Tarentī, Sipontī.** *He stationed one legion each at Brundisium, Tarentum and Sipontum.*
> **Bīna hastīlia ferunt.** *They carry two spears each.*

Distributives are also used with words which have a special meaning in the plural (8.1/4), except that **ūnus** replaces **singulī**. Here they have the same meaning as cardinals: **duae litterae** *two letters of the alphabet*; **bīnae litterae** *two letters (epistles)*; **ūna castra** *one camp*; **sēna castra** *six camps*.

12.2 Latin reading

1 Latrante uno, latrat statim et alter canis.
2 Tertio anno senae litterae a Cicerone scriptae ad senatum advenerunt.
3 Terra mutata non mutat mores.
4 Hannibal, patriam defensum revocatus, bellum gessit adversus P. Scipionem.
5 Magna in dato beneficio laus est.
6 Eum alii deprehensi non terruerunt.
7 Aeneas urbe et sociis et classe relicta
  sceptra Palatini sedemque petit Euandri.
8 Capti oppidi signum e muro tollunt.
9 Herbas congerunt formidulosas dictu, non esu solum.
10 Hannibal, nuntiato hostium adventu, castra movit.
11 Violati hospites, legati necati, fana vexata, hanc tantam effecerunt vastitatem.
12 Consul triumphans in urbem venit, Cluilio duce Volscorum vincto et ante currum ambulante.
13 Horatius, respiciens, tres Curiatios magnis intervallis venientes vidit.
14 Antonius, repudiata sorore Octaviani, Cleopatram uxorem duxit.
15 Dionysius, cultros metuens tonsorios, candente carbone sibi adurebat capillum.

Horatiana

Quintus Horatius Flaccus (65–8 BC), known in English as Horace, was a contemporary of Vergil and achieved almost as great a reputation in lyric poetry as Vergil in epic. The passages below are from his *Odes*.

16 Damna tamen celeres reparant caelestia lunae:
>   nos ubi decidimus
> quo pater Aeneas, quo Tullus dives et Ancus,
>   pulvis et umbra sumus.   4

>   . . . .

> cum semel occideris et de te splendida Minos
>   fecerit arbitria,
> non, Torquate, genus, non te facundia, non te
>   restituet pietas.   8

The Favour of the Muse

17   Quem tu, Melpomene, semel
> nascentem placido lumine videris,
>   illum non labor Isthmius
> clarabit pugilem, non equus impiger   4
>   curru ducet Achaico
> victorem, neque res bellica Deliis
>   ornatum foliis ducem,
> quod regum tumidas contuderit minas,   8
>   ostendet Capitolio:
> sed quae Tibur aquae fertile praefluunt
>   et spissae nemorum comae
> fingent Aeolio carmine nobilem.   12

Notes

7 The ablative absolute has three subjects **urbe, sociīs, classe,** but the participle **relictā** agrees with the nearest one only; translate **sceptra** as singular (see note on 8.2, 11); **Euander, -drī** *Evander* the king of Pallanteum on the Palatine hill (**Palātium, -ī**; adj. **Palātīnus**) at Rome.

15 **sibi** is dative of advantage (see 28.1/1*e*); literally *used to singe hair for himself*, i.e. *used to singe his hair*.

16 In the preceding lines Horace has described the transition from the joy of spring to the gloom of winter, *but*, he says, *swift moons*

(i.e. *the passing of time*) *restore the losses caused by the heavens* (lit. *celestial losses* – the heavens were regarded as causing the changes of the seasons). *l.*2 **dēcidimus** perfect *have descended*. *l.*3 after **quō** supply **dēcidērunt**; **Aenēās** see note on Vergil in 8.2; **Tullus, Ancus** early kings of Rome. *ll.*5f. **cum** is here a conjunction *when*; **occīderis** and **fēcerit** are future perfect, as is **vīderis** in the next passage – 5.1/3; **Mīnōs** one of three judges of the Underworld; the pronouncements of such an eminent legal figure were naturally **splendida** *august*; **arbitria** to be translated by a singular (cf. **sceptra** in 7 above). *l.*7 **nōn** and **tē** are repeated for emphasis.

17 *l.*1 The antecedent of **quem** is **illum** (*l.*3). *l.*2 **nascentem** (from **nascor** deponent; 14.1/4) *being born*; **lūmine** here *eye*. *l.*3 **illum** is to be taken with **clārābit, dūcet, ostendet** and **fingent**; **victōrem** and **ducem** are in apposition to **illum**; **labor Isthmius** *toil in the Isthmian Games*. *l.*5 **Achāicō** = **Graecō**. *l.*6 **rēs bellica** lit. *the military thing*, i.e. *the business of war*; **Dēlius, -a, -um** *of Delos*, Greek island sacred to Apollo; his special tree was the laurel, which is referred to here. *l.*8 **contuderit** future perfect of **contundō** but translate *has crushed* (5.1/3). *l.*9 A victorious general offered a sacrifice at the temple of **Iuppiter optimus maximus** on the Capitol after coming in triumph through Rome. *l.*10 Translate as though the order were **aquae quae** *the waters which*. *l.*12 **Aeolius, -a, -um** *Aeolian*, i.e. resembling the poetry of Sappho and Alcaeus, who wrote in Aeolic Greek.

UNIT 13

13.1 Grammar

13.1/1 Subjunctive mood

Of the finite forms of verbs (i.e. those that can stand alone in clauses), we have up to now dealt only with the indicative mood, which is used to express facts, e.g. **heri tē vīdī** *I saw you yesterday*; **nunc Rōmae maneō** *now I am staying in Rome*. The subjunctive, one of the two other moods, expresses a possibility, i.e. what might happen in the future, be happening now, or have happened in the past, e.g. **sī tū essem, nōn illud dīcerem** *if I were you I would not say that* (the reference is to the present). We still have a very few single-word subjunctive verb forms in English (as *were* in *if I were you*), but in the vast majority of cases where Latin has a subjunctive we use an auxiliary such as *should*, *would* or *might*. There are four tenses of the subjunctive in Latin: present, imperfect, perfect and pluperfect; there is no future subjunctive (although a periphrastic form is possible; see 16.1/*la*), and when reference to the future is required the present subjunctive is normally used. The meaning of the subjunctive depends on the construction in which it is used, and single-word English equivalents cannot be given.

13.1/2 Present subjunctive active

In the second, third and fourth conjugations we add the endings **-am**, **-ās**, **-at**, **-āmus**, **-ātis**, **-ant**, to the present stem. In the first conjugation we drop the final **a** of the present stem, and, to avoid confusion with the present indicative, a different set of endings is used: **-em**, **-ēs**, **-et**, **-ēmus**, **-ētis**, **-ent**. **Sum** is irregular.

		I	II	III	IV	sum
SINGULAR	1	ámem	móneam	régam	aúdiam	sim
	2	ámēs	móneās	régās	aúdiās	sīs
	3	ámet	móneat	régat	aúdiat	sit
PLURAL	1	amémus	moneámus	regámus	audiámus	sĩmus
	2	amétis	moneátis	regátis	audiátis	sĩtis
	3	áment	móneant	régant	aúdiant	sint

The first person singular active of the present subjunctive and of the future indicative are the same in the third and fourth conjugations. This is because the future of these conjugations is in origin an old subjunctive which coincides at this point with the present subjunctive of Classical Latin.

13.1/3 Imperfect and pluperfect subjunctive active
(see pp. 281 and 283.)

Both tenses are regular for all verbs. The endings **-m, -s, -t, -mus, -tis, -nt** are added to the present infinitive active to form the imperfect subjunctive active, and so we have **amárem, monérem, régerem, audĩrem, éssem,** etc. For the pluperfect subjunctive active the same endings are added to the perfect infinitive active, which is formed by adding **-isse** to the perfect stem:

	PERFECT STEM	PERFECT ACTIVE INFINITIVE		PLUPERFECT ACTIVE SUBJUNCTIVE
I	amāv-	amāvísse	*to have loved*	amāvíssem, -ēs, etc.
II	monu-	monuísse	*to have warned*	monuíssem, -ēs, etc.
III	rex-	rexísse	*to have ruled*	rexíssem, -ēs, etc.
IV	audĩv-	audĩvísse	*to have heard*	audĩvíssem, -ēs, etc.
sum	fu-	fuísse	*to have been*	fuíssem, -ēs, etc.

In both tenses the final **e** is lengthened before the endings of the second singular and the first and second plural: **amárēs, amárémus, amārétis, monuíssēs, monuissémus, monuissétis,** etc.

13.1/4 Perfect subjunctive active (see p. 282)

To the perfect stem we add **-erim, -erīs, -erit, -erīmus, -erītis, -erint**: **amáverim, monúerim, réxerim, audĩverim, fúerim,** etc. Notice that the perfect subjunctive active of all verbs is similar to the future perfect indicative active except that:

(a) The first person singular endings are **-erim** and **-erō** respectively. It is easy to distinguish these as *all* tenses of the subjunctive have a first person singular active ending in **-m**.

(b) The endings **-erīs, -erīmus, -erītis** of the perfect subjunctive have **-erī-**, not **-eri-**; the accent is therefore different in the first and second persons plural: **amāverímus** (perf. subj.), **amāvérimus** (fut. perf.), etc.

13.1/5 Adverbial clauses of purpose

English has several ways of expressing purpose. We can use a phrase, as in *he is arming his soldiers to attack the enemy/in order to attack the enemy/for the purpose of attacking the enemy*. We can also use a clause, as in *the ship was coated with pitch so that the salt water would not affect it*. These constructions are not always interchangeable, although it is possible to use the second in all cases, e.g. *he is arming his soldiers so that he may attack the enemy*. What we find in Latin is similar. Certain constructions involving a phrase (as the supine in **-um** – 12.1/3; see also 18.1/2) are used to express purpose in particular contexts. A purpose clause, however, which is introduced by **ut** *so that* or **nē** *lest, so that. . . not*, can be used anywhere. As a purpose is something desired but which will not necessarily happen, it is natural that the verb in a purpose clause is always in the subjunctive.

> **Laelius veniēbat ad cēnam ut satiāret dēsīderia nātūrae.** *Laelius used to dine to satisfy the needs of nature* (lit. *used to come to dinner so that he might satisfy…*).
> **Dionȳsius, nē collum tonsōrī committeret, tondēre fīliās suās docuit.** *Dionysius, in order not to entrust* (lit. *so that he might not entrust*) *his neck to a barber, taught his daughters to cut hair* (**tondēre**).
> **Edō ut vīvam, nōn vīvō ut edam.** *I eat to live, I do not live to eat.*
> **Tē domum praemittō ut haec uxōrī meae nuntiēs.** *I am sending you home ahead to announce these things to my wife.*

As we cannot realise a purpose before taking action to bring it about, the verb in a purpose clause must be either imperfect subjunctive (where the reference is to the past) or present subjunctive (where the reference is to the present or future). No distinction is made here between present and future as the difference between what may or could be happening now and what may or could happen in the future is often vague, and sometimes no distinction is possible.

The relationship of the tense used in a subordinate clause to that of the main verb is called *sequence of tenses* (see 16.1/2 and 23.1/3).

Notes

1   A second purpose clause, if negated, must be introduced by **nēve** or **neu**.

   Caesar hās mūnītiōnēs auxit ut mūrī tūtī essent neu hostēs imprōvīsō impetum facerent. *Caesar enlarged these fortifications so that the walls would be safe and the enemy would not unexpectedly attack.*

2   When a comparative adjective or adverb (see 19.1/1–2) occurs in a positive purpose clause, **ut** is replaced by the conjunction **quō**.

   Caesar, quō facilius equitātum Pompeiānum ad Dyrrachium continēret, aditūs duōs praemūnīvit. *Caesar fortified the two approaches so that he might more easily* (**facilius**) *tie down Pompey's cavalry* (lit. *the Pompeian cavalry*) *at Dyrrachium.*

3   Negative purpose clauses are introduced by **nē** (or occasionally **ut nē**), *never* by **ut nōn** (which has a different use, 16.1/1). Consequently, if such a clause begins in English with *so that no one, so that never, so that nowhere*, etc. we must in Latin have *lest* (**nē**) *anyone, lest ever, lest anywhere*, etc.; for the Latin words see 16.1/1.

4   The infinitive to express purpose, which we use so often in English, occurs only in Latin poetry, and there only after verbs of motion (in prose we could have a supine, 12.1/3): **vēnerat aurum petere** *he had come to seek gold.*

13.1/6 Phrases expressing time (2)

In addition to phrases expressing *time how long*, *time when*, and *time within which* (5.1/4), we have the following:

(*a*) phrases answering the questions *how long before?* and *how long after?*, which can be expressed by either:

   (i) **ante** and **post** used as prepositions governing the accusative (3.1/4):

   Ante trēs diēs. *Before three days* or *three days before.*
   Post decem annōs. *After ten years* or *ten years after.*

(ii) **ante** and **post** used as adverbs meaning *previously* and *afterwards* (in other contexts we would usually have **anteā** and **posteā**) with an ablative of measure of difference (cf. 19.1/4*b*) to express the interval of time:

Tribus ante diēbus. *Three days before* (lit. *previously by* [*the measure of*] *three days*).
Decem post annīs. *Ten years after* (lit. *afterwards by* [*the measure of*] *ten years*).

In the second construction **ante** and **post** never come first in the phrase. There is no difference in meaning between the two constructions.

(*b*) phrases answering the question *how long ago?*, which are expressed by the adverb **abhinc** *ago*, *back from the present* and an accusative expressing time how long:

Abhinc septem mensēs. *Seven months ago.*

13.1/7 Phrases of spatial extent and dimension

Spatial extent can be either:

(*a*) distance travelled, which occurs with verbs of motion and is expressed by the accusative:

Decem mīlia passuum contendērunt. *They marched ten miles* (lit. *ten thousands of paces*).

(*b*) distance between or from, which is expressed by either the accusative or ablative:

Dux Gallōrum duo mīlia (or **duōbus mīlibus**) **passuum aberat.** *The leader of the Gauls was two miles away* (**absum** *be distant, away*).

Dimension, which tells us *how high, deep, broad* or *long* something is, is expressed by the accusative with the appropriate adjective (**altus** *high* or *deep*, **lātus** *broad*, **longus** *long*):

Erant mūrī Babylōnis ducentōs pedēs altī. *The walls of Babylon were two hundred feet high.*

This use of the accusative is close to that in phrases expressing time how long (5.1/4): **ducentōs pedēs altī** means literally *high* (*to the extent of*) *two hundred feet*. Dimension and size may also be expressed by the genitive (27.1/4*c*).

13.2 Latin reading

1 Legatos misit ut pacem peterent.
2 Ubi Romae erat, numquam ab uxore pedem discedebat.
3 Caesar singulis legionibus singulos legatos praefecit, ut eos testes suae quisque virtutis haberet.
4 Quaestor fuisti abhinc quattuordecim annos.
5 Ut iugulent hominem, surgunt de nocte latrones.
6 Produxit servos quos in pabulatione paucis ante diebus exceperat.
7 Cur non mitto meos tibi, Pontiliane, libellos?
   ne mihi tu mittas, Pontiliane, tuos.
8 Ratem ducentos longam pedes, quinquaginta latam in flumen porrexerunt.
9 Ne omnino metum sui reditus tolleret atque ut barbarorum auxilia tardaret, partem ultimam pontis rescidit.
10 Caesar milia passuum tria ab eorum castris castra posuit.
11 Centuriones, ne partam rei militaris laudem amitterent, fortiter pugnantes conciderunt.
12 Milites aggerem altum pedes octoginta exstruxerunt.
13 Hi rursus invicem anno post in armis sunt, illi domi remanent.

Caesar sails to Britain

14 **Gaius Iūlius Caesar** (100–44 BC), in addition to his military and political activities, was a writer of considerable distinction. In his work *dē Bellō Gallicō* he described the campaigns he conducted in Gaul, during which he made a brief and successful assault on East Kent.

His rebus gestis Labienum in continenti cum tribus legionibus et equitum milibus duobus reliquit ut portus defenderet et rei frumentariae provideret. ipse, cum quinque legionibus et pari numero equitum quem in continenti relinquebat, ad solis occasum naves solvit. et leni Africo provectus media circiter   5
nocte, vento intermisso, cursum non tenuit et longe delatus aestu, prima luce, sub sinistra Britanniam relictam conspexit. tum, aestu commutato, remis contendit ut eam partem insulae caperet ubi facilis erat egressus. . . Caesar, exposito exercitu et loco castris idoneo capto, ubi ex captivis cognovit quo in loco hostium copiae 10
consedissent, cohortibus decem ad mare relictis et equitibus trecentis ut naves custodirent, ad hostes contendit.

Notes

1 **lēgātōs** *envoys*; in 3 the military context tells us that the word there has its other meaning *legate* (a rank in the Roman army).

3 **praeficiō (prae + faciō)** *put in charge of* takes the accusative of the person appointed and dative of what he is put in charge of, here **singulīs legiōnibus**.

5 **dē nocte** lit. *from* [*the time of*] *night*, i.e. *while it is still night*.

7 **tibi, mihi** datives of advantage (28.1/1e), lit. *for you, for me*; **libellōs** self-deprecating use of a diminutive (**libellus** <**liber** *book*).

9 **reditūs** is genitive singular; **rescidit** <**rescindō**.

11 **partam** (with **laudem**) *acquired* (<**pariō** *acquire*), tr. *which they had won*; **concidērunt** from **concidō** *fall*, not **concīdō** *kill*.

14 *l.*2 **relīquit** the subject is *Caesar*, who in his war commentaries always wrote in the third person. *ll.*3ff. **prōvideō** *provide for, take care of* is followed by the dative; **parī ... quem** a condensed expression for *a number of horsemen equal* [*to the number*] *which*, translate *the same number ... as*; **sōlis occāsum** i.e. *the west*. *ll.*5f. **Āfricō** (supply **ventō**) *south-west wind*; **prōvectus** *carried along*; **mediā ... nocte** *middle of the night* (see 21.1/3). *l.*6 **dēlātus** past participle of **dēferō** *bear away*. *l.*7 **sub sinistrā** (i.e. **manū**) *on the left* [*hand*]. *l.*9 **castrīs** dative *for a camp* (28.1/1h). *l.*10 **quō in locō** *in what place*. *l.*11 **cōnsēdissent** (<**cōnsīdō**) translate as though indicative – the construction (indirect question, 23.1/3) requires the subjunctive.

13.3 Excursus

The days of the week

The idea of using a seven-day cycle as a measure of time originated in the Middle East, as is exemplified in the Jewish (and Christian) Sabbath; and it is to the Babylonians that we owe the names of individual days. As astrologers, they believed that the seven celestial bodies, the moon, Mercury, Venus, the sun, Mars, Jupiter, Saturn,[1] which they conceived as revolving around an immovable earth, were

[1] The planets Uranus, Neptune and Pluto were unknown in antiquity.

divine beings influencing earthly affairs. This belief was combined with the already existing system of counting days – the coincidence in number obviously helped – and it was supposed that each celestial body in turn governed the first hour of a day and hence should give that day its name.

The countries of the Middle East were brought into direct contact with the West as a result of the conquests of Alexander the Great (d. 323 BC), and Eastern beliefs and superstitions began to trickle through to the northern shores of the Mediterranean. As a result the Babylonian week became known in Greece and Italy, but at first its use was probably restricted to believers in astrology. The only change made was that the names of the Babylonian gods and goddesses were replaced with those of the corresponding local divinities. The system gradually became more popular and it was officially adopted by the Roman emperor, Constantine, in AD 321.

The Latin names of the days of the week, starting with Sunday, are:

> **diēs Sōlis** day of the sun (**sōl**)
> **diēs Lūnae** day of the moon (**Lūna**)
> **diēs Martis** day of the war god (**Mars**)
> **diēs Mercurī** day of the messenger god (**Mercurius**, Mercury)
> **diēs Iovis** day of Jupiter (6.1/2 note 5)
> **diēs Veneris** day of the love goddess (**Venus**)
> **diēs Sāturnī** day of Saturn, father of Jupiter.

It will be seen how most have come down into French and Italian with little change, except that **diēs** and the divinity change places (Fr. *lundi*, It. *lunedì*, etc.). In northern Europe the Roman gods were replaced with their Germanic equivalents, and so in English we have *Sunday* (day of the sun), *Monday* (day of the moon) etc.; the only exception is Saturday where the name of the Roman god was kept.

UNIT 14

14.1 Grammar

14.1/1 Present, future and imperfect passive

In a clause where the verb is active the subject is the doer (*the man bit the dog; the consul is hurrying through the forum*). There may or may not be an object, depending on whether the verb is transitive or intransitive (see **Glossary of grammatical terms**). In a clause with a passive verb the subject is the sufferer (*the dog was bitten by the man; in the previous year the Roman army had been defeated at Cannae; I am being bored with your chatter*). The agent (11.1/4) or instrument (7.1/4) may or may not be specified. In English all passive forms are made up of the past passive participle of a verb preceded by the appropriate part of the verb *to be* (*was bitten, had been defeated, am being bored*); the part of the verb *to be* may itself contain an auxiliary, as in the second and third examples (*had been, am being*). In Latin, however, such composite tenses occur only in the perfect, pluperfect and future perfect passive. In the present, imperfect and future we have single-word forms.

For the indicative of the present, imperfect and future passive we employ the same stem as for the active. Only the ending (or part of it) is changed, and that in a very regular way. Where in the active we have **-ō/-am, -s, -t, -mus, -tis, -nt**, in the passive we get **-or/-ar, -ris, -tur, -mur, -minī, -ntur**. Full tables will be found on pp. 284–5. There are only two complications. In the future of the first and second conjugations and in the present of the third we get, in the second person singular, **amāberis, monēberis, régeris**, not forms in **-iris**, as we might have expected. Secondly, in the same tenses of these conjugations the vowel before **-tur** in the third singular is not lengthened as happens elsewhere, hence **amā́bitur** (fut.) but **amā́tur** (pres.) and **amābā́tur** (impf.); **monḗbitur** (fut.) but **monḗtur** (pres.) and **monēbā́tur** (impf.); **régitur** (pres.) but **regḗtur** (fut.) and **regēbā́tur** (impf.).

The meaning of these passive forms can be seen from the following examples, all of which are first person singular:

> **ámor** (pres.) *I am loved, I am being loved.*
> **amā́bor** (fut.) *I shall be loved.*
> **amā́bar** (impf.) *I was being loved, I used to be loved.*

> **régor** (pres.) *I am ruled, I am being ruled.*
> **régar** (fut.) *I shall be ruled.*
> **regḗbar** (impf.) *I was being ruled, I used to be ruled.*

The present and imperfect subjunctive passive are formed by replacing the active endings of these tenses of the subjunctive with **-r, -ris, -tur** (with the vowel before this ending lengthened), **-mur, -minī, -ntur**. There is no future subjunctive passive.

Notes

1 In the future indicative passive and the present subjunctive passive of the third and fourth conjugations, the first person singular coincides, **regar, audiar**; the same occurs in the active (13.1/2).
2 **Amor** can be first singular present indicative passive of **amō**, as above, or nominative and vocative singular of **amor, amōris** *love*; such a coincidence does not occur elsewhere.
3 For the second person singular forms of the above passive tenses there is a less common alternative in **-re** (for **-ris**), e.g. **amāre** (= **amāris**), **monēbere** (= **monēberis**); in the present tense these alternative forms coincide with the imperative passive (21.1/1) and also with the present infinitive active.

14.1/2 Perfect, pluperfect and future perfect passive
(see pp. 286–7)

These tenses of the passive are *not* made by varying the endings of the corresponding active forms. They are all composite tenses consisting of the perfect participle and a part of the verb **sum**. The elements are written separately, just as composite tenses in English. The tense of

sum employed is different from that of the verb *to be* in English and can cause confusion:

The *perfect indicative passive* requires the present indicative of **sum**, e.g. **amātus sum** *I have been loved*, or *was loved*, not *I am (being) loved* which is **amor**.

The *pluperfect indicative passive* requires the imperfect indicative of **sum**, e.g. **amātus eram** *I had been loved*, not *I was loved* which is **amātus sum**.

The *future perfect indicative passive* requires the future of **sum**, e.g. **amātus erō** *I shall have been loved*, not *I shall be loved* which is **amābor**.

For the perfect and pluperfect subjunctive passive we simply substitute the subjunctive of **sum** for the indicative, e.g. **amātus sim**, **amātus essem**. There is no future perfect subjunctive passive.

As the perfect participle is declinable and, in composite tenses, qualifies the subject, it must agree with the subject in number, gender and case. **Amātus sum, amātus es, amātus est** can only be used if the subject is masculine (and singular); if the subject is feminine singular we must have **amāta sum, amāta es, amāta est**, and if neuter singular, **amātum est**, etc. The same applies in the plural and a distinction is made that is not possible in English. **Amātī sunt** means *they* (masculine) *have been loved*, **amātae sunt** *they* (feminine) *have been loved*. Where, however, a mixed group is referred to, the masculine form of the participle is used.

14.1/3 Infinitives

So far we have had only the present infinitive active (2.1/1) and perfect infinitive active (13.1/3). Latin has passive infinitives for both these tenses as well as a future infinitive active and a future infinitive passive. The present infinitive passive is formed by adding **-rī** to the present stem in the first, second and fourth conjugations, and **-ī** to the present stem in the third:

I	**amā́rī**	*to be loved*	III **régī**	*to be ruled*
II	**monérī**	*to be warned*	IV **audī́rī**	*to be heard*

The perfect infinitive passive is formed, like the perfect indicative passive, from the perfect participle and the appropriate part of **sum**, viz the present infinitive:

I amátus ésse *to have been loved*   III réctus ésse *to have been ruled*
II mónitus ésse *to have been warned*   IV audítus ésse *to have been heard*

The perfect participle must agree with the subject of the infinitive as we shall see when treating the construction where this infinitive is most commonly used (17.1/2). The same applies to the future participle, which joins with **esse** to form the future infinitive active:

I amātúrus ésse *to be going to love*   III rectúrus ésse *to be going to rule*
II monitúrus ésse *to be going to warn* IV audītúrus ésse *to be going to hear*

As the future participle of **sum** is **futūrus** (11.1/2 note 3), its future infinitive is **futūrus esse** *to be going to be*. **Sum**, however, has another future infinitive, **fore** (the only single-word future infinitive in Latin); there is no distinction in meaning between the two. As one would expect, **sum** has no passive infinitives.

The future infinitive passive consists of the supine in **-um** and the present infinitive passive of **eō** (15.1/6*b*): **amātum īrī** *to be going to be loved*. As it is the supine, not a participle, that is used in this infinitive, there is no agreement with the subject. This infinitive is rare in all periods of Latin.

14.1/4 Deponent verbs

A linguistic phenomenon for which we have no parallel in English is the deponent verb. These verbs, which occur in all four conjugations, have the peculiarity of being passive in form but active in meaning. Except for the five forms noted below, they are not conjugated in the active voice. A wholly satisfactory explanation for this bizarre phenomenon has yet to be discovered, but some deponents are among the most common verbs in Latin. Deponent verbs also occur in ancient (and modern) Greek. **Tūtor (tūtārī)**, a regular deponent verb of the first conjugation, means *I protect*. The Latin, therefore, for *I will protect* is **tūtābor**, for *I was protecting* is **tūtābar**, for *I protected* is **tūtātus sum**. Other examples are:

Inter sē adversīs luctantur cornibus haedī. *Young goats struggle*
(**luctor, luctārī**) *with each other with opposing horns.*
Quod rectum et honestum et cum virtūte est, id sōlum opīnor
bonum. *What is proper, honourable and virtuous* (lit. *with virtue*),
that alone I consider (**opīnor, opīnārī**) *good.*

Quācumque incessērunt, lātē populātī sunt tecta agrōsque.
Wherever they went, they pillaged (**populor, populārī**) *buildings and fields over a wide area* (**lātē** lit. *broadly*).
Numquam omnēs hodiē moriēmur inultī. *Never today shall we all die* (**morior, morī**) *unavenged.*

Deponents can be transitive (**opīnor, populor**) or intransitive (**luctor, morior**). Transitive deponents can take a direct object, but there is no way we can turn **id sōlum opīnor bonum** around so that the verb is passive in sense (*that alone is considered good by me*), since we have no special endings to give deponents a passive meaning. They can only be used in an active sense; and if we want to say *that alone is considered good by me* in Latin, we must use a normal verb which has the same meaning as **opīnor** (e.g. **putō**). There are, however, four active forms of a normal verb which have no corresponding passive, viz present participle, future participle, supine, and gerund. Each of these, though active in form, can also be formed from deponents, which would otherwise be deprived of these important parts. From **opīnor** we have: **opīnans** present participle *thinking*; **opīnātūrus** future participle *going to think*; **opīnātum** supine (*act of*) *thinking*; and, a part of the Latin verbal system we have not yet treated, the gerund **opīnandum** (for its meaning see 18.1/2 note 1). Also, for the future infinitive we have, somewhat illogically, **opīnātūrus esse** *to be going to think*, which is active in form; since normal verbs do have a future passive infinitive (see last subsection), we might have expected **opīnātum īrī** but this never occurs. Gerundives (another verbal form not yet treated) of deponents behave in the same way as those of normal verbs (18.1/2 note 1).

The perfect participle of deponents warrants special attention because, although passive in form, it is active in meaning and so provides something lacking in normal verbs, a perfect participle active, e.g. **opīnātus** *having thought*, **populātus** *having ravaged*. We do not, however, have any form of these verbs with the passive meaning *having been thought, having been ravaged*.

The deponents used in the following examples will be found in the subsequent list:

Vulcānus ea verba locūtus optātōs dedit amplexūs. *Having spoken these words Vulcan gave the desired embraces.*

P. Sulpicius, profectus ab urbe, Brundisium vēnit. *Publius Sulpicius,*
having set out from the city, came to Brundisium.
Dictātor absentem M. Valerium Corvum, trēs et vīgintī annōs
nātum, consulem renuntiāvit. *The dictator declared the absent*
23-year-old (lit. *born three and twenty years*) *Marcus Valerius*
Corvus consul.

Very often the perfect participle of deponents is used with a present
sense:

Caesar insidiās veritus exercitum equitātumque in castrīs continuit.
Caesar, fearing (we might have expected **verens**) *an ambush, kept*
the army and cavalry in the camp.

The principal parts of deponents are given thus: **tūtor, tūtārī, tūtātus**
sum. The supine (which here is **tūtātum**) is not cited because its stem
is the same as that of the perfect participle (11.1/2), which we know
from **tūtātus sum.**

Among the most frequently used deponents are:

First conjugation (and regular)
arbitror, arbitrārī, arbitrātus sum	*consider, judge*
cōnor, cōnārī, cōnātus sum	*try*
cunctor, cunctārī, cunctātus sum	*delay*
opīnor, opīnārī, opīnātus sum	*consider, suppose*
populor, populārī, populātus sum	*ravage*

Second conjugation
fateor, fatērī, fassus sum	*confess*
reor, rērī, ratus sum	*think*

Third conjugation
loquor, loquī, locūtus sum	*speak*
nascor, nascī, nātus sum	*be born*
proficiscor, proficiscī, profectus sum	*set out*
sequor, sequī, secūtus sum	*follow*

Mixed conjugation (see 7.1/3)
ēgredior, ēgredī, ēgressus sum	*go out*
ingredior, ingredī, ingressus sum	*go into*
morior, morī, mortuus sum	*die*
patior, patī, passus sum	*suffer, allow*
prōgredior, prōgredī, prōgressus sum	*advance*

Fourth conjugation
    experior, experīrī, expertus sum   *try*
    orior, orīrī, ortus sum   *arise*

As examples of deponents, **cōnor** and **patior** are conjugated on pp. 291–2. Note that the imperfect subjunctive (**cōnārer, paterer**, etc.) is formed from a hypothetical present infinitive active **cōnāre, patere**. With a second conjugation deponent, e.g. **fateor**, the imperfect subjunctive is **fatērer**, and from the fourth conjugation **experior** has **experīrer**.

14.2 Latin reading

1 Partem suarum copiarum traducere coacti sunt.
2 Duos qui sequitur lepores, neutrum capit.
3 Ut Romae consules, sic Karthagine quotannis bini reges creabantur.
4 Parturiunt montes, nascetur ridiculus mus.
5 Tempora mutantur, nos et mutamur in illis.
6 Quem di diligunt, adulescens moritur.
7 Felices sequeris, Mors, miseros fugis.
8 Nascentes morimur, finisque ab origine pendet.
9 Curae leves loquuntur, ingentes stupent.
10 Augescunt aliae gentes, aliae minuuntur.
11 Nec amor nec tussis celatur.
12 Fortuna, cum blanditur, captatum venit.
13 Ex auribus cognoscitur asinus.
14 Legati se ad pedes Caesaris proiecerunt suppliciterque locuti flentes pacem petiverunt.
15 Spectatum veniunt: veniunt, spectentur ut ipsae.

Epigrams from Martial
16 Versiculos in me narratur scribere Cinna.
        non scribit, cuius carmina nemo legit.
17 Hesterno fetere mero qui credit Acerram
        fallitur: in lucem semper Acerra bibit.

Martial's jealous rival
18 Rumpitur invidia quidam, carissime Iuli,
        quod me Roma legit, rumpitur invidia.

rumpitur invidia quod turba semper in omni
monstramur digito, rumpitur invidia.
rumpitur invidia, tribuit quod Caesar uterque 5
ius mihi natorum, rumpitur invidia.
rumpitur invidia quod rus mihi dulce sub urbe est
parvaque in urbe domus, rumpitur invidia.
rumpitur invidia quod sum iucundus amicis,
quod conviva frequens, rumpitur invidia. 10
rumpitur invidia quod amamur quodque probamur:
rumpatur quisquis rumpitur invidia.

Notes

2 Here, as in 17, *l*.1, the relative pronoun is not placed at the beginning of the clause it introduces; **lepus, leporis** *hare*.
5 In poetry **et**, when joining clauses, is often placed after the first word of the second clause. In this line **nōs et** would be **et nōs** in prose.
6 **adulescens** is predicative after **moritur**.
9 **levēs** <**levis** adj. *light*, not **lēvis** *smooth*.
12 **captātum** 12.1/3.
18 *l*.1 **cārissime** *dearest* (19.1/1) vocative with **Iūlī**; **invidiā** is ablative in every place it occurs in this poem. *l*.4 **monstrāmur** to be translated as singular (also **amāmur, probāmur** in *l*.11); Latin authors often use the royal plural (in English *we* for *I*). *l*.5 **Caesar uterque** the emperors Titus and Domitian. *l*.6 **iūs (trium) nātōrum** to encourage procreation, parents of three children were given certain privileges. As a mark of special favour these were sometimes given to people, such as Martial, who were childless. *l*.7 **rūs** here *country estate*. *l*.12 **rumpātur** subjunctive to express a command (22.1/1*c*), *let whoever . . . burst!*

UNIT 15

15.1 Grammar

15.1/1 *Possum* can, be able (see p. 294)

The principal parts of **possum** are: **possum, posse, potuī,** *no supine.* In origin it is a compound of the stem of **pote** *able* and **sum**, but the latter element has been eliminated from the perfect stem (**potu-**). In the present, future and imperfect, **pot-** is prefixed to the appropriate part of **sum** with a change of **t** to **s** before a following **s**: **potest, poterat** but **possum, possunt**. The only irregularity is that the present infinitive is **posse** (not **potesse**) and the imperfect subjunctive is therefore **possem, possēs**, etc. The perfect, pluperfect and future perfect are formed from the stem **potu-** with the regular endings. There are no participles (**potens** *capable, powerful* is not part of **possum** and is only used as an adjective). **Possum**, like *be able* in English, is followed by the infinitive.

> **Fēlix quī potuit rērum cognoscere causās!** *Happy* [*the man*] *who was able to discover the causes of things!*
> **Mīlitēs, dum parī certamine rēs gerī potuit, magnum hostium numerum sustinuērunt.** *While the battle could be fought on equal terms* [lit. *the thing could be done in equal contest*], *the soldiers withstood a large number of the enemy.*

15.1/2 Other compounds of *sum*

Sum forms several other compounds, but all are simple combinations of a prepositional prefix and **sum**; in **prōsum**, but not elsewhere, a **d** is inserted where otherwise two vowels would come together: **prōdest, prōderam** but **prōsunt, prōsit.**

dēsum	*be lacking to, fail*	**praesum**	*be in command of*
intersum	*be among*	**prōsum**	*be of benefit to, help*
obsum	*be a trouble to, bother*	**supersum**	*survive*

Of the English meanings given *fail, bother, help* and *survive* are normal transitive verbs while the others involve the use of prepositions. All the Latin verbs, however, are intransitive and are followed by the dative. In some cases it is easy to see the reason, e.g. **prōsum** strictly means *be of benefit* and the following dative is one of advantage (see 28.1/1*e*). These verbs can never be followed by an accusative even if their English equivalent is transitive.

> **Nōn modo igitur nihil prōdest sed etiam obest Clōdī mors Milōnī.** *Therefore the death of Clodius not only benefits Milo in no way* (**nihil**) *but is even a trouble to him.*
> **L. Fūrius Purpūriō tum prōvinciae praeerat.** *Lucius Furius Purpurio was then in command of the province.*

15.1/3 *Fīō* be made, become (see p. 294)

Except for its one infinitive **fierī** and its imperfect subjunctive **fierem**, etc., **fīō** is very similar to a fourth conjugation verb. In its first meaning *be made*, which is passive, it is a deponent in reverse as, except for **fierī**, it is active in form. It exists only in the present, imperfect and future where it must be used as the passive of **faciō**, which has no passive forms of its own in these tenses. In the perfect, pluperfect and future perfect **faciō** has the expected forms **factus sum, factus eram, factus erō**, etc.

In its second meaning *become*, **fīō** is always followed by the nominative because it is acting as a copulative verb (i.e. a verb which predicates something of the subject) as opposed to normal transitive verbs which, when active, signify the action which the subject is inflicting on the object. Other copulative verbs are *be, seem, appear,* and the passives of various verbs such as *be called, be voted,* etc. When an adjective or noun is used after these verbs it must be in the nominative (cf. 2.1/4). Examples of each meaning of **fīō** are:

> **Concursus fit ad praetōria consulum.** *A crowd forms* (lit. *is made*) *at the headquarters of the consuls.*
> **Quod fierī ferrō liquidōque potest ēlectrō . . .** [*That*] *which can be made from iron and molten electrum . . .*
> **Vae! deus fīō!** *Alas! I'm becoming a god!*
> **Ille fit lupus et veteris servat vestigia formae.** *He becomes a wolf and preserves traces of his old appearance.*

Note

Compounds of **faciō** with prepositional prefixes (e.g. **interficiō** *kill*) all have normal passive forms: **interficitur, interficiēbātur**, etc. Other compounds of **faciō** (e.g. **calefaciō** *make warm*; **cale-** is not a preposition) have passive forms with **fīō: calefīō, calefit**, etc.

15.1/4 *Ferō* carry, bear

Ferō belongs to the third conjugation. Its principal parts are irregular: **ferō, ferre, tulī, lātum**. Its present infinitives and some forms of its present indicative have suffered contraction:

ACTIVE			PASSIVE		
s. **férō**	pl.	**férimus**	s. **féror**	pl.	**férimur**
fers		**fértis**	**férris**		**ferímini**
fert		**férunt**	**fértur**		**feríntur**
INFINITIVES **férre**			**férrī**		

Because the present infinitive active is **ferre**, the imperfect subjunctive is **férrem, férrēs**, etc. in the active, and **férrer, ferrēris**, etc. in the passive. All other forms (except for the imperative – 21.1/1 note 1) are regular. **Ferō** must be carefully distinguished from a completely separate verb **feriō, -īre** *strike*, which only exists in tenses formed from the present stem.

15.1/5 *Volō, nōlō, mālō* (see p. 294)

Volō *wish, want* has two compounds which follow it closely: **nōlō** (**nōn** + **volō**) *not to want, be unwilling*, and **mālō** (**magis** + **volō** lit. *I want more*) *prefer*. Their principal parts are parallel and all lack a supine: **volō, velle, voluī; nōlō, nolle, nōluī; mālō, malle, māluī**. All three verbs are irregular only in the tenses formed from the present stem. They differ from each other in that **mālō** has no present participle and only **nōlō** has imperatives (21.1/1*c*). Each can be followed by a noun or pronoun, **hoc volō** *I want this*, or an infinitive, **Rōmam nāvigāre nōlō** *I do not want to sail to Rome*.

15.1/6 *Eō* go (see p. 294)

The principal parts of **eō** are: **eō, īre, iī** (rarely **īvī**), **itum**. Like **volō**, **eō** is irregular in the tenses formed from the present stem, but it has certain other peculiarities:

(*a*) In forms made from the shorter perfect, **iis-** is contracted to **īs-**. This involves the second singular and plural perfect indicative **istī** and **istis**, the perfect infinitive **isse** and all the pluperfect subjunctive **issem, issēs**, etc. The initial **i** of these forms is long but, because it is followed by two consonants, it is not marked as such (see p. xiv).

(*b*) There are three finite passive forms of **eō**: **ītur** (pres.), **ībātur** (impf.) and **itum est** (perf.). Their use is explained at 20.1/3. Transitive compounds of **eō**, however, are conjugated fully in the passive, e.g. **adeō** *I approach*, **adeor** *I am approached*. **Eō** has also a present infinitive passive **īrī**; as this is only used to form the future passive infinitive (14.1/3) it cannot be given an independent meaning.

15.2 Latin reading

1 Nec mortem effugere quisquam nec amorem potest.
2 Stultum facit Fortuna quem vult perdere.
3 Lucrum sine damno alterius fieri non potest.
4 Sapientia sine eloquentia parum prodest civitatibus.
5 Romani, qui caedibus superfuerant, in arcem confugerunt.
6 Abii ante lucem ne me illi viderent.
7 Ducunt volentem fata, nolentem trahunt.
8 Nunc eas ab saxo fluctus ad terram ferunt.
9 Lusum it Maecenas, dormitum ego.
10 Poeta nascitur, non fit.
11 Omnia pontus erant, deerant quoque litora ponto.
12 Stultum est vicinum velle ulcisci incendio.
13 Qui pergit ea, quae vult, dicere, ea, quae non vult, audiet.
14 Dum tecum vixi, dum me levis aura ferebat
       haec mea per placidas cumba cucurrit aquas.
15 Ibo ut, erus quod imperavit, Alcumenae nuntiem.
16 Omnibus negotiis non interfuit solum, sed praefuit.
17 Ex quovis ligno non fit Mercurius.

Florus to the emperor Hadrian and the latter's reply
18 *Florus*   Ego nolo Caesar esse,
                   ambulare per Britannos
                   Scythicas pati pruinas.   3

Hadrian Ego nolo Florus esse
        ambulare per tabernas,
        latitare per popinas,
        culices pati rotundos.

19 Eo mortuo, ad neminem unum summa imperii rediit.
20 Nemo potest triduo septingenta milia passuum ambulare.

Epigrams from Martial
21 Cana est barba tibi, nigra est coma. tingere barbam
        non potes (haec causa est), et potes, Ole, comam.
22 Non amo te, Sabidi, nec possum dicere quare:
        hoc tantum possum dicere, non amo te.

Notes

  8 **eās** (<**is**) *the women* (acc.).
  9 **lūsum** (<**lūdō**) and **dormītum** are supines; **Maecēnās** (nom. s.) patron of Vergil and Horace.
 12 **stultum est** impersonal expression *it is stupid*; **vīcīnum** m. acc. s.
 14 **vixī** <**vīvō**; **levis** *light, gentle*.
 15 **Alcumēnae** dative singular.
 17 **quōvīs** (<**quī** + **vīs** the second element is indeclinable) *any sort of*; **Mercurius** here not the god himself but . . .
 18 *ll*.3 & 7 **patī** 14.1/4; the **culicēs** (here probably *mosquitoes*) are round because they have gorged themselves.
 19 **eō** <**is**.
 22 **Sabidī** vocative singular of **Sabidius** (3.1/2); **tantum** *only*.

15.3 Extra reading

From this point extra reading will be included with certain units. Because it will consist of longer passages it will necessarily be somewhat more difficult than the other exercises. If you are not confident enough to tackle it when working your way through the grammar for the first time, it may be conveniently reserved until later. Most passages will be selected on their literary merit.

Orpheus and Eurydice (1)

Orpheus, the musician who *with his lute made trees, and the mountain tops that freeze, bow themselves when he did sing*, was so affected by the death of his wife, Eurydice, that he went down to the Underworld and persuaded the Nether Gods to let him bring her back to the land of the living. His venture, however, ended in failure. The story is told by Vergil in the *Georgics*.

Ipse cava solans aegrum testudine amorem
te, dulcis coniunx, te solo in litore secum,
te veniente die, te decedente canebat.
Taenarias etiam fauces, alta ostia Ditis,
et caligantem nigra formidine lucum   5
ingressus, Manisque adiit regemque tremendum
nesciaque humanis precibus mansuescere corda.
at cantu commotae Erebi de sedibus imis
umbrae ibant tenues simulacraque luce carentum,
quam multa in foliis avium se milia condunt,   10
vesper ubi aut hibernus agit de montibus imber,
matres atque viri defunctaque corpora vita
magnanimum heroum, pueri innuptaeque puellae,
impositique rogis iuvenes ante ora parentum,
quos circum limus niger et deformis harundo   15
Cocyti tardaque palus inamabilis unda
alligat et novies Styx interfusa coercet.
quin ipsae stupuere domus atque intima
Leti Tartara caeruleosque implexae crinibus anguis
Eumenides, tenuitque inhians tria Cerberus ora,   20
atque Ixionii vento rota constitit orbis.

l.1 **cavā** with **testūdine**. *l*.3 **dēcēdente** supply **diē**. *l*.4 **Taenariās** adjective of **Taenarus**, a promontory in southern Greece where there was a cave supposed to lead down to the Underworld; **ostia** plural for singular; **Dītis** gen. of **Dīs**, another name of **Plūtō,** the king of the Underworld. *l*.5 **nigrā** with **formīdine**. *l*.6 **-que . . . -que** *both . . . and*; **tremendum** (<**tremō** 18.1/2*a*) *fearsome*. *l*.9 **ībant** *began to go* (inceptive use of imperfect); **careō** *lack* takes the abl. not the acc. (20.1/1). *l*.10 lit. *as* (**quam**) *many [as] the thousands of birds hide . . .* i.e. *as numerous as the thousands of birds which hide . . . l*.11 **vesper ubi** i.e. **ubi vesper** (supply

est). *l.*12 **vītā** (abl.) is governed by **dēfuncta** (<**dēfungor** deponent *be finished with* takes the abl. like **careō**). *l.*13 **magnanimum** old form of gen. pl. (3.1/3*a*) agreeing with **hērōum** (gen. pl. of **hērōs** *hero* an adapted Greek word). *l.*14 **impositī . . . rogīs** *placed on funeral pyres*. *l.*15 **circum** adv. *round about*. *ll.*16, 17 **Cōcȳtus** and **Styx** were two of the five Underworld rivers; **tardā undā** instrumental abl.; **alligat** has three subjects but agrees only with the nearest, **palūs**. *ll.*18f. **quīn** *indeed, in fact*; **ipsae** agrees with **domūs** (nom. pl.); **intima Lētī Tartara** *Death's inmost region*, **Tartara** (neut. nom. pl.; usually *Tartarus* in English) was the lowest part of the Underworld; there wrong-doers were punished under the supervision of the three Furies (the **Eumenides**). To present a suitably horrific appearance the latter had blue snakes in their hair; hence **caeruleōs implexae crīnibus anguīs**; **implexae** (**implectō, -ere** *intertwine*) can here be translated as active (see 27.1/3*b*), lit. *having intertwined blue snakes in their hair*, i.e. *with blue snakes intertwined in their hair*. *l.*21 lit. *the wheel of Ixionian rotation* (**orbis**), etc., i.e. *the revolving wheel of Ixion* (Vergil uses the adjective of his name; Ixion was a mortal who, for attempting to seduce Juno (9.3), was spread-eagled on a constantly turning wheel); **constitit** <**consistō**.

UNIT 16

16.1 Grammar

16.1/1 Adverbial clauses of result

Result in English is generally expressed by a subordinate clause of the type (*he was so tired*) *that he couldn't move a step*, and Latin has a similar construction. In English we may also say *he was so tired he couldn't move a step*, but in Latin the conjunction is never omitted. In both languages there is usually an anticipatory word (in English *so, such,* etc.) in the main clause. The Latin conjunction introducing these clauses, whether positive or negative, is **ut** and it is followed by the subjunctive. We would not, on logical grounds, have expected the subjunctive here as result clauses generally express facts, not possibilities, but languages, including Latin, are not necessarily consistent or logical.

Examples of result clauses are:

> **Tantus repente pavor omnīs cēpit ut abiectīs armīs fugerent.** *So great* (**tantus**) *a panic suddenly seized everyone that they threw away their arms and fled* (lit. *arms having been thrown away they fled*).
>
> **Quis tam dēmens est ut suā voluntāte maereat?** *Who is so* (**tam**) *mad that he willingly* (lit. *by his own choice*) *grieves?*
>
> **In nātūrīs hominum dissimilitūdinēs sunt ut aliōs dulcia, aliōs subamāra dēlectent.** *In the natures of human beings there are differences, with the result that sweet things please some, tart things others.*
>
> **Nōn adeō virtūtum sterile erat saeculum ut nōn et bona exempla prōdiderit.** *The age was not so* (**adeō**)[1] *barren of virtues that it did not produce* (**prōdiderit** <**prōdō**) *good examples as well* (**et**).

---

[1]This **adeō** has no connection with **adeō** (**ad** + **eō**) *approach*.

There is a certain similarity with purpose clauses, but, while a negative purpose clause must be introduced by **nē** (or **ut nē**), a negative result clause is always introduced by **ut** followed by **nōn** or certain other negatives. The following list and examples will clarify this:

PURPOSE	RESULT	MEANING
nē	**ut nōn**	*that not*
nē quis	**ut nēmō**	*that no one*
nē umquam	**ut numquam**	*that never*
nē usquam	**ut nusquam**	*that nowhere*
nē ullus (homō)	**ut nullus (homō)**	*that no (person)*

Praesidium in vestibulō relīquit nē quis adīre Cūriam iniussū suō nēve inde ēgredī posset. *He left a guard in the vestibule so that no one could approach the Senate house without his orders* (lit. *with his non-command*) *or go out from there.* (Purpose)

Adventus eius compressit Etruscōs adeō ut nēmō extrā mūnīmenta ēgraderētur. *His arrival checked the Etruscans so much* (**adeō**) *that no one went out beyond the fortifications.* (Result)

A certain type of result is expressed in English by an infinitive phrase, e.g. *he is not so clever as to understand Plato* (we could also say *he is not clever enough to understand Plato*). We can turn this phrase into a clause: *he is not so clever that he understands Plato.* Although this is somewhat different from *he was so tired he could not move a step* (*he understands Plato* is what does *not* result), Latin uses the same construction: **nōn est tam sapiens ut Platōnem intellegat.** For sentences of the type *he is too stupid to understand Plato* see 19.1/4d.

The tense of the verb in result clauses is basically the same as in English, although the mood is different. The following points deserve attention:

(*a*) Where a result is specified as going to take place in the future, Latin uses a composite tense (composite future subjunctive) consisting of the future participle and the present subjunctive of **sum**: **adeō fessus sum ut crās tē nōn vīsūrus sim** *I am so tired that I shall not see you tomorrow.*

(*b*) The difference between the imperfect and perfect subjunctive in result clauses is small. The imperfect stresses the logical connection between the subordinate clause and the main clause, the perfect stresses that the result actually happened: **tantus terror omnēs occupāvit ut nullus mīles arma caperet et ipse rex ad flūmen nāvēsque perfūgerit** *so great a panic gripped everyone that no soldier took up arms and the king himself actually escaped to the river and ships.* In this context the force of the perfect **perfūgerit** can be brought out by inserting *actually*.

16.1/2 Classification of tenses

To analyse the use of tenses in certain constructions it is useful to classify them into two groups:

(*a*) *Primary tenses*, which have reference to the present or future, i.e. present, future, perfect when used to express a present state, and future perfect.

(*b*) *Historic* (or *secondary*) *tenses*, which have reference to the past, i.e. imperfect, perfect when used to express a simple action or state in the past, and pluperfect.

The perfect is in both groups because of its twofold meaning (4.1/6). In **quod domī es, portam iam clausī** *because you are home I have already closed the door,* the perfect **clausī** (<**claudō, -ere**) *I have closed* indicates a present state; the door is now closed as a result of my action. But in **multīs ante diēbus servus portam clausit** *many days previously the slave closed the door,* a simple past act is described. Nothing is indicated about the present state of the door, which might, for all we know from this statement, have been blown away in the meantime.

Why do we translate the perfect of **claudō** in these two different ways? In each sentence the context gives us the clue. In the second, the phrase **multīs ante diēbus** indicates that **clausit** must be taken as indicating a simple past action; *many days previously the slave has closed the door* would be absurd. It would also be absurd to take the first example as meaning *because you are home I already closed the door*; we know we are dealing with the present because of **iam** and the tense of **es**. Hence **clausī** in this example is classified as primary, while **clausit** in the other is historic.

The classification of tenses can be tabulated as follows:

PRIMARY	HISTORIC
future future perfect present perfect (translated with *have*)	imperfect perfect (translated without *have*) pluperfect

16.1/3 The conjunction *cum*

In addition to the preposition **cum** *with*, Latin has a subordinating conjunction **cum**. The two have completely separate origins and are very easily distinguished. The conjunction has the basic meaning of *when* but is often used in the sense of *because* or *since* (but not *since* in the meaning *from the time when*), and this difference is to some extent reflected in the mood of the verb in the **cum** clause. In Classical Latin the rules governing its use are:

(*a*) **Cum** meaning *since, because* always takes the subjunctive: **diūtius cum sustinēre nostrōrum impetūs nōn possent, Helvētiī sē in montem recēpērunt** *because they were not able to withstand the attacks of our men any longer* (**diūtius**), *the Helvetii retreated* (lit. *took themselves back*) *to a hill.*

(*b*) **Cum** meaning *when* takes the indicative if its verb is in a primary tense: **sīdera multa, cum tacet nox, furtīvōs hominum vident amōrēs** *the many stars see the stolen loves of men when the night is silent.*

(*c*) **Cum** meaning *when* takes the subjunctive when its verb is in a historic tense (with certain exceptions mentioned below):

   Zēnōnem, cum Athēnīs essem, audiēbam frequenter. *When I was in Athens I often used to hear Zeno.*
   Cum Caesar Ancōnam occupāvisset, Rōmam relīquimus. *When Caesar had captured Ancona we left Rome.*

   In sentences such as these, the tense of the verb in the **cum** clause must reflect its temporal relationship to the main verb. Because Caesar's capture preceded our leaving Rome the pluperfect **occupāvisset** must be used, though in English we could say *when Caesar captured Ancona* (note the difference from the construction of **ubi, postquam, antequam, simulac** and **ut** 5.1/2). In this category it is often difficult to decide whether **cum** should be translated by *when* or *since*. Sometimes, but not always, when the relationship between the subordinate and main clauses is purely temporal the indicative is used and any possible causal interpretation is thereby excluded: **cum Caesar in Galliam vēnit, alterīus factiōnis prīncipēs erant Haeduī, alterīus Sēquanī** *when Caesar came to Gaul the leaders of one of the two factions were the Haedui, the Sequani of the other.* A subjunctive in the **cum** clause would imply there was a causal connection between it and the main clause and thereby alter the meaning.

(d) **Cum** meaning *whenever* takes the indicative (the subjunctive is sometimes used in Silver Latin (1.3)). The perfect is normally used in the **cum** clause if the main verb is present, the pluperfect if the main verb is in the past: **cum rosam vīderat, tum incipere vēr arbitrābātur** *whenever he saw a rose he used then to think spring to be beginning.*

(e) Sometimes, for stylistic reasons, the **cum** clause describes the more important event, while the main clause describes something of less importance (so-called inverted **cum**). This can only occur in past narration. The **cum** clause then takes the indicative: **iam vēr appetēbat cum Hannibal ex hibernīs mōvit** *already spring was approaching when Hannibal moved from his winter camp* (**hiberna**), i.e. *when spring was already approaching, Hannibal . . .*

(f) **Cum prīmum** *as soon as* takes the indicative: **cum prīmum Rōmam vēnī, hās litterās scrīpsī** *as soon as* (lit. *when first*) *I came to Rome, I wrote this letter.*

(g) **Cum** with the subjunctive is occasionally used in the sense of *although*; the more usual words are **quamquam** and **quamvīs** (29.1/4b): **nōn poterant tamen, cum cuperent, Aprōnium imitārī** *however* (**tamen**), *they were not able to imitate Apronius, although they wanted to.*

The following is a table of these uses:

INDICATIVE	SUBJUNCTIVE

cum = *when* (primary)
cum prīmum = *as soon as*
  (primary and historic)
inverted **cum** (only occurs in
  historic tenses)
cum = *whenever* (primary
  and historic)
	cum = *when* (historic, except
	  as indicated in (c) above)
	cum = *since* (primary
	  and historic)
	cum = *although* (primary
	  and historic)

16.2 Latin reading

1 Ita currus collocant ut expeditum ad suos receptum habeant.

2 Alexander Magnus, cum ad Achillis tumulum venisset, 'O fortunate' inquit 'adulescens, cum tuae virtutis Homerum praeconem inveneris!'

3 Avarus, nisi cum moritur, nihil recte facit.

4 Custodes circa omnes portas miserunt ne quis ex urbe egrederetur.

5 Bene vixit is qui potuit, cum voluit, mori.

6 Aqua, quae flumine Nilo fertur, adeo est limosa ac turbida ut multos variosque morbos efficiat.

7 Caesar castella constituit ibique tormenta collocavit ne, cum aciem instruxisset, hostes ab lateribus pugnantes suos circumvenire possent.

8 Quis tam perditus ut dubitet Senecam praeferre Neroni?

9 Tarquinius sic Servium diligebat ut is eius vulgo haberetur filius.

10 Tanta tempestas coorta est ut naves cursum tenere non possent.

11 Factum est opportunitate loci, hostium inscientia ac defatigatione, virtute militum et aliarum pugnarum exercitatione, ut ne unum quidem nostrorum impetum ferrent ac statim terga verterent.

12 Nemo adeo ferus est ut non mitescere possit.

13 Verres Siciliam ita perdidit ut ea restitui non possit.

14 Cum cohors impetum fecerat, hostes refugiebant.

15 Cum solitudo et vita sine amicis insidiarum et metus plena sit, ratio ipsa monet amicitias comparare.

16 Socrates, cum facile posset educi e custodia, noluit.

17 Tua res agitur, paries cum proximus ardet.

Catullus to Lesbia

18   Ille mi par esse deo videtur,
    ille, si fas est, superare divos,
    qui sedens adversus identidem te
        spectat et audit   4
    dulce ridentem, misero quod omnis
    eripit sensus mihi: nam simul te,
    Lesbia, aspexi, nihil est super mi
        vocis in ore,   8

lingua sed torpet, tenuis sub artus
flamma demanat, sonitu suopte
tintinant aures, gemina teguntur
   lumina nocte.   12

Notes

2 **inquit** *said* (25.1/5*a*, i).
3 **nisi** *except*.
7 **pugnantēs** with **hostēs**, which is the subject of the **nē** clause.
8 **perditus** supply **est**; **Seneca**, a writer under the emperor Nero.
9 Servius and Tarquin were the two last kings of Rome (6th cent.
   BC); **is** i.e. Tarquin, **eius** i.e. Servius; **habērētur** *was considered*.
11 **nē . . . quidem** *not even*; **nē** here is an adverb, it does not introduce
   a purpose clause.
15 **plēna** + gen.; **sit** agrees with the closer element of the double
   subject (**vīta**) – English requires *are*.
18 *l.*1 **mī** (also *l.*7) shorter form of **mihi**; **pār** + dat. *equal to*; **vidētur**
   the passive of **videō** can mean *seem* as well as *be seen*. *l.*2 supply
   vidētur with **superāre**. *l.*5 **dulce rīdentem** lit. *laughing a sweet thing*,
   i.e. *laughing sweetly* (27.1/3*e*); **quod** *a thing which*; **omnīs** with
   sensūs (*l.*6). *l.*6 **mihi** dative of disadvantage (28.1/1*e*) lit. *to the*
   disadvantage of me, i.e. *from me*; **simul** = **simulac** *as soon as*. *ll* 7f.
   nihil . . . vōcis lit. *nothing of voice*, i.e. *no voice* (27.1/4*k*); **est super**
   = **superest**. *l.*10 **suōpte** = **suō**, an emphatic form. *l.*11 **geminā** with
   nocte.

16.3 Extra reading

Orpheus and Eurydice (2)

Iamque pedem referens casus evaserat omnis,
redditaque Eurydice superas veniebat ad auras
pone sequens (namque hanc dederat Proserpina legem),
cum subita incautum dementia cepit amantem,
ignoscenda quidem, scirent si ignoscere Manes: 5
restitit, Eurydicenque suam iam luce sub ipsa
immemor, heu! victusque animi respexit. ibi omnis
effusus labor atque immitis rupta tyranni

foedera, terque fragor stagnis auditus Avernis.
illa 'quis et me' inquit 'miseram et te perdidit, Orpheu,
quis tantus furor? en iterum crudelia retro
fata vocant, conditque natantia lumina somnus.
iamque vale: feror ingenti circumdata nocte
invalidasque tibi tendens, heu non tua, palmas.'
dixit et ex oculis subito, ceu fumus in auras
commixtus tenuis, fugit diversa, neque illum
prensantem nequiquam umbras et multa volentem
dicere praeterea vidit: nec portitor Orci
amplius obiectam passus transire paludem.

Notes

*l.*1 **pedem referens** i.e. *returning*; **omnīs** with **cāsūs**. *l.*3 **pōne** adv. *behind*;
Prōserpina (9.3) wife of Pluto and queen of the Underworld; the **lex**
was that Orpheus should not look at Eurydice until they were both
back in the upper world. *l.*5 **ignoscenda** (18.1/2*a*) *pardonable* with
dēmentia; scīrent (<**sciō**); this line is a condensed form of [*which would
have been*] *pardonable if the Shades knew how to pardon* with both
verbs in the subjunctive (22.1/2). *l.*6 **restitit** (<**resistō**) *he stopped*;
Eurydicēn Greek accusative of **Eurydicē** (25.1/4*e*; the story and names
were Greek); **lūce sub ipsā** = **sub lūce ipsā**. *l.*7 **victus animī** lit.
conquered in mind (**animī** locative), i.e. *with mind overcome*. *ll.*8f.
supply **est** with **effūsus** and **audītus, sunt** with **rupta; foedera** plural for
singular. *l.*10 **inquit** *said* (25.1/5*a*, i); **Orpheu** vocative (25.1/4*e*, i). *l.*12
vocant supply **mē**. *l.*13 **valē** *farewell* (21.1/1); **circumdata** *surrounded*.
*l.*14 **tua** with the understood subject **ego** (Eurydice). *l.*16 **dīversa** *in the
opposite direction* (i.e. back to the Underworld). *l.*19 **amplius** *further,
again*; **obiectam** (<**obiciō**) with **palūdem** *the swamp that stood in his
way*; **passus** (<**patior**) supply **est**.

UNIT 17

17.1 Grammar

17.1/1 Indirect speech (1)

There are two ways in which we can relate what someone has said. We can either give the exact words: *'I am', the candidate for the consulship announced, 'going to make important changes in the organisation of the water supply.'* or we can subordinate his words to a verb of saying (here *announced*) and make the necessary changes in pronouns and verbs: *The candidate for the consulship announced that he was going to make important changes*, etc. The first we call *direct speech*, and second *indirect* (or *reported*) *speech*. The latter is divided into three sub-categories, which reflect corresponding differences in the former:

Indirect statement: *He said that he was sick.* (Original *I am sick.*)
Indirect question: *She asked where she was.* (Original *Where am I?*)
Indirect command and petition: *She ordered him to leave immediately.* (Original *Leave immediately!*)

In the first two the reported speech is, in English, expressed by noun clauses; *that he was sick* and *where she was* could, from a grammatical point of view, be replaced by nouns, e.g. *three words* and *a question* respectively. An indirect command in English is normally expressed by an infinitive phrase, as in the third example, but here too we can use a noun clause [*she ordered*] *that he leave immediately*. In Latin, for indirect questions and indirect commands and petitions we use noun clauses (23.1/3 and 21.1/2); but for indirect statement we have the *accusative and infinitive* construction.

17.1/2 Indirect statement

In English we can say, with the same meaning, *I know that he is honest* or *I know him to be honest*. The latter is exactly the Latin accusative and infinitive. The noun clause *that he is honest* has been converted into an infinitive phrase by putting its subject into the accusative (*he* to *him*) and changing its finite verb *is* to the infinitive *to be*; the conjunction *that* is no longer required. *I say that you are foolish* becomes in Latin **dīcō tē stultum esse.** As *foolish* qualifies *you*, the accusative **stultum** is necessary as it must agree with **tē**, which is itself accusative. **Tē**, however, although accusative, is the subject of the infinitive **esse.** This feature is even more obvious in the following examples:

> **Mīlitēs renuntiant Caesarem castra Gallōrum cēpisse.** *The soldiers report that Caesar has captured the camp of the Gauls.*
> **Consul dīcit novās copiās crās ventūrās esse.** *The consul says that reinforcements* (**novae cōpiae**) *will come tomorrow.*

Why do we have a perfect infinitive in the first example and a future infinitive in the second? Because these were the tenses used by the speakers in their original statements, which were **Caesar castra Gallōrum cēpit** *Caesar has captured the camp of the Gauls*, and **novae cōpiae crās venient** *reinforcements will come tomorrow*. The rule is: *the tense of the infinitive in accusative and infinitive must reflect that of the original statement*. A present infinitive represents the present tense in the original statement, a future infinitive represents the future tense, and a perfect infinitive represents a past tense. We must always go back to the *original* statement. In *he said that the dog was sick* (**dixit canem aegrōtāre**), the original statement was *the dog is sick* (**canis aegrōtat**) not *the dog was sick* (**canis aegrōtāvit**); if the original statement had been the latter we would have *he said that the dog had been sick* (**dixit canem aegrōtāvisse**).

Since the infinitive in this construction can, if from a transitive verb, have an object, which must be in the accusative, we may ask how we are to distinguish the subject of the infinitive from its object if we have both. In cases like **dīcunt Egnātium dentēs saepe lāvāre** *they say that Egnatius cleans* (lit. *washes*) *his teeth often*, we have two accusatives, but the sense tells us which is subject and which is object of the infinitive. It is obvious, however, that ambiguity is possible. The most celebrated example was the elusive reply of the priestess at Delphi to Pyrrhus, king of Epirus, when he asked her about his chances against the Romans: **aiō tē Rōmānōs vincere posse.** As word order is no guide, does this mean *I say that you can conquer the Romans* or *I say that the Romans can conquer you*? Pyrrhus, rather egotistically, did not take the second possibility into account and suffered accordingly. Ambiguities of this sort are avoided by Latin authors.

The reflexive pronoun **sē** (9.1/4) is of especial importance in this construction. If we report Caesar's words **vēnī, vīdī, vīcī** *I came, I saw, I conquered*, we get **Caesar dixit sē vēnisse, vīdisse, vīcisse**, lit. *Caesar said himself to have come*, etc. If instead of **sē** we write **eum**, the meaning becomes *Caesar said that he* (someone else) *had come*, etc., reflecting an original **vēnit, vīdit, vīcit.** The rule is: **sē**, *when used as the subject of an accusative and infinitive, refers to the subject of the verb introducing the construction.*

In the following examples the **esse** of the perfect passive and future active infinitives is omitted. This is a very common use (cf. 3.1/7).

> **Caesar sē eōs in fidem receptūrum et conservātūrum dixit.** *Caesar said that he would take them into his protection and look after them.*
>
> **Lēgātī haec sē ad suōs relātūrōs dixērunt.** *The envoys said that they would report back* (**referre**) *these things to their people.*
>
> **Dēsertōs sē ac prōditōs ā vōbīs dīcunt.** *They say that they have been deserted and betrayed by you.*

To establish what participles (and adjectives) agree with the reflexive pronoun, we must first see to what word it refers, and then determine the gender and number of this word (it will always be in the nominative case). In the first example **sē** refers to **Caesar**, and therefore is masculine singular (acc.); hence **receptūrum** and **conservātūrum** agree with **sē**. In the second example **sē** refers to **lēgātī**, and therefore is masculine plural (acc.); hence **relātūrōs** agrees with it.

Notes

1 An indirect statement, if negated, cannot be introduced by **dīcō**. **Negō** *deny* must be used, and the negative dropped from the

accusative and infinitive: **negat vēnisse sē cum multitūdine ad iānuam meam** *he says that he did not come with a mob to my door* (lit. *denies himself to have come . . .*). There is no similar restriction on other verbs that can introduce this construction.

2 The accusative and infinitive construction is also used after verbs of thinking, feeling, perceiving, knowing, believing, where in English we would normally have a clause: **deum aliquem prōtectūrum vōs raptūrumque hinc putātis?** *do you think that some god is going to protect you and carry you off from here?*

3 It is also used with verbs of hoping, promising, swearing and threatening. When these verbs have a future reference (as they generally do), they are often followed in English by a present infinitive, but in Latin an accusative and a future infinitive must be used: **spērat adulescens sē diū victūrum** *a young man hopes to live for a long time* (lit. *himself to be going to live*).

4 When direct speech is converted into indirect speech, any verbs in the indicative mood in subordinate clauses are changed into the subjunctive. This can be best seen in adjectival clauses:

Original: **Triumphum postulō dē Gallīs quōs vīcī.** *I claim a triumph over the Gauls whom I have defeated.*

Reported: **Dīcit sē triumphum postulāre dē Gallīs quōs vīcerit.** *He says he is claiming a triumph over the Gauls whom he has defeated.*

This change is made so that we can distinguish between the words of the original speaker and any comments made by the person reporting him. **Quōs vīcit** would be additional information supplied by the person making the report and would not represent anything in the original statement.

17.1/3 Adverbs

A large number of adverbs in Latin are derived from adjectives. With first and second declension adjectives, **-ē**, or, less commonly, **-ō**, is added to the stem: **dūrē** *harshly* (**dūrus**), **pulchrē** *beautifully* (**pulcher**), **tūtō** *safely* (**tūtus**). **Bene** *well* (**bonus**) and **male** *badly* (**malus**) have a short final **e**; **magnopere** *greatly* (from **magnus**) is irregular. With third declension adjectives, **-iter**, or **-er** (after **nt**) is added to the stem: **ferōciter** *fiercely* (**ferox**), **fortiter** *bravely* (**fortis**), **prūdenter** *prudently*

(**prūdens**). The neuter nominative and accusative singular of a few
third declension adjectives is used as the adverb: **facile** *easily* (**facilis**).
A few adverbs end in **-im**: **statim** *immediately*, **partim** *partly*; and in
-um: **paulum** *little*, **multum** *much*, **parum** *too little*. Of the remainder,
which we need not classify by ending, adverbs of place can be
conveniently tabulated here:

PLACE WHERE

ubi	*where?*	**ibi**	*there*
hīc	*here*	**illīc**	*there*

PLACE TO WHICH

quō	*to where?*	**eō**	*to there*
hūc	*to here*	**illūc**	*to there*

PLACE FROM WHICH

unde	*from where?*	**inde**	*from there*
hinc	*from here*	**illinc**	*from there*

The second of each of the pairs in the right-hand columns is more
emphatic.

In English we normally use *place where* adverbs in the sense of *place
to which*: *he came here yesterday*; *where are you going?* In Latin we
must use *place to which* adverbs in these cases: **heri hūc vēnit**; **quō
vādis?** Latin often uses adjectives where we would have adverbs in
English: **citī ad aedēs Circae vēnimus** *we came quickly to Circe's house*;
the adverb **cito** *quickly* would be equally correct.

17.2 Latin reading

A graffito from Pompeii

1 Admiror, paries, te non cecidisse ruinis,
     cum tot scriptorum taedia sustineas.

Four epigrams from Martial

2 Inscripsit tumulis septem scelerata virorum
     'se fecisse' Chloe. quid pote simplicius?

3 Esse negas coctum leporem poscisque flagella.
     mavis, Rufe, cocum scindere quam leporem.

4 Sordida cum tibi sit, verum tamen, Attale, dicit,
     quisquis te niveam dicit habere togam.

5 In thermis sumit lactucas, ova, lacertum,
 et cenare domi se negat Aemilius.

6 Aristoteles ait bestiolas nasci quae unum diem vivant.

7 Illi, supplicia cruciatusque Gallorum veriti quorum agros vexaverant, remanere se apud eum velle dixerunt.

8 A. Ubi ea mulier habitat? B. hic. A. unde eam esse aiunt? B. Samo.

9 Caesar, cum de natura moribusque Nerviorum quaereret, sic repperit: nullum esse aditum ad eos mercatoribus: nihil pati vini reliquarumque rerum ad luxuriam pertinentium inferri, quod his rebus relanguescere animos existimarent: esse homines feros magnaeque virtutis atque incusare reliquos Belgas qui se populo 5 Romano dedidissent patriamque virtutem proiecissent: confirmare se neque legatos missuros neque ullam condicionem pacis accepturos.

10 P. Scipio Nasica, cum ad poetam Ennium venisset et ancilla negavisset Ennium domi esse, sensit illam domini iussu dixisse et illum intus esse. paucis post diebus, cum ad Nasicam venisset Ennius et eum a ianua quaereret, exclamat Nasica se domi non esse. tum Ennius 'quid? ego non cognosco vocem' inquit 'tuam?' 5 hic Nasica 'homo es impudens. ego, cum te quaererem, ancillae tuae credidi te domi non esse. tu mihi non credis ipsi?'

Notes

1 **tot** *so many* indeclinable adjective qualifying **scriptōrum** (<**scriptor** *writer*).

2 **Chloē** nom. s. (Greek female name). What Chloe actually wrote was **Chloē fēcit**; **faciō** can mean *make* or *do* – Chloe meant that she herself had made the gravestones, but others maliciously misunderstood **Chloē fēcit** as signifying that she had killed her husbands; **quid pote** = **quid potest esse**; **simplicius** *more naïve* comparative of **simplex** (19.1/1).

3 **quam** *rather than*.

4 **cum** *although*; **niveus** has two meanings (*a*) *white as snow*, (*b*) *cold as snow* – only (*b*) is really applicable as Attalus's toga is filthy and, presumably, threadbare; **quisquis** (= **quīcumque**, 10.1/1*j*) *whoever* (only this form and the neuter **quidquid** are in common use).

5 **thermae [aquae]** lit. *warm waters* another name for **balneae** *baths*.

6 **ait** *says* from the defective verb **aiō** (25.1/5*a*, i).

7 **cruciātūs** acc. pl. *tortures*.

8 **hīc** (the adverb, not **hic** *this*) answers the preceding question, as does **Samō** (the Aegean island Samos).

9 *l.*2 **mercātōribus** dat. *for merchants*; **nihil** with **vīnī** and **rērum** lit. *nothing of wine and . . .*, i.e. *no wine and . . .* (27.1/4*k*); **patī** from **patior** *allow*. *l.*3 **pertinentium** with **rērum** *things pertaining to*. *l.*5 **magnae virtūtis** 6.1/3. *l.*6 **patriam** <**patrius**.

10 *l.*1 **ad** here and in *l.*3 means *to the house of*. *l.*4 **exclāmat** is a vivid present (a very common use to enliven narrative) and should be translated by the past tense in English. *l.*5 **inquit** *said* (25.1/5*a*, i). *l.*6 **hīc Nāsīca** *at this point* (lit. *here*) *Nasica* [*said*]. *l.*7 **crēdidī** and **crēdis** from **crēdō** *believe*, which is intransitive and takes the dative, not the accusative (20.1/1), hence **ancillae tuae** and **mihi ipsī**.

17.3 Extra reading

Sacrilege

Marcus Tullius Cicerō (in English *Cicero*, though up to the eighteenth century he was sometimes called *Tully*) lived from 106 to 43 BC and is one of the most important figures in Latin literature. His surviving works consist of treatises on philosophy and rhetoric, political and legal speeches, a large collection of letters, and some poetry. His speeches in particular have always been regarded as models of Latin prose. The following is from his prosecution of Verres, a former Roman provincial governor, whom he is upbraiding for plundering the temple of Apollo at Delos.

Illine tu templo Apollinis, tam antiquo, tam sancto, tam religioso manus impias ac sacrilegas afferre conatus es? si in pueritia non his artibus et disciplinis institutus eras, ut ea, quae litteris mandata sunt, disceres atque cognosceres, ne postea quidem, cum in ea ipsa loca venisti, potuisti accipere id, quod est proditum memoriae ac litteris? 5 Latonam ex longo errore et fuga confugisse Delum atque ibi Apollinem Dianamque peperisse: qua ex opinione hominum illa insula eorum deorum sacra putatur: tantaque eius auctoritas religionis et est et semper fuit, ut ne Persae quidem, cum bellum toti Graeciae, dis hominibusque indixissent et mille numero navium 10 classem ad Delum appulissent, quidquam conarentur aut violare aut attingere. hoc tu fanum depopulari audebas? fuit ulla cupiditas tanta, ut tantam exstingueret religionem?

Notes

*l.*1 **Illī** (dat.) + **-ne**; **templō** dat. of disadvantage (28.1/1*e*), *to the disadvantage of*, i.e. *against*. *l.*4 **nē . . . quidem** *not even*; **loca** the plural of **locus** is normally neuter (25.1/4*b*). *l.*6 **Lātōnam**, etc. acc. and inf. *that Latona . . .*; **Dēlum** see 12.2, 17 note on *l.*6. *l.*7 **quā** with **opīniōne** lit. *from which opinion*; Latin very often joins a sentence to the preceding one in this way with the relative (adj. or pron.), but we would translate into English *from this opinion*. *ll.*9f. **tōtī Graeciae, dīs hominibusque** dat. of disadvantage as in *l.*1, (*had declared war*) *on all Greece, gods and men*. *l.*11 **ad Dēlum** *at Delos*; if *to Delos* were meant we would have simply **Dēlum** as in *l.*6.

UNIT 18

18.1 Grammar

18.1/1 Gerund

We have already seen that the Latin supine is a verbal noun with a very restricted use (12.1/3). The other verbal noun, which has a wide range of uses, is the gerund. To form it we add **-ndum** to the present stem of the first and second conjugations and **-endum** to that of the third and fourth. The result is a second declension neuter noun: **amá-ndum** [*the act of*] *loving,* **moné-ndum** [*the act of*] *warning,* **reg-éndum** [*the act of*] *ruling,* **audi-éndum** [*the act of*] *hearing* (on the two functions of English verbal forms in -*ing* see 11.1/2 note 1). The gerund is active in meaning and has no plural. Because it is a noun it can be declined, but as it is also a verbal form it can be qualified by an adverb; if it is from a transitive verb it can, within certain limits, govern an object. The following analysis of its uses is arranged according to case:

(*a*) The gerund cannot be used in the *nominative*. Instead, we must use the infinitive, a construction we also have in English: **crrārc cst hūmānum** *to err* (i.e. *the act of erring*) *is human.*

(*b*) In the *accusative* the gerund is only used after prepositions such as **ad**, with which it expresses purpose (for restrictions on this use see end of 18.1/2): **ad bene vīvendum breve tempus satis est longum** *for living well a short time is long enough.* Where English has a verbal noun as the direct object of a verb, Latin generally has an infinitive: **tēcum vīvere amō** *I love living with you.*

(*c*) The *genitive* of the gerund is used after adjectives which are followed by the genitive, and after nouns: **vir bonus dīcendī perītus** *a good man experienced in speaking*; **difficultās nāvigandī** *difficulty* *in sailing*; **cupiditās videndī deōs hominēsque** *desire of seeing gods and men.*

(*d*) The ***dative*** of the gerund is rare.

(*e*) In the ***ablative*** the gerund is commonly used with prepositions which take the ablative (**ā/ab, dē, ē/ex, in**), and by itself, where it expresses instrument or cause:

> **Lex est recta ratiō in iubendō et vetandō.** *The law is the correct method in ordering and forbidding.*
>
> **Ūnus homō nōbīs cunctandō restituit rem.** *One man restored our fortunes* (lit. *restored the thing for us*) *by delaying.*

18.1/2 Gerundive

The gerundive is a verbal adjective for which there is no single-word equivalent in English. It is formed by taking the stem of the gerund and adding the endings of first and second declension adjectives: **amánd-us, -a, -um; monénd-us, -a, -um; regénd-us, -a, -um; audiénd-us, -a, -um**. It has three uses:

(*a*) As an attributive adjective with the sense of *able to be loved, worthy of being loved,* etc.; i.e. it is an adjective, passive in sense and expressing what could or should happen: **vir laudandus** *a worthy-to-be-praised man*, i.e. *a praiseworthy man*; **rēs metuendae** *things worthy-to-be-feared*, i.e. *terrible things*; **Mānīsque adiit rēgemque tremendum** *he approached both the shades and their fearsome* (lit. *worthy-to-be-feared*) *king* (from **Orpheus and Eurydice** 15.3 *l.*6).

(*b*) As a predicative adjective with the same basic sense, except that it always expresses the idea of necessity, i.e. what should happen, not what could happen. This use involves part of **sum**:

> **Mulier audienda est.** *The woman must be heard* (lit. *is needing-to-be-heard*).
>
> **Soror amanda est.** *A sister must be loved* (lit. *is needing-to-be-loved*).
>
> **Dōna Gallōrum nōn recipienda sunt.** *The presents of the Gauls must not be received* (lit. *are not needing-to-be-received*).
>
> **Exercitus ad Italiam dūcendus erat.** *The army had to be led to Italy* (lit. *was needing-to-be-led*).

Because a gerundive cannot be changed to indicate time, we must vary the tense of **sum**. Also, as the last example shows, a different expression must be used for the past in English as *must* does not have a past tense.

In this construction an agent is expressed by the dative without a preposition (dative of agent, 28.1/1*c*), not by **ā/ab** and the ablative: **gens dūra atque aspera dēbellanda tibi est** *a hard and tough race must be subdued by you*, i.e. *you must subdue*, etc. When, however, there is another dative in the clause and confusion would result from a dative of agent, **ā/ab** and the ablative is used: **obsidēs Rōmānīs ab hostibus dandī erant** *hostages had to be given to the Romans by the enemy*, i.e. *the enemy had to give*, etc. These two examples also show how a Latin gerundive clause where an agent is specified can often be translated into idiomatic English by changing the verb from passive to active.

A gerundive main clause can be put into the accusative and infinitive construction in the same way as any other main clause: **dixit obsidēs Rōmānīs ab hostibus dandōs fuisse** *he said that the enemy had had to give hostages to the Romans*.

Since the gerundive is passive it is obvious that only transitive verbs can be used in sentences such as the above, where we have a normal subject. If we take an intransitive verb such as *come*, we cannot make up a sentence where it is used in the passive with a proper subject. To take an example, *lift* is a transitive verb, and a sentence where it is used actively *you must lift this stone* can be put into the passive *this stone must be lifted by you* (which can be translated directly into Latin with a gerundive). *Come*, however, which can never have a direct object, is intransitive, and *you must come to Rome* cannot be put into a passive form resembling *this stone must be lifted by you*. The same is true for Latin; but, as we shall see later (20.1/2), the Romans had a liking for impersonal expressions (*it is raining, it is necessary*[1]) where there is no true subject, and so the gerundives of intransitive verbs can be used impersonally: **Rōmam tibi veniendum est** *it is to-be-come (must-be-come) by you to Rome,* i.e. *you must come to Rome.* This construction can also be used with transitive verbs: **nunc nōbīs bibendum est** *now it is to-be-drunk by us,* i.e. *now we must drink.*

---

[1]The pronoun *it* is used in such expressions because in English virtually all finite verbs, except imperatives (21.1/1), must be provided with a subject.

The gerundive, in this and its other uses, is one of the trickiest parts of Latin grammar because we have nothing similar to it in English. If you do not master it at first **nōn tibi dēspērandum est** *it is not to-be-despaired by you*, i.e. *you must not despair!* Its impersonal use has parallels elsewhere in intransitive verbs (20.1/3).

(*c*) In this remaining use the gerundive has the sense of a present or future passive participle, but, with one exception, it is only employed in the same type of grammatical contexts as the gerund; consequently, we do not find it in the nominative in this meaning. It has here no sense of obligation or necessity and is always combined with a noun or pronoun to form an abstract expression parallel to what we have already encountered at 12.1/2. **Caesar occīsus** can mean *the murder of Caesar*; **Caesarem occīdendum** (we take the accusative because the nominative only occurs in uses (*a*) and (*b*)) can also mean *the murder of Caesar*, but the two are not interchangeable as Latin makes a distinction we do not have in English. **Caesar occīsus** describes an action occurring before that of the finite verb of its clause; **Caesarem occīdendum** refers to something which is happening at the same time as the action of the finite verb, or may happen subsequently.

> **Brūtus ad Cūriam vēnit ad Caesarem occīdendum.** *Brutus came to the Senate house for the murder of Caesar* (lit. *for Caesar going-to-be-murdered*).
> **Haec arma ad bellum gerendum ūtilia sunt.** *These weapons are useful for the waging of war* (lit. *for war going-to-be-waged*).

In both examples we would go a stage further for an idiomatic English translation and use a present active infinitive or a verbal noun in *-ing* without the article: *Brutus came to the Senate house to murder Caesar; these weapons are useful for waging war.* We shall see that the English verbal noun so used is generally the best way of translating a gerundive of this sort.

We can now analyse this use case by case:

(i) The *accusative* of the gerundive in this sense is used after prepositions taking the accusative, most commonly **ad**, with which it expresses purpose (see the two examples already given). The accusative of the gerundive also occurs after a few verbs (mainly **cūrō, dō, mittō**) and agrees with the object. This construction has the sense *X arranges* (**cūrat**), *gives* (**dat**), *sends* (**mittit**) *something to be done.*

Caesar pontem in Ararī faciendum cūrāvit. *Caesar arranged the building of a bridge on the Arar* (lit. *arranged a bridge going-to-be-built*).

Dant eum Vestae ēducandum. *They give him to Vesta to rear* (lit. *give him going-to-be-reared, the rearing of him*).

This use has no parallel among those of the gerund.

(ii) The gerundive (with the noun it qualifies) is often used in the *genitive* after an adjective or noun: **regendae reī pūblicae scientissimus** *most knowledgeable in governing the state* (lit. *of the state being governed*); **cupiditās bellī gerendī** *desire of waging war* (lit. *of war being waged*). A very frequent construction is **grātiā** or **causā** (each is ablative and has the meaning *for the sake of, by reason of*) with a preceding noun or pronoun and gerundive to express purpose. **Grātiā** and **causā** always come at the end of the phrase: **Menapiī lēgātōs ad eum pācis petendae causā mīsērunt** *the Menapii sent envoys to him for the sake of seeking peace* (lit. *of peace being sought, i.e. to seek peace*). The same construction is also used with the gerund.

(iii) The *dative* is used where it is required by a verb or adjective (28.1/1*a, b*): **mons pecorī bonus alendō erat** *the mountain was good for feeding livestock* (lit. *for livestock being fed*). It can also be used to express purpose (28.1/1*h*): **diem praestituit operī faciendō** *he fixed a day for doing the work* (lit. *for the work going-to-be-done*).

(iv) As with the gerund (18.1/1*e*), the *ablative* of the gerundive is common both with and without prepositions:

Multa sunt dicta ab antīquīs dē contemnendīs ac despiciendīs rēbus hūmānīs. *Many things were said by the ancients about disregarding and despising human affairs* (lit. *about human affairs being condemned and despised*).

Loquendī ēlegantia augētur legendīs ōrātōribus et poētīs. *Elegance in speaking is increased by reading orators and poets* (lit. *by orators and poets being read*).

When we compare these uses of the gerundive with those of the gerund (18.1/1) we see a considerable overlap, and this occurs where we could theoretically have a gerund governing an accusative. In the last example we could have **legendō ōrātōrēs et poētās**. Latin authors prefer the gerundive construction in such cases, particularly when the other construction would involve a gerund in the accusative. **Ad pācem petendam** *for seeking peace* is what Latin authors always use, never **ad petendum pācem**.

Notes

1 As noticed in 14.1/4, deponent verbs have both gerunds and gerundives. The gerund of a deponent verb is active in meaning, the gerundive is passive; consequently they are not different in any way from the gerund and gerundive of normal verbs: **opīnandum** [*the act of*] *thinking* (from **opīnor**); **mīlitēs cohortandī erant** *the soldiers were needing-to-be-encouraged*, i.e. *had to be encouraged* (from **cohortor**).
2 In the third conjugation an older form of the gerund/gerundive stem in **-und-** is sometimes used: **gerundum** (< **gerō**), **dūcundus** (< **dūcō**).

18.2 Latin reading

1 Diu apparandum est bellum, ut celeriter vincas.
2 Bellum nec timendum nec provocandum est.
3 Cato, cum in Curia orationem habebat, semper dicebat 'Karthago delenda est'.
4 Dissimulandi causa in senatum veniebat.
5 De gustibus non est disputandum.
6 Amare et sapere vix deo conceditur.
7 Nox ruit, Aenea, nos flendo ducimus horas.
8 O discipuli, ea, quae dixistis, vera sunt, exceptis excipiendis et mutatis mutandis.
9 Deliberandum est saepe, statuendum est semel.
10 Ratione, non vi, vincenda adulescentia est.
11 Adhibenda est in iocando moderatio.
12 Cavendi nulla est dimittenda occasio.
13 Prope cottidie cum omni equitatu Indutiomarus sub castris

vagabatur, alias ut situm castrorum cognosceret, alias colloquendi
aut territandi causa.

Caesar in a tight corner
14   In the second year (57 BC) of his campaigning in Gaul, Caesar
     took his army to what is now north-eastern France to subdue the
     Nervii, a fierce tribe of Germanic origin. Learning of his
     approach, they made a sudden and unexpected attack on Caesar's
     vanguard when it was building a camp in anticipation of the
     arrival of the remainder of his army. Out of the subsequent
     pandemonium Caesar emerged victorious.

Caesari omnia uno tempore erant agenda: vexillum
proponendum, signum tuba dandum, ab opere revocandi milites:
qui e castris aggeris petendi causa processerant, arcessendi, acies
instruenda, milites cohortandi. quarum rerum magnam partem
temporis brevitas et incursus hostium impediebat . . . Caesar,   5
necessariis rebus imperatis, ad cohortandos milites decucurrit et
ad legionem decimam devenit. milites brevi oratione cohortatus,
proelii committendi signum dedit. atque in alteram partem item
cohortandi causa profectus, pugnantibus occurrit. temporis tanta
fuit exiguitas hostiumque tam paratus ad dimicandum animus ut   10
non modo ad insignia accommodanda sed etiam ad galeas
induendas scutisque tegimenta detrahenda tempus defuerit.
quam in partem quisque ab opere devenit et quae signa prima
conspexit, ad haec constitit, ne in quaerendis suis pugnandi
tempus dimitteret.   15

Notes

3   **habēbat** here *delivered, gave.*
7   **Aenēā** vocative (25.1/4*e*) *O Aeneas*; **dūcimus** *draw out, waste.*
13 **aliās . . . aliās** *at one time . . . at another time* (**aliās** is here an
    adverb).
14 In the first four lines the appropriate part of **sum** must be supplied
    with each gerundive except **agenda** and **petendī**. *l.*3 the subject of
    arcessendī is the understood antecedent of **quī** (*l.*3). *l.*4 **quārum** see
    note on **quā** in 17.3 (*l.*7). *l.*9 **profectus** from **proficiscor**, not
    prōficiō; **pugnantibus** (dat.) **occurrit** *ran into men fighting. l.*12
    scūtīs ablative of separation (see 28.1/2*e*) *from shields.*

18.3 Extra reading

Ulysses, come home!

Publius Ovidius Nāsō (43 BC–AD 17), known in English as Ovid, was the last great poet of the Augustan age. In AD 8, as the result of a mysterious scandal about which we are ill-informed, he was banished by the Emperor Augustus to Tomis, an outpost of the Roman Empire on the west coast of the Black Sea (now *Constanta* in Romania), where he died. One of his most attractive works, the *Hērōides*, is a collection of poems, each of which is in the form of a letter, in most cases from a woman of the heroic age to her absent husband or lover, in a few from the absent man. The following is part of Penelope's letter to Ulysses, whose return to Ithaca after the sack of Troy was delayed by the hostility of Neptune.

Argolici rediere duces, altaria fumant,
    ponitur ad patrios barbara praeda deos
 grata ferunt nymphae pro salvis dona maritis:
    illi victa suis Troia fata canunt.
mirantur iustique senes trepidaeque puellae:
    narrantis coniunx pendet ab ore viri.
atque aliquis posita monstrat fera proelia mensa,
    pingit et exiguo Pergama tota mero.
hic ibat Simois, hic est Sigeia tellus,
    hic steterat Priami regia celsa senis.   1(
 . . . .
diruta sunt aliis, uni mihi Pergama restant,
    incola captivo quae bove victor arat.
iam seges est ubi Troia fuit, resecandaque falce
    luxuriat Phrygio sanguine pinguis humus.
semisepulta virum curvis feriuntur aratris   1:
    ossa. ruinosas occulit herba domos.

Notes

*l.*1 **Argolicī** Greek; **rediēre** (<**redeō**) = **rediērunt** (4.1/6 note 1). *l.*3 **prō salvīs . . . marītīs** *for* [*their*] *safe husbands,* i.e. *because their husbands are safe.* *l.*4 With **suīs** supply **fātīs** *the Trojan destiny* (lit. *fates*) *conquered by their own,* a somewhat complicated way of saying *Troy* *conquered by them*; **Trōïa** (3 syllables) is an adjective with **fāta** (but in *l*.13 **Troia** (2 syllables) is the noun *Troy*). *l*.6 **narrantis** with **virī** (gen.). *l*.7 **positā . . . mensā** ablative absolute. *l*.8 **pingit et** = **et pingit.** *l*.9 **hīc** *here*; **Sīgēia tellūs** *the Sigean land, the land of Troy. l*.11 **aliīs, ūnī mihi** *for others, for me alone. l*.12 The prose order would be **quae incola victor captīvō bove arat**; **victor** used here as adj. *victorious. l*.13 **resecanda** with **humus.** *l*.14 **Phrygiō** (= Trojan) **sanguine** *with Phrygian blood* is instrumental ablative (7.1/4) with **luxuriat.** *l*.15 **virum** gen. pl. (3.1/3*a*).

19.1 Grammar

19.1/1 Comparison of adjectives

Adjectives have three *degrees*: *positive* good, hard, beautiful; *comparative* better, harder, more beautiful; and *superlative* best, hardest, most beautiful. To give the three degrees of an adjective is to *compare* it. Some adjectives in English are compared regularly (*hard, beautiful*), some irregularly (*good*). The same applies in Latin. All regular adjectives, whether of the first and second declension or of the third, form their comparative by adding **-ior** to their stem, and their superlative by adding **-issimus**:

POSITIVE	STEM	COMPARATIVE	SUPERLATIVE
dūrus *hard*	**dūr-**	**dūrior** *harder*	**dūríssimus** *hardest*
fórtis *brave*	**fort-**	**fórtior** *braver*	**fortíssimus** *bravest*
ámans *loving*	**amant-**	**amántior** *more loving*	**amantíssimus** *most loving*
félix *fortunate*	**félīc-**	**fēlícior** *more fortunate*	**fēlicíssimus** *most fortunate*

All superlative adjectives belong to the first and second declension. All comparatives belong to the consonantal stem division of third declension adjectives (9.1/2); but, unlike normal adjectives of this class, comparatives have a separate form for the neuter singular nominative. **Dūrior** is declined as follows:

	SINGULAR		PLURAL	
	M. & F.	N.	M. & F.	N.
N. & V.	**dūrior**	**dūrius**	**dūriórēs**	**dūrióra**
Acc.	**dūriórem**	**dūrius**	**dūriórēs**	**dūrióra**
Gen.	**dūrióris**	**dūrióris**	**dūriórum**	**dūriórum**
Dat.	**dūriórī**	**dūriórī**	**dūrióribus**	**dūrióribus**
Abl.	**dūrióre**	**dūrióre**	**dūrióribus**	**dūrióribus**

Two groups of adjectives have a slight irregularity. All adjectives in -er, whether of the first and second declension (**pulcher, tener**) or of the third (**ācer**), form their superlative in **-errimus**. In the comparative they are regular, and only adjectives like **tener** keep their final **e** as they do in the declension of their positive forms:

púlcher	púlchrior	pulchérrimus
téner	tenérior	tenérrimus
ácer	ácrior	ācérrimus

Six third declension adjectives ending in **-ilis** form their superlative in **-illimus**. These are: **facilis** *easy*, **difficilis** *difficult*, **similis** *similar*, **dissimilis** *dissimilar*, **gracilis** *slender*, **humilis** *low*. **Facilis** is compared: **fácilis, facílior, facíllimus**. Some adjectives are quite irregular, and of these the most important are:

bónus *good*	**mélior** *better*	**óptimus** *best*
málus *bad*	**péior** *worse*	**péssimus** *worst*
mágnus *great*	**máior** *greater*	**máximus** *greatest*
párvus *small*	**mínor** *smaller*	**mínimus** *smallest*
múltus *much*	**plūs** *more*	**plúrimus** *most*
ínferus *lower*	**inférior** *lower*	**ínfimus** or **ímus** *lowest*
súperus *upper*	**supérior** *upper*	**suprēmus** or **súmmus** *highest*

Maior and **peior** are pronounced **maiior** and **peiior** (see p. xv).

Notes

1 **Multus** in the singular is often best translated *a lot of*. The plural of **multus** means *many*: **multī mīlitēs** *many soldiers*. Its comparative, **plūs**, only exists in the following forms:

	SINGULAR	PLURAL	
		M. & F.	N.
N. & V.	plūs	plūrēs	plūra
Acc.	plūs	plūrēs	plūra
Gen.	plūris	plúrium	plúrium
Dat.	lacking	plúribus	plúribus
Abl.	plúre	plúribus	plúribus

The plural forms function as normal adjectives: **cum plūribus mīlitibus** *with more soldiers*. They can also be used as nouns: **ē plūribus ūnum** *one [created] from many* (lit. *more*). In the singular,

plūs is only used as a neuter noun, and expressions such as *more money* become **plūs pecūniae** lit. *more of money*. **Plūris** can be used in genitive of value expressions (see 7.1/5): **hic servus plūris est quam tū** *this slave is of a greater value than you* (for **quam** see 19.1/4). **plūs** can also be used as an adverb (see next subsection).

2 **Inferus** and **superus** are used in contexts where a comparison or contrast is at least implied: **Inferī** *the inhabitants of the lower world*, i.e. *the dead and the gods of Hades*; **Superī** *the gods who live in the sky* (cf. *lower storey, upper storey*). Often these forms are interchangeable with the comparative forms **inferior** and **superior**, but the latter are much more frequently used.

3 Adjectives ending in **-eus, -ius** and (sometimes) **-uus**, which would produce awkward vowel combinations with the comparative and superlative endings, are not compared as above. Instead, they are qualified by the adverbs **magis** *more*, and **maximē** *most*: **idōneus** *suitable*, **magis idōneus** *more suitable*, **maximē idōneus** *most suitable*. This method of comparison is sometimes used with other adjectives.

4 Some adjectives denoting spatial relationships only exist in the comparative and superlative, but with a preposition corresponding to each pair. An example is **intrā** *within*, **interior** *interior, inner*, **intimus** *innermost, inmost*: **intima Lētī Tartara** *Death's inmost region*, i.e. *the deepest part of Hades* (15.3 *ll*.18–19).

5 **Prior** *earlier, former* has no positive or superlative.

6 An alternative to **-imus** in superlatives is **-umus**: **maxumus** (= **maximus**).

19.1/2 Comparison of adverbs

The positive degree of an adverb is formed from the positive degree of the corresponding adjective: **tardus, tardē**; **fortis, fortiter** (17.1/3). The comparative adverb is the same as the neuter nominative singular of the corresponding comparative adjective, and for the superlative adverb we add **-ē** to the stem of the superlative adjective.

ADJECTIVE ADVERB

	POSITIVE	COMPARATIVE	SUPERLATIVE
tárdus slow	**tárdē** slowly	**tárdius** more slowly	**tardíssimē** most slowly
fórtis brave	**fórtiter** bravely	**fórtius** more bravely	**fortíssimē** most bravely
fácilis easy	**fácile** easily	**facílius** more easily	**facíllimē** most easily
bónus good	**béne** well	**mélius** better	**óptimē** best
párvus small	**paúlum** little	**mínus** less	**mínimē** least
múltus much	**múltum** much	**plūs** more	**plúrimum** most
mágnus great	**magnópere** greatly	**mágis** more	**máximē** most

The last three are the commonest of the few irregular adverbs. The difference between **plūs/plūrimum** and **magis/maximē** was originally that between frequency or quantity and degree: **plūs quam semel** *more than once*; **magis ambitiō quam avāritia animōs hominum exercēbat** *ambition used to occupy men's minds more (to a higher degree) than greed*. This distinction is obvious in most of the regular uses of these words (e.g. **magis/maximē** are the pair used in comparing adjectives in **-eus**, etc.), but even in Classical Latin it had started to become blurred. Out of the confusion of Late Latin come the French **plus beau** and Italian **più bello** *more beautiful*.

Notes

1 **Diū** *for a long time*, **diūtius**, **diūtissimē** have no corresponding adjectives. **Potius** *rather*, **potissimum** *especially* have no positive degree.
2 Adjectives which are compared with **magis/maximē** have adverbs formed in the same way: **magis idōneē** *more suitably*, etc.

19.1/3 Meaning of the comparative and superlative

Latin comparatives and superlatives are not always to be understood as meaning *more x* and *most x*. A comparative adjective or adverb is often used where no comparison is expressed, and indicates a higher degree than the positive. English here uses *rather* or *too*:

> **Quī plūra loquitur, is ineptus esse dīcitur.** *He who speaks too much* (lit. *more things*) *is said to be stupid.*
> **Senectūs est nātūrā loquācior.** *Old age is by nature rather talkative.*
> **Soror, quam dīxī, ad flammās accessit imprūdentius.** *The sister, whom I mentioned, rather incautiously went up to the fire.*

Likewise, the superlative is often used to express a very high degree: **grātissimae mihi tuae litterae fuērunt** *your letter* (8.1/4) *was extremely pleasing to me.*

19.1/4 Constructions involving the comparative

(*a*) In comparisons in English we must follow a comparative adjective or adverb by *than*: *he is taller than his sister.* **Quam** in Latin is used in the same way:

> **Dīvitiae ā stultīs magis quam ā sapientibus expetuntur**. *Riches are sought by fools more than by wise men.*
> **Cicerō disertior quam Brūtus fuit.** *Cicero was more eloquent than Brutus.*

Quam here is a conjunction, and what follows it must be in the same case as what precedes. Whereas in English we can say *this man is taller than me*, in Latin we must have **hic altior est quam ego**; as **hic**, the first member of the comparison, is nominative, the second member, **ego**, must be the same. There is, however, another construction which can be used if the first member is nominative or accusative. The second member is put into the ablative and **quam** is not required. This is the *ablative of comparison.*

> **Quid est in homine ratiōne dīvīnius?** *What is there in a human being more divine than reason?*
> **Nēminem Lycurgō maiōrem Lacedaemōn genuit.** *Sparta (Lacedaemon) gave birth to no one greater than Lycurgus.*

(*b*) A comparative can be accompanied by an ***ablative of measure of difference***: **est Hibernia dīmidiō minor quam Britannia** *Ireland is half as big as* (lit. *smaller by half than*) *Britain.* Here **dīmidiō** tells us by how much Ireland is smaller. **Multō** *by much* is often used in the same way: **multō breviōre itinere illī ad Hiberum pervenīre poterant** *they were able to get to the [River] Ebro by a much shorter route* (lit. *route shorter by much*).

(*c*) For the construction used when a comparative occurs in a purpose clause see 13.1/5 note 2.

(*d*) In sentences of the type *he is too stupid to understand Plato*, Latin uses a comparative adjective followed by **quam** and a result clause (16.1/1): **stolidior est quam ut Platōnem intellegat** (lit. *he is more stupid than that he may understand Plato*).

19.1/5 Constructions involving the superlative

(*a*) In expressions of the type *as quickly as possible*, Latin uses the superlative, viz **quam celerrimē potest** (note that here we should think of **quam** as meaning *as* – see 30.1/1 note 4). **Potest** (or **poterat**, etc.) is often omitted. As in English, this idiom is also used with adjectives.

> **Relinquēbātur ut quam plūrimōs collēs occupāret Caesarisque cōpiās, quam maximē posset, distinēret.** *What remained was* (lit. *it was left*) *that he should seize as many hills as possible and keep Caesar's forces apart as much as possible.*

(*b*) When a noun is qualified by a superlative adjective and an adjectival clause, as in *Themistocles sent to Xerxes the most trustworthy slave he had*, Latin puts the adjective in the adjectival clause: **Themistoclēs servum, quem habuit fidēlissum, ad Xerxem mīsit.**

(*c*) The superlative is used with **quisque** *each* to express a class: **Epicūreōs doctissimus quisque contemnit** *all the most learned men despise Epicureans.*

19.2 Latin reading

1 Vilius argentum est auro, virtutibus aurum.
2 Sueborum gens est longe maxima et bellicosissima Germanorum omnium.
3 Video meliora proboque, deteriora sequor.
4 Plura faciunt homines e consuetudine quam e ratione.
5 Philosophia, non illa de natura, quae erat antiquior, sed haec in qua de hominum vita et moribus disputatur, a Socrate inventa esse dicitur.
6 Quid magis est saxo durum, quid mollius unda?
7 Discipulus est prioris posterior dies.
8 Aspiciunt oculis Superi mortalia iustis.
9 A bove maiore discit arare minor.
10 Frumentum omne combusserunt ut, reditionis spe sublata, paratiores ad omnia pericula subeunda essent.
11 Bona opinio hominum tutior est pecunia.
12 Haedui Caesarem certiorem fecerunt sese depopulatis agris non

facile ab oppidis vim hostium prohibere.

13 Germanorum civitatibus maxima laus erat quam latissime vastatis finibus circum se solitudines habere.

14 Impedimenta in Italia reliquerunt et expediti naves conscenderunt quo maior numerus posset imponi.

15 Optimum quidque rarissimum est.

16 Verres misit ad Antiochum regem rogatum vasa quae pulcherrima viderat.

17 Sol multis partibus maior atque amplior est quam terra universa.

18 Caesar litteris Labieni certior fiebat omnes Belgas contra populum Romanum coniurare.

19 Isocrates maiore ingenio est quam ut cum Lysia comparetur.

20 Corruptio optimi pessima.

Horace's claim to immortality

21 Exegi monumentum aere perennius
    regalique situ Pyramidum altius,
    quod non imber edax, non Aquilo impotens
    possit diruere aut innumerabilis
    annorum series et fuga temporum.

Notes

5 **disputātur** lit. *it is discussed* (impersonal construction 20.1/3), i.e. *there is discussion*; **Sōcrate** abl. of **Sōcratēs** (25.1/4e).

6 **undā** ablative.

7 With **priōris** supply **diēī**.

9 With **minor** supply **bōs**.

10 **sublātā** <**tollō** here *remove*; **subeunda** gerundive of **subeō** (see Appendix 4).

11 **pecūniā** ablative.

12 **Caesarem certiōrem fēcērunt** . . . lit. *made Caesar more certain that* . . ., i.e. *informed Caesar that* . . .; **certiōrem aliquem faciō** + acc. and inf. *I inform someone that* . . . is a common idiom (cf. sentence 18); **sēsē = sē**.

13 **cīvitātibus** *among the states* dat. of reference (28.1/1f); **quam lātissimē** (19.1/5a).

14 **quō** introduces a purpose clause containing a comparative (13.1/5 note 2).

17 **multīs partibus** i.e. *many times.*
19 See 19.1/4*d*. **Isocratēs** nom. s.; **ingeniō** abl. of quality (6.1/3); **Lӯsiā**
    abl. of **Lӯsiās** (25.1/4*e*).
20 Supply **est**.
21 *l.*1 **Exēgī** <**exigō** *complete*; **aere** <**aes, aeris** (n) *bronze*. *l.*2 **sitū**
    <**situs** *structure*. *l.*3 **nōn . . . nōn** performs the same function as **nec**
    . . . nec but is more emphatic; **Aquilō impotens** *the raging North*
    Wind. *l.*4 **possit** potential subjunctive (22.1/1*b*) *could (if it tried)*.
    *l.*5 **temporum** plural for singular.

19.3 Extra reading

Ovid's childhood

Sulmo mihi patria est, gelidis uberrimus undis,
    milia qui novies distat ab urbe decem.
editus hic ego sum, nec non ut tempora noris,
    cum cecidit fato consul uterque pari.
nec stirps prima fui: genito sum fratre creatus,   5
    qui tribus ante quater mensibus ortus erat.
Lucifer amborum natalibus adfuit idem:
    una celebrata est per duo liba dies.
protinus excolimur teneri curaque parentis
    imus ad insignes urbis ab arte viros.   10
frater ad eloquium viridi tendebat ab aevo,
    fortia verbosi natus ad arma fori.
at mihi iam puero caelestia sacra placebant,
    inque suum furtim Musa trahebat opus.
saepe pater dixit 'studium quid inutile temptas?   15
    Maeonides nullas ipse reliquit opes.'
motus eram dictis, totoque Helicone relicto
    scribere temptabam verba soluta modis.
sponte sua carmen numeros veniebat ad aptos,
    et quod temptabam dicere versus erat.   20

Notes

*l.*1 **gelidīs undīs** *in cool waters.* *l.*2 **noviēs . . . decem** i.e. 90; poets often
had difficulty in fitting numbers into verse (cf. *l.*6); **urbe** i.e. Rome (cf.

l.10). *l*.3 **nec nōn** *and indeed* the negatives cancel each other, as always in Latin; **nōris** contracted for **nōveris** (25.1/5*b*) (*so that*) *you may know*. *l*.4 this establishes the year as 43 BC; **cecidit** <**cadō** (not **caedō**). *l*.6 **ortus erat** <**orior** (here a synonym for **nascor** *be born*). *ll*.7–8 the brothers had the same birthday. *l*.9 **prōtinus** *from the start*; **cūrā(que)** is abl.; the verbs in this line and next are in the present for vividness (vivid present) and should be translated by the simple past; **tenerī** *tender, at a young age* agrees with the subject *we*. *l*.12 the forum was the centre of the Roman political and legal world. *l*.13 **caelestia sacra** *divine rites* a deliberately vague expression which is clarified in the next line; poetry was sometimes regarded as a sacred rite performed in honour of the Muse or Muses; **placeō** *be pleasing to, please* takes the dative, here **mihi** (20.1/1). *l*.14 with **trahēbat** supply **mē**. *l*.15 **quid** *why*. *l*.16 i.e. Homer (Maeonides) himself died poor; Homer was regarded as the greatest of the Greek and Roman poets. *l*.17 Helicon, the mountain in Greece where the Muses were supposed to live, here symbolises poetry. *l*.18 **verba solūta modīs** i.e. prose; **modīs** is ablative of separation (see 28.1/2*e*) *freed* (**solūta**) *from metre(s)*. *l*.19 **sponte suā** *of its own accord*; **numerōs . . . ad aptōs** *in suitable rhythms*.

UNIT 20

20.1 Grammar

20.1/1 Verbs governing cases other than the accusative

A transitive verb is defined as one that can be followed by the accusative case. As both the English verb *love* and the Latin **amō** are transitive, in the sentences *Cicero loves the girl* and **Cicerō puellam amat** both *girl* and **puellam** are direct objects and hence accusative. We might at first suppose that if a verb is transitive in English its Latin equivalent should be the same; but, although this is true for the greater number of verbs, there are some which are transitive in one language but intransitive in the other. The Latin **spectō** *look at* is transitive and we can say **tē spectō** *I am looking at you*; but we cannot say in English *I look you* because *look* is an intransitive verb and must be followed by a preposition, not a direct object (in *I am looking at you*, *you* is accusative after the preposition *at*). Similarly we have other verbs which are transitive in English but intransitive in Latin. Such Latin verbs are not followed by a preposition; the noun or pronoun they govern is put into a case other than the accusative. Most verbs of this sort take the dative, a few take the genitive or ablative. As will be seen below, virtually all the corresponding verbs in English are transitive. In no case is the meaning a guide to the Latin construction.

Among the most common verbs taking the dative are the following:

crēdō, -ere, crēdidī, crēditum *believe*
faveō, -ēre, fāvī, fautum *favour*
ignoscō, -ere, ignōvī, ignōtum *forgive*
imperō, -āre *order*
invideō, -ēre, invīdī, invīsum *envy*

irascor, -ī, irātus sum *be angry with*
minor, -ārī *threaten*
noceō, -ēre *harm*
nūbō, -ere, nupsī, nuptum *marry* (only with a woman as subject)

pāreō, -ēre *obey*

persuādeō, -ēre, persuāsī, persuāsum
persuade

placeō, -ēre *please*

resistō, -ere, restitī (no supine) *resist*

serviō, -īre *serve, be of use to*

suādeō, -ēre, suāsī, suāsum *advise*

subveniō, -īre, subvēnī, subventum
come to help, help

Invideō, minor, suādeō take the accusative of the thing envied, threatened or advised; but the person who is envied, threatened or advised must be in the dative. The same applies to **crēdō** in the sense of *entrust*. For compounds of **sum** which take the dative see 15.1/2.

> **Subvēnistī hominī iam perditō.** *You have helped a man already destroyed.*
>
> **Metuī nē Libyae tibi regna nocērent.** *I was afraid lest the kingdoms of Libya might harm you.*
>
> **Ascaniōne pater Rōmānās invidet arcēs?** *Does his father begrudge Ascanius the citadels of Rome?* (lit. *envy A. the Roman citadels*)

The genitive is taken by verbs meaning *remember* and *forget*; these can also take the accusative:

> **meminī** *remember* (25.1/5a, ii)   **reminiscor, -ī** (n.o.p.) *remember*
>
> **obliviscor, -ī, oblītus sum** *forget*

The only important other verbs taking the genitive are certain impersonals (see next subsection) and the following, which can also take the ablative:

> **abundō, -āre** *be rich in*
>
> **egeō, -ēre, eguī** (no supine) *lack, be in need of*
>
> **indigeō, -ēre, indiguī** (no supine) *lack, be in need of*
>
> **potior, -ī, potītus sum** *make oneself master of, capture*

> **Nōn adeō maiestātis populī Rōmānī oblītus sum.** *I have not so forgotten the dignity of the Roman people.*
>
> **Spē praedae mīlitēs accensī oppidō** (or **oppidī**) **potiuntur.** *The soldiers, fired by hope of booty, capture the town.*

A few verbs can only be followed by the ablative (except **vescor,** which can also be followed by the accusative):

> **careō, -ēre** *lack, be free of*   **ūtor, -ī, ūsus sum** *use*
>
> **fruor, -ī, fructus sum** *enjoy*   **vescor, -ī** (n.o.p.) *feed on*
>
> **fungor, -ī, functus sum** *perform, discharge*

Carmina morte carent. *Poetry does not die* (lit. *poems are free from death*).

Quattuor tribūnī creātī sunt, omnēs iam functī eō honōre. *Four tribunes were appointed, all having already discharged that office.*

20.1/2 Impersonal verbs

An impersonal verb is one that has no real subject. Prime examples are weather expressions such as **pluit** *it is raining* and **ningit** *it is snowing* where there is no subject either expressed or understood in Latin, and in English *it* is simply a subject of grammatical convenience as it does not refer to anyone or anything. We have other types in English such as *it is necessary, it suits* (*does it suit you to do this?*), the old-fashioned *it behoves*, etc. The corresponding Latin impersonals can be classified according to the construction they take. In many cases this is easily remembered from the construction of the English equivalent given below. Most impersonal verbs have forms only for the third singular active of each tense, for the infinitives and, sometimes, a gerund.

(*a*) *Impersonals followed by an accusative and an infinitive*

decet *it becomes, befits*	**iuvat** *it pleases*
dēdecet *it does not become, befit*	**oportet** *it behoves*

Iuvat is part of **iuvō, -āre** *help*, but is used impersonally in this special sense. The other three belong to the second conjugation (infinitives **decēre, dēdecēre, oportēre**; perfect **decuit, dēdecuit, oportuit**; no supines):

Heia, mea Iūnō, non decet esse tē tam tristem tuō Iovī. *Hey, my Juno, you should not be* (lit. *it does not become you to be*) *so unfriendly to your Jupiter.*

Decet and **dēdecet** can be used in the third person singular or plural with a subject but no infinitive:

Neque tē ministrum dēdecet myrtus. *Nor is myrtle unbecoming for you as a servant.*

Togae tenuēs eum decent. *Fine togas suit him.*

Oportet is often to be translated by *ought* or *must*:

Oportet mē hoc facere. *I ought to do this,* or *I must do this.*
Oportuit mē hoc facere. *I ought to have done this.*

In the second example the fact that the obligation existed in the past is indicated in Latin by the perfect tense of **oportuit**, whereas in English we use the perfect infinitive *to have done.*

(*b*) *Impersonals with the accusative of person and genitive of cause*

mē **miseret** *I pity*   mē **pudet** *I am ashamed*
mē **paenitet** *I regret*   mē **taedet** *I am tired of*
mē **piget** *I am displeased*

The first singular pronoun has been added to bring out the meaning as we do not have corresponding impersonal expressions in English (*it pities me* is not intelligible). All five belong to the second conjugation.

Mea māter, tuī mē miseret, meī piget. *I am sorry for you, mother,*
   I am displeased with myself (**mē** is understood with **piget**).
Eōrum nec virtūtis nec fortūnae populum Rōmānum paenituit.
   The Roman people has regretted neither the bravery nor the
   success of those men.

These verbs may also, if appropriate, be followed by an infinitive: **pudet mē hoc fēcisse** *I am ashamed to have done this*; we could also have, in the same sense, **pudet mē huius factī** (lit. *I am ashamed of this deed*).

(*c*) *Impersonals followed by a dative and infinitive*

Libet *it is pleasing* and **licet** *it is allowed*, which both belong to the second conjugation (**licet** is also used as a subordinating conjunction; see 29.1/4*b*): **magistrātūs eī petere licēbit** *he will be allowed to seek public offices.* Several normal verbs are used impersonally in this way, as **expedit (expediō, -īre)** *it is expedient*; **convenit (conveniō, -īre)** *it befits, it is agreed.* Except for **libet**, these verbs may in appropriate contexts be followed by the accusative and infinitive. They may all have a neuter singular pronoun as subject instead of being followed by an infinitive.

Convenit Euandrī victōs discēdere ad urbem. *It is agreed that the*
   conquered leave for the city of Evander.
Nīl vident nisi quod libet. *They see nothing except what is pleasing*
   (i.e. to them).

(*d*) **Rēfert** *and* **interest**

Rēfert *it concerns, it matters* (perfect **rētulit**) does not come from **referō** *bring back*, but was regarded as a compound (a strange one) of the ablative singular of **rēs** and the third person singular of **ferō**. It is not used with the first person and second person pronouns but with the feminine singular ablative of the possessive adjectives (**meā, tuā**, etc.) which were regarded as agreeing with **rē**. **Meā rēfert** means literally *it bears on my business*. **Rēfert** is normally followed by an accusative and infinitive, but it can also have a neuter singular pronoun as subject.

> **Tuā et meā maximē rēfert tē valēre.** *It concerns you and me very much that you are well.*
> **Quid id nostrā rēfert?** *How does this concern us?*

Interest (from **intersum**) is used as an impersonal with the same sense and construction as **rēfert**. The use of **meā, tuā**, etc. here is quite illogical. **Interest** is also followed by the genitive in the case of nouns and third person pronouns (this is possible with **rēfert** but rarely occurs).

> **Quid Milōnis intererat interficī Clōdium?** *What concern was it of Milo's that Clodius be killed?*
> **Meā nihil interest scīre sed illīus multum.** *It matters nothing to me to know but [it matters] to that man very much.*

(*e*) *Weather impersonals*

In this category are **pluit** *it is raining*, **tonat** *it is thundering* and similar words.

(*f*) *Impersonal expressions with* **est**

As in English, we can have impersonal expressions involving an adjective such as **difficile est** *it is difficult* and **facile est** *it is easy*. The neuter singular of the adjective must always be used, except in **necesse est** *it is necessary* where **necesse** is an adverb and is not used elsewhere (the normal adjective is **necessārius, -a, -um**). The noun **opus, operis** (n) *work* is used in **opus est** *there is need*, which is followed by the dative of the person in need and the ablative of what is needed.

> **Difficile est saturam nōn scrībere.** *It is difficult not to write satire.*
> **Mihi necesse est īre hinc.** *It is necessary for me to go from here.*

162 LATIN

Graecīs iīs librīs mihi opus est. *I need those Greek books* (lit. *there is work for me with those Greek books*).

(g) **Vidētur** *as an impersonal*

Vidētur can have the expected meaning of *it seems*. It can also have the sense of *it seems good to, seems proper to, is the decision of*; it is often to be translated as *X decides*: **visum est mihi dē senectūte aliquid conscrībere** *I have decided* (lit. *it has seemed good to me*) *to write something on old age*.

20.1/3 Passive of intransitive verbs

From a logical point of view we might think that the passive of an intransitive verb was impossible since, for a clause to be turned from active to passive, its verb must have a direct object and therefore be transitive. When we turn *Scipio defeated Hannibal at Zama* into a passive construction, we get *Hannibal was defeated by Scipio at Zama*; but how can we make the verb passive in *Scipio returned to Rome*? Obviously this is not possible in English, but in Latin intransitive verbs can be used in the third singular passive in an impersonal construction: **Rōmam ā Scīpiōne reditum est**, lit. *it was returned to Rome by Scipio*. Similarly, **ītur in antīquam silvam** literally means *it is gone into an ancient wood* but we must tell from the context (*Aeneid VI*, 179) who did the going and translate accordingly: *they go into an ancient wood*. Sometimes a different translation is possible: **ad arma mīlitēs cucurrērunt ācriterque ibi pugnātum est.** *The soldiers ran to their arms and there was a fierce battle in that place* (lit. *it was fought fiercely there*).

This is the only passive construction possible with verbs taking the dative, which, because they cannot be followed by an accusative, are naturally intransitive. This possibility occasionally arises with verbs taking the genitive and ablative (for deponents this is limited to the impersonal use of the gerundive, 18.1/2*b*):

Decimae legiōnī ā Caesare indulgēbātur. *Caesar used to indulge the tenth legion* (lit. *it used to be indulged by Caesar to the tenth legion*).
Ā bonīs cīvibus pārētur lēgibus. *Good citizens obey the laws* (lit. *it is obeyed to the laws by good citizens*).
Omnibus argūmentīs ūtendum est. *Use must be made of all arguments*, i.e. *all arguments must be used*.

20.2 Latin reading

1 Adulescentem verecundum esse decet.
2 Quid tua id refert?
3 Avidum esse oportet neminem, minime senem.
4 Excelsis multo facilius casus nocet.
5 Mulier quae multis nubit, multis non placet.
6 Est proprium stultorum aliorum vitia cernere, oblivisci suorum.
7 Monere, non punire, stultitiam decet.
8 Necesse est minima maximorum esse initia.
9 Virtuti melius quam fortunae creditur.
10 Illis artificio opus est ut turpia facta oratione tegant.
11 Nullum caruit exemplo nefas.
12 Diu cum esset pugnatum, impedimentis castrisque nostri potiti sunt.
13 Cui peccare licet, peccat minus.
14 Nostra nihil interest iterum aut alio modo haec narrare.
15 Bonis nocet quisquis parcit malis.
16 Audiit Omnipotens oculosque ad moenia torsit
   regia et oblitos famae melioris amantes.
17 Bella suscipienda sunt ob eam causam, ut sine iniuria in pace
   vivatur.
18 Famae laboranti non facile succurritur.
19 Suo cuique iudicio utendum est.
20 Mortuo leoni et lepores insultant.
21 Sic itur ad astra, dis genite et geniture deos.

Egnatius and his teeth
22 Egnatius, quod candidos habet dentes,
   renidet usquequaque. si ad rei ventum est
   subsellium, cum orator excitat fletum,
   renidet ille: si ad pii rogum fili
   lugetur, orba cum flet unicum mater,
   renidet ille. quidquid est, ubicumque est,   5
   quodcumque agit, renidet: hunc habet morbum,
   neque elegantem, ut arbitror, neque urbanum.
23 Varias audit voces fruiturque deorum colloquio.
24 Cassandrae quia non creditum, ruit Ilium.
25 Decet imperatorem stantem mori.
26 Nihil est sanitati multo vino nocentius.

Notes

4 **cāsus** *a fall*.
6 **proprium** could be omitted without changing the sense.
10 **illīs** dat. with **opus est**.
14 **modō** abl. sing. of **modus** *way, manner*.
16 **audiit** 4.1/6 note 2; **Omnipotens** *the Almighty*, i.e. Jupiter.
19 **Suō . . . iūdiciō** ablative.
20 **et** *even*.
21 **genite** and **genitūre** are vocatives; these words (*Aeneid IX*, 641–2) are spoken to Iulus (son of Aeneas) whose grandmother was the goddess Venus; he was also the supposed ancestor of Julius Caesar and the emperor Augustus, both of whom were deified; **dīs** ablative of origin (28.1/2*f*).
22 *ll*.2f. the prose word order would be **sī ad subsellium reī ventum est**; **reī** <**reus** *defendant*. *l*.5 **lūgētur** as the agent is not specified we must translate *there is lamentation* (lit. *it is lamented*). *l*.8 **ut** + indicative *as*.
24 Cassandra, daughter of Priam, king of Troy, was a prophetess whose predictions, though always true, were never believed; with **crēditum** supply **est**; **ruit** perfect tense.

20.3 Excursus

Latin expressions in English

Because Latin had a central place in Western culture and education from the Middle Ages up to the recent past, many Latin expressions gained such a currency in English that they are still in normal use. Only a few were set phrases in antiquity, and one or two have developed meanings that would have puzzled a Roman (e.g. **ad hoc**). The following list is by no means exhaustive. In many cases the current pronunciation is a parody of what would have come from Roman lips (e.g. **locum**), and some expressions have been clipped of a word or more (e.g. **status quo**). Others (**pāce, rē, viā, vice**) would be followed by a genitive in Latin and hence the literal translations *with the pardon of*, etc.

addenda (neut. pl. of the gerundive of **addō**) *things to be added.*
ad hoc *for this [purpose only], special.*
ad īnfīnītum *to infinity.*
ad nauseam *to [the point of] nausea, to a disgusting degree.*
ā fortiōrī[1] *from [what is] stronger, with stronger reason.*
agenda (neut. pl. of the gerundive of **agō**) *things to be done.*
ā posteriōrī *from [what is] later, argument from effect to cause.*
ā priōrī *from [what is] earlier, argument from cause to effect.*
argumentum ad hominem *argument [directed] to the [individual] person.*
compōs mentis *sound of mind.*
dē factō *from the act (but without legal recognition), not legally recognised.* Normally used with an implied contrast to **dē iūre** *from law, legal.*
errātum (perf. pple. of **errō**) *a mistake.*
ex cathedrā *from the seat (of office), with authority.*
ex officiō *by virtue of one's office.*
ex parte *from [one] side, biased.*
in tōtō *in all, totally.*
ipsō factō *by [virtue of] the fact itself.*
locum [tenēns] *person holding another's position as a temporary substitute.*
magnum opus *great work, crowning work of one's career.*
memoranda (neut. pl. of the gerundive of **memorō**) *things to be remembered.*
modus vīvendī *manner of living [together], compromise.*
mūtātīs mūtandīs (abl. absolute) *things to be changed having been changed, with the necessary changes.*
nōn sequitur *it does not follow, false conclusion.*
pāce *with the pardon (peace) of, with apologies to.*
per annum *by the year, annually.*
per capita *according to heads, individual, by the individual.*
per sē *in itself.*
persōna nōn grāta *an unacceptable person.*
post mortem *[medical examination] after death.*
primā faciē *on first appearance, superficially.*

---

[1]The ablative singular of comparatives occasionally has the ending **-ī** (also **posteriōrī** and **priōrī**).

quā *in the capacity of.*

quid prō quō *something for something, recompense.*

rē *in the matter* (**rēs**) *of, with reference to.*

sīc! *thus* [*written or spoken by the person quoted*]. Used when reporting an error, usually a false spelling.

sine quā nōn [*thing*] *without which* [*something is*] *not* [*able to be done*], *essential condition.* **Rēs** is to be understood as the antecedent of **quā**.

status quō *state in which* [*things are and have been*], *existing state of affairs.*

stet (3rd s. subjunctive act. of **stō**) *let it stand.* Written in the margin of copy for printing to cancel a correction.

suī generis *of own kind, unique.*

ultrā vīrēs *beyond the* [*legal*] *powers* [*of a person or body*].

viā (abl. s. of **via**) *by way of, through.*

vice *in place of, deputy.*

vice versā (abl. absolute) *interchange having been effected, conversely.*

UNIT 21

21.1 Grammar

21.1/1 Imperative mood, positive and negative commands

The imperative mood expresses a command:

Ī, puer, atque meō citus haec subscrībe libellō. *Go, slave, and quickly add these things to my little book.* (on **citus** see 17.1/3)

It can also express what is really a request:

Dā, pater, augurium. *Father, give [us] a sign.*

As in English, the normal Latin imperative exists only in the second person, though with a distinction between singular and plural. There is only one tense, called the present (but see below, note 3), although virtually all commands refer to the future. Its forms are:

	I	II	III	IV	Mixed
			ACTIVE		
s.	**ámā** *love!*	**mónē** *warn!*	**rége** *rule!*	**aúdī** *hear!*	**cápe** *take!*
pl.	**amā́te**	**monḗte**	**régite**	**audī́te**	**cápite**
			PASSIVE		
s.	**amā́re**	**monḗre**	**régere**	**audī́re**	**cápere**
	be loved!	*be warned!*	*be ruled!*	*be heard!*	*be taken!*
pl.	**amā́minī**	**monḗminī**	**regíminī**	**audī́minī**	**capíminī**

As English makes no distinction between second person singular and second person plural we translate both **amā** and **amāte** by *love!* etc. The passive is not much used except with deponents. In its plural the same form is used for the imperative as for the indicative; and its singular coincides with the present infinitive active and with the alternative second person singular present indicative passive (14.1/1 note 3).

While positive commands are simply put into the imperative, negative commands are expressed in one of three ways:

(a) **Nē** with the imperative, a construction only used in Classical Latin by poets: **equō nē crēdite, Teucrī!** *do not trust the horse, Trojans!*

(b) **Nē** with the perfect subjunctive (for the use of the subjunctive to express commands see 22.1/1c); **nē** is here an adverb and is translated by *not*: **nē amāverīs Iūliam** *do not love Julia.*

The adverbial use of **nē** in these two constructions is to be distinguished from its function as a subordinating conjunction introducing negative purpose clauses and certain types of noun clauses (21.1/2, 26.1/2).

(c) A periphrasis consisting of the imperative of **nōlō** *be unwilling*, s. **nōlī**, pl. **nōlīte** (15.1/5) and the present infinitive: **nōlī eam vexāre!** *don't disturb her!* (lit. *be unwilling to disturb her*). This is the more common prose construction. Negative commands are often unpleasant both to give and receive, and the use of **nōlī/nōlīte** and the infinitive was originally a form of politeness meant to sugar the pill.

Notes

1 Four verbs, through frequent use, lost the second singular imperative ending: **dīc** *say!* **fac** *do!* **dūc** *lead!* **fer** *carry!* (from **dīcō, faciō, dūcō, ferō**; the old schoolboy mnemonic was *Dick's fat duck's fur*). **Ferō** also has an irregular second plural imperative **ferte**. The imperative of **sum** is **es, este** *be!* and of **eō, ī, īte** *go!*

2 The imperative is used in the following greetings:
   salvē, salvēte *hail! hello!* (from a verb not otherwise used except in the infinitive **salvēre**)
   valē, valēte *farewell! goodbye!* (**valeō** *be in good health*)
   avē, avēte either *hello!* or *goodbye!* (from a verb not otherwise used except in the infinitive **avēre**).

3 There is another form of the imperative, not much used in Classical Latin except in legal documents and with certain verbs (as **mementō** 25.1/5a,ii; **scītō**, from **sciō**) and normally called, by way of distinction, the future imperative. Its forms in the active are:

	I	II	III	IV	Mixed	**sum**
			SINGULAR			
2	amā́tō	monḗtō	régitō	audī́tō	cápitō	éstō
3	amā́tō	monḗtō	régitō	audī́tō	cápitō	éstō
			PLURAL			
2	amātṓte	monētṓte	regitṓte	audītṓte	capitṓte	estṓte
3	amántō	monéntō	regúntō	audiúntō	capiúntō	súntō

The second person forms have the same meaning as the normal imperative. The third person forms in the singular mean *let him/her love,* etc., in the plural *let them love,* etc., but for these meanings Latin normally uses the subjunctive (22.1/1*c*). Passive forms exist but are extremely rare.

21.1/2 Indirect command and petition

This construction is one of the three divisions of indirect speech (17.1/1). Indirect commands come after verbs of ordering; indirect petitions, which Latin expresses in the same way, follow verbs meaning *encourage, exhort, induce, persuade, urge,* etc. Both represent either an imperative or a jussive (or optative) subjunctive (22.1/1*c, a*) in the original direct speech. In English we normally use an infinitive after verbs of both classes: *he ordered me to go to Rome*; *I persuaded them not to hijack the ship.* Some verbs, however, can also be followed by a subordinate clause introduced by *that*: *he ordered that I go to Rome*; *I persuaded them that they should not hijack the ship.* Latin, except for the verbs mentioned below in note 1, always uses a subordinate clause which is identical in every way with purpose clauses (13.1/5), i.e. **ut/nē** with the subjunctive. As with purpose clauses, if the main verb has a present or future reference (i.e. is in a primary tense, 16.1/2*a*), the verb of the indirect command is in the present subjunctive; but if the main verb has a past reference (i.e. is in a historic tense, 16.1/2*b*), the verb of the indirect command is in the imperfect subjunctive.

> **Fīnitimīs imperāvit ut ab iniūriā et maleficiō sē suōsque prohibērent.** *He ordered the neighbouring peoples* (**imperō** takes the dative, 20.1/1) *to restrain themselves and their men from injury and crime.*[1]

---

[1] On the use of the reflexive **sē** and **suus** in indirect speech, see 31.1/2.

Tōtī exercituī imperāvit nē iniussū suō concurrerent. *He ordered the whole army not to charge without his order.*

Tum cuidem ex equitibus Gallīs magnīs praemiīs persuādet ut ad Cicerōnem litterās dēferat. *Then, by large rewards, he persuades a certain man (**persuādeō** takes the dative, 20.1/1) from the Gallic cavalry to take a letter to Cicero.*

Labiēnus, mīlitēs cohortātus ut suae pristīnae virtūtis et tot secundissimōrum proeliōrum memoriam retinērent, dedit signum pugnae. *Labienus, having encouraged the soldiers to preserve the memory of their former courage and of so many very successful encounters, gave the battle signal.*

Notes

1 **iubeō, -ēre, iussī, iussum** *order* and **vetō, -āre, vetuī, vetītum** *forbid, order . . . not* are followed by an accusative and infinitive just as in English. **Vetō** is always used for **iubeō . . . nōn.**

Pompeius mīlitēs silentiō nāvēs conscendere iussit. *Pompey ordered the soldiers to board the ships in silence.*
Labiēnum fugientēs longius prōsequī vetuit. *He ordered Labienus not to pursue the fugitives further.*

2 Among other verbs that can take the normal indirect command and petition construction (although the meanings of some are not covered by this description) are:

caveō, -ēre, cāvī, cautum *take care*	**ōrō, -āre** *beg*
cūrō, -āre *see to it* [*that*]	**permittō, -ere, permīsī, permissum**
dēcernō, -ere, dēcrēvī, dēcrētum	(with dative of person) *allow*
decree	**rogō, -āre** *ask, request*
hortor, -ārī *urge*	

3 **Ut** is sometimes omitted: **Caesar huic imperāvit adīret cīvitātēs** *Caesar ordered this man to approach the states.*

4 A few verbs can be followed by either the indirect command and petition construction or an accusative and infinitive, depending on the sense.

Eīs persuāsum est Rōmānōs nōn sōlum itinerum causā sed etiam perpetuae possessiōnis culmina Alpium occupāre cōnārī. *They were convinced (it was persuaded to them) that the Romans were trying to occupy the peaks of the Alps for the sake not only of travel (journeys) but also of continual occupation.*

For **persuādeō** with the other construction see above.

21.1/3 *Medius* and similar adjectives

Medius *middle,* **summus** *highest,* **īmus** *lowest,* **prīmus** *first,* **ultimus** *last,* as well as expressing order in place or time (*the middle house, the first battle*) are also used to indicate a part of the noun they qualify:

> **prīmus digitus** *the first [part] of the finger, fingertip*
> **summus mons** *the top [part] of the mountain*
> **media via** *the middle [part] of the road*

In the latter use the adjective normally precedes the noun, in the former it follows: **medius digitus** the middle of the finger, **digitus medius** the middle finger. *The middle finger, the highest mountain* can also be expressed by **medius digitōrum** (lit. *the middle [one] of the fingers*), **summus montium.**

21.2 Latin reading

1 Vade ad formicam, o piger, et considera vias eius et disce sapientiam.
2 Crede ratem ventis, animam ne crede puellis.
3 Non est, crede mihi, sapientis dicere 'vivam'.
  sera nimis vita est crastina. vive hodie!
4 Exigis ut nostros donem tibi, Tucca, libellos.
  non faciam: nam vis vendere, non legere.
5 Lex universa est quae iubet nasci et mori.
6   'procul, o procul este, profani'
  conclamat vates 'totoque absistite luco:
  tuque invade viam vaginaque eripe ferrum:
  nunc animis opus, Aenea, nunc pectore firmo.'
7 I, sequere Italiam ventis, pete regna per undas.
8 Mediam mulierem complectitur.
9 Gaditanis, ut naves longas decem facerent, Varro imperavit:
  complures praeterea Hispali faciendas curavit.

10 Ambiorix in Nervios pervenit hortaturque ne sui in perpetuum liberandi atque ulciscendi Romanos occasionem dimittant.

11 Caesar se recepit suisque imperavit ne tela in hostes reicerent.

12 Saepius ventis agitatur ingens
pinus et celsae graviore casu
decidunt turres feriuntque summos
fulgura montes.

Catullus at the tomb of his brother

13 Multas per gentes et multa per aequora vectus
advenio has miseras, frater, ad inferias,
ut te postremo donarem munere mortis
et mutam nequiquam alloquerer cinerem.
quandoquidem fortuna mihi tete abstulit ipsum,
heu miser indigne frater adempte mihi,
nunc tamen interea haec, prisco quae more parentum
tradita sunt tristi munere ad inferias,
accipe fraterno multum manantia fletu,
atque in perpetuum, frater, ave atque vale.

14 Galbae permisit uti in his locis legionem hiemandi causa collocaret, si opus esse arbitraretur.

15 Neque tamen Indutiomarus ulli civitati Germanorum persuadere potuit ut Rhenum transiret.

16 Te, Fortuna, sequor. procul hinc iam foedera sunto:
credidimus satis his, utendum est iudice bello.

17 Ave, Caesar, morituri te salutant.

Notes

1 **viās** *ways* here used metaphorically.

4 Supply **eōs** with **vendere** and **legere**.

5 In this general statement we can supply either **nōs** or **vōs** as the subject of **nascī** and **morī**.

6 *l*.3 **vāgīnā** *from its scabbard* (abl. of separation 28.1/2*e*). *l*.4 with **opus** supply **tibi est**; **animīs** (plural for singular) <**animus** *courage*; **Aenēā** vocative of **Aenēās** (25.1/4*e*).

7 **regna** plural for singular.

9 **faciendās cūrāvit** 18.1/2*c*, i.

10 The verbs are in the vivid present and should be translated by the past tense in English; **suī** is the genitive of **sē** (not a part of **suus**)

and is to be taken with **līberandī** – it refers to the subject of **dīmittant**.

12 **dēcidunt** <**dēcidō** (not **dēcīdō**).

13 *l*.2 **ad** *for* [*the purpose of*], also in *l*.8; the **inferiae** were offerings of wine, milk and honey poured on a grave. *l*.3 **mūnere mortis** *due gift of death*, i.e. *gift due to the dead*. *l*.4 **cinerem** the Romans practised cremation. *l*.5 **mihi** dative of disadvantage *from me*, also in *l*.6 (28.1/1*e*); **tētē** = **tē**. *l*.6 **indignē** adverb; **adempte** vocative. *l*.7 **haec** is the object of **accipe**. *l*.8 **tristī mūnere** ablative of manner *by way of sad gift* (28.1/2*j*). *l*.9 **mānantia** with **haec** (*l*.7) lit. *much dripping with fraternal weeping.*

14 **Galba** male cognomen; **utī** = **ut**; **arbitrārētur** is subjunctive because it is in a subordinate clause in reported speech (17.1/2 note 4).

16 **hinc iam** lit. *now henceforth*, i.e. *from now*; **suntō** 21.1/1 note 3.

17 The words addressed to the emperor by gladiators before fighting; **moritūrī** (from **morior** 11.1/2 note 4).

21.3 Excursus

Latin abbreviations in English

What has been said about the persistence of Latin expressions in English applies **ā fortiōrī** to those phrases which were so familiar in the past that they now exist only in an abbreviated form. The following list contains the most common:

A.D. **Annō Dominī** *in the year of* [*our*] *Lord.*

a.m. **ante merīdiem** *before midday.*

c. **circā** *about.* Used of uncertain dates.

cf. **confer** (imperative of **conferō**) *compare.*

D.V. **Deō volente** (abl. absolute) *God being willing*, i.e. if nothing unforeseen (bad weather, etc.) occurs.

e.g. **exemplī grātiā** *for the sake of an example.*

et al. **et aliī** *and others.*

etc. **et cētera** *and the other things, and the rest.*

fl. **flōruit** (from **flōreō**) *he/she flourished.* Used to indicate the high point of a person's life or career, usually when the dates of birth and death are unknown.

ibid. **ibidem** *in the same book* (lit. *in the same place*).

i.e. **id est** *that is.*

loc. cit. **locō citātō** *in the passage* [*already*] *cited.*

n.b. **notā bene** *note well.*

nem. con. **nēmine contrādīcente** (abl. absolute) *with no one speaking in opposition.*

op. cit. **opere citātō** *in the book* [*already*] *cited.*

per cent **per centum** *by the hundred, in* [*every*] *hundred.*

p.m. **post merīdiem** *after midday.*

pros and cons (from **prō** and **contrā**) [*arguments*] *for and against.*

pro tem. **prō tempore** *for the* [*present*] *time, temporary.*

p.s. **postscriptum** [*something*] *written afterwards.*

q.v. **quod vidē** (imperative of **videō**) *which see.*

R.I.P. **requiescat in pāce** *may he/she rest in peace.*

sc. *or* scil. **scīlicet** (= **scīre licet**) *that is to say, namely.*

s.v. **sub vōce** *under the word.* Used in connection with alphabetically arranged reference works.

v. **vidē** (imperative of **videō**) *see, look up.*

v. inf. **vidē infrā** *see below.*

viz (*not* **viz.** as **z** here is not a letter but a sign of contraction) **vidēlicet** (= **vidēre licet**) *that is to say, namely.*

vs. **versus** *against.*

v. sup. **vidē suprā** *see above.*

UNIT 22

22.1 Grammar

22.1/1 Uses of the subjunctive in main clauses

When used in a main clause the subjunctive can express what is willed, wished or considered possible. Within this range we include:

(a) wishes (*optative subjunctive*: *may this happen!*);
(b) simple possibility (*potential subjunctive*: *we would be happier* [*if you were here*);
(c) certain types of command or exhortation (*jussive subjunctive*: *let there be light!*);
(d) deliberative expressions (*deliberative subjunctive*: *what am I to do?*);
(e) suppositions and concessions (*concessive subjunctive*: *suppose this were to happen*).

In actual speech some of these uses (e.g. wishes and commands) would have been differentiated by tone of voice, but in writing the context will always tell us which use is involved. In nearly every case the meaning of these subjunctives is indicated in English by an auxiliary verb or some expanded expression (*may this happen!* or *I wish this would happen*). The negative is **nē** (adv. *not*, cf. 21.1/1*b*) or **nōn** (**nē** is used in the constructions expressing a desire or command, i.e. optative, jussive, concessive; **nōn** is used in those expressing possibility or uncertainty, i.e. potential, deliberative).

(a) *Optative subjunctive* (negated by **nē**)

The name of this use comes from the verb **optō, -āre** *desire*. It can be used by itself (**sīs fēlix** *may you be fortunate!*), or it may be reinforced by **utinam**, an adverb which has no equivalent in English except the normally unacceptable *hopefully*; **utinam** appears more commonly with the imperfect and pluperfect and need not be translated by any particular word. The use of tenses, which is the same as in conditional sentences taking the subjunctive (22.1/2), can cause confusion.

(i)   The present subjunctive expresses a wish for the future:

Dī ōmen āvertant! *May the gods avert the omen!*
Absit ōmen! *May the omen be invalid!* (lit. *be absent*)
Dī tē ērādīcent quī mē hinc extrūdis! *May the gods destroy you who are pushing me from here!*
Nē istud Iuppiter optimus maximus sinat! *May Jupiter best [and] greatest not allow that!*

The translation of any of the above can be put in the form: *I wish (hope) that the gods would (will) avert the omen.* This is, in fact, the normal way we express a wish in modern English.

(ii) The imperfect subjunctive expresses a wish for the present. As the distinction between wishes for the future and for the present is not always made clear by the form of the verb in English, we sometimes use the adverb *now* with the latter to make the time reference unambiguous. This is not necessary in Latin.

A. Homō hic ēbrius est, ut opīnor. B. utinam ita essem! *A. This man is drunk, (as) I think. B. I wish I were* (lit. *would that I were so!*).
Utinam haec dīcerent! *I wish they were saying this* [*now*]*!*

(iii) The pluperfect subjunctive expresses a wish for the past:

Utinam istam calliditātem hominibus dī nē dedissent! *I wish the gods had not given, that craftiness to men* (lit. *would that the gods had not given, etc.*).
Utinam rēs pūblica stetisset nec in hominēs ēvertendārum rērum cupidōs incidisset! *I wish the state had stood and had not fallen to men who wanted to create turmoil* (lit. *men desirous of things being overturned*).

In the nature of things only wishes for the future can be fulfilled. Wishes for the present and past are futile protests against what is happening or has happened.

Notes

1   The perfect subjunctive is rare in wishes. It expresses a wish that something may turn out to have happened: **utinam haec mūta facta sit!** *I hope this woman has been struck* (lit. *made*) *dumb.*
2   For **utinam** we sometimes in verse have **ō sī**, which may be translated *if only*: **ō mihi praeteritōs referat sī Iuppiter annōs!** *if only Jupiter would bring back my past years!*

(*b*)   *Potential subjunctive* (negated by **nōn**)

This subjunctive expresses an action or state which has or had the potentiality of happening. In English we most commonly use the auxiliary *would*, though others (as *could* and *should*) are possible: *you would have thought him crazy; would he dare to say that?* It is most commonly found in conditional sentences of the type *if I were you I would not do that* (this use is treated separately in 22.1/2).

When this subjunctive is used without an accompanying conditional clause (i.e. one beginning with **sī** *if* or **nisi** *unless*), the time reference of the tenses is somewhat different from that of the optative subjunctive.

(i)   As in English no distinction is made between present and future time. Both are expressed by the present (or perfect) subjunctive.

   Quis hoc dīcere audeat? *Who would dare to say this?* (the time reference is to the future).
   Migrantīs cernās tōtāque ex urbe ruentīs. *You could see them leaving and rushing from the whole city* (the time reference is to the present).
   Quod tibi suādeō, suādeam meō patrī. *What I am recommending to you, I would recommend to my father* (the time reference is either present or future).
   Ego cum Platōne nōn invītus errāverim. *I would not unwillingly err with Plato* (perfect subjunctive used in the same sense as present subjunctive; the time reference is either present or future).

(ii)   When the time reference is to the past the imperfect subjunctive is employed. This use is different from that of the optative subjunctive and also from that of the potential subjunctive when used with a conditional clause. It is not particularly common: **putārēs Sullam vēnisse in Italiam nōn bellī vindicem sed pācis**

auctōrem *you would have thought that Sulla had come to Italy not as a champion of war but as a maker of peace.*

Notes

1 Very common examples of the potential subjunctive are **velim** *I would like,* **nōlim** *I would not like,* **mālim** *I would prefer.*

2 When the second person singular is used, it normally has a general sense and may be translated by *one.* The example above in (*b*) (ii) could also be translated as *one would have thought. . .*

3 The pluperfect subjunctive is not found here. It is, however, very common in the other use of the potential subjunctive (i.e. with conditional clauses).

4 The potential subjunctive is also common in adjectival clauses (30.1/2).

(*c*) *Jussive subjunctive* (negated by **nē**)

The name of this use comes from the supine of **iubeō**. We can easily imagine that a jussive subjunctive would have been spoken with a tone different from that of an optative subjunctive. Because we have the imperative mood for giving orders directly to other people, the jussive subjunctive of the second person in positive commands is something of a superfluity but does occur: **cautus sīs!** *be careful!* In negative commands the present subjunctive expresses a general prohibition: **actum nē agās** *one should not do* [*what is already*] *done* (cf.21.1/1*b*). For the other persons we have the following uses:

(i) The first person plural expresses self-exhortation or self-encouragement and is translated *let us . . .*

   Amēmus patriam, praesentēs frūctūs neglegāmus. *Let us love our country, let us ignore immediate profits.*
   Nē difficilia optēmus. *Let us not desire difficult things.*

   The first person singular in this sense (*let me . . .*) is possible but rare.

(ii) The third person singular and plural express commands and are to be translated by either *let him/her/it/them . . .* or *he/she/it/they should . . .*

   Dōnīs impiī nē plācāre audeant deōs. *Let not the wicked dare to appease the gods with gifts* (or *the wicked should not dare . . .*).

Caveat emptor. *Let the buyer beware.*
Cēdant arma togae. *Let arms yield to the toga.*

Note

We would not have expected a jussive subjunctive with a past sense, but the imperfect subjunctive is so used, with the meaning *should have*.

At tū dictīs, Albāne, manērēs. *But you, man of Alba, should have remained true to your word* (lit. *remained in your words*).
A. Cūr nōn eum occīdistī extemplō? B. gladius nōn erat. A. caperēs aut fustem aut lapidem. *A. Why didn't you kill him on the spot? B. There was no sword. A. You should have taken a stick or a rock.*

Three other constructions, which are in fact more common, may be used instead of this type of the jussive subjunctive. For the last clause we could have a gerundive to express necessity (18.1/2*b*) **aut fustis aut lapis tibi capiendus erat**; **dēbeō** + infinitive **aut fustem aut lapidem capere dēbuistī**; or **oportet** + acc. and infinitive (20.1/2*a*) **aut fustem aut lapidem capere tē oportuit**.

(*d*) *Deliberative subjunctive* (negated by **nōn**)

This subjunctive is used exclusively in questions and indicates the uncertainty of the speaker about the future and what must be done.

A. Per Venerem hanc iūrandum est tibi. B. quid iūrem? A. quod iubēbō. *A. You must swear by this [statue of] Venus. B. What am I to swear? A. What I shall order.*
Nōs nōn poētārum vōce moveāmur? *Are we not to be moved by the voice of poets?*
Quid faciam? maneam an abeam? *What am I to do? Am I to stay or (an* 23.1/1*f) go away?*

The imperfect subjunctive can be used in the same way: **haec cum vidērem, quid agerem, iūdicēs?** *when I saw these things, what was I to do, O judges?*

(*e*) *Concessive subjunctive* (negated by **nē**)

This use, which is really a development of the jussive, expresses concession, and is to be translated by adding *granted that, I concede that*: **sit fūr, sit sacrilegus, sit flāgitiōrum omnium vitiōrumque princeps: at est bonus imperātor** *I concede that he is a thief; that he is a temple robber, that he is a leader in all debaucheries and vices; but he is a good commander.*

22.1/2 Conditional sentences

Conditional sentences contain at least one main clause and one adverbial clause of condition; the latter is introduced by **sī** *if* or **nisi** *unless, if . . . not*. They fall into two clearly defined categories in both English and Latin:

(*a*) English has *would* or *should* (or occasionally *could*) as part of the main verb, and Latin uses the subjunctive mood for the verb of both the main and the conditional clause.

(*b*) English does not have *would* or *should* as part of the main verb, and Latin uses the indicative mood for the verb of both the main and the subordinate clause.

There is a clear difference between the two categories. The first is used in cases where something could have happened in the past, could be happening now, or could happen in the future. The second is used in cases which are also hypothetical; but here, by not using *would* or *should* with the main verb in English or two subjunctives in Latin, we express ourselves in a more positive and confident way. Examples are:

(*a*) **Sī Rōmam veniās, hīc maneam.** (Future reference) *If you were to come to Rome, I would stay here.*
Sī hīc essēs, nōn legerem. (Present reference) *If you were here, I would not be reading.*
Sī Rōmae fuissēs, saepe tē vīdissem (Past reference) *If you had been in Rome, I would have seen you often.*

(*b*) **Sī in forum mēcum vēneris, Cicerōnem audiēs.** (Future reference) *If you come to the forum with me, you will hear Cicero.*
Sī aegrōtās, doleō. (Present reference) *If you are sick, I am sorry.*
Sī id dixistī, errāvistī. (Past reference) *If you said that, you were wrong.*

The time reference of the tenses in (*a*) is the same as for the optative subjunctive, but different from that of the potential subjunctive used without a **sī/nisi** clause. It is essential to equate the use of *would/should* in the main clause in English with the subjunctive in both clauses in Latin, and the absence of *would/should* in English with the indicative in both clauses in Latin. The following table shows the same basic example in each construction and tense (all are not equally common):

	CATEGORY 1	CATEGORY 2
English	*would/should* in main clause	verb without *would/should* in main clause
Latin	subjunctive in both clauses	indicative in both clauses

FUTURE

Latin construction	present subjunctive in both clauses	future/future perfect indicative in **sī/nisi** clause (see 5.1/3) future indicative in main clause
	Sī id dīcās, errēs.	**Sī id dīcēs, errābis.**
	If you were to say that, you would be wrong.	*If you say that, you will be wrong.*

PRESENT

Latin construction	imperfect subjunctive in both clauses	present indicative in both clauses
	Sī id dīcerēs, errārēs.	**Sī id dīcis, errās.**
	If you were (now) saying that, you would be wrong.	*If you say that, you are wrong.*

PAST

Latin construction	pluperfect subjunctive in both clauses	imperfect or perfect indicative in **sī/nisi** clause imperfect or perfect indicative in main clause
	Sī id dixissēs, errāvissēs.	**Sī id dīcēbās, errābās.**
	If you had said that, you . would have been wrong	*If you used to say that, you were (used to be) wrong.*
		Sī id dixistī, errāvistī.
		If you said that, you were wrong.

Notes

1 In category 1, English does not distinguish between main clauses relating to the future and present (*you would be wrong* in both cases). Certain other overlaps are possible in English, but in Latin each verbal form has a precise reference.

2 It is possible, within limits, to combine different time references within one sentence:

Sī peccāvissēs, poenam merērēs. *If you had done wrong, you would deserve punishment.*

Sī peccābās, poenam merēs. *If you used to do wrong, you deserve punishment.*

3 It was often felt that, if the main clause of a category 1 sentence contained an infinitive with **possum/dēbeō/oportet** or a gerundive, no subjunctive was needed. **Possum/dēbeō/oportet** and the gerundive were considered sufficient in themselves to convey the idea of potentiality and so make the subjunctive superfluous (cf. 22.1/1*c* note).

Consul nōn esse potuī, nisi eum cursum vītae tenuissem ā pueritiā.
I would not have been able (lit. *was not able*) *to be consul if I had not followed* (lit. *held to*) *this course of life from childhood.*
Sī ūnum diem morātī essētis, moriendum omnibus fuit. *If you had delayed for one day, all must have died.*

4 In category 2 (past) a pluperfect indicative in the **sī/nisi** clause and an imperfect indicative in the main clause express something that happened often (cf. the similar use with **cum**, 16.1/3*d*): **sī peccāverās, poenās dabās** *if ever you had done wrong, you used to be punished.*.

22.2 Latin reading

1 Fiat iustitia, ruat caelum!
2 Vilicus primus surgat, postremus cubitum eat.
3 Si tacuisses, philosophus mansisses.
4 Pereas ultimus tuorum!
5 Cito rumpas arcum, semper si tensum habeas.
6 Fiat experimentum in vili corpore.
7 Si hanc viam asperam esse negem, mentiar.
8 Omnia vincit amor: et nos cedamus amori.
9 Pereant qui ante nos nostra dixerunt!
10 Utinam populus Romanus unam cervicem haberet!
11 Qui non vult fieri desidiosus, amet.
12 Si quod grande vas aut maius opus inventum erat, laeti auferebant.
13 Qui dedit beneficium, taceat: narret qui accepit.
14 Avaro quid mali optes, nisi 'vivat diu'?
15 Multa ante temptes quam virum invenias bonum.
16 Nubere Paula cupit nobis, ego ducere Paulam
   nolo: anus est. vellem, si magis esset anus.
17 Omnes quas habuit, Fabiane, Lycoris amicas
   extulit. uxori fiat amica meae!

18 Paulum deliquit amicus, quod nisi concedas, habeare insuavis.
19 Bibamus, moriendum est.
20 Ante victoriam ne canas triumphum.
21 Non id fecissem nisi necesse fuisset.
22 Frustra, cum ad senectutem ventum est, repetas adulescentiam.
23 Si Pompeius privatus esset hoc tempore, tamen ad tantum bellum is erat deligendus.
24 Memoriam ipsam cum voce perdidissemus, si tam in nostra potestate esset oblivisci quam tacere.
25 Expedit esse deos et, ut expedit, esse putemus:
       dentur in antiquos tura merumque focos.
26 Si vir bonus habeat hanc vim, ut digitorum percussione nomen suum in locupletum testamenta inserere possit, hac vi non utatur.
27 Nemo saltat sobrius, nisi forte insanit.
28 Dixit Deus 'fiat lux' et facta est lux.

Notes

4 **tuōrum** 4.1/4.
8 **et** *too* emphasising **nōs**.
12 **sī** + pluperfect *if ever, whenever*; **quod** indefinite adjective (10.1/1*i*); **opus** here has a concrete meaning; translate **laetī** as adverb (17.1/3).
14 **Avārō** dative; **quid malī** *what of evil*, i.e. *what evil* (27.1/4k).
15 **ante . . . quam** = **antequam**; subj. because it expresses something anticipated (29.1/3*b*).
16 **nūbō** + dat. *marry* with woman as subject, **dūcō** + acc. *marry* with man as subject; **nōbīs** plural for singular.
17 **Lycōris** (nominative) female name; **extulit** <**efferō** *carry out* (for cremation), translate *dispose of*.
18 **quod** is accusative after **concēdās** and should be translated here *and . . . it*; the passive of **habeō** means *be considered*.
19 **moriendum** impersonal gerundive (18.1/2*b*).
23 The main clause has its verb in the indicative because of the gerundive (22.1/2, note 3); the imperfect **erat** is used because we would otherwise have the imperfect subjunctive as the time reference is to the present.
24 **tam . . . quam** *as much . . . as* (see 30.1/1).

25 **in** + acc. lit. *on to* because the offerings were poured on to the altars; translate *on*.
26 **digitōrum percussiōne** i.e. *by snapping his fingers.*

22.3 Extra reading

Caesar's description of the Ancient Britons

Ex his omnibus longe sunt humanissimi qui Cantium incolunt, quae regio est maritima omnis, neque multum a Gallica differunt consuetudine. interiores plerique frumenta non serunt, sed lacte et carne vivunt pellibusque sunt vestiti. omnes vero se Britanni vitro inficiunt, quod caeruleum efficit colorem, atque hoc horribiliores sunt   5 in pugna aspectu: capilloque sunt promisso atque omni parte corporis rasa praeter caput et labrum superius. uxores habent deni duodenique inter se communes, et maxime fratres cum fratribus parentesque cum liberis: sed qui sunt ex iis nati eorum habentur liberi ad quos primum virgo quaeque deducta est.   10

Notes

*ll.*1f. **Ex hīs omnibus** i.e. inhabitants of Britain; **quae regiō** *which region*, **quae** is the relative adjective and consequently agrees with **regiō** although the antecedent is **Cantium** – this construction, which is a type of parenthesis, is the equivalent of **regiōnem quae est** . . . *a region which is* . . . where **regiōnem** would be in apposition to **Cantium** (and hence accusative) and **quae** the normal relative pronoun. *l.*3 **interiōrēs** *those further from the coast. l.*4 **verō** *indeed* emphasises the fact that while the Britons differed from each other in some ways they all used woad – it need not be translated in English as, to make the same emphasis, we would raise our voice on *all. ll.*5ff. **hōc** abl. *through, because of, this*; **aspectū** ablative of respect (28.1/2*l*) *in appearance*; **capillō** . . . **prōmissō, omnī parte** . . . **rāsā** ablatives of description (6.1/3). *ll.*7f. **dēnī duodēnīque** distributive numerals (12.1/4) *groups of ten and twelve each*; the object of **habent** is **uxōrēs . . . commūnēs**.

UNIT 23

23.1 Grammar

23.1/1 Direct questions (2)

We have already seen that direct questions can be introduced by:

(*a*) interrogative adverbs such as **cūr** *why*, **quōmodō** *how* (3.1/8)
(*b*) the interrogative **-ne** attached to the first word (3.1/8)
(*c*) the interrogative pronoun **quis** *who* and the interrogative adjective **quī** *what* (10.1/1*g,h*). For other interrogative pronouns and adjectives see 30.1/1 note 1.

There are several other types of questions:

(*d*) Questions expressed in such a way as to invite a negative answer: *he hasn't done this, has he?* or *surely he hasn't done this?* Of course, we may try to assert pressure in this way, but we will not necessarily get the answer we want. Latin introduces these questions with **num**, and would express the above question as **num hoc fēcit?**

Num lūmina flexit? num lacrimās dedit? *Surely he didn't turn his eyes? Surely he didn't shed* (lit. *give*) *tears?*

(*e*) Questions expressed in such a way as to invite a positive answer: *he has done this, hasn't he?* or *surely he has done this?* Here Latin uses **nōnne: nōnne hoc fēcit?**

Nōnne respondēbis? *You will reply, won't you?*

(*f*) Alternative questions such as *will you come to Rome or will you remain at Athens?* Latin normally introduces the first question with **utrum** or **-ne**, but we can dispense with an introductory word; the second clause must begin with **an** or **anne** (*not* **aut**). We can, therefore, have:

Utrum Rōmam veniēs an (anne) Athēnīs manēbis?
or   **Rōmamne veniēs an (anne) Athēnīs manēbis?**
or   **Rōmam veniēs an (anne) Athēnīs manēbis?**

If the second question is abridged to *or not*, we have in Latin **an nōn** (sometimes written **annōn**): **ille est quem quaerō an nōn?** *is he the one I am looking for or not?*

(*g*) Deliberative questions – see 22.1/1*d*.

23.1/2 Yes and No

Latin does not have exact equivalents for *yes* and *no*. Instead, the key word of the question is repeated, in an affirmative reply sometimes with a strengthening word such as **vērō** *in truth* or **sānē** *indeed*, in a negative reply always with **nōn**.

> **A. Nōn dīxī hoc futūrum esse? B. Dixistī.** *A. Didn't I say this would happen? B.* Yes (lit. *you said* [*it*]).
> **A. Estne frāter meus intus? B. nōn est.** *A. Is my brother inside? B.* No (lit. *he is not*).

Less frequently **sānē, etiam** or **ita** are used by themselves for an affirmative answer, **nōn ita, nōn vērō** or **minimē** (rarely **nōn** by itself) for a negative one.

23.1/3 Indirect questions

Indirect questions are another form of indirect speech (17.1/1). In Latin the verb in an indirect question must always be in the subjunctive (cf. indirect command and petition 21.1/2).

DIRECT	INDIRECT (a)	INDIRECT (b)
Valetne Caesar?	**num Caesar valeat.**	**num Caesar valēret.**
Is Caesar well?	**valeatne Caesar.**	**valēretne Caesar.**
	if Caesar is well.	*if Caesar was well.*
Quis est iste?	**quis iste sit.**	**quis iste esset.**
Who is that man?	*who that man is.*	*who that man was.*
Rogat	**Rogāvit**	
He asks	*He asked*	
Quō it Brūtus.	**quō Brūtus eat.**	**quō Brūtus īret.**
Where is Brutus going?	*where Brutus is going.*	*where Brutus was going.*
Cūr vēnērunt?	**cūr vēnerint.**	**cūr vēnissent.**
Why have they come?	*why they have come.*	*why they had come.*

The word introducing the question remains unchanged, except that instead of **-ne** we may, and more often do, have **num**, which in indirect questions normally performs exactly the same function (the distinction between questions expecting a positive answer and those expecting a negative one is not common in indirect speech; **nōnne** is only used with **quaerō** *ask*).

The above examples which follow **rogāvit** show that the tense of the original direct question is changed if the verb introducing the indirect version is past; the translations illustrate the same in English. We have already seen this idiom (sequence of tenses) in operation in indirect commands and petitions and purpose clauses, but here a greater variety of tenses is possible. Sequence of tenses prescribes that the tense of the subjunctive in certain subordinate clauses is restricted by the tense of the main verb according to the following table (for the terms *primary* and *historic* see 16.1/2):

Table 1

	MAIN CLAUSE	SUBORDINATE CLAUSE
PRIMARY	Present Future Perfect with *have* Future perfect	Present subjunctive Composite future subjunctive Perfect subjunctive
HISTORIC	Imperfect Perfect without *have* Pluperfect	Imperfect subjunctive Pluperfect subjunctive Composite future-in-the-past subjunctive

For the distinction between the perfect with and without *have* see 16.1/2. The composite future subjunctive (e.g. **factūrus sit**) is also used in result clauses (16.1/1*a*); the composite future-in-the-past subjunctive is of the same formation, but has the imperfect subjunctive of **sum**, e.g. **factūrus esset** (**rogāvī quid factūrus esset** *I asked what he would do* – the original question was **quid faciet?** *what will he do?*).

Within each group the tense of the subjunctive in the subordinate clause depends on the context; but we cannot use a primary subjunctive tense in a subordinate clause in conjunction with a historic tense in a main clause or vice versa. The two tables overleaf are mutually exclusive:

Table 2
PRIMARY SEQUENCE

Original question	Possible main clause	Indirect question
(a) **Quid agis?**	**Rogō** *I am asking*	(a) **quid agās.**
How are you? (lit. *how are you doing?*)	**Rogāvī** *I have asked*	*how you are*
	Rogābō *I shall ask*	
(b) **Quid ēgistī**	**Rogāverō** *I shall have asked*	(b) **quid ēgerīs.**
How have you been? or *How were you?*		*how you have been* or *how you were.*
(c) **Quid agēs?**		(c) **quid actūrus sīs.**
How will you be?		*how you will be*

Each direct question in column 1 is converted to the corresponding indirect question of column 3 in primary sequence. **Rogō, rogāvī** (only in the sense *I have asked*), **rogābō** and **rogāverō** can each be combined with any indirect question in column 3, giving us twelve possibilities: **rogō quid agās, rogō quid ēgerīs,** etc. Note that while **rogāvī** in the main clause can only have the sense *I have asked*, the perfect subjunctive in the indirect question may represent the perfect with or without *have*.

Table 3
HISTORIC SEQUENCE

Original question	Possible main clause	Indirect question
(a) **Quid agis?**	**Rogābam** *I was asking* or *used to ask*	(a) **quid agerēs.**
How are you?		*how you were.*
(b) **Quid ēgistī**	**Rogāvī** *I asked*	(b) **quid ēgissēs.**
How have you been? or *How were you?*	**Rogāveram** *I had asked*	*how you had been.*
(c) **Quid agēs?**		(c) **quid actūrus essēs.**
How will you be?		*how you would be.*

The original questions here are the same, but their indirect forms must have a historic tense of the subjunctive. We have nine possibilities: **rogābam quid agerēs, rogābam quid ēgissēs,** etc.

Notes

1 In Latin indirect questions are never introduced by **sī** although in English they can be introduced by *if*. The Latin for *I asked if you were wrong* is **rogāvī num errārēs.**

2 Indirect questions occur in contexts where no verb of asking is involved, e.g. **incertum est num Cicerō Rōmae sit** *it is uncertain if Cicero is in Rome.* With some verbs we may have an indirect question or an adjectival clause; *I do not know what he is doing* can be **nesciō quid faciat** (indirect question) or **nesciō id quod facit** (adjectival clause, lit. *that which . . .*).

3 Two idiomatic expressions containing **an** (not **num** or **-ne**) to introduce an indirect question are: **haud**[1] **sciō an** (or **nesciō an**) which means *I am inclined to think that*, not *I don't know if* (which would be **haud sciō/nesciō num**); and **forsitan** (**fors sit an** lit. *there may be a chance that*) *it is possible that.* **Dubitō, -āre** *doubt* may also be followed by **an** but has the same meaning as **haud sciō an** (26.1/2*b*). This use of **an** to introduce indirect questions is extended in Silver Age Latin to other verbs.

4 *When* in questions, both direct and indirect, is always **quandō**, never **cum** or **ubi** which, in the sense of *when* (i.e. at the time when), are only used to introduce adverbial clauses (**ubi** can also mean *where . . .?*).

5 Alternative indirect questions are introduced in the same way as alternative direct questions, but **necne** is used instead of **an nōn** for *or not*: **quaeram utrum id ēmerit necne** *I shall ask whether he has bought it or not.*

6 In direct questions we can have a deliberative subjunctive (22.1/1*d*) or a potential subjunctive (**quid fēcisset sī hīc fuisset?** *what would he have done if he had been here?*). As we have only one subjunctive mood, these uses, when occurring in indirect questions, cannot be formally distinguished from subjunctives which represent an original indicative. Where ambiguity is possible a periphrasis is used. Thus an impersonal gerundive can represent an original deliberative subjunctive: **quid faciam?** *what should I do?* **rogō quid mihi faciendum sit** *I am asking what I should do.*

7 Because of the restrictions imposed by sequence of tenses, there are some combinations of tenses which, though possible in English, are not possible in Latin, e.g. *he is asking what you were doing yesterday.* Here we must content ourselves with **rogat quid heri fēcerīs** (lit. *he is asking what you did yesterday*), as an imperfect subjunctive cannot follow a present indicative.

---

[1]**Haud** is a negative only used in certain expressions; it has the same meaning as **nōn**.

23.1/4 Shortened verbal forms

Many parts of the tenses formed from perfect stems in -v- (i.e. all first and fourth conjugation verbs with regular principal parts and some verbs from the second and third conjugations) can be shortened so that **-vi-**, **-vē-** and **-ve-** are lost. Examples are:

from	**amō**	*from*	**dēleō**
	amástī (amāvistī)		**dēléstī (dēlēvistī)**
	amā́runt (amāvērunt)		**dēlḗrunt (dēlēvērunt)**
	amā́ram (amāveram)		**dēlḗram (dēlēveram)**
	amásset (amāvisset)		**dēlésset (dēlēvisset)**
from	**noscō** (see 25.1/5*b*)	*from*	**audiō**
	nóstī (nōvistī)		**audístī (audīvistī)**
	nŏ́runt (nōvērunt)		
	nŏ́ram (nōveram)		
	nóssem (nōvissem)		**audíssem (audīvissem)**

From perfects in **-īvī** (mainly fourth conjugation verbs) only forms with the sequence **-īvi-** are shortened (cf. 4.1/6 note 2). Shortened forms are particularly common with verbs of the first conjugation.

23.2 Latin reading

1 Videamus ea quae sequuntur, primum, deorumne providentia mundus regatur, deinde, consulantne di rebus humanis.
2 Quid est, Catilina? num dubitas id, me imperante, facere quod iam tua sponte faciebas?
3 Nonne vides etiam guttas in saxa cadentis
   umoris longo in spatio pertundere saxa?
4 Bene dormit qui non sentit quam male dormiat.
5 Me si caelicolae voluissent ducere vitam,
   has mihi servassent sedes.

Funeral arrangements of Diogenes
6 Diogenes philosophus, cum amici ab eo quaererent quomodo eum sepulturi essent, proici se iussit inhumatum. tum amici 'volucribusne et feris?' 'minime vero' inquit 'sed bacillum prope me ponite ut eas abigam.' 'quomodo poteris? non enim senties.' 'quid igitur mihi oberit ferarum laniatus nihil sentienti?'

7   Si omnes Athenienses delectarentur tyrannicis legibus, num
     idcirco hae leges iustae haberentur?

Catullus to Caesar
8   Nil nimium studeo, Caesar, tibi velle placere
         nec scire utrum sis albus an ater homo.

Only the good man is happy
9   Socrates, cum esset ex eo quaesitum nonne Archelaum, regem
     Macedonum, beatum putaret, 'haud scio' inquit 'numquam enim
     cum eo collocutus sum.'
     'aliter id scire non potes?'
     'nullo modo.'
     'tu igitur ne de Persarum quidem rege magno potes dicere
     beatusne sit?'
     'non possum, cum ignorem utrum sit vir bonus necne.'
     'quid? tu in eo sitam esse vitam beatam putas?'
     'ita existimo, bonos esse beatos, improbos miseros.'
     'miser ergo Archelaus?'
     'certe, si iniustus.'
10   Anaxagoras quaerentibus amicis, velletne in patriam, si quid
     accidisset, auferri, 'non necesse est' inquit 'undique enim ad
     inferos tantundem viae est.'

Cicero writes to his friend Trebatius who was serving under
Caesar in Gaul
11   Iam diu ignoro quid agas, nihil enim scribis: neque ego ad te his
     duobus mensibus scripsi. quod cum Quinto fratre meo non eras,
     quo litteras mitterem aut cui darem, nesciebam. cupio scire quid
     agas et ubi sis hiematurus.

Narcissus
12   As the result of a curse the handsome youth Narcissus fell in love
     with his own reflection, which he saw in a pool, and became the
     first victim of narcissism. In the story, as told by Ovid in the
     course of his poem ***Metamorphōsēs*** (*Transformations*; see 30.3),
     he addresses his image as follows:

         Quisquis es, huc exi! quid me, puer unice, fallis
         quove petitus abis? certe nec forma nec aetas
         est mea quam fugias, et amarunt me quoque nymphae.
         spem mihi nescioquam vultu promittis amico,

cumque ego porrexi tibi bracchia, porrigis ultro: ~
cum risi, arrides: lacrimas quoque saepe notavi
me lacrimante tuas: nutu quoque signa remittis.
iste ego sum! sensi: nec me mea fallit imago:
uror amore mei, flammas moveoque feroque!
quid faciam? roger, anne rogem? quid deinde rogabo?   1(
iamque dolor vires adimit, nec tempora vitae
longa meae superant, primoque exstinguor in aevo.
nec mihi mors gravis est, posituro morte dolores:
hic, qui diligitur, vellem, diuturnior esset!
nunc duo concordes anima moriemur in una.   1~

Notes

1 **prōvidentiā** ablative.
2 **tuā sponte** *of your own will*; **sponte** is a defective noun which
   occurs only in the ablative (25.1/4*d*).
3 **vidēs** is followed by an accusative (**guttās . . . cadentīs**) and
   infinitive (**pertundere**).
5 **hās . . . sēdēs** plural for singular.
6 With **quaerō** the person asked is put into the ablative with **ā/ab**;
   volucribus . . . ferīs dative; **sentiēs** i.e. *will have power of feeling, will
   be conscious*; **quid** *how*.
8 **Nīl** emphatic for **nōn**.
9 **in eō sitam** lit. *dependent on that*.
10 **quaerentibus amīcīs** dative, *said* (**inquit**) *to his friends enquiring . . .*;
   tantundem viae lit. *the same amount of road*.
11 **iam diū ignōrō** lit. *already for a long time I do not know*, i.e. *I
   haven't known for a long time*; **quid agās** *how you are*.
12 *l*.1 **exī** <**exeō**; **quid** *why*. *l*.2 **quōve** = **quō** + **-ve**. *l*.3 **fugiās** potential
   subj. (22.1/1*b*). *l*.5 **tibi** *towards you* the dative can be used in poetry
   to express motion (28.1/1*j*). *l*.7 **mē lacrimante** abl. absolute
   (12.1/1). *l*.8 **iste** *that person of yours*, i.e. *you*. *l*.9 **ūror** lit. *I am being
   burnt*; **ūrō** can only be transitive but as the English *burn* is either
   transitive (*I am burning my rubbish*) or intransitive (*I am burning
   with anger*) we can translate **ūror** by *I burn*; **meī** genitive of **ego**
   (not from **meus**); **flammās** *flames of passion*. *l*.10 both **roger** and
   rogem are deliberative subjunctives (22.1/1*d*). *l*.11 **tempora** plural
   for singular. *l*.13 **positūrō** with **mihi** lit. *for me going to lay aside*.
   l.14 with **vellem** supply **ut** *I would wish that*, i.e. *my wish is that*. *l*.15
   animā with **ūnā**.

24.1 Grammar

24.1/1 The nature of Latin verse, long and short syllables

Classical Latin poetry (as distinct from Christian and Medieval Latin poetry) was composed on a completely different principle from that employed in English. It was not constructed by arranging stressed syllables in patterns, and rhyme was never used. The Roman poets used a number of different metres, all of which consist of certain fixed arrangements of long and short syllables. In English verse, whether rhymed or not, the length and rhythm of a line is determined by the number and arrangement of its stressed syllables:

> Knów ye the lánd where the cýpress and mýrtle
> Are émblems of deéds that are dóne in their clíme?

In Latin verse we have a succession of long and short syllables whose number and order are prescribed by the metre used. Syllables are marked with a macron (‾) when long and a micron (˘) when short (see also 24.1/2 note 1):

ărmă vĭrūmquĕ cănō Trōiaē quī prīmŭs ăb ōrīs

The rules for determining the length of syllables within words are given on pp. xvif. These apply for poetry with two important additions:

(*a*) When the final syllable of a word contains a short vowel followed by a consonant (e.g. **annus**) and the word immediately following begins with a consonant (except **h**), the final syllable of the first word counts as long: **ānnūs nŏvŭs**. When, however, the second word begins with a vowel (or **h**), the final syllable of the first remains short: **ānnŭs ōc-tā-vŭs**.

(*b*) In verse, **r** and **l** may begin a syllable within a word, and we may have either **pa-tris** (the pronunciation of normal speech) or **pat-ris**. In this word **a** is a short vowel, but, according to the syllable division adopted by a poet in a particular line, the syllables can count as **pă-tris** or **pāt-ris**. Simply stated, this means that if a short vowel is followed by two consonants of which the second is either **r** or **l**, the syllable containing the short vowel may be either long or short. This does not apply between words: **frangit remum** always counts as **frān-gĭt rē-mŭm**.

In determining the length of syllables, it is essential to remember that **h** never counts, **qu** counts as only one consonant, and **x** and **z** (which is rare) count as two (p. xvi).

For purposes of Latin verse, all long syllables are presumed to take the same time to articulate, and, in the metres described below, all short syllables are presumed to take exactly half that time. Consequently, in certain places in a line of verse, a long syllable may be replaced with two short syllables, except at the end, where either a long syllable or a single short syllable may stand.

24.1/2 Metrical feet, the hexameter

A foot is made up of a certain combination of long and short syllables. Of the numerous possibilities we can confine ourselves to the following:

Dactyl   — ‿ ‿
Spondee   — —
Trochee   — ‿

Names for Latin metrical feet have been taken into English, but with a changed meaning because of the different nature of English poetry. A trochee becomes in English a foot of two syllables where the first bears a stress accent (e.g. *keéper*); but in Latin these terms always refer to combinations of long and short syllables without any reference whatsoever to the accent of individual words.

The metre used for epic, pastoral, satire, and certain other poetic genres was the hexameter. This metre consists of six feet. The first four can be either dactyls or spondees, the fifth must be a dactyl,[1] and the sixth can be either a spondee or trochee. This can be represented as follows:

— ‿‿ | — ‿‿ | — ‿‿ | — ‿‿ | — ‿‿ | — ‿

The upright lines show the syllable division between one foot and the next; they do *not* necessarily coincide with word division. Examples of scanned hexameters are:

ūrbs ān-|tī-quă fŭ-|īt Tў-rĭ-|ī tĕ-nŭ-|ē-rĕ cŏ-|lō-nī

quām Iū-|nō fēr-|tūr tēr-|rīs mă-gĭs| ōm-nĭ-bŭs| ū-năm

hīc cūr-|rūs fŭ-ĭt| hōc rēg-|nūm dĕ-ă| gēn-tĭ-bŭs| ēs-sĕ

The scansion of Latin poetry faithfully reflects pronunciation. A poet could not write a line where **coloni** (first line above) was scanned as, say, **cŏlŏnĭ**, because his audience would not have recognised the word any more than we could recognise *mind* in an English poem if it were pronounced to rhyme with *sinned*. Whether a vowel was long or short was fixed by normal everyday usage. Consequently, whenever a syllable is made up of a vowel followed either by no consonant, or by only one consonant, and its quantity therefore depends on whether the vowel is long or short, this can be discovered from a dictionary or the vocabulary at the back of this book. Generally, however, we can go a long way by small pieces of detective work, even without knowing, or looking up, the quantity of each vowel. To scan a hexameter from first principles we proceed in the following way:

1   2   3 4   5 6   7   8   9   10 11 12 13   14
tan-tae mo-lis er-at Ro-ma-nam con-de-re gen-tem

We can immediately mark syllables 1, 6, 9, 10, 13 as long because each contains a vowel followed by two consonants. Also, 2 must be long because of the diphthong **ae**, and we have:

tān-taē mo-lis er-āt Ro-ma-nām cōn-de-re gēn-tem

---

[1] A spondee occurs very occasionally in the fifth foot (often in a Greek name) but this can be ignored for present purposes.

The first two syllables are long and therefore make up a spondee, not a dactyl; we can put a vertical stroke after **tantae** to indicate the end of the first foot. We can also put a stroke before syllable 13; the last foot always contains two, and only two, syllables. The fifth foot now stands revealed; the last two syllables of a hexameter must always form the sixth foot, and the three preceding syllables must constitute the fifth, which is a dactyl. We have already identified syllable 10 as long and we can now mark syllables 11 and 12 as short:

I | | V | VI
tān-tae| mo-lis er-āt Ro-ma-nām| cōn-dĕ-rĕ| gēn-tem

Here we realise that syllable 3 must be long because it begins the second foot, and whether this foot is a spondee or dactyl (as allowed by the metrical scheme), it will always begin with a long syllable. We next attack 8; this must be part of the fourth foot because it is only one syllable before the fifth. The fourth foot can be either a dactyl or spondee. If it ends with a long syllable (we have already marked 9 as long) it must be a spondee. Therefore 8 is long. Next 7; we now know that both 6 and 8 are long and we see from the metrical scheme that no possible combination of feet in a hexameter will result in a short syllable being wedged between two long ones. Therefore 7 is long. We record our results and, counting from the end, number the feet we have identified:

I | | III | IV | V |VI
tān-tae| mō-lis er-| āt Rō-|mā-nām|cōn-dĕ-rĕ|gēn-tem

Only the second foot remains. For it we have syllables 3, 4, 5. It must therefore be a dactyl because a dactyl has three syllables, a spondee only two. The complete scansion of the line is:

I | II | III | IV | V |VI
tān-tae| mō-lĭs ĕr-| āt Rō-|mā-nām|cōn-dĕ-rĕ|gēn-tem

The final syllable of a hexameter is either long or short (the sixth foot being either a spondee or trochee). As we have here a vowel followed by a single consonant, we cannot say whether this constitutes a long or short syllable without knowing whether the **e** is long or short. The length of vowels in terminations is always consistent within declensions (and conjugations); and when we look up the third declension (the exact parallel to **gentem** would be the accusative singular of **mons** 7.1/1), we find that the **e** of the accusative singular ending has no long mark over it and is therefore short. Consequently the syllable **-em** is short.

This last step could be the model for all the preceding ones except the first. If we consult the vocabulary (or a dictionary) we find **Rōmānus**, and so can mark syllables 7 and 8 of the worked example as long because they contain long vowels. For terminations and parts of verbs (e.g. is the **e** of **erat** long or short?) we must consult the appropriate paradigms. Sometimes, when deduction cannot help, we must do this in any case. If we already know the correct pronunciation of each word (as e.g. that **Romanus** is pronounced with a long **o** and a long **a**) every line will scan automatically. The one complication, elision, will be explained in the next unit.

Notes

1 The macron (⁻) is used in two ways. In all other contexts it is employed to mark long vowels, but in scansion it marks long syllables and, as we have seen, a long syllable does not necessarily contain a long vowel. When it is used in the latter way for a long syllable made up of a short vowel followed by two consonants, as syllable 6 of the worked example, we must not imagine this vowel is to be pronounced as long; the **a** of **erat** is always short, but here, where the following word (**Rōmānam**) begins with a consonant, it is part of a long syllable.

2 There are a number of rules to determine whether vowels are long or short, but these only apply in certain contexts and do not cover every vowel of every Latin word. These rules fall into two categories:

  (i) those relating to terminations, e.g. the accusative plural of masculine and feminine nouns in all declensions has a long vowel. These rules can be observed from paradigms.

  (ii) those relating to the following sound. The most important is that where two vowels occur together and do not form a diphthong the first is short; the few exceptions include **diēī** (three syllables, from **diēs**) and similar fifth declension forms; some parts of **fīō** and some Greek names, e.g. **Aenēās**.

3 It is frequently essential to scan a line of poetry to discover the length of final vowels. This applies particularly to final **a**'s.

24.2 Latin reading

Aeneas and the Sibyl enter the Underworld

In Vergil's epic (8.2), Aeneas, when close to his destination, lands at Cumae in southern Italy and is taken by the Sibyl, a local priestess, to the realm of the dead in order to see his father Anchises. The following passage describes the first part of their journey.

Ibant obscuri sola sub nocte per umbram
perque domos Ditis vacuas et inania regna:
quale per incertam lunam sub luce maligna
est iter in silvis, ubi caelum condidit umbra
Iuppiter, et rebus nox abstulit atra colorem. 5
vestibulum ante ipsum primisque in faucibus Orci
Luctus et ultrices posuere cubilia Curae,
pallentesque habitant Morbi tristisque Senectus.
. . . .
Hinc via Tartarei quae fert Acherontis ad undas.
turbidus hic caeno vastaque voragine gurges 10
aestuat atque omnem Cocyto eructat harenam.
portitor has horrendus aquas et flumina servat,
terribili squalore Charon, cui plurima mento
canities inculta iacet, stant lumina flamma,
sordidus ex umeris nodo dependet amictus. 15
ipse ratem conto subigit velisque ministrat
et ferruginea subvectat corpora cumba,
iam senior, sed cruda deo viridisque senectus.
huc omnis turba ad ripas effusa ruebat,
matres atque viri defunctaque corpora vita 20
magnanimum heroum, pueri innuptaeque puellae,
impositique rogis iuvenes ante ora parentum:
quam multa in silvis autumni frigore primo
lapsa cadunt folia, aut ad terram gurgite ab alto
quam multae glomerantur aves, ubi frigidus annus 25
trans pontum fugat et terris immittit apricis.
stabant orantes primi transmittere cursum
tendebantque manus ripae ulterioris amore.
navita sed tristis nunc hos nunc accipit illos,
ast alios longe submotos arcet harena. 30

Scan (i.e. mark the metrical feet in) the first five lines. The metre here, as in all Vergil's poems, is the hexameter.

Notes

*l.*1 we tell from the metre that **sola** is scanned **sōlā**, i.e. that it is ablative singular feminine, and therefore agrees with **nocte**. *l.*2 **vacuās, inānia** the Underworld is, in a sense, empty because, apart from its ruling divinities, it contains nothing of substance, only the shades of the dead; **domōs** and **regna** are both plural for singular. *l.*3 **quāle** (<**quālis** see 30.1/1) with **iter**, lit. *of what sort is a journey* – translate *as [on] a journey . . .* and omit **est**. *l.*4 **umbrā** we cannot tell from the metre that this is ablative but as **Iuppiter** can only be nominative (and therefore is the subject of **condidit**) it cannot fit into the clause in any other way. *l.*5 **rēbus** ablative of separation (see 28.1/2e), translate *from the world* (lit. *things*). *l.*7 **posuēre** = **posuērunt** (4.1/6 note 1). *l.*9 with **via** supply **est** and take **Tartareī** with **Acherontis**; **fert** *leads to. l.*10 **hīc** *here*; we see from the metre that we have **vastā** ablative feminine singular, which therefore goes with **vorāgine**. *l.*11 **Cōcȳtō** dative of motion (28.1/1*j*) *into Cocytus. l.*12 **horrendus** attributive use of the gerundive (18.1/2*a*) *fearsome, dread. l.*13 **terribilī squālōre** ablative of description (6.1/3); **cui**, dative of possessor (8.1/5), introduces the clauses containing **iacet, stant** and **dēpendet**, *on whose chin* (lit. *for whom on the chin*) *. . . whose eyes . . . from whose shoulders (for whom from shoulders) . . .*, it is better in English to convert each of these adjectival clauses into main clauses and translate *on his chin . . . his eyes . . . from his shoulders . . . l.*14 again we cannot tell from the metre whether the last syllable of the line is short or long (**flamma** or **flammā**), but as the verb of the clause formed by the last three words is plural (**stant**) we cannot have a nominative singular and so must analyse the last word as **flammā**. *l.*16 **vēlīs** dative with **ministrat** *attends to the sails. l.*17 metre tells us that **ferrūginea** must be scanned **ferrūgineā** (fem. abl. s.), but do we have **cumba** or **cumbā** at the end of the line? As **ipse** (*l.*16) is the subject of **subvectat**, **cumba** (nom.) is ruled out (we could also argue that **ferrūgineā** must have a feminine noun in the ablative singular to agree with). *l.*18 **deō** dative of possessor (8.1/5). *ll.*20–22 see 15.3 (*ll.*12 14). *l.*23 lit. *as* (**quam**) *many [as] the leaves fall and drop (having fallen drop)*, i.e. *as numerous as the leaves which . . .* The same construction is in *l.*25. *l.*25 **frīgidus annus** *the cold [part of the] year. l.*26 **terrīs . . . aprīcīs** *to sunny lands* dative of motion (see 28.1/1*j*). *l.*27 the construction here after **ōrantēs** (we would expect a clause of indirect petition with **ut** and the subjunctive – 21.1/2) is poetical and exactly the same as in English – *begging to cross the passage first. l.*28 the sense alone tells us that we have the accusative plural **manūs**. *l.*30 **harēnā** abl. of place from which (28.1/2*d*) *from the sand.*

24.3 Excursus

A medieval Latin poem

Most medieval Latin poetry was written in rhymed stanzas and with lines whose rhythm depends, as in English poetry, on stress accent – no attention was paid to the long and short syllables of Classical poetry. The following five stanzas are from a poem of the twelfth century by the Archipoeta (his real name is unknown), in which he expresses the conflict he felt between worldly pleasures and Christian prescriptions and beliefs. The poem has come to typify the attitudes of the wandering students and scholars of the Middle Ages who moved about Europe from one university town to another. Its language is very close to Classical Latin; in our extract the original spelling, which reflects medieval pronunciation, has been changed to the classical norm.

Aestuans interius		Feror ego veluti	
ira vehementi		sine nauta navis,	
in amaritudine		ut per vias aeris	
loquor meae menti:	4	vaga fertur avis:	20
factus de materia,		non me tenent vincula,	
cinis elementi,		non me tenet clavis:	
similis sum folio,		quaero mihi similes,	
de quo ludunt venti.	8	et adiungor pravis.	24
Cum sit enim proprium		Mihi cordis gravitas	
viro sapienti		res videtur gravis:	
supra petram ponere		iocus est amabilis	
sedem fundamenti,	12	dulciorque favis:	28
stultus ego comparor		quidquid Venus imperat,	
fluvio labenti		labor est suavis,	
sub eodem tramite		quae numquam in cordibus	
numquam permanenti.	16	habitat ignavis.	32

Via lata gradior
more iuventutis,
implicor et vitiis
immemor virtutis: 36
voluptatis avidus
magis quam salutis,
mortuus in anima
curam gero cutis.   40

Notes

*l.*1 **interius** is used here as an adverb *inwardly, inside (myself)*. *l.*2 **īrā**.
*l.*6 **cinis** is in apposition to the understood subject *I*. *l.*7 **similis** + dative
(**foliō**) *similar to*. *l.*8 **dē quō** *with which*. *l.*9 **cum** *whereas*. *l.*12 **sēdem**
fundāmentī lit. *the seat* (i.e. *bottom*) *of his foundation*. *l.*13 **comparor** +
dative (**fluviō**) *I am matched with*, i.e. *I am like*. *l.*15 **sub** *on* (a medieval
use). *l.*19 **āeris** (3 syllables) from **āēr** (2 syllables) *air*. *l.*31 the
antecedent of **quae** is **Venus**. *l.*33 **viā lātā**. *l.*35 **implicor et** = **et implicor**.
*l.*38 **salūs** here in the Christian sense *salvation*. *l.*40 **cutis** in Classical
Latin means *skin* but here *the [needs of the] flesh*.

UNIT 25

25.1 Grammar

25.1/1 Elision

When a vowel (or diphthong) at the end of a word is followed by a word beginning with a vowel (or diphthong), the former is elided, i.e. is not pronounced and does not count metrically. When scanning we enclose elided vowels in brackets:

Āl-bā-|nī-quĕ pă-|trēs āt-|qu(e) āl-taē| moē-nĭ-ă| Rō-maē

īm-pŭ-lĕ-|rīt tān-|taēn(e) ă-nĭ-|mīs caē-|lēs-tĭ-bŭs| ī-raē

As **h** does not count metrically, elision also occurs when a word beginning with **h** is preceded by a word ending in a vowel:

tū mĭ-hĭ| quōd-cūm-|qu(e) hōc rēg-|nī tū| scēp-tră Iŏ-|vēm-quĕ

Further, we even have elision with words ending in a vowel and **m**. This reflects the weak pronunciation of final **m** in Latin:

lī-tŏ-ră| mūl-t(um) īl-|l(e) ēt tēr-|rīs iāc-|tā-tŭs ĕt| āl-tō

Absence of elision, which is called **hiatus**, occurs, but is rare. The purpose of elision is to facilitate pronunciation by eliminating the slight pause necessary when two vowels come together (compare **ill(e) et** with **ille et**). It does not, however, take place inside words or between lines.

25.1/2 Caesura in the hexameter

A hexameter in which the end of each foot coincides with the end of a word, such as

spār-sīs| hās-tīs| lōn-gīs| cām-pūs| splēn-dĕt ĕt| hōr-rĕt

was regarded by Classical Latin poets as ugly and lacking in rhythm (this example is from the early poet Ennius). To avoid this they wrote their hexameters in such a way that there was a break between words after the first syllable of the third foot or after the first syllables of the second and fourth feet. This break is called the **caesura** (*cutting*) and is marked by two vertical lines. It is of value in observing the rhythm, but does not help in determining the sense of a line:

prō-gĕ-nĭ-|ēm sĕd ĕ-|nĭm||Trō-|iā-n(o) ā| sān-guĭ-nĕ| dū-cī

īd mĕ-tŭ-|ēns||vĕ-tĕ-|rīs-quĕ mĕ-|mōr||Sā-|tūr-nĭ-ă| bēl-lī

25.1/3 The pentameter

One hexameter followed by one pentameter forms an elegiac couplet, a metre used for love poetry, epigrams (as in the poems of Martial we have read) and elsewhere. The pentameter is never used by itself. An elegiac couplet normally forms a sense unit; the pentameter, which by convention is indented from the left-hand margin, generally concludes with a strong mark of punctuation (see the passage from Ovid in 18.3). The pentameter consists of two halves of two and a half feet each; the division between the two is marked by a break in words (here called **diaeresis** *division*, not **caesura**, because it occurs at the end, not in the middle, of a metrical unit; it is also marked by two vertical lines). Its metrical pattern is:

Examples (taken from 18.3 and 21.2, 13) are:

lū-xŭ-rĭ-|āt Phrȳ-gĭ-|ō|| sān-guĭ-nĕ| pīn-guĭs hŭ-|mŭs

ōs-să rŭ-|ī-nō-|sās|| ōc-cŭ-lĭt| hēr-bă dŏ-|mōs

ād-vĕ-nĭ-|(o) hās mĭ-sĕ-|rās|| frā-tĕr ăd| īn-fĕ-rĭ-|ās

āt-qu(e) īn| pēr-pĕ-tŭ-|ūm|| frā-tĕr ăv-|(e) āt-quĕ vă-|lē

25.1/4 Oddities in nouns

(*a*) A few second declension nouns in **-us** are neuter: **pelagus, -ī** *sea*, **vīrus, -ī** *poison*, **vulgus, -ī** *the common people* (the last is occasionally masculine). Some others are feminine, as **humus, -ī** *ground, earth* (already mentioned at 8.1/3) and names of trees:

cedrus, -ī *cedar*, **ulmus, -ī** *elm*, etc. (**quercus** *oak* and **pīnus** *pine* are also feminine but belong to the fourth declension).

(*b*) **locus, -ī** *place* and **iocus, -ī** *joke* can have the plural neuter forms **loca** (example at 6.2, 13), **ioca**, as well as **locī, iocī**, etc.

(*c*) A few nouns are declined in two ways: **plebs, plēbis** (f) or **plēbēs, plēbeī** (f) *the common people*; **māteria, -ae** (f) or **māteriēs, -eī** (f) *material, matter* (some other nouns vacillate between the first and fifth declensions). Several have a slight difference of meaning between forms, as **pecus, -oris** (n) *livestock, farm animals* and **pecus, -udis** (f) *an individual domestic animal*.

(*d*) Many nouns are not used in every possible form. Sometimes the same is true of the corresponding English word: **aurum, -ī** (n) *gold* is not used in the plural, **arma, -ōrum** (n) *arms* does not occur in the singular (for other plural-only words see 8.1/4).

A few do not have a nominative singular and are listed under either a hypothetical nominative singular or their genitive singular. The two most common are **opem** (gen. **opis**, no dative, abl. **ope**) *aid* (the plural, which exists in all cases, means *resources*), and **vicem** (gen. **vicis**, no dative, abl. **vice**) *interchange* (the plural exists in all cases, gen. **vicium**). In the vocabulary (following the practice of the *Oxford Latin Dictionary*) the former is listed under **ops**, the latter under **vicis**.

Fās *right* and **nefās** *wrong* (both neuter) only occur in the nominative and accusative singular.

The following only exist in the ablative singular: **nātū** (m) *by birth* (**maior/minor nātū** *elder/younger*); **iussū** (m) *by command*; **iniussū** (m) *without the order (of)*; **sponte** (f) *of (my, your, etc.) own accord*. The last three are normally accompanied by a possessive adjective or a genitive (examples in 19.3 *l.*19; 21.1/2; 23.2, 2).

Nēmō *no one* is usually combined with **nullus** (10.1/1*e*) to give **nēmō, nēminem, nullīus, nēminī, nullō**.

(*e*) As Roman literature was written in the Greek tradition, we encounter many Greek words in Latin authors, but these are almost always common nouns or proper names. Some of the former and many of the latter keep features of their original Greek declension (there are only three declensions in Classical Greek).

In the **first declension** nearly all nouns that preserve anything of their Greekness are proper names. These include male names, which always have -s in the nominative singular. There are three types:

Nom.	Aenéās (m)	Anchīsēs (m)	Círcē (f)
Voc.	Aenéā	Anchísā	Círcē
Acc.	Aenéān	Anchísēn	Círcēn
Gen.	Aenéae	Anchísae	Círcēs
Dat.	Aenéae	Anchísae	Círcae
Abl.	Aenéā	Anchísā	Círcē

The above declension of **Aenēās** and **Anchīsēs** is that used by Vergil, but the degree of Latinisation in nouns of this category varies; **Círcē**, for example, can be declined purely as a Latin word: **Circa, Circa, Circam, Circae, Circae, Circā.**

Second declension Greek nouns (here too mostly proper names) sometimes keep their original ending in the nominative and accusative singular: **Dēlos, Dēlon** (f) the island of Delos; **Pēlion** (n) a mountain in northern Greece.

The Greek **third declension** shows an even greater variety than its Latin counterpart. Of the following eccentricities only (iv) applies to neuter nouns:

(i) Nouns in **-ēs, -eus** and **-is** can form their vocative by dropping their final s: **Sōcratē** (<**Sōcratēs**), **Orpheu** (<**Orpheus**), **Pari** (<**Paris**).

(ii) Nouns in **-ēs,** and some in **-is,** can have an accusative singular in **-n** or **-m**: **Sōcratēn** or **Sōcratem, Parin** or **Parim.**

(iii) Many nouns (including some in -is) can have an accusative singular in **-a**: **lampada** (<**lampas** *torch*), **Agamemnona** (<**Agamemnōn**), **Parida** (another possible accusative of **Paris**).

(iv) Occasionally we get **-os** in the genitive singular: **Pānos** (<**Pān**), **Aenēidos** (<**Aenēis** *the Aeneid*); but the normal Latin **-is** is much more common.

(v) **-es** (not **-ēs**) is the ending in the nominative plural, and **-as** often occurs for the accusative plural: **Cyclopes, Cyclopas** (<**Cyclops**); **hērōes, hērōas** (<**hērōs** *hero*). **Crātēr** (m) *mixing-bowl* is declined as follows:

	SINGULAR	PLURAL
N. & V.	crātēr	crātēres
Acc.	crātēra (or -em)	crātēras
Gen.	crātēros (or -is)	crātērum
Dat.	crātērī	crātēribus
Abl.	crātēre	crātēribus

25.1/5 Oddities in verbs

(*a*) Some common Latin verbs do not occur in every possible form. They fall into two groups:

(i) Five verbs exist in a very limited number of forms scattered over various tenses and moods:

for, fārī, fātus sum *speak*, which is regular. The forms **fātur** and **fātus** are very common.

aiō *say, affirm* (on the pronunciation when **ai** is followed by a vowel see p. xv). Present indicative, **aiō, ais, ait, aiunt** (all 2 syllables). Imperfect indicative, **aiēbam**, etc.

inquam *say* (**inquam** and **sum** (2.1/4) are the only two Latin verbs with the **-m** ending for the first person singular of the present indicative active). The most common form is the third singular **inquit** which can be either present or perfect. This verb is only used with direct speech and is always placed after the first word or later: **'nōn tacēs' inquit 'gladiātor obscēne?'** *'Won't you shut up'* (lit. *aren't you keeping quiet*), *he said, 'you filthy gladiator?'*

queō *be able,* **nequeō** *be unable,* which are both conjugated, in the few forms that occur, as though they were compounds of **eō** (15.1/6). Hence we have **queō, quīs, quit, quīmus, quītis, queunt**.

(ii) Three verbs do not have a present stem and, consequently, have no present, future or imperfect forms. Of these, **coepī** (2 syllables) *I began, have begun* has a true perfect meaning, and its other tenses are supplied by **incipiō, -ere** *begin.* However, **ōdī** *I hate* and **meminī** *I remember,* though perfect in form, are present in meaning; consequently their future perfect has the sense of a simple future and their pluperfect the sense of an imperfect or perfect (there are no forms which mean *I had hated* or *I had remembered*).

INDICATIVE

Perfect	**coépī** *I began, have begun*	**ṓdī** *I hate*	**mémínī** *I remember*
Pluperfect	**coéperam** *I had begun*	**ṓderam** *I hated, was hating*	**memíneram** *I remembered, was remembering*
Future perfect	**coéperō** *I shall have begun*	**ṓderō** *I shall hate*	**meminerō** *I shall remember*

SUBJUNCTIVE

Perfect	**coéperim**	**ṓderim**	**memínerim**
Pluperfect	**coepíssem**	**ṓdíssem**	**meminíssem**

The above tenses and moods are conjugated in the singular and plural and in all persons.

OTHER FORMS

Perfect infinitive	**coepísse** *to have begun*	**ṓdísse** *to hate*	**meminísse** *to remember*
Imperative	none	none	s. **meméntō** *remember!* pl. **mementṓte**

Of the few other occurring forms the most common are the participles **coeptus** *having been begun* (the neuter **coeptum** is often used as a noun in the sense of *undertaking, scheme*) and **ṓsus** which, like the past participle of deponents, has a present active sense *hating* (cf. 14.1/4).

(*b*) **Noscō** (**-ere, nṓvī, nṓtum**) and its compound **cognoscō** (**-ere, cognṓvī, cognitum**; note the different supines) both mean *get to know, find out* in the present tense. Their perfect tense is often used with the present sense *I know* (= *have found out*), and likewise **nṓveram, cognṓveram** can mean *I knew* (= *I had found out*). See also **consuescō** in the vocabulary.

(*c*) Only two compounds of **dō** (2.2/1), **circumdō** *surround* and **vēnumdō** *sell*, belong to the first conjugation. The remainder are third conjugation, e.g. **prōdō, prōdere, prōdidī, prōditum** *betray*; **ēdō, ēdere, ēdidī, ēditum** *bring forth, produce*.

(*d*) **Edō** *eat* has some forms which have the same spelling as those from either **ēdō** *bring forth* or **sum** *be*, but in every case the length of the initial **e** is different. Of its forms the following should be noted (for the sake of clarity the hidden quantities in **ēst, ēstis** and **ēsse** are marked but because no vowel quantities are indicated in editions of Latin authors these forms are very easily confused):

> Present indicative active: **edō, ēs, ēst, edimus, ēstis, edunt**
> Present infinitive active: **ēsse**

(e) Four common verbs (and a few others) are semi-deponents; in their primary tenses they have active forms and active meanings, but their historic tenses (16.1/2) are passive in form although active in meaning:

> **audeō, -ēre, ausus sum** *dare* (an alternative present (originally perfect) subjunctive follows **sum: ausim, ausīs, ausit, ausīmus, ausītis, ausint**)
> **fīdō, -ere, fīsus sum** (+ dat.) *trust*
> **gaudeō, -ēre, gāvīsus sum** *rejoice*
> **soleō, -ēre, solītus sum** *be accustomed*

(f) The following resemble **fīō** (15.1/3) inasmuch as they are also active in form but only passive in meaning:

> **vapulō, -āre** *be beaten*
> **vēneō, vēnīre, vēniī, vēnitum** *be sold*

> **vēneō** is a compound of **eō** (15.1/6) and follows its conjugation: **vēneō, vēnīs, vēnit**, etc. (cf. **queō** and **nequeō** above).

(g) An archaic form of the present passive infinitive (14.1/3) in which **-ier** replaces **-ī** is sometimes used by poets: **amārier** (= **amārī**), **monērier** (= **monērī**), **regier** (= **regī**), **audīrier** (= **audīrī**). There is no difference in meaning.

25.2 Latin reading

1 Hectora quis nosset, felix si Troia fuisset?
2 Tu regere imperio populos, Romane, memento
      (hae tibi erunt artes) pacisque imponere morem,
      parcere subiectis et debellare superbos.
3 Odi et amo. quare id faciam, fortasse requiris.
         nescio, sed fieri sentio et excrucior.
4 Inventa sunt specula ut homo ipse se nosset.
5 Vixere fortes ante Agamemnona
   multi, sed omnes illacrimabiles
      urgentur ignotique longa
         nocte, carent quia vate sacro.

6 Romulus, arma ad caelum tollens, 'Iuppiter, tuis' inquit 'iussus
avibus hic in Palatio prima urbi fundamenta ieci.'

7 Sic fatus validis ingentem viribus hastam contorsit.

8 Aenean fundantem arces ac tecta novantem conspicit.

9 Forsan et haec olim meminisse iuvabit.

10 Aut amat aut odit mulier: nihil est tertium.

11 Flectere si nequeo Superos, Acheronta movebo.

12   Tu, Tityre, lentus in umbra
formosam resonare doces Amaryllida silvas.

13 Mecum una in silvis imitabere Pana canendo.

14 Augur cum esset, dicere ausus est optimis auspiciis ea geri quae
pro rei publicae salute gerantur.

15 Nil ait esse prius, melius nil, caelibe vita.

16 Non ego mendosos ausim defendere mores.

17 Quis caelum posset, nisi caeli munere, nosse,
et reperire deum nisi qui pars ipse deorum?

18 Canis caninam non est.

Notes

1 **nosset** (= **nōvisset**) is the equivalent of an imperfect subjunctive
(25.1/5*b*).

2 **populōs** the various peoples whom the Romans had incorporated
into their empire.

5 *l*.1 **vixēre** <**vīvō**. *ll*.2–4 the prose order would be **omnēs,
illacrimābilēs ignōtīque, longā nocte** (instrumental ablative 7.1/4)
urgentur, quia vāte sacrō carent; **carent** with abl. (20.1/1). *l*.4 **vāte
sacrō** a poet was sacred because he was divinely inspired.

9 **et** *even*.

11 **Acherōn**, a river of the Underworld, is used here to signify the
gods of the Underworld.

13 **ūnā** the feminine ablative singular of **ūnus** is regularly used as an
adverb meaning *together*.

17 **mūnere** <**mūnus**; after **quī** supply **est**.

18 With **canīnam** supply **carnem** (<**carō**) *flesh*; **ēst** see above 25.1/5*d*.

25.3 Extra reading

Leander to Hero

Leander, a youth of Abydos on the south side of the Hellespont, was in love with Hero, a girl from Sestos on the opposite shore, and swam across each evening to visit her. Here, in a letter to his beloved written while he was confined to Abydos by bad weather, Leander describes his first crossing. The passage is from Ovid's *Heroides* (see 18.3). The story, which ends in Leander's death, was the subject of a poem begun by the Elizabethan dramatist, Christopher Marlowe (*On Hellespont, guilty of true love's blood,/ In view and opposite two cities stood . . .*).

> Nox erat incipiens (namque est meminisse voluptas)
>   cum foribus patriis egrediebar amans.
> nec mora, deposito pariter cum veste timore,
>   iactabam liquido bracchia lenta mari.
> unda repercussae radiabat imagine lunae,
>   et nitor in tacita nocte diurnus erat.
> iamque fatigatis umero sub utroque lacertis
>   fortiter in summas erigor altus aquas.
> ut procul aspexi lumen, 'meus ignis in illo est:
>   illa meum' dixi 'litora numen habent.'
> et subito lassis vires rediere lacertis,
>   visaque, quam fuerat, mollior unda mihi.
> excipis amplexu, feliciaque oscula iungis,
>   oscula, di magni! trans mare digna peti.

The metre is the elegiac couplet. Scan the first six lines.

Notes

*l.*1 **erat incipiens** = **incipiēbat** *was beginning. l.*2 **foribus patriīs** lit. *from paternal door* (ablative of place from which 28.1/2*d*; **forēs** plural because the front door on Roman buildings was usually double) i.e. *from my father's door*; **amans** lit. *loving* (with *I*, the understood subject of **ēgrediēbar**) but this is not in accord with English idiom and we would normally use a phrase such as *full of love. l.*3 supply **erat** with **mora** *there was no delay*, i.e. *I did not delay. l.*4 **iactābam** *I started to toss*, the imperfect is sometimes used in the sense *begin to, start to* (2.1/3 note). *l.*5 **unda** lit. *wave* but often used in poetry to mean simply *water.* *l.*6 **nitor . . . diurnus** *the day-brightness,* i.e. *the brightness of day.* *l.*8 **ērigor** vivid present *I raise myself* (the passive is used here for an action done to oneself); **in summās . . . aquās** plural for singular *to the top of the water* (21.1/3), Leander wants to see how close he is to Sestos. *l.*9 **meus ignis** *my flame,* i.e. the person who is inspiring him with love; **in illō** *in it,* i.e. the light he sees – Leander somewhat fancifully supposes that his flame, Hero, is creating the light which guides him to Sestos. *l.*11 **lassīs lacertīs** *to my weary shoulders,* dative of motion (28.1/1*j*). *l.*13 both verbs are vivid presents; with **excipis** supply **mē**.

UNIT 26

26.1 Grammar

26.1/1 Further uses of the infinitive

(a) We have already seen how an infinitive can be the subject of a verb (18.1/1): **nihil agere mē dēlectat** *to do nothing pleases me.*[1] An infinitive can also be used as the object of a verb: **errāre, nescīre, et malum et turpe dūcimus** *we consider to make mistakes, to be ignorant, both wrong and disgraceful.* After prepositions the gerund, not the infinitive, is used (18.1/1).

(b) A large number of verbs in Latin can be followed by an infinitive, and in almost every case English idiom is the same. These verbs can express:

  (i) ability and inability, as **possum, queō, nequeō**: **iam fragilīs poteram ā terrīs contingere rāmōs** *already I was able to touch brittle twigs from the ground.*

  (ii) wish, intention, effort, as **volō, mālō, optō, statuō, cōnor, temptō, audeō**: **nocte silentī fallere custōdēs foribusque excēdere temptant** *in the silent night they try to deceive the guards and go out by the doors.*

  When the infinitive after a verb of wishing has its own subject, we have an accusative and infinitive: **volō tē hoc facere** *I want you to do this.* Because, however, such sentences can be regarded as virtual orders, we can instead have an indirect command (**ut/nē** + subj., 21.1/2) with no difference in sense: **volō ut hoc facias.**

---

[1]In English we can also use a verbal noun as a subject: *doing nothing pleases me.* This is not possible in Latin.

    (iii) obligation, habit, as **dēbeō, soleō**: **scīre suōs fīnēs mātrōna dēbet** *a matron should know her limits.*[1]

    (iv) beginning, stopping, as **incipiō, dēsinō, dēsistō**: **dēsine fāta deum flectī spērāre precandō** *cease to hope that the will* (lit. *fates*) *of the gods is bent by praying.*

    (v) knowing, teaching, learning. In English, when *know* and sometimes *teach* and *learn* are followed by an infinitive, *how* is inserted; no similar word is used in Latin: **vincere scīs, Hannibal: victōriā ūtī nescīs** *you know how to conquer, Hannibal; you do not know how to use victory.*

(c) Verbs in categories (b) (i) – (iv) can be followed by **esse** *to be* and an adjective, e.g. *I want to be happy.* As the adjective refers to the subject it must be in the nominative: **volō laetus esse**. In place of an adjective we may have a noun: **morī mālō quam servus esse** *I prefer to die than to be a slave.* The same construction occurs with verbal forms meaning *be said, be thought, seem* (cf. 15.1/3): **dīcitur Homērus caecus fuisse** *Homer is said to have been blind.*

(d) An infinitive is often used to replace the imperfect indicative in narration (**historic infinitive**). This was regarded as producing a vivid effect (cf. vivid present), and it occurs in both prose and verse. Nouns, pronouns and adjectives are in exactly the same case as they would be if the verb were finite. The construction is usually confined to main clauses. A number of infinitives can be used in a single sentence without any conjunction:

    Intereā Catilīna cum expedītīs in primā aciē versārī, labōrantibus succurrere, integrōs prō sauciīs arcessere, omnia prōvidēre, multum ipse pugnāre, saepe hostem ferīre. *Meanwhile Catiline was busy in the front line with the light-armed troops, was helping those in difficulty, calling up fresh men in place of the wounded, looking after everything, fighting much himself, often striking the enemy.*

---

[1]**Dēbeō** can duplicate the gerundive in sentences of this kind. We can have, with exactly the same meaning, **suī fīnēs mātrōnae sciendī sunt** (**suus** can be used with the subject in passive clauses where the person referred to by it is in another case); cf. 22. 1/1c note.

26.1/2 Noun clauses

Noun clauses function as nouns, to which they bear the same relation as adjectival clauses to adjectives, and adverbial clauses to adverbs. Their use, however, is restricted. Except for **quod** clauses (below (*d*)), they only occur with certain types of verbs and verbal expressions and can be classified accordingly. These include indirect command and petition (21.1/2) and indirect questions (23.1/3); in *he asked whether I had been to Greece*, the indirect question *whether I had been to Greece* is the object of the verb *ask* and so is performing the function of a noun.

(*a*) *Verbs of fearing, as* **metuō, vereor, timeō**

A noun clause after a verb expressing fear is introduced by **nē** and has its verb in the subjunctive. The tense will depend on the sequence of tenses table given in 23.1/3, except that the present subjunctive is normally used to express a fear for the future in primary sequence:

> **Metuit nē uxor resciscat.** *He is afraid that* (lit. *lest*) *his wife may find out.*
> **Metuō nē nimis stultē fēcerim.** *I am afraid that I may have acted particularly stupidly.*
> **Veritus sum nē facerēs idem quod multī servī solent.** *I was afraid that you might do the same as many slaves normally do* (lit. *which many slaves are accustomed* i.e. *to do*).
> **Verēbāminī nē nōn id facerem?** *Were you afraid that I might not do it?*

As in the last example, the **nē** clause can contain a negative. Often, however, **nē nōn** is replaced by **ut**, as though the two negatives cancelled each other. Sentences with this use of **ut** have the opposite meaning to what we might think at first sight:

> **Vidēris verērī ut epistulās tuās accēperim.** *You seem to be afraid that I have not received your letters.*
> **Metuō ut fierī possit.** *I am afraid that it could not happen.*

Where in English a verb of fearing is followed by an infinitive, Latin has the same construction: **equitēs intrāre fūmum et flammam densissam timēbant** *the horsemen were afraid to enter the smoke and very thick fire.*

(b) **Dubitō** *and expressions of doubting*

When **dubitō** *doubt* and expressions of doubting such as **dubium est** *it is doubtful* or **incertum est** *it is uncertain* are used positively and followed by a clause, the latter is treated as an indirect question (23.1/3): **dubitāvī utrum hōs hominēs emerem necne** *I was doubtful whether I should buy these people or not.*

Dubitō an has the special sense of *I am inclined to think that* (cf. **haud sciō an** 23.1/3 note 3; **dubitō num** means *I doubt if*): **Dārīus dubitābat an dēdecus fugae honestā morte vītāret** *Darius was inclined to think that he should avoid the disgrace of flight by a noble death.*

When **dubitō** and **dubium est** are negated[1] or occur in questions, a following clause is always introduced by **quīn** and has its verb in the subjunctive. This conjunction, which has other uses (see below), means *how not/but that*, but is here more naturally translated by *that*:

> **Haud dubium est quīn Chremēs tibi nōn det nātam.** *There is no doubt that Chremes won't give you his daughter.*
> **Nōn dubium est quīn uxōrem nōlit fīlius meus.** *There is no doubt that my son does not want a wife.*
> **Nōn dubitārī dēbet quīn fuerint ante Homērum poētae.** *It ought not be doubted that there were poets before Homer.*

Other similar expressions such as **contrōversia nōn est** *there is no dispute* and **nōn ambigitur** *it is not uncertain* are also followed by **quīn** and the subjunctive.

(c) *Verbs of hindering, preventing and forbidding*

In English *hinder, prevent* and similar verbs are followed by the preposition *from* and a verbal noun: *I prevented him from going. Forbid* is normally followed by an infinitive: *I forbid you to do this.* In Latin all such verbs (except for **vetō** and, sometimes, **prohibeō** – see below) must be followed by a subordinate clause with its verb in the subjunctive. If the main clause is positive the subordinate clause is introduced by **nē** or **quōminus**; the latter literally means *by which* (**quō**) *not* (**minus** *less* is used here as an adverb of negation), but is synonymous with **nē** in the sense *so that . . . not*:

---

[1]The obsolescent negative **haud** (= **nōn**) is very often used with both.

Impedior dolōre animī nē dē huius miseriā plūra dīcam. *I am prevented by my grief of mind from saying more about this man's unhappiness.*

Tē infirmitās valētūdinis tuae tenuit quōminus ad lūdōs venīrēs. *The weakness of your health prevented you from coming to the games.*

When the main clause is negated **quōminus** or **quīn** is used:

Nōn tē impediō quōminus susceptum negōtium gerere possīs. *I am not hindering you from being able to do the business you have undertaken.*

Germānī retinērī nōn potuērunt quīn in nostrōs tēla conicerent. *The Germans could not be restrained from hurling weapons at our men.*

Vetō *forbid* takes an accusative and infinitive (21.1/2 note 1); **prohibeō** *prevent* can either follow **vetō** or take the above construction: **prohibuērunt signum ab hoste capī** or **prohibuērunt quōminus** (or **nē**) **signum ab hoste caperētur** *they prevented the standard from being captured by the enemy.*

(d) *Noun clauses introduced by* quod

Quod has three functions as a pronoun and adjective (10.1/1*f–i*) and can also be a subordinating conjunction meaning *because* (29.1/2). In addition, in the sense of *(the fact) that*, it serves as the conjunction to introduce a certain type of noun clause which always expresses fact and has its verb in the indicative. Such clauses can stand as the subject or object of a verb:

Percommodē factum est quod dē morte et dē dolōre disputātum est. *It has happened very opportunely that death and pain have been discussed* (lit. [*the fact*] *that it has been discussed about death and pain has happened . . .*).

Adicite ad haec quod foedus aequum dedimus. *Add* (adicite <adiciō) *to these things* [*the fact*] *that we granted an equal treaty.*

They may also be in apposition to a preceding noun or pronoun: **hōc ūnō praestāmus maximē ferīs, quod colloquimur inter nōs** *we are most superior to beasts in this one thing,* [*namely*] *that we talk with each other.*

(e) *Noun clauses introduced by* ut (nōn)

Indirect commands and petitions have exactly the same construction as purpose clauses (**ut/nē** and the subjunctive, 21.1/2). This is also the construction used after a number of other verbs such as **caveō** *take care* and **hortor** *urge* (21.1/2 note 2), where the following noun clause expresses what the subject of the main verb does or does not want. We can, however, have sentences of the type **accidit ut in forō heri essem** *it happened that I was in the forum yesterday* in which a simple fact is stated. Such noun clauses are treated in the same way as result clauses, where we also have a subjunctive expressing a fact (16.1/1). Consequently **ut nōn, ut nēmō**, etc. (not **nē, nē ullus**, etc.) are used when the clause is negated. This construction can occur after:

(i)   **faciō** and certain of its compounds[1] with the sense *bring it about* [*that*];
(ii) certain impersonal uses as **accidit, fit, ēvenit** (all meaning *it happens*), and **restat** *it remains*;
(iii) various expressions consisting of **est** (**erat**, etc.) with a word or phrase which is explained or defined by the following noun clause.
      Ut here can often be translated by *that*, but sometimes the clause it introduces is best rendered by a phrase.

Perfēcit Dēmosthenēs ut nēmō plānius locūtus esse putārētur.
Demosthenes's achievement was (lit. *D. brought it about*) *that no one was thought to have spoken more clearly.*

Ita fit ut omnīnō nēmō esse possit beātus. *Thus it happens that no one can be completely happy.*

Fuit occāsiō ut argentum daret. *There was an opportunity for him to give the money.*

Nōn mōs erat Graecōrum ut in convīviō virōrum accumberent mulierēs. *It was not the custom of the Greeks that women should have a place* (lit. *lie down*) *at a men's banquet.*

---

[1] Usage with **faciō** and its compounds can vary; and when the intention of the subject, rather than the result, is emphasised, the other construction is used. In practice this only means that we have **nē**, and not **ut nōn** if the noun clause is negated: **efficiam posthāc nē quemquam vōce lacessās** *I shall see to it* (lit. *cause*) *that after this you will not challenge anyone to sing* (lit. *with your voice*).

(f) *Other uses of* quīn

Quīn + subjunctive is also used after various other expressions, all of which involve a negative but are not covered by categories (*b*) and (*c*). In most cases it is the equivalent of **ut nōn** when used to introduce noun clauses or result clauses and must be translated by *that . . . not.*[1]

> **Nullō modō potest fierī quīn dōs dētur virginī.** *In no way can it happen that a dowry is not given to the girl.*
> **Nīl tam difficile est quīn quaerendō investīgārī possit.** *Nothing is so difficult that it cannot be tracked down by searching.*

In **nēmō est quīn** . . . *there is no one who does not* . . . and similar expressions, **quīn** is the equivalent of a relative pronoun followed by **nōn**: **nēmō Lilybaeī fuit quīn hoc vīderit, nēmō in Siciliā quīn audierit** *there was no one at Lilybaeum who did not see this, there was no one in Sicily who did not hear of it.*

In its remaining uses **quīn** functions as an adverb introducing main clauses but these may conveniently be mentioned here. In its original sense of an interrogative adverb *how not/why not*, it can be used in direct questions: **quīn ego hoc rogem?** *why should I not ask this?* (**rogem** deliberative subjunctive, 22.1/1*d*).

As an emphasising adverb (sometimes with **etiam**) it is placed at the beginning of a statement which corroborates and reinforces what precedes. Here it is to be translated *further, indeed, in fact,* and has no negative force:

> **Troiae sub moenibus altīs**
> **tot nātī cecidēre deum. quīn occidit ūnā**
> **Sarpēdōn, mea prōgeniēs.**
> *So many sons of gods fell beneath the lofty walls of Troy. Indeed, Sarpedon, my offspring, died with them* (**ūnā** *together*).

Also, as an emphasising adverb, it can strengthen an imperative. We may translate this use by *well*: **quīn ergo rape mē: quid cessās?** *well, then, seize me; why are you delaying?*

---

[1] The difference between **quīn** here and in (*b*) where it is to be translated by *that* is confusing. Its basic meaning as a conjunction *but that* can be used in both cases to give a rough translation.

26.2 Latin reading

1 Pallida mors aequo pulsat pede pauperum tabernas
    regumque turris. o beate Sesti,
  vitae summa brevis spem nos vetat incohare longam.
2 Aetas non impedit quominus litterarum studia teneamus usque
  ad ultimum tempus senectutis.
3 Adde quod non horam tecum esse potes.
4 Incipe, parve puer, risu cognoscere matrem.
5 Intellexi te vereri ne superiores litterae mihi redditae non essent.
6 Quod spiro et placeo, si placeo, tuum est.
7 Ornamenta quae locavi, metuo ut possim recipere.
8 Dubitandum non est quin numquam possit utilitas cum honestate
  contendere.
9 Quod formas hominum habetis, indignantur. quin etiam, si dis
  placet, nefas aiunt esse consulem plebeium fieri.
10 In castello nemo fuit omnino militum quin vulneraretur.
11 Fit ut in somnis facere hoc videatur imago.
12 Milites aegre tunc sunt retenti quin oppidum irrumperent,
  graviterque eam rem tulerunt, quod stetisse per Trebonium
  quominus oppido potirentur videbatur.

A confused battle
13 Ceterum facies totius negoti vana, incerta, foeda atque
  miserabilis. dispersi a suis, pars cedere, alii insequi: neque signa
  neque ordines observare: ubi quemque periculum ceperat, ibi
  resistere ac propulsare: arma, tela, equi, viri, hostes atque cives
  permixti: nihil consilio neque imperio agi: fors omnia regere.
14 Est mos hominum ut nolint eundem pluribus rebus excellere.

A nasty trick foiled
15 Qua in fuga Fabius Paelignus quidam ex infimis ordinibus de
  exercitu Curionis primum agmen fugientium consecutus magna
  voce Varum nomine appellans requirebat, uti unus esse ex eius
  militibus et monere aliquid velle ac dicere videretur. ubi ille
  saepius appellatus aspexit ac restitit et quis esset aut quid vellet   5
  quaesivit, umerum apertum gladio appetivit paulumque afuit
  quin Varum interficeret: quod ille periculum sublato ad eius
  conatum scuto vitavit. Fabius a proximis militibus circumventus
  interficitur.

16   Nil habet infelix paupertas durius in se
     quam quod ridiculos homines facit.
17   In omni calamitate infelicissimum est genus infortunii, fuisse felicem.
18   Absurdum est ut alios regat qui se ipsum regere nescit.

Notes

1   Death does not knock politely at the door of either poor or rich;
he kicks it with his foot.

2   **litterārum** *literature*; **studia** we would use the singular *pursuit* in
English.

3   **hōram** acc. to express time how long (5.1/4).

5   **redditae . . . essent** here **reddō** means *give*, not *give back*.

9   **sī dīs placet** lit. *if it pleases the gods*, an expression used to avert
divine anger at what might possibly be seen as human
presumption (cf. **sī fas est** in Catullus's poem to Lesbia, 16.2, 18);
here, as often, it is used ironically.

11   **in somnīs** *during sleep*.

12   The adverb **aegrē** *with difficulty* with a verb of hindering or
preventing is followed by the same construction as **nōn**; the idiom
per aliquem stat *it is due to someone* [*that*] is followed by **quōminus**
(or **nē**) to express an action that is prevented.

13   This passage comes from the *Jugurtha* of Sallust, a contemporary
of Caesar and Cicero who affected a terse, epigrammatic style;
this is particularly evident here in his use of the historic infinitive
(26.1/1*d*). In the first sentence supply **erat**; after **dispersī** (nom. pl.)
we would have expected **aliī . . . aliī** *some . . . others*, but for variety
Sallust uses **pars . . . aliī** *part . . . others* with the same sense.

14   **plūribus** *too many* (19.1/3).

15   *l.*1 **Quā in fugā** connects this sentence with the preceding one. *l.*2
consecūtus would be better translated into English as a finite verb.
*l.*4. **monēre aliquid . . . ac dīcere** *to warn something and say*
[*something*], i.e. *to give some warning and say something*; **ubi ille**
translate *when Varus*; as Latin has a more flexible system of
pronouns than English, confusion can often result if we translate
all Latin pronouns by pronouns in English (the same applies in
*l.*7). *l.*5 **restitit** <**resistō** *stop*. *ll.*6f. **paulum āfuit** (<**absum**) **quīn**, etc.,
it was little lacking but that he killed, i.e. *he almost killed . . . l.*9
interficitur vivid present.

26.3 Extra reading

Gyges and the magic ring of invisibility

Gyges, cum terra discessisset magnis quibusdam imbribus, descendit
in illum hiatum, aëneumque equum, ut ferunt fabulae, animadvertit,
cuius in lateribus fores erant: quibus apertis, hominis mortui vidit
corpus magnitudine inusitata anulumque aureum in digito: quem ut
detraxit, ipse induit – erat enim regius pastor – tum in concilium se   5
pastorum recepit. ibi cum palam eius anuli ad palmam converterat, a
nullo videbatur, ipse autem omnia videbat: idem rursus videbatur,
cum in locum anulum inverterat. itaque hac opportunitate anuli usus
regem dominum interemit, sustulitque quos obstare arbitrabatur: nec
in his eum facinoribus quisquam potuit videre. sic repente anuli   10
beneficio rex exortus est Lydiae.

Notes

*l.*1 **imbribus** abl. of cause (7.1/4). *l.*2 **ferunt** *say, tell. l.*3 **quibus apertīs**
which having been opened (referring back to **forēs**) i.e. *when he opened
them*; Latin often joins a sentence to the previous one by the relative
pronoun or adjective (see note on 17.3); **apertīs** we know that it was
Gyges who opened the doors because he is the subject of the main
verb **vīdit** (if someone else had done it this would have been
mentioned – see 11.1/3). *l.*4 **inūsitātā; quem** refers to **anulum** – the
literal translation of this and the following words is *which when he
took off, he put on himself* (the relative pronoun is used as in *l.*3). *l.*6
(and *l.*8) **cum** + pluperfect indicative *whenever* (16.1/3*d*). *ll.*7f. **īdem** (lit.
the same man) is used here in a weakened sense *likewise, he. l.*8 **hāc
opportūnitāte ūsus** lit. *using the opportunity of* (i.e. *given by*) *the ring.
ll.*9f. **nec . . . quisquam** *and no one* (3.1/6).

UNIT 27

27.1 Grammar

27.1/1 Introduction to further uses of cases in Latin

All the Latin cases, except the vocative, can be used in more than one way. Some of these have already been described; others have been mentioned in notes on sentences and passages for translation. In this unit and the next all their main uses are listed, together with a description of those not previously treated. This list is undoubtedly formidable, and an attempt to absorb it in its entirety on first reading could lead to severe indigestion. A better plan is to get a general idea of the range of uses of each case (particularly those where English idiom is different), and then to refer back when confronted with particular instances. The name given to each use is traditional and in nearly every instance is an adequate short description.

Here, as elsewhere, it is necessary to fit linguistic phenomena into pigeon-holes. This can give the impression that distinctions are more clear-cut than is sometimes the case. As indicated below, there is an overlap between certain uses, and we frequently meet examples that can be classified in more than one way.

27.1/2 Nominative and vocative (see 1.1/3*a*, *b*)

The nominative is used for the predicate of a finite copulative verb as well as for the subject of a finite verb: **is nōnnumquam stultus putātur** *he was sometimes thought a fool* (see 2.1/4 and 15.1/3).

27.1/3 Accusative

Apart from its use as the case of the direct object of transitive verbs (1.1/3*c*) and after most prepositions (3.1/4), the accusative can function in a number of ways, some of which require rephrasing to be turned into normal English.

(*a*) *Accusative and infinitive* (see 17.1/2)

(*b*) *Accusative of respect*

This use (chiefly poetical) qualifies adjectives and verbs. Its literal meaning is obtained by prefixing the noun involved with the words *in respect of*; but, as we do not have a similar construction in English, some rearrangement is necessary for an idiomatic translation. In **fēminae nūdae bracchia** *women naked* [*in respect of*] *arms*, **bracchia** is accusative of respect and qualifies **nūdae**; the idiomatic translation would be *women with naked arms*. **Tremis ossa pavōre** means literally *you are trembling from fear* (**pavōre**) [*with respect of*] *bones*, but idiomatic English requires *your bones are trembling from fear*. Other examples are:

Percussa novā mentem formīdine māter . . . *The mother, smitten* [*in respect of*] *mind by a new fear . . .* i.e. *the mother, her mind smitten by a new fear . . .*

Terga et pectora tēlīs transfīgitur. *He is pierced* [*in respect of*] *back and chest* (both plural for singular) *by weapons*, i.e. *his back and chest are pierced with weapons*.

When the accusative is used in this way with the passive of verbs meaning *put on* (**induō**), *take off* (**exuō**) and the like, the verb is to be translated as active; this is an imitation of a Greek construction used for actions done to oneself:

Clipeum aurōque trilīcem lōrīcam induitur. *He puts on his shield and corselet triple-threaded with gold.*

Terrificōs umerīs Aetōlus amictūs exuitur. *The Aetolian takes off the terrifying cloak* (plural for singular) *from his shoulders.*

Caeruleōs implexae crīnibus anguīs Eumenidēs (15.3 *ll*.19–20).

(*c*) *Accusative of exclamation*

This is used in expressions of amazement, admiration or distress; it is normally, but not always, preceded by **Ō, heu** or a similar word: **Ō hominem impūrum!** *O the vile man!* **Ō occāsiōnem mīrificum!** *What a wonderful opportunity!* (lit. *O wonderful opportunity!*) **Heu mē infēlīcem!** *Alas unhappy me!* This use is different from a vocative; **Ō homō impūre!** is used for addressing a vile man, **Ō hominem impūrum!** for deploring him.

(*d*) *Cognate accusative*

This is a noun etymologically related to the verb (nearly always otherwise intransitive) by which it is governed. Its simplest form is of the type **vītam vīvere** *to live a life,* **cursum currere** *to run a race,* but it is normally accompanied by an adjective or by a noun in the genitive:

>**Cūr nōn eōsdem cursūs cucurrērunt?** *Why did they not run the same courses?*
>**Mīrum atque inscītum somniāvī somnium.** *I have dreamt a remarkable and strange dream.*
>**Hannōnem īre iter ūnīus diēī iussit.** *He ordered Hanno to go on a one-day journey.*

Also included under this heading are accusatives used in exactly the same way but with nouns not etymologically related to the preceding verb: **semper longam incomitāta vidētur īre viam** *she always seems to be going unaccompanied* (**incomitāta**) *on a long journey* (**longam viam** = **longum iter**).

(*e*) *Adverbial accusative*

This is a neuter singular pronoun or a neuter adjective used as an adverb. **Nihil** *nothing* is very frequently so used and has the sense of an emphatic negative: **nihil verēmur istōs** *we are not at all afraid of those men.* Likewise the interrogative **quid?** *what?* is used to mean *in respect to what?* i.e. *why?* **quid hīc nunc stās?** *why are you standing here now?* With adjectives this construction is poetical: **dulce rīdentem Lalagēn amābō, dulce loquentem** *I shall love Lalage laughing sweetly, talking sweetly* (from Horace).

(*f*) *Verbs taking two accusatives*

These occur in Latin as in English (*they made him king; she asked me my opinion*) and can be divided into two categories:

(i) Verbs of making, calling, thinking, etc. (factitive verbs), after which the first word in the accusative can be followed by a predicate, which is also in the accusative: **is mē hērēdem fēcit** *he made me an heir*; **omnēs Vercingetōrigem probant imperātōrem** *all approve of Vercingetorix as commander*; **hominēs caecōs reddit cupiditās** *greed makes men blind.* When such clauses are put into the passive, both accusatives become nominative: **ab eō hērēs factus sum** *I was made an heir by him* (cf. 15.1/3).

(ii) **Doceō** *teach*, **rogō** *ask* (*a question*),[1] and a few others can be followed by one accusative stating who is being taught, asked, etc. and another indicating what is being taught, asked, etc. (English usage is the same with *teach* and *ask* but varies with other verbs):

> **Posteā Racilius mē prīmum sententiam rogāvit.** *Afterwards Racilius asked me first for my opinion.*
> **Is hunc hominem cursūrum docuit.** *He taught this man [the art of] running.*

If clauses of this type are put into the passive with the person taught or asked as the subject, the case of the noun expressing what is taught or asked is not altered (***retained accusative***): **ā Raciliō sententiam rogātus sum** *I was asked my opinion by Racilius.*

(*g*) *Accusative to express time how long* (see 5.1/4*a*)

(*h*) *Accusative to express motion towards* (see 8.1/3)

In poetry the accusative can be used in this sense with any nouns indicating a place:

> **Arma virumque canō, Troiae quī prīmus ab ōrīs**
> **Ītaliam, fātō profugus, Lāvīniaque vēnit**
> **lītora** (Vergil, *Aeneid I*, 1–3).
> *I sing of arms and of the man who, an exile by fate, first came from the shores of Troy to Italy and the Lavinian coasts.*

(*i*) *Accusative to express spatial extent and dimension* (see 13.1/7)

27.1/4 Genitive

A noun in the genitive in Latin can qualify another noun, an adjective, a verb, or even an adverb. Most of its uses are to be translated by *of*; the possessive genitive can also be rendered by the normal English genitive (*man's, Rome's*), while in a few senses some supplement or change is necessary.

---

[1]On the meaning and construction of two verbs **quaerō** and **petō**, which also mean *ask*, see the vocabulary.

(a) **Possessive genitive**
This use normally indicates simple possession: **domus Cicerōnis** *the house of Cicero* (or *Cicero's house*). It can also be used for the author of a book or, more generally, for a person who has made something: **Aenēis Vergilī** *Vergil's Aeneid*, **statua Pheidiae** *a statue by Pheidias*. In some cases the relationship between the genitive and the other noun is one of association rather than actual possession: **commoda pācis** *the advantages of peace*, **labor obsidiōnis** *the toil of a siege*.

A possessive genitive (usually of a pronominal adjective) can be used together with a possessive adjective: **meus ipsīus pater** *my own father* (we might have expected a Latin expression like *the father of me myself*).

In certain very restricted contexts the genitive of a proper noun qualifies a missing word such as *wife, son, daughter, house*, etc., which can be supplied from a knowledge of the story or circumstances involved (cf. *If there's one place where I refuse to eat it's Colonel Sander's*): **Dēiphobē Glaucī, fātur quae tālia rēgī . . .** *Deiphobe* [*the daughter*] *of Glaucus, who says such things to the king . . .*

(b) **Genitive of characteristic** (see 6.1/4)
A possessive genitive can be used predicatively, as: **omnia, quae mulieris fuērunt, virī fīunt nōmine dōtis** *everything which belonged to a woman becomes her husband's by way of dowry* (lit. *all things which were of a woman become of her man under the title of dowry*) and the genitive of characteristic is a special case of this.

(c) **Genitive of quality or description** (see 6.1/3)
This can also be used to express:
(i) age: **puella annōrum undecim** *a girl eleven years old* (we can also say **puella undecim annōs nāta**, 5.1/4*a*), **Falernum annōrum centum** *Falernian* [*wine*] *a hundred years old*;
(ii) size: **pons pedum quinquāgintā** *a bridge of fifty feet* (or **pons pedēs quinquāgintā longus** lit. *a bridge fifty feet long* – 13.1/7);
(iii) number: **classis centum nāvium** *a fleet of a hundred ships*.
In all cases the genitive must be accompanied by an adjective.

(d) **Genitive of value** (see 7.1/5)
As this genitive describes the noun of which it is predicated it is close in meaning to (*c*).

(*e*) *Attributive genitive*
This genitive performs the same function as an attributive adjective;
we may say *a crown of gold* or *a golden crown*. This use too is similar
to (*c*), but the term is confined to genitives giving the content or
material of the noun qualified and need not be accompanied by an
adjective: **praemia pecūniae** *rewards of money* or *monetary rewards*;
acervus frūmentī *a pile of grain*.

(*f*) *Appositional genitive*
This genitive (sometimes called *genitive of definition*) defines more
precisely what is meant by the noun it governs, and stands in the same
relation to it as a noun in apposition. It is sometimes to be translated
by *of*, sometimes simply by using apposition: **virtūtēs continentiae,**
gravitātis, iustitiae *the virtues of self-restraint, sobriety, justice* (or *the*
virtues, self-restraint, sobriety, justice); **familia Scīpiōnum** *the family of*
the Scipios; **haec vox voluptātis** *this word 'pleasure'*. In English it is the
genitive used with place-names in expressions such as *the city of*
Rome, but here Latin normally uses apposition: **urbs Rōma**.

(*g*) *Genitive with verbs*
This genitive falls under three headings:

(i) intransitive verbs followed by the genitive (see 20.1/1);
(ii) impersonal verbs followed by the genitive (see 20.1/2*b*);
(iii) verbs followed by an accusative and a genitive.

Most of the last group are legal terms, and often the English
equivalent has the same construction. The most important are:

absolvō, -ere *acquit*	**condemnō, -āre** *condemn*
accūsō, -āre *accuse*	**convincō, -ere** *convict*
arguō, -ere *charge*	**damnō, -āre** *condemn*

Aedīlēs aliquot mātrōnās probrī accūsāvērunt. *The aediles accused*
some married women of disgraceful conduct.
Tē convincō nōn inhūmānitātis sōlum sed etiam āmentiae. *I convict*
you not only of cruelty but also of madness.

(*h*) *Genitive with adjectives*

The genitive was used with a certain range of adjectives by Cicero and
his contemporaries, but this was considerably extended by the time of
Silver Latin (see 1.3). Most adjectives followed by a genitive in Golden

Age prose are best treated under the broader heading of *objective genitive* (see below); apart from these we have adjectives denoting fullness or deficiency, which may take either the genitive or the ablative (see 28.1/2*l*): **omnia plēna consiliōrum, inānia verbōrum, vidēmus** *we see everything full of plans* [*but*] *empty of words.*

From Vergil and Horace onwards the genitive with adjectives was used with the meaning *in respect of* (*genitive of respect*): **atrox odiī Agrippīna** *Agrippina, cruel in respect of her hatred,* i.e. *cruel in her hatred* (see also 28.1/2*l*).

(*i*) *Objective genitive*

In this construction, which we also have in English, a genitive stands in the same relation to a noun or adjective as an object does to a transitive verb. In *Nero's love of orgies exceeded all bounds,* the genitive *of orgies* is objective because the sense connection between *orgies* and *love* is the same as between an object and a verb. We could say, with the same meaning, *Nero loved orgies; this exceeded all bounds.* Other examples, where English and Latin idiom coincide, are:

> **interfectōrēs Caesaris** *Caesar's murderers*; **amor suī** *love of oneself,* i.e. *self-love*; **metus mortis** *fear of death*; **apēs, ventūrae hiemis memorēs** *bees, mindful of the coming winter*; **Mettius foederis Rōmānī Albānīque ruptor est** *Mettius is the breaker of the Roman and Alban treaty.*

This use is more widely extended in Latin and we must sometimes translate it by *for* or some other preposition:

> **Avidum pugnae Ascanium prohibent.** *They restrain Ascanius* [*who is*] *eager for battle.*
> **Uterque patefēcit eārum ipsārum rērum aditum.** *Each of the two has opened up an approach to these very things.*

On the use of **nostrī/vestrī** as objective genitives see 8.1/1 note 3.

(*j*) *Subjective genitive*

This genitive stands in the same relation to a noun as a subject does to a verb: **coniūrātiō Catilīnae** *the conspiracy of Catiline*; **minae Clōdiī** *the threats of Clodius.* This use is really only a variety of the possessive genitive; it merits special mention because a genitive can sometimes be interpreted as either subjective or objective, and a choice must be made from the context. **Metus hostium** can mean *the fear inspired by the enemy* (*fear of the enemy*) or *the fear felt by the enemy* (*the enemy's fear*).

(*k*) *Partitive genitive*

This use is not satisfactorily named, as it suggests that the genitive here is used to express a part. In fact, in phrases involving this construction (which consists of a noun, pronoun, adjective, or adverb used as a noun followed by a genitive), the genitive expresses the whole and the other word a part of that whole: **multī Gallōrum** *many of the Gauls*; **trēs nostrum** *three of us*[1] (on the use of **nostrum/vestrum** here, see 8.1/1 note 3).

This genitive frequently follows the neuter singular of a pronoun or of an adjective of quantity where English uses a noun with an accompanying adjective: **multum temporis** (= **multum tempus**) *much of time*, i.e. *much time*; **quid novī?** (= **quid novum?**) *what news?*; **aliquid sollicitūdinis** (= **aliqua sollicitūdō**) *some worry*. The most common pronouns and adjectives used are: **aliquid, id, quid** (interrogative and indefinite), **quicquam, nihil, hoc, quod, tantum, quantum, multum, minus**. This construction is obligatory with **plūs** *more*, which is regarded as a noun (19.1/1 note 1). It also occurs with some adverbs, particularly **satis** *sufficiently*, **nimis** *excessively*, and **parum** *insufficiently*, which in this use can be regarded as indeclinable nouns meaning *sufficiency*, *excess* and *insufficiency* respectively. Other examples are:

> **multum aurī** *much gold*; **tantum spatiī** *so much distance*; **satis ēloquentiae** *sufficient eloquence*; **sapientiae parum** *insufficient wisdom*; **quid negōtiī?** *what business?*; **plūrimum speī** *very much hope*; **nihil vōcis** *no voice* (16.2, 18 *ll.*7f.).

Such phrases occur as the subject or object of a verb. The partitive genitive is also used with certain adverbs to form an adverbial phrase: **tum temporis** *at that time*; **ubi gentium . . .?** *where of* (= *among*) *peoples*, i.e. *where on earth . . . ?* **Eō** *to there, to that point* (17.1/3) gives us expressions such as **eō stultitiae vēnit ut . . .** *he came to such a* (lit. *that*) *point of stupidity that . . .*

---

[1] Phrases of this type can also be expressed by **ē/ex** or **dē** and the ablative with no difference in meaning, **multī ē (dē) Gallīs, trēs ē (dē) nōbīs.**

27.2 Latin reading

In addition to translating, define the use of each accusative (except direct objects of verbs) and genitive.

1 Horti Caesaris; Hectoris Andromache; fuga Pompeii; laus recte factorum; libri Platonis; ars scribendi.
2 His animum arrecti dictis et fortis Achates
  et pater Aeneas iamdudum erumpere nubem
  ardebant.
3 Dic quibus in terris inscripti nomina regum
  nascantur flores, et Phyllida solus habeto.
4 Linguas hominum sensusque docebit aerias volucres.
5 Mirabar quid maesta deos, Amarylli, vocares.
6 Liber sum et liberae civitatis.
7 Imperatoris est non minus consilio quam gladio superare.
8 Auctoritas Commii in his regionibus magni habebatur.
9 Quid mulieris uxorem habes!
10 Germanis neque consilii habendi neque arma capiendi spatium datum est.
11 Magna opinio fuit L. Crassum non plus attigisse doctrinae quam quantum prima puerili institutione potuisset, M. autem Antonium omnino omnis eruditionis expertem atque ignarum fuisse.
12 T. Roscius plurimarum palmarum vetus ac nobilis gladiator habetur.
13 Ex Africa semper aliquid novi.
14 It pectore summo flexilis obtorti per collum circulus auri.
15 Propono spem meis hospitibus ac necessariis quo tutiorem sese vitam meo praesidio victuros esse arbitrentur.
16 O fortunatam natam me consule Romam!
17 Catilina admonebat alium egestatis, alium cupiditatis suae.
18 Iustum et tenacem propositi virum
   non civium ardor prava iubentium,
       non vultus instantis tyranni
           mente quatit solida.
19 Tantum religio potuit suadere malorum.
20 Homo sum: humani nil a me alienum puto.

Notes

1   In what relation did Andromache stand to Hector?

2   **pater** *father* is an epithet Vergil regularly gives Aeneas; **iamdūdum**
    . . . **ardēbant** *were already burning for a long time*, i.e. *had been
    burning for a long time*.

3   **Dīc** 21.1/1 note 1; **Phyllida** <Phyllis 25.1/4*e*; **sōlus** *alone*, i.e. *for
    yourself*; **habēto** 2nd s. fut. imp. act. (21.1/1 note 3).

4   **linguās** *languages*.

5   Translate **maesta** by an adverb (17.1/3); **Amarylli** <Amaryllis
    25.1/4*e*.

11 **quantum** is here a relative pronoun (30.1/1 note 1), lit. *how much*,
    but translate by *what*; with **potuisset** supply **attingere** from
    attigisse but translate by a different verb to avoid repetition.

13 Supply **est**.

14 Take **flexilis** with **circulus** (it could be taken as genitive singular
    with **aurī** but Vergil and subsequent Roman poets avoided putting
    two adjectives or participles with one noun); **per** here *around*, not
    through.

15 **quō** introduces a purpose clause containing a comparative (13.1/5
    note 2).

17 **alium** . . . **alium** *one* . . . *another* (10.1/1*c*).

18 **nōn** . . . **nōn** emphatic for **nec** . . . **nec**; **mente** . . . **solidā** *in his firm
    mind* (28.1/2*c*).

27.3 Extra reading

The greatest pleasure

Titus Lucrētius Cārus (c. 94–55 BC) wrote a long philosophical poem
entitled *dē Rērum Nātūrā* (*on the Nature of the Universe*). In this he
expounds the theories of the Greek philosopher Epicurus on the
nature of the material world, and the significance of these theories for
humankind. Into his seemingly intractable subject-matter Lucretius
infuses a poetic fervour which marks him as one of the greatest
didactic poets of antiquity.

Suave, mari magno turbantibus aequora ventis,
e terra magnum alterius spectare laborem:
non quia vexari quemquamst iucunda voluptas,
sed quibus ipse malis careas quia cernere suave est.
suave etiam belli certamina magna tueri
per campos instructa tua sine parte pericli.
sed nil dulcius est, bene quam munita tenere
edita doctrina sapientum templa serena,
despicere unde queas alios passimque videre
errare atque viam palantis quaerere vitae,
certare ingenio, contendere nobilitate:
noctes atque dies niti praestante labore
ad summas emergere opes rerumque potiri.
o miseras hominum mentis, o pectora caeca!
qualibus in tenebris vitae quantisque periclis
degitur hoc aevi quodcumquest!

The *dē Rērum Nātūrā* is in hexameters (24.1/2).

Notes

l.1 supply **est** with **suāve** (also in *l*.5); **marī magnō** abl. of place where
(28.1/2*c*); **turbantibus . . . ventīs** abl. absolute, with the other words
between the commas forming part of the phrase. *l*.3 **quemquamst** =
quemquam est. *l*.4 **quibus . . . careās** is an indirect question (23.1/3)
after **cernere**. *l*.6 scansion shows that we have **tuā**, which therefore
must go with **parte** (the only feminine singular noun in the ablative in
the sentence), lit. *without your part of danger*, i.e. *without any danger
yourself*. *ll*.7f. **bene** with **mūnīta**; as a pre-Vergilian poet Lucretius
sometimes piles up epithets with one noun (cf. note on 27.2, 14), and
mūnīta, ēdita and **serēna** all agree with **templa** (here *regions*, not
temples); scan the line to discover whether we have **doctrīna** or
doctrīnā. *l*.9 take **despicere** after **queās**. *l*.10 the infinitives in this line
(and the next two) should be translated as present active participles;
pālentīs (= **pālentēs**) accusative plural with **aliōs**. *l*.11 **ingeniō** and
nōbilitāte are instrumental ablatives (7.1/4) but may be translated by
in. *l*.13 **ēmergere** and **potīrī** depend on **nītī** (*striving to . . .*); **opēs** *power*;
rērum (genitive after **potīrī** – 20.1/1) here means *things around us, the
(physical) world* (in the title of Lucretius's poem it has a still broader
sense, *the universe*). *l*.14 **miserās . . . mentīs** and **pectora caeca** are

accusatives of exclamation (27.1/3*c*). *l.*15 **quālibus** and **quantīs** here introduce an exclamation (30.1/1 note 1), *in what darkness . . . and in what great dangers . . .! l.*16 **hoc aevī quodcumquest** (= **quodcumque est**) *this of life* (partitive genitive) *whatever it is*, i.e. *this life, such as it is.*

UNIT 28

28.1 Grammar

28.1/1 Dative

A noun in the dative is generally to be translated by *to* or *for*. It may go in sense with a verb, an adjective or, very occasionally, a noun or adverb. It indicates the person involved in an action or state (recipient, person advantaged or disadvantaged, etc.) and, in the case of things, a purpose or goal.

(*a*) *Verbs governing the dative*
Most verbs can be accompanied by a dative of one sort or another, but we refer here only to those with which a dative is required by Latin idiom:

(i) Verbs followed by a direct object (accusative) and an indirect object (dative – 1.1/3*e*)

These include verbs of saying, giving, promising, showing, etc. where English idiom is similar. There are some other verbs (mainly compounds), such as **praeficiō** *put in charge of*, which also take an accusative and dative but whose English equivalent generally has a different construction.

Labiēnum exercituī praefēcit. *He put Labienus in charge of the army.*
Magnum nostrīs terrōrem iniēcit. *He instilled great fear into our men.*
Nōs sibi amīcōs iunget. *He will join us to himself as friends.*

The English construction by which the indirect object of a verb in the active voice can become the subject of the same verb when made passive (*I was given the horse*; *we were told the news*) does not exist in Latin. Only direct objects of active verbs can be transformed into the subjects of passive ones. **Mihi equum dedit** *he* *gave me the horse* becomes **equus ab eō mihi datus est** *the horse was given to me by him,* and no other passive version is possible in Latin. **Datus sum** means *I was given,* i.e. *handed over* (*to the slave-traders, to the lions in the Colosseum* or the like).

(ii) Intransitive verbs followed by the dative (15.1/2 and 20.1/1)

(iii) Impersonal verbs followed by the dative (20.1/2*c*)

(*b*) *Dative with adjectives, nouns and adverbs*
A group of adjectives whose English equivalent can usually be followed by *to* or *for* is used with the dative. This includes **ūtilis** *useful*, **aptus** *suitable*, **fidēlis** *faithful*, **amīcus** *friendly*, **similis** *similar* and other such adjectives, together with their opposites: **alta quiēs simillima mortī** *deep sleep most like to death*; **vēr ūtile silvīs** *spring, useful to forests.* Most adjectives of this sort can also be followed by a genitive (as **pār** *like*) with no difference in meaning.

A few nouns and adverbs can be followed by a dative: **obtemperātiō lēgibus** *obedience to laws*; **convenienter nātūrae vīvere** *to live in accordance with nature.*

(*c*) *Dative of agent* (see 18.1/2*b*)
This is occasionally found in contexts not containing a gerundive: **carmina quae scrībuntur aquae pōtōribus** *songs which are written by teetotallers* (lit. *drinkers of water*). Where the dative of agent is used it is obvious from the broader context that agency is involved. In the above example **pōtōribus** could theoretically be taken as dative of advantage (*for teetotallers*), but the passage where the words occur (Horace, *Epistles I*, 19, 2f.) shows that *by teetotallers* is the intended meaning.

(*d*) *Dative of possessor* (see 8.1/5)

(*e*) *Dative of advantage and disadvantage*
The dative is used for a person who is affected by the action expressed by a verb, whether advantageously or the reverse. This use can sometimes be translated by *for*, but often we must adapt our translation to the English idiom suitable to the context.

> **Tibi quisquam in Cūriam venientī assurexit?** *Did anyone stand for you [as you were] coming into the Senate House?*

Neque sōlum nōbīs dīvitēs esse volumus, sed līberīs, propinquīs, amīcīs, maximēque reī pūblicae. *Nor do we wish to be rich only for ourselves, but for our children, relatives, friends, and, most of all, the state.*

Quid tibi dēlīquī? *What did I do wrong to you?*

Nōbīs curvātur Apollinis arcus. *Apollo's bow is bent against us* (lit. *for us*, i.e. *to our disadvantage*).

With verbs meaning *take away* and the like, the dative is translated *from*: **nihil equidem tibi abstulī** *indeed I took away nothing from you* (lit. *to your disadvantage*). With such verbs this use overlaps with the ablative of separation (28.1/2e). The normal difference between the two is that the former is used with living beings, the latter with things; but sometimes, with forms that can be either dative or ablative, it is impossible to make a distinction: **is frātrem non potuit ēripere fātō** *that man was not able to snatch his brother from death.* Here **fātō** could be either dative of disadvantage or ablative of separation according to whether we regard death as a divinity or a physical condition.

(f) *Dative of reference*

This gives the person who is interested or involved in the action or state expressed by a verb. The use overlaps to some extent with the previous one. Sometimes this dative is used to mean *in the eyes of, in the judgement of.*

Tuī virō oculī dolent. *Your husband has sore eyes* (lit. *for your husband the eyes are sore*; **virō** could also be taken as a dative of disadvantage).

Estne ille mihi līber cui mulier imperat? *Is that man, in my judgement, free who takes orders from his wife* (*to whom his wife gives orders*)?

Hoc est oppidum prīmum Thessaliae venientibus ab Ēpīrō. *This is the first town of Thessaly for those coming from Epirus.*

(g) *Ethic dative*

This term is traditional and the use has no relation to ethics. It occurs with the first and second person pronouns only. There is no great difference in meaning between the two as each draws the attention of the person addressed and stands apart from the construction of the remaining words. The ethic dative occurred in Elizabethan English (*he plucked me ope his doublet,* i.e. *he plucked open his doublet, I tell you*), but has now long since disappeared, and we must translate it by some other expression: **quid mihi Celsus agit?** *how, tell me, is Celsus doing?*

(*h*) **Dative of purpose**
When used with things, the dative expresses the end or goal for which something exists or is done. The goal can be concrete, as **Caesar locum castrīs dēlēgit** *Caesar chose a place for a camp,* but, more commonly, it is abstract: **mūnītiōnī castrōrum tempus relinquī volēbat** *he wished time to be left for the fortification of the camp.*

It can also consist of a noun and a gerundive (18.1/2*c,* iii).

(*i*) **Predicative dative**
This is close in meaning to the preceding but is generally accompanied by a dative of advantage or disadvantage. Instead of *this was a disgrace to him,* Latin prefers **hoc eī dēdecorī fuit,** lit. *this was for a disgrace for him,* where the predicative dative **dēdecorī** expresses the end result. Other examples are:

> **Exitiō est avidum mare nautīs.** *The greedy sea is death to sailors.*
> **Quinque cohortēs castrīs praesidiō relinquit.** *He leaves five cohorts as a guard for the camp.*
> **Cui bonō?** *To benefit whom?* (lit. *to whom for a benefit?*)

(*j*) **Dative to express motion towards**
This is a frequent construction in poetry to express the place towards which motion is directed. It is the equivalent of **ad** + acc.:

> **Multōs Danaum dēmittimus Orcō.** *We send down many of the Greeks to the Underworld.*
> **Facilis descensus Avernō.** *The descent to Hades (**Avernus**) is easy.*

The dative of a person after a verb of motion is better taken as a dative of advantage (examples in 13.2,7), but exceptions occur (as in 23.2, 12 *l.*5).

28.1/2 Ablative

The reason why the Latin ablative has so many, and often unrelated, uses is that it is an amalgam of three cases:

(i) the original ablative, which expressed removal and separation;

(ii) almost all the original locative, which expressed *place where* and *time when* (what remains of the locative in Latin is a small fragment of its former self);

(iii) an old instrumental case, which expressed both agent (without any preposition) and instrument.

Because so many uses were combined, some were distinguished and made more precise with prepositions (3.1/4), a need that was not felt with the genitive or dative. In a few of these uses, prepositions were not consistently used, particularly in poetry, which reflects, to some extent, an earlier stage of the language.

(*a*) *Ablative with intransitive verbs* (see 20.1/1)
The ablative with some verbs can be classified as one of separation (see (*e*) below). Elsewhere (e.g. with **ūtor** *use*), no useful analysis is possible.

(*b*) *Ablative of time when and time within which* (5.1/4)

(*c*) *Ablative of place where*
Position is normally expressed by prepositions (3.1/4), except where the locative is appropriate; but, as noted in 8.1/3, we sometimes get the plain ablative, especially in poetry. This use is virtually the same as (*b*). It is easily distinguished from (*d*) because it does not occur with verbs of motion: **celsā sedet Aeolus arce** *Aeolus sits in his lofty citadel.*

(*d*) *Ablative of place from which*
This only occurs with verbs of motion. In prose it has the same restrictions as the locative and the accusative of motion towards (8.1/3), but, like (*c*), it is used more freely in verse: **iam nox ūmida caelō praecipitat** *already damp night is coming quickly* (**praecipitat**) *from the sky.* In prose we could have **ā, dē** or **ē** with **caelō**.

(*e*) *Ablative of separation*
This is very close to (*d*). It is generally to be translated by *from* or *of* and occurs in four similar contexts:

(i) with transitive verbs indicating removal or separation such as **līberō, -āre** *free*, **solvō, -ere** *release*, **abstineō, -ēre** *restrain*:

Ostreīs et mūraenīs mē facile abstineō. *Without difficulty* (**facile**) *I restrain myself from oysters and eels.*

L. Brūtus cīvitātem dominātū rēgiō līberāvit. *Lucius Brutus freed the state from the rule of kings* (lit. *regal rule*).

(ii) with a few intransitive verbs indicating shortage or lack such as **egeō, indigeō** *lack, be in want of,* which can also take the genitive, and **careō** *lack, be free of* (20.1/1);

(iii) with adjectives with a meaning corresponding to some verbs in (i) and (ii), as **vacuus** *destitute of, free of*: **nec ullum in hīs malīs consilium perīculō vacuum invenīrī potest** *nor in these troubles can any plan free of danger be found.* These adjectives may also take the genitive (27.1/4h).

(iv) with the adverb **procul** *far from*: **haud procul Cremōnā** *not far from Cremona.*

In all these categories except (ii) we sometimes get the plain ablative replaced by **ā/ab** + ablative with no difference in meaning.

(f) *Ablative of origin*
This ablative is also akin to *(d)* and is used with past participles such as **nātus** (<**nascor** be born), **ortus** (<**orior** *arise, come from, be born of*): **Apollō Iove nātus et Lātōnā** *Apollo, born of Jupiter and Latona.*

(g) *Ablative of comparison* (see 19.1/4a)

(h) *Ablative of measure of difference* (see 13.1/6a and 19.1/4b)

(i) *Ablative of quality or description* (6.1/3)

(j) *Ablative of manner and ablative of attendant circumstances*

These are both used in adverbial phrases: *he walked **with a bad limp*** (manner); *no gladiator ever died **amid greater shouting*** (attendant circumstances). The two are combined here because they have the same construction, which is:

(i) If the noun involved is qualified by an adjective (or another noun in the genitive), it is put into the ablative with or without **cum**. If used, **cum** comes between the two words.

(ii) If the noun is alone we must have **cum** + ablative. The few exceptions are virtually adverbs, as **iūre** *rightly* (lit. *by law*; opposite **iniūriā** *wrongly*); **silentiō** *in silence.*

These uses are generally translated by a preposition (normally *in, with* or *to*):

Polliceor hoc vōbīs bonā fidē (manner). *I promise you this in good faith.*

Cum perīculō ex castrīs ēgredī coactus est (attendant circumstances). *In dangerous circumstances he was forced to go out of the camp.*

Verrēs signum abstulit magnō cum luctū cīvitātis (attendant circumstances). *Verres removed the statue to the great grief of the community.*

(k) *Ablative of accompaniment*

Accompaniment is normally expressed by **cum** + ablative: **cum uxōre meā** *with my wife*. The plain ablative is used in military contexts for the troops, ships, etc. with which a leader makes a journey or expedition: **decem nāvibus Rōmam rediit** *he returned to Rome with ten ships.*

(l) *Ablative of respect*

We have already met the accusative of respect (27.1/3*b*) and the genitive of respect (27.1/4*h*). The former was a foreign import, the latter a poetical development. The normal classical construction is the ablative, and it may follow nouns, adjectives and verbs. Its basic meaning is *in respect of* and is to be translated by a preposition, most commonly *in*: **superō Crassum dīvitiīs** *I surpass Crassus in riches*; **umerō saucius** *wounded in the shoulder*; **formā similis** *similar in appearance*; **maior nātū** *older by birth*; **Cicerō nōmine** *Cicero by name.*

This ablative also occurs with:

(i) adjectives denoting fullness and abundance (which can also take the genitive – 27.1/4*h*): **erant plēna laetitiā et grātulātiōne omnia** *everything was full of happiness and rejoicing.*

(ii) **dignus** *worthy of*: **utinam patribus nostrīs dignī sīmus** *may we be worthy of our fathers.*

(m) *Ablative of instrument and ablative of cause* (7.1/4)

In the idiom **opus est** *there is need* (20.1/2*f*) the ablative is one of instrument: **mihi gladiō opus est** *I need a sword* (lit. *there is work for me with a sword*).

The adjective **frētus** *relying on, trusting in* (originally *supported by*) is followed by an ablative, and this too is one of instrument: **impudentiā atque audāciā frētus** *relying on shamelessness and audacity.*

(*n*) *Ablative of price* (7.1/5)

(*o*) *Ablative of agent* (11.1/4)

(*p*) *Ablative absolute* (12.1/1)

28.1/3 Identification of case uses

Some Latin case uses present no problem because of the similarity of the equivalent English construction, e.g. objective genitives can usually be translated by *of*; most uses of the dative are rendered by *to* or *for*. The following considerations will help determine the nature of more difficult instances:

(*a*) The meaning of a noun often gives a clue to the way in which it is used, e.g. the accusative to express time how long and the ablative to express time when can only be used with nouns which denote a period of time (*day, autumn*, etc.).

(*b*) Far more often than not, a noun is governed by an adjacent word. The meaning of the words immediately preceding and following may indicate the case use involved.

(*c*) The overall context is our final resort. When in doubt about why a noun is in a particular case, or, if an ending is ambiguous, what the case of a noun is, we should analyse and translate all other words. In the following sentences (all from Vergil) we have **caelō** used in three different ways:

(i) **It caelō clāmorque virum clangorque tubārum.**

(ii) **Nova prōgeniēs caelō dēmittitur.**

(iii) **Caelō cava nūbila rumpit.**

Caelō is either dative or ablative singular, and its meaning, *sky*, indicates that some sort of spatial relationship may be involved. The meaning of the other words is:

(i) *Both shout of men and blast of trumpets go . . .*

(ii) *A new race is sent down . . .*

(iii) *He bursts the hollow clouds . . .*

If we are correct in our hypothesis about a spatial relationship (the verbs in (i) and (ii) seem to confirm this) the only possibilities are: dative to express motion towards (28.1/1*j*), ablative of place from which (28.1/2*d*), and ablative of place where (28.1/2*c*). As shouts of men can only go *to the sky*, a new race can only be sent down *from the sky*, and he (in this case Jupiter) bursts clouds *in the sky*, the uses involved are in the order given.

28.2 Latin reading

In addition to translating, define the use of each dative and ablative (except ablatives after prepositions).

1 In id studium, in quo estis, incumbite, ut et vobis honori et amicis utilitati et rei publicae emolumento esse possitis.
2 Victrix causa deis placuit sed victa Catoni.
3 Iam veniet tacito curva senecta pede.
4 Receptui signum audire non possumus.
5 Desperanda tibi salva concordia socru.
6 Quod tibi libet, fac, quoniam pugnis plus vales.
7 Barbarus hic ego sum quia non intellegor ulli.
8 Nemo potest nudo vestimenta detrahere.
9 Q. Fabius comitia censoribus creandis habuit.
10 Quae sunt uncis unguibus ne nutrias.
11 Quintia formosa est multis. mihi candida, longa,
        recta est: haec ego sic singula confiteor.
12 Si sine uxore vivere possemus, omnes ea molestia careremus.
13 Cum toga signum dedero, tum mihi undique clamore sublato turbam invadite ac sternite omnia ferro.
14 Ubi is finem fecit, extemplo ab ea turba, quae in comitio erat, clamor flebilis est sublatus manusque ad Curiam tendebant orantes ut sibi liberos, fratres, cognatos redderent. feminas quoque metus ac necessitas in foro turbae virorum immiscuerat.
15 Post meum discessum, metum bonis, spem audacibus, servitutem depulit civitati.
16 Eodem die legati ab hostibus missi ad Caesarem de pace venerunt. his Caesar numerum obsidum, quem ante imperaverat, duplicavit eosque in continentem adduci iussit.
17 Multorum calamitate vir moritur bonus.

Vergiliana
18 Vix ea fatus erat, geminae cum forte columbae
    ipsa sub ora viri caelo venere volantes,
    et viridi sedere solo.
19 Nate, quis indomitas tantus dolor excitat iras?
    quid furis? aut quonam nostri tibi cura recessit?
    non prius aspicies ubi fessum aetate parentem
    liqueris Anchisen, superet coniunxne Creusa
    Ascaniusque puer?

20 Aude, hospes, contemnere opes et te quoque dignum
    finge deo rebusque veni non asper egenis.
21 Quis te, nate dea, per tanta pericula casus
    insequitur? quae vis immanibus applicat oris?
    tune ille Aeneas quem Dardanio Anchisae
    alma Venus Phrygii genuit Simoentis ad undam?
22 Muscosi fontes et somno mollior herba,
    solstitium pecori defendite: iam venit aestas
    torrida, iam lento turgent in palmite gemmae.

Notes

2   In this famous line (***Bellum Civile I***, 128) from his epic on the civil
    war between Julius Caesar and Pompey, the Silver Age poet
    Lucan contrasts the support each side enjoyed. That of Caesar
    had the favour of the gods and so won; that of Pompey lost but
    had attracted the support of one of the most respected figures of
    the day, the younger Cato.

5   Scan this hexameter to discover the lengths of final **a**'s; the second
    vowel of **tibi** is here long.

6   **fac** 21.1/1 note 1.

11 With **haec sīc singula** supply **esse**.

13 **ferrum** is frequently used, as here, to mean *sword(s)*.

14 **sibi** refers back to the subject of the main clause, not to the
    subject of **redderent** (for this use of the reflexive in indirect speech
    see 31.1/2); the subject of **redderent** is the men inside the **Cūria**,
    the senators, and to avoid ambiguity we should supply this in
    English; **līberōs, frātrēs, cognātōs** in enumeration of this sort
    Latin either puts a word for *and* after each member except the
    last, or has no conjunction at all (another example in 15);
    immiscuerat is singular because, when we have a double subject
    (**metus ac necessitās**), the verb may agree with the nearer one only.

18 **fātus erat** 25.1/5*a*; **ōra** (<**ōs, ōris** n. *face*) plural for singular.

19 *l*.4 the interrogative **-ne** is attached to the second word of the
    indirect question; **superet** see note on **immiscuerat** in 14.

21 *l*.1 **quis . . . cāsus** *what fortune*; scan this hexameter to discover
    whether we have **dea** or **deā**. *l*.3 **tūne** i.e. **tū** + **-ne**.

22 *l*.2 scan this hexameter to discover whether we have **venit** (pres.) or
    vēnit (perf.).

28.3 Extra reading

The Emperor Galba

The greatest prose writer of the Silver Age was the historian Tacitus
(c. AD 55–116). His extremely dense and epigrammatic Latin puts him
in the class of more difficult authors, but his style and general manner
of writing more than compensate for any extra effort needed to
understand him. The final words of this passage are a splendid
example of his teasing brevity and his caustic attitude towards some
of the great figures of the Roman past.

Hunc exitum habuit Servius Galba, tribus et septuaginta annis
quinque principes prospera fortuna emensus et alieno imperio felicior
quam suo. vetus in familia nobilitas, magnae opes: ipsi medium
ingenium, magis extra vitia quam cum virtutibus. famae nec
incuriosus nec venditator: pecuniae alienae non appetens, suae
parcus, publicae avarus: amicorum libertorumque, ubi in bonos
incidisset, sine reprehensione patiens: si mali forent, usque ad culpam
ignarus. sed claritas natalium et metus temporum obtentui, ut, quod
segnitia erat, sapientia vocaretur. dum vigebat aetas, militari laude
apud Germanias floruit. pro consule Africam moderate, iam senior   1(
citeriorem Hispaniam pari iustitia continuit, maior privato visus dum
privatus fuit, et omnium consensu capax imperii nisi imperasset.

Notes

Tacitus had a very real dislike of using the verb *to be* where it could
be avoided. Some part of **sum** is to be understood in nearly every
sentence of this passage.

*ll.*1–3 this sentence consists of only one clause and its verb is **habuit**;
in **tribus . . . suō** we have two phrases, the first dependent on **ēmensus**,
the second on **fēlīcior**, and both words agree with **Servius Galba**;
tribus . . . annīs time within which (5.1/4c); **prosperā fortūnā** abl. of
manner (28.1/2j); **aliēnō** is an adjective but often is to be translated *of
another's* or *of others*. *l.*3 **ipsī** dative of possessor (8.1/5), lit. *to [him]
himself*. *ll.*4f. **fāmae** objective genitive with **incūriōsus** and **venditātor**.
*l.*5 **pecūniae** objective genitive with **appetens, parcus** and **avārus**. *ll.*6f.
amīcōrum lībertōrumque objective genitives with **patiens**; freed slaves
(**lībertī** *freedmen*) were often employed as officials by the emperors;

ubi is followed by the subjunctive on the analogy of **cum**. *l.*7 **sine reprehensiōne** *without* [*giving cause for*] *blame*; **forent** an alternative form of the imperfect subjunctive of **sum** which is formed by adding the normal endings to the future infinitive **fore** (14.1/3) – there is no difference in meaning between **forem** and **essem**; the subjunctive is used here to express something happening often (a Silver Age use), *if ever, whenever, they were bad*; **usque ad** lit. *right to* but translate simply by *to*. *l.*10 **Germāniās** the Roman empire included the provinces **Germānia superior** and **Germānia inferior** which together took up only a part of modern Germany; **prō consule** *proconsul, governor* a phrase which is used as a noun. *l.*11 **vīsus (est)** *he seemed.*

UNIT 29

29.1 Grammar

29.1/1 Further adverbial clauses

Adverbial clauses of purpose (13.1/5), result (16.1/1) and condition (22.1/2) need concern us no further. Of the other varieties some have already been treated in part. For adverbial clauses of comparison see 30.1/1.

29.1/2 Adverbial clauses of reason

Latin has several conjunctions meaning *because* or *since*. **Cum** in this sense always takes the subjunctive (16.1/3a), but the mood after **quod** and **quia** can vary. If they are followed by the indicative the speaker or writer is giving a reason which he sees as genuine:

> **Tibi agō grātiās quod mē vīvere coēgistī.** *I thank you because you have forced me to live.*
>
> **Quia nūda fuī, sum vīsa parātior illī.** *Because I was naked, I seemed more ready to him.*

If a **quod** or **quia** clause occurs in indirect speech, its verb is put into the subjunctive because of the overall rule relating to reported subordinate clauses (17.1/2 note 4): **hīs Caesar respondit sē minus dubitāre quod eās rēs memoriā tenēret** *Caesar replied to them that he was less hesitant because he remembered* (lit. *held in memory*) *these things*. **Quod/quia** + subjunctive are used elsewhere if the speaker or writer wishes to ascribe a reason or motive to somebody but does not vouch for it himself. This type of expression is called *virtual indirect speech*, as no verb of saying, thinking, etc. is involved. **Quod/quia** are to be translated here by *on the grounds that, thinking that*:

Rōmānī, quia consulēs ibi prosperē rem gererent, minus hīs clādibus commovēbantur. *The Romans, thinking that the consuls were acting successfully there, were less concerned by these disasters.*
Laudat Panaetius Āfricānum quod fuerit abstinens. *Panaetius praises Africanus on the grounds that he was temperate.*

Quod and **quia** are often preceded by the adverbs **ideō, idcircō, proptereā** or **eō** (abl. neut. sing. of **is** used as an ablative of cause), all of which in this context mean *for this reason* and anticipate the following clause. These words often need not be translated: **eō miser sum quod male illī fēcī** *I am miserable because* (lit. *for this reason, because*) *I have done wrong to him.*

Quoniam is used in the same ways as **quod** and **quia** (though rarely with the subjunctive) and with the same meaning. **Quandō**, the interrogative (*when . . . ?*) and indefinite adverb of time (**sī quandō** *if ever*), can also mean *because*, but in this sense is often combined with **quidem** *indeed* to form **quandōquidem**.

29.1/3 Adverbial clauses of time

These clauses express the temporal relationship between one action, state or event, and another. Each possibility (before, after, during, etc.) has its own subordinating conjunction. The most common is **cum** (16.1/3). The rest can be divided into two classes:

(*a*) subordinating conjunctions of time followed by the indicative (except in indirect speech – 17.1/2 note 4):

(i) **ubi** *when*, **ut** *when, as*, **simulac** *as soon as* (5.1/2);

(ii) **postquam** *after*, **posteāquam** *after*, which have no difference in meaning or use; both can be split into two words, **post/posteā . . . quam** (30.1/1 note 4);

(iii) **quotiens** *as often as, whenever* (30.1/1).

(*b*) subordinating conjunctions of time followed by either the indicative or subjunctive.

The overall rule for these conjunctions is that when they introduce a subordinate clause which describes something that has happened, is happening, or will happen, and which has a purely temporal connection with its main clause, they are followed by the indicative (except in indirect speech where the subjunctive is always used and no such distinction is possible, 17.1/2 note 4): **in**

forō mansī dōnec Caesar vēnit *I waited in the forum until Caesar came.* When the subordinate clause expresses something anticipated (but which does not eventuate) or implies purpose or intention, its verb is in the subjunctive: **in forō mansī dōnec Caesar venīret** *I waited in the forum for Caesar to come* (lit. *until Caesar should come*).

The examples given below (and in the reading) illustrate this rule, but there was a tendency, which we see beginning in Cicero, to use the subjunctive in many cases where we would expect the indicative.

(i) **Antequam** and **priusquam** both mean *before*, but when following a negated main clause they are sometimes to be translated *until.* They may be split up into **ante/prius . . . quam.**

> **Antequam tuās lēgī litterās, hominem īre cupiēbam.** *Before I read your letter I wanted the man to go.*
>
> **Hostēs nōn prius fugere destitērunt quam ad flūmen Rhēnum pervēnērunt.** *The enemy did not stop fleeing until they came to the River Rhine.*
>
> **Numidae, priusquam ex castrīs subvenīrētur, in proximōs collēs discessērunt.** *The Numidians went off to the nearest hills before help might come* (lit. *it might be helped* – 20.1/3) *from the camp.*

(ii) **Dōnec** and **quoad** with the indicative mean either *until (an event takes/took place)* or *while, as long as.* It is always obvious from the context which sense is meant:

> **Dōnec rediit Marcellus, silentium fuit.** *There was silence until Marcellus returned.*
>
> **Quoad dēdita arx est, caedēs tōtā urbe factae sunt.** *Massacres were committed in the whole of the city until the citadel was surrendered.*
>
> **Dōnec grātus eram tibi, Persārum viguī rēge beātior.** *While I was pleasing to you, I flourished in greater happiness* (lit. *happier*) *than the king of the Persians.*
>
> **Quoad vixit, crēdidit ingens pauperiem vitium.** *As long as he lived, he believed poverty a terrible vice.*

When used with the subjunctive **dōnec** and **quoad** mean *until (an event may/might take place)*: **ea continēbis quoad ipse tē videam** *you will keep these things to yourself until I see you myself.*

(iii) **Dum** can mean *until* and be used in exactly the same way as **dōnec** and **quoad**. In the sense of *while, during the time that,* it is followed by the *present* indicative whatever the tense of the main verb: **haec dum aguntur, Cleomenēs iam ad Pelōrī lītus pervēnerat** *while these things were being done, Cleomenes had already arrived at the shore of Pelorus.* This purely idiomatic use is not to be explained on logical grounds but is probably akin to the vivid present.

When **dum** means *as long as, all the time that,* it is followed by the logically required tense. Here the extent of time taken by the main clause is the same as that of the **dum** clause, while in the above use the main clause takes up only part of the time indicated by the latter: **neque, dum eram vōbīscum, animum meum vidēbātis** *nor used you to see my soul as long as I was with you.*

Dum can also mean *provided that.* In this sense it always takes the subjunctive and is sometimes reinforced by **modo**[1] (lit. *only*). This use of **dum** is an extension of its meaning *as long as*: **omnia recta et honesta neglegunt, dummodo potentiam consequantur** *they neglect everything right and honourable, provided they achieve power.* This use of **dum** is negated by **nē**: **quidvīs cupiō dum nē ab hōc mē fallī comperiam** *I am willing for anything provided I do not discover that I am being deceived by this man.*

29.1/4 Adverbial clauses of concession

Concessions may be expressed by a main clause with the concessive subjunctive (22.1/1*e*), but a subordinate clause is more common. These fall into two broad categories, one with conjunctions meaning *even if*; the other with conjunctions meaning *although*. The distinction between the two is not always clear-cut, and conjunctions of the first type are sometimes to be translated by *although*.

(*a*) **Etsī, tametsī, etiamsī** *even if* are all compounds of **sī** and have the same construction as conditional clauses (22.1/2):

---

[1] **modo** can be used by itself as a conjunction with the subjunctive in the same sense. **Tantum ut** + subj. (lit. *only that*) also has this meaning.

Erat raptor etiamsī negābat. *He was a robber even if he used to deny it.*

Facerem improbē etiamsī alius lēgem tulisset. *I would be acting wrongly even if another man had proposed the law.*

(b) **Quamquam** *although* was originally followed by the indicative, and this is still the normal use in Golden Age Latin. In the Silver Age the subjunctive is very common.

Quamquam animus meminisse horret luctūque refūgit, incipiam (from Vergil). *Although my mind shudders to remember and has recoiled in grief, I shall begin.*

Quamquam ēdictō monuisset nē quis quiētem eius irrumperet, tamen sē in insulam abdidit (from Tacitus). *Although he had, by proclamation, given warning that no one should disturb his rest, he nevertheless hid himself away on an island.*

Quamvīs is a combination of the conjunction **quam** *as* and **vīs** (<**volō**) in the sense *as (much as) you wish, however much you wish,* and came to be used as a subordinating conjunction meaning *although.* It is generally followed by the subjunctive: **illa quamvīs rīdicula essent, mihi tamen rīsum nōn mōvērunt** *although those things were absurd, they did not, however, make me laugh* (lit. *arouse laughter for me*).

Licet we have already seen as an impersonal verb meaning *it is allowed* (20.1/2c). In addition to its normal construction with an infinitive, it can be followed by a subjunctive with or without **ut**: **licet (ut) bibās** *you are allowed to drink* (lit. *it is allowed that you drink*). This sentence (without **ut**) can be accompanied by a clause of an adversative nature: **licet bibās, ego tamen ēsse volō** lit. *you can drink, I, however, want to eat.* Here **licet** is used as a subordinating conjunction with the sentence meaning *although you are drinking, I want to eat.* In this construction **licet** is always followed by the subjunctive: **licet superbus ambulēs pecūniā, fortūna nōn mūtat genus** *although you walk proudly because of your money, luck does not change your origin* (lit. *birth*).

Notes

1   **cum** + subj. can also mean *although* (16.1/3g).

2   **quamquam** and **quamvīs** can be used with adjectives, adverbs or
    phrases: **ego, quamquam perfectus asinus, sensum tamen retinēbam
    hūmānum** *I, although wholly a donkey* (lit. *a complete donkey*),
    nevertheless retained human understanding.

29.2 Latin reading

1   Urbs, quia postrema aedificata est, Neapolis nominatur.
2   Noctu ambulabat Themistocles quod somnum capere non posset.
3   Ita fit ut adsint propterea quod officium sequuntur, taceant
    autem idcirco quia periculum vitant.
4   Donec eris felix, multos numerabis amicos.
5   Atque ea diversa penitus dum parte geruntur,
    Irim de caelo misit Saturnia Iuno
    audaccm ad Turnum. luco tum forte parentis
    Pilumni Turnus sacrata valle sedebat.
6   Plus dolet quam necesse est qui ante dolet quam necesse est.
7   Postremo in scelera ac dedecora prorupit postquam, remoto
    pudore et metu, suo tantum ingenio utebatur.
8   Ambiguae si quando citabere testis
    incertaeque rei, Phalaris licet imperet ut sis
    falsus, et admoto dictet periuria tauro,
    summum crede nefas animam praeferre pudori
    et propter vitam vivendi perdere causas.
9   Hunc ad egrediendum nequaquam idoneum locum arbitratus,
    dum reliquae naves eo convenirent, ad horam nonam in ancoris
    exspectavit.
10 Oderint dum metuant.
11 Plebs, quamquam agitata multis eo anno et variis motibus erat,
    non plures quam tres tribunos creavit.

A lover's complaint
12 Etsi perque suos fallax iuravit ocellos
            Iunonemque suam perque suam Venerem,
    nulla fides inerit: periuria ridet amantum
            Iuppiter et ventos irrita ferre iubet.   4
    quam vellem tecum longas requiescere noctes
            et tecum longas pervigilare dies,

perfida, nec merito nobis inimica rependens,
    perfida, sed, quamvis perfida, cara tamen.   8
13 Prius ad hostium castra pervenit quam, quid ageretur, Germani
    sentire possent.
14 Hasdrubal, Poenorum imperator, procul ab hoste se tenebat
    quoad multum ac diu obtestanti quattuor milia peditum et
    quingenti equites in supplementum missi ex Africa sunt.
15 Nostri, tametsi ab duce et a fortuna deserebantur, tamen omnem
    spem salutis in virtute ponebant.
16   Dum me Galatea tenebat,
    nec spes libertatis erat nec cura peculi.
    quamvis multa meis exiret victima saeptis,
    pinguis et ingratae premeretur caseus urbi,
    non umquam gravis aere domum mihi dextra redibat.
17 Horum omnium fortissimi sunt Belgae, propterea quod a cultu
    atque humanitate Provinciae longissime absunt.

Notes

1 **Neāpolis** is Greek for *New City*.
4 **eris** should be translated by a present (5.1/3).
5 *l.*1 scan this hexameter to discover the quantities of the final **a**'s;
    penitus follows the word it qualifies; **dum** in prose would come
    before **ea**; *l.*4 scan.
7 **tantum** adverb, *only, exclusively*; **ūtēbātur** *started to use* (inceptive
    imperfect).
8 *l.*1 **citābere** = **citāberis** 14.1/1 note 3; *l.*2 **Phalaris** a tyrannical ruler
    of Agrigentum in Sicily who roasted live dissidents in a hollow
    bronze bull; as he lived in the seventh century BC, the meaning
    here is *a [person like] Phalaris*; *l.*5 take **vīvendī** with **causās**.
9 **hōram nōnam** the Romans divided the time when the sun was
    visible each day into twelve equal parts (**hōrae**) (and consequently
    an hour in summer was longer than an hour in winter); here
    translate *ninth hour*.
10 A quotation from the tragedian Accius; **ōderint** (25.1/5*a*, ii) is
    jussive subjunctive (22.1/1*c*).
12 *l.*1 the poet is talking about his girl-friend. *l.*2 **suam ... suam** as
    female deities, Juno and Venus were sometimes regarded as more
    the concern of women than men. *l.*7 **nec** negates only **meritō**, *and
    not deservedly*; **nōbīs** etc. lit. *repaying hostile things to us*.

14 **in** + acc. is here used to express purpose; translate *for*.
16 *l.*3 scan this hexameter to discover the quantities of the final **a**'s;
   *l.*4 **pinguis et** = **et pinguis** (postponed **et**, which is often used by
   poets for reasons of metre).
17 **Prōvinciae** the original Roman province in southern Gaul (hence
   the district *Provence* in modern France).

29.3 Extra reading

Two poems of Horace

These two love poems illustrate the meticulous aptness of expression,
the **cūriōsa fēlīcitās** which a later Roman author ascribes to Horace.
In the first he reflects on the fickleness of a former love, Pyrrha, from
whom he has escaped in the way a shipwrecked sailor might escape
from a violent storm. The second is a clever seduction poem playing
on the well-worn theme of life's shortness. We have no other
information about the ladies addressed (both of whom have Greek
names), if in fact they ever existed outside Horace's imagination. A
different lyric metre is used in each poem.

(*a*) Quis multa gracilis te puer in rosa
    perfusus liquidis urget odoribus
        grato, Pyrrha, sub antro?
           cui flavam religas comam,
    simplex munditiis? heu quotiens fidem   5
    mutatosque deos flebit et aspera
        nigris aequora ventis
           emirabitur insolens,
    qui nunc te fruitur credulus aurea,
    qui semper vacuam, semper amabilem   10
        sperat, nescius aurae
           fallacis! miseri, quibus
    intemptata nites. me tabula sacer
    votiva paries indicat uvida
        suspendisse potenti   15
           vestimenta maris deo.

(*b*) Tu ne quaesieris, scire nefas, quem mihi, quem tibi
finem di dederint, Leuconoe, nec Babylonios
temptaris numeros. ut melius, quidquid erit, pati,
seu pluris hiemes seu tribuit Iuppiter ultimam,
quae nunc oppositis debilitat pumicibus mare   5
Tyrrhenum: sapias, vina liques, et spatio brevi
spem longam reseces. dum loquimur, fugerit invida
aetas: carpe diem, quam minimum credula postero.

Notes

(*a*) *ll.*1–3 Horace imagines that Pyrrha's present lover is in the prime
of youth and is courting her in the highly romantic setting of a grotto
scattered with roses; **multā** ablative with **rosā**; **liquidīs . . . odōribus**
liquid scents, Roman men were less squeamish about using perfume
(particularly on their hair) than the normal Anglo-Saxon male. *l.*4 **cui**
interrogative *for whom . . .? l.*5 Pyrrha, being presumably young as
well as beautiful, had no need of any elaborate hair-style or beauty
treatment, and so was *simple in her elegance* (**mund_itiīs** ablative of
respect, 28.1/2*l* and plural for singular); **fidem** [*lack of*] *faith. ll.*6–8
Pyrrha is to lovers what a storm is to sailors; **nigrīs . . . ventīs** ablative
of cause (7.1/4) with **aspera**; the unfortunate lover is **insolens**
unaccustomed because Pyrrha is a completely new experience. *ll.*9f. the
antecedent of **quī . . . quī** is the subject of **flēbit** and **ēmīrābitur** (i.e. the
lover); **tē . . . aureā** ablative after **fruitur** (20.1/1) – Pyrrha is described
as golden because of her beauty and because she has honey-blonde
hair **flāvam comam** (this is also the meaning of her name). *ll.*11f. **aurae**
fallācis objective genitive (27.1/4*i*) after **nescius**; **miserī** [**sunt**] [*they are*]
unhappy; **quibus** dative of reference (28.1/1*f*), *to whom, in whose eyes.*
*ll.*13–16 shipwrecked sailors sometimes dedicated the clothes in which
they were rescued to the god that had saved them (the clothes were
hung up in his temple with an appropriately inscribed plaque) –
Horace here carries the metaphor to its conclusion; **tabulā . . . vōtīvā**
ablative of instrument (7.1/4); **vōtīvā** *votive*, during the storm a sailor
would vow to make such a dedication if the god saved him; the wall is
sacer because it is part of a temple; **ūvida** with **vestīmenta**; **maris**
objective genitive (27.1/4*i*) after **potentī**; **deō** i.e. Neptune.

(b) *ll*.1–3 **nē quaesieris . . . nec . . . temptāris** (shortened form 23.1/4)
are two negative commands with the perfect subjunctive (21.1/1b);
scīre nefas [est] a parenthesis; **Leuconoē** name of person addressed;
Babylōniōs . . . numerōs i.e. calculations made according to
Babylonian astrology (13.3) to determine one's horoscope and so
predict the date of one's death; **ut** the exclamatory *how* (there is no
exclamation mark at the end of the sentence because of its length). *l*.4
plūrīs accusative plural with **hiemēs**; with **ultimam** supply **hiemem** –
the full expression would be [*as our*] *last* [*winter, the one*] *which . . .*
ll.5–7 **oppositīs . . . pūmicibus** ablative of instrument (7.1/4) *with rocks
set opposite* [*to the sea*]; **mare Tyrrhēnum** (accusative after **dēbilitat**)
the sea on the west coast of Italy; **sapiās . . . liquēs . . . resecēs** jussive
subjunctives; **vīna liquēs** ancient wine was not pre-strained. *l*.8 **quam
minimum** *as little as possible* (19.1/5a); **crēdula** is feminine because it
agrees with the understood subject *you* (Leuconoe); **posterō [diēī]** is
dative after **crēdula**, which, like **crēdō** (20.1/1), takes the dative.

UNIT 30

30.1 Grammar

30.1/1 Correlatives and clauses of comparison

Correlatives in Latin are pairs of words, one a normal adjective or adverb, the other a relative adjective/pronoun or a conjunction. They are used in sentences expressing a comparison. In the sentence *there are not as many ships in the harbour today as there were last week*, the words *as many . . . as* are functioning as correlatives.

Latin has three pairs of correlative adjectives referring to quantity, quality and number:

	NORMAL ADJECTIVE	RELATIVE ADJECTIVE
Quantity	**tantus, -a, -um**	**quantus, -a, -um**
	so much, as much	*how much*
Quality	**tālis, -is, -e**	**quālis, -is, -e**
	such, of such a sort	*of what sort*
Number	**tot** (indeclinable)	**quot** (indeclinable)
	so many, as many	*how many*

The relative adjectives can be conveniently remembered with the meanings given (which they have when used in other connections; see below note 1), but when used with their correlatives they are often to be translated by *as*:

> **Quot hominēs, tot sententiae.** [*There are*] *as many opinions as* [*there are*] *men.*
> **Quālis dominus, tālis servus.** *A slave* [*is*] *of such a sort as his master* [*is*] (i.e. *like master, like slave*).

In both cases the *as* introducing the second clause in English is a conjunction, not, like **quot** and **quālis** (or **quantus**), a relative adjective;

English does not, in fact, have relative adjectives of this sort. A literal translation of these two sentences would be: [*there are*] *so many opinions, how many* [*there are*] *men*; *a slave* [*is*] *of such a sort, of what sort* [*is*] *his master* (the appropriate part of **sum** must be supplied twice in each sentence).

Tantus . . . quantus are used in the same way: **nōn mihi est tantum ingenium quantum Themistoclī erat** *I do not have as much talent as Themistocles had* (lit. *there is not for me so much talent, how much there was for Themistocles*).

Similarly **īdem . . . quī** (*the same . . . who*) function as correlatives when used together and can be translated *the same . . . as*: **certō īdem sum quī semper fuī** *certainly I am the same as I always have been.*

Correlatives consisting of an adverb and conjunction are **tam . . . quam** *so . . . as*, **ita (sīc) . . . ut** *so, in such a way . . . as*:

> **Nihil est tam populāre quam bonitās.** *Nothing is so winning as kindness.*
> **Nōn ita amō ut sānī solent hominēs.** *I do not love in such a way as sane men are accustomed to.*

This use is different from that of **ita** and **tam** to anticipate result clauses (*I was so tired that I couldn't move a step* – see 16.1/1), where the following **ut** is to be translated by *that* and is followed by the subjunctive.

Another pair of adverb and conjunction correlatives is **totiens . . . quotiens** *so often . . . how often*. In English we would normally render **quotiens** by *whenever* and leave **totiens** untranslated: **quotiens fugās et caedēs iussit princeps, totiens grātēs deīs actae sunt** *whenever the emperor ordered banishments and executions, thanks were made to the gods* (lit. *how often . . . so often*). **Totiens** can in fact be omitted in Latin: **quotiens forās īre volō, mē retinēs** *you detain me whenever I want to go outside.*

Notes

1   **Quantus, quālis** and **quot** can be used by themselves:
    (i)   as relatives with the appropriate correlative to be understood:
          crās et quot diēs erimus in Tusculānō, agāmus haec *let us do these things tomorrow and for as many days as we will be on the*

Tusculan estate (the full expression would be **tot diēs quot erimus . . .**).

(ii) as interrogatives meaning *how much/big/great . . .? of what sort . . .? how many . . .?*

Hoc quantum est? *How big is this?*
Quāle tibi consilium Pompeiī vidētur? *How does Pompey's plan seem to you?* (lit. *of what sort does P's plan . . .*)
Quot annōs nāta dīcitur? *How old* (lit. *born how many years*) *is she said to be?*

(iii) to introduce exclamations. In speech the difference between this use and the previous one would have been simply one of tone: **at quantus ōrātor!** *but how great a speaker!*

2 **Tantus, tālis** and **tot**, like **tam** and **ita**, can be used to anticipate result clauses (16.1/1): **tantus est clāmor exortus ut hostēs ē castrīs excīret** *so great a shout arose that it drew the enemy from their camp.*

3 The neuter **tantum** is used as an adverb in the sense of *only*: **inter bīna castra ūnum flūmen tantum intererat** *between the two camps there was only a single river.*

4 **Quam** can be:
(i) the correlative of **tam** as given above;
(ii) the accusative feminine singular of the relative, interrogative and indefinite pronoun and adjective (10.1/1*f–i*);
(iii) an interrogative adverb meaning *how . . .?* and an exclamatory adverb meaning *how . . .!*: **quam mox vir meus redit domum?** *how soon is my husband coming home?*
(iv) a conjunction meaning *than* which is used after comparatives (19.1/4*a*) and certain other words such as **aliter** *otherwise*, **posteā** *later*, **prius** *earlier*. Like **antequam** and **priusquam** (29.1/3*b*,i), **posteāquam** and **postquam** (both conjunctions mean *after*; see 5.1/2) can be used as single words or divided into **posteā/post . . . quam** with no difference in sense: **nihil post accidit quam litterās tuō lībertō dedī** *nothing happened after I gave the letter to your freedman* (**nihil accidit postquam . . .** would have the same meaning).
(v) the conjunction used with superlatives in expressions of the type **quam celerrimē potest** *as quickly as possible* (19.1/5*a*).

5   **Ac/atque**, which has the basic meaning *and* (3.1/5), is also used after words expressing similarity and dissimilarity as the link between the two elements compared: **coactus est aliter ac superiōribus annīs, exercitum in hībernīs collocāre** *he was forced to put his army in winter quarters in a way different from (otherwise than) in previous years.* In this use **ac/atque** coincides to some extent with use (iv) of **quam**.

6   **Sī** is combined with various words meaning *as* to introduce clauses which express something unreal or untrue and therefore have their verb in the subjunctive. These combinations (**quasi, tamquam sī, ut sī, velut sī**) are translated by *as if, as though*: **tamquam sī claudus sim, fuste ambulō** *I am walking with a stick as if I were lame.* Such clauses (which are similar to **sī** clauses in category 1 conditional sentences – 22.1/2) imply a comparison (*I am walking with a stick in such a way as I would do if*, etc.).

7   Proportional comparison, *the more/the less . . . the more/the less*, is expressed by **tantō . . . quantō** or **eō . . . quō** (all ablatives of measure of difference – 19.1/4*b*) with the appropriate adjectives or adverbs:

> **Quantō speī est minus, tantō magis amō.** *The less hope there is, the more I love* (lit. *by how much there is less of hope, by so much I love more*).

> **Quō plūrēs erant Veientēs, eō maior caedēs fuit.** *The more Veians there were, the greater was the slaughter* (lit. *by what [amount] there were more Veians, by that [amount] the slaughter was greater*).

There is no difference in meaning between these correlatives when used in this way. The same sense may also be expressed by **ita/tam . . . ut/quam** and two superlatives: **quam citissimē conficiēs, tam maximē expediet** *the quicker you finish [it], the more profitable it will be* (lit. *how most quickly you finish [it], so it will be most profitable*).

30.1/2 *Quī* with the subjunctive

A normal adjectival clause expresses a plain fact. Its verb is in the indicative, except when it is part of indirect speech and the subjunctive must be used (17.1/2 note 4). The subjunctive occurs in other types of adjectival clauses, where it either expresses something which is not a fact (i.e. something which could/might happen or have happened), or shows that the fact it states must be interpreted with reference to the main clause. We distinguish the following categories:

(*a*) *Adjectival clauses of purpose*

Lēgātōs Rōmam mīsērunt quī senātuī grātiās ēgērunt. *They sent envoys to Rome who thanked the senate.* (fact)

Lēgātōs Rōmam mīsērunt quī senātuī grātiās agerent. *They sent envoys to Rome who might thank the senate,* i.e. *to thank the senate.* (purpose)

Agerent in the second sentence expresses something that was intended to happen, but does not necessarily imply that it did. This use of **quī** with the subjunctive has the same meaning as **ut** with the subjunctive to express purpose (13.1/5), with which it can always be replaced. The subjunctive here is potential (22.1/1*b*); only the present and imperfect tenses are used with **quī** (or **ut**) in this sense.

(*b*) *Generalising adjectival clauses*

In the sentence **puellās dētestor quae in forō cunctantur** *I loathe the girls who are loitering in the forum* the indicative **cunctantur** shows we are dealing with a fact and that therefore specific girls are meant; for this reason we translate *girls* with the definite article. But in **puellās dētestor quae in forō cunctentur** *I loathe girls who* (*would*) *loiter in the forum* the subjunctive (here also potential) indicates what could happen and so shows that a type of girl is meant, not particular individuals.

Generalising adjectival clauses also occur in expressions such as **nēmō est quī ...** *there is no one who ...* and **nihil est quod ...** *there is nothing which ...* : **nihil est quod timeās** *there is nothing you should fear.* The use is extended to clauses indicating a general class or group where the potential force of the subjunctive is, at best, weak. A common example is **sunt quī ...** *there are people who ...* which is always followed by the subjunctive: **sunt quī discessum animī ā corpore putent esse mortem** *there are people who think that the departure of the soul from the body is death.*

(*c*) *Adjectival clauses expressing a consequence or result*

Here the **quī** clause can be the equivalent of **ut** with the subjunctive to express result (16.1/1) and must be so translated: **quis homō est tantā confidentiā quī sacerdōtem audeat violāre?** *what man is so audacious* (*is with so much audacity*) *that he would dare to violate a priestess?*

Similarly, after the adjectives **dignus** *worthy*, **indignus** *unworthy* and **idōneus** *suitable*, we find the subjunctive in clauses introduced by the relative pronoun or by **ut**, but the former is more common: **Līviānae fābulae nōn dignae sunt quae iterum legantur** *the plays of Livius* (*the Livian plays*) *are not worth reading twice* (*not worthy that they should be read again*). The two constructions are equally possible and common after a comparative and **quam** (for an example with **ut** see 19.1/4*d*): **maior sum quam cui possit Fortūna nocēre** *I am too great for Fortune to be able to harm* (lit. *greater than whom Fortune could harm*; **noceō** + dat. 20.1/1). In other cases a simple substitution of **ut** for **quī** would not be possible: **nōn is sum quī mortis perīculō terrear** *I am not a man who would be frightened by danger of death*. In this sentence, which is a common type, the **quī** clause expresses the result of the subject of the main clause being a certain type of person. To use **ut** here, a preceding **tālis** would be necessary.

(*d*) *Causal and concessive adjectival clauses*

Adverbial clauses can be used for both causes and concessions (29.1/2 & 4). An author employs adjectival clauses in these senses when he wishes to be less emphatic or to vary his style. Either the indicative or subjunctive is possible, but the latter is more common. Both causes and concessions are generally facts, and the use of the subjunctive here, which is not potential, is comparable with the construction of **cum** with the subjunctive in the senses of *because* and *although*. With either mood we must deduce from the context what the connection between the main clause and the adjectival clause is; the subjunctive shows that such a connection is intended, whereas the indicative does not.

Amant tē omnēs mulierēs, quī sīs tam pulcher. *Women love you since you are so handsome* (lit. *you who are . . .*).

Ego, quī sērō ac leviter Graecās litterās attigissem, tamen complūrēs Athēnīs diēs sum commorātus. *Although I had taken up Greek literature late* [*in life*] *and superficially, nevertheless I stayed in Athens several days* (lit. *I, who had . . .*).

In both cases, if the indicative had been used (**es, attigeram**), we would translate the relative clauses as such (*you who are . . .; I, who had . . .*) and leave the reader to decide from the broader context if there was a closer connection between them and the main clauses.

Causal adjectival clauses with the subjunctive are sometimes introduced by **quippe quī** (less commonly **ut quī, utpote quī**), which means *because-he-is-one who* (**quippe** is an adverb with no one-word English equivalent). This makes the clause emphatically causal: **convīvia cum patre nōn inībat, quippe quī nē in oppidum quidem, nisi perrārō, venīret** *he used not to go to banquets with his father since he did not even come into the town, except very rarely.*

30.2 Latin reading

1 Esse quam videri bonus malebat.
2 Quot contorsit spicula virgo, tot Phrygii cecidere viri.
3 Forte ita eo anno evenit ut, quotienscumque dictator ab exercitu recessisset, hostes in Samnio moverentur.
4 Exploratores mittit qui locum idoneum castris deligant.
5 Mihi, quanto plura recentium seu veterum revolvo, tanto magis ludibria rerum mortalium cunctis in negotiis observantur.
6 Nihil tam firmum est cui periculum non sit etiam ab invalido.
7 Nil adeo magnum neque tam mirabile quidquam
   quod non paulatim minuant mirarier omnes.
8 Homo totiens moritur quotiens amittit suos.
9 Nihil est quod magis deceat quam constantia.
10 Parthi, quo plus bibunt, eo plus sitiunt.
11 Qualis artifex pereo!
12 Aleator quanto in arte est melior, tanto est nequior.

Caratacus
13 Caratacus was a British chieftain taken to Rome in AD 51 after a prolonged resistance to the invasion of Britain by the Emperor Claudius (AD 43). According to Tacitus, he was granted a pardon after the following address to the emperor.

Si, quanta nobilitas et fortuna mihi fuit, tanta rerum prosperarum moderatio fuisset, amicus potius in hanc urbem quam captus venissem, neque dedignatus esses claris maioribus ortum,

plurimis gentibus imperitantem foedere in pacem accipere.
praesens sors mea ut mihi informis sic tibi magnifica est. habui   5
equos, viros, arma, opes: quid mirum si haec invitus amisi? nam si
vos omnibus imperitare vultis, sequitur ut omnes servitutem
accipiant? si statim deditus traherer, neque mea fortuna neque tua
gloria inclaruisset, et supplicium mei oblivio sequeretur: at si
incolumem servaveris, aeternum exemplar clementiae ero.   10

14 Solis candor illustrior est quam ullius ignis, quippe qui in
immenso mundo tam longe lateque colluceat.

15 Tam de se iudex iudicat quam de reo.

16 Maiores arbores caedebant quam quas ferre miles posset.

17 Qui modeste paret, videtur, qui aliquando imperet, dignus esse.

18 Stultissimum est in luctu capillum sibi evellere quasi calvitio
maeror levetur.

19 Multo aliter ac sperarat, rem publicam se habentem cognovit.

20 Utinam lex eadem, quae uxori est, viro!

21 Mendicus aequo censu, atque ille opulentissimus, censetur ad
Acherontem mortuus.

Notes

2 **Phrygii** Phrygian, i.e. *Trojan* (cf. 18.3 *l.*14).

3 **ēvēnit** perfect; **movērentur** *moved* (intr.), *made a move*, because
moveō is normally transitive, the passive can be used reflexively
(**moveor = mē moveō** *I move myself*, i.e. *I move* intr.).

4 The vivid presents should be translated by the English past tense.

5 **mihi** dat. of agent (28.1/1*c*) with **observantur**; **recentium seu
veterum** partitive genitive (27.1/4*k*); **lūdibria** lit. *mockeries, acts of
derision* – the author of this sentence, Tacitus, sees human affairs
as manipulated by a malign Fate or Chance; **rērum mortālium**
objective genitive (27.1/4*i*).

6 The subjunctive **sit** (and **minuant** in the next sentence) is in a
generalising adjectival clause (30.1/2*b*) and should be translated
by an indicative.

7 **mīrārier** archaic pres. inf. pass. (25.1/5*g*).

11 In this sentence (the dying words of the emperor Nero) **artifex**
artist is meant in a broad sense.

13 *ll.*1f. the two elements of the comparison are **nōbilitās et fortūna**
and **moderātiō**; **fuit** is indicative because it expresses a fact while

fuisset (supply **mihi**) is subjunctive because it does not and is the verb of a category 1 conditional sentence; **moderātiō** is preceded by an objective genitive (27.1/4*i*) and so means *control over*. *ll.*3f. there are two main verbs **vēnissem** and **dēdignātus essēs** after the **sī** clause; with **ortum** supply **mē** and with this take **imperitantem**. *l.*5 **ut . . . sīc** link the parallel and contrasted adjectives **informis** and **magnifica** (**sīc** may be left untranslated). *l.*8 **sī . . . traherer** lit. *if, having been surrendered immediately* (i.e. at the beginning of his resistance against the Romans), *I were being dragged* [*here*]; Caratacus had been betrayed and handed over to the Romans by a fellow Briton but only after he eluded them for eight years. *l.*10 **incolumem** supply **mē**.

19 **aliter** qualifies **habentem**.

30.3 Extra reading

The cave of Sleep

This description is from Ovid's long poem *Metamorphōsēs* (*Transformations*), a collection of stories, mainly from mythology, all of which tell of, or allude to, a change in bodily form.

Est prope Cimmerios longo spelunca recessu,
mons cavus, ignavi domus et penetralia Somni,
quo numquam radiis oriens mediusve cadensve
Phoebus adire potest. nebulae caligine mixtae
exhalantur humo dubiaeque crepuscula lucis.   5
non vigil ales ibi cristati cantibus oris
evocat Auroram, nec voce silentia rumpunt
sollicitive canes, canibusve sagacior anser.
non fera, non pecudes, non moti flamine rami,
humanaeve sonum reddunt convicia linguae.   1(
muta quies habitat. saxo tamen exit ab imo
rivus aquae Lethes, per quem cum murmure labens
invitat somnos crepitantibus unda lapillis.
ante fores antri fecunda papavera florent,
innumeraeque herbae, quarum de lacte soporem   1<
nox legit, et spargit per opacas umida terras.
ianua, ne verso stridorem cardine reddat,

nulla domo tota: custos in limine nullus.
at medio torus est ebeno sublimis in antro,
plumeus, unicolor, pullo velamine tectus,   20
quo cubat ipse deus, membris languore solutis.
hunc circa passim, vanas imitantia formas,
somnia vana iacent totidem, quot messis aristas,
silva gerit frondes, eiectas litus harenas.

Notes

*l.*1 **longō . . . recessū** abl. of description (6.1/3). *ll.*3f. **medius . . .**
Phoebus is the sun at noon. *l.*6 **cristātī. . . ōris** (with **āles**) abl. of
description (6.1/3). *l.*8 **anser** the value of geese as sentinels was
illustrated for the Romans by the famous story of how the sacred
geese on the Capitol had alerted the guards to a night attack by
invading Gauls (390 BC). *l.*11 **saxō . . . īmō** *the deepest* [*part of the*] *rock*
(21.1/3). *l.*12 **Lēthēs** gen. of **Lēthē** (25.1/4*e*). *l.*14 **papāvera** the soporific
effect of the seed of the opium poppy was well known in antiquity.
*l.*16 **legit** here *collects, takes*; **ūmida** goes with **nox** and should be
translated with it; **terrās** *the earth* (the prose expression is **orbis**
terrārum lit. *the circle of lands*). *l.*17 **cardine** doors in antiquity were
hinged by two pins (**cardinēs**), one projecting up into the frame in
which the door swung, the other projecting down into the threshold
beneath; this system is still standard for very large doors, but the
absence of precision engineering and proper bearings meant that a
Roman door always squeaked unless the pins were constantly
lubricated. *l.*18 scan this hexameter to discover the case of the first
and third words. *l.*19 **mediō** with **antrō**; **ebenō** abl. of origin (28.1/2*f*)
with **torus** [*made*] *of ebony*. *l.*21 **quō** *on which* has **torus** as its
antecedent. *l.*22 **hunc circā** = **circā hunc**. *ll.*23f. the dreams are
compared in number with ears of corn (**aristās**), leaves (**frondēs**) and
grains of sand (**harēnās**); **quot** is to be taken with each, lit. *how many*
ears of corn the harvest [*bears*], [*how many*] *leaves the forest bears*, etc.

UNIT 31

31.1 Grammar

31.1/1 Indirect speech (2)

Some Latin authors often report long speeches indirectly where in English we would think it stylistically bizarre not to give the speaker's actual words. Some of the following details elaborate on the earlier descriptions of the constructions involved; others set out complications which can occur in more extensive passages of indirect speech.

Subsection 2 has reference only to reports made by a third party, not by the original speaker or by someone addressing him. **Heri togam ēmī** *yesterday I bought a toga* can be reported in any one of the three persons:

> **Dixī mē heri togam ēmisse.** *I said that I had bought a toga yesterday.* (report by the original speaker)
> **Dixistī tē heri togam ēmisse.** *You said that you had bought a toga yesterday.* (report by a person addressing the original speaker)
> **Dixit sē heri togam ēmisse.** *He said he had bought a toga yesterday* (report by a third party about the original speaker)

The third type is by far the most common in Latin literature and involves problems that the other two do not. Combinations of the above types are possible (*you said that he . . .* , etc.), but present no special difficulty.

31.1/2 Change of pronouns, adverbs, etc. in indirect speech

In converting direct speech to indirect speech (as reported by a third party) certain words require adjustment because of the changed point of view.

ego, nōs	become	**sē** or are the unexpressed subjects of finite verbs in the third person.
meus, noster	become	**suus**.
tū, vōs	become	**ille, illī** (or the accusative, **illum, illōs**, when the subject of an infinitive).
tuus, vester	become	**illīus, illōrum**.
hic, iste	become	**is** or **ille** (or the accusative when the subject of an infinitive).

Likewise, certain adverbs (and adverbial phrases) of time and place may require change. If appropriate to the context of the indirect speech, **nunc** *now* becomes **tunc** *then*, **hodiē** *today* becomes **illō diē** *on that day*, **hīc** *here* becomes **illīc** *there*, etc.

> **Herī amīcum tuum Bāiīs vīsī sed nunc cum uxōre meā Rōmae sum.**
> *Yesterday I visited your friend at Baiae but now I am with my wife in Rome.*

> **Dīxit sē prīdiē amīcum illīus Bāiīs vīsisse sed tunc cum uxōre suā Rōmae esse.** *He said that on the previous day he had visited the friend of that man at Baiae but that he then was with his wife in Rome.*

Notice that while we can have ambiguity in English with third person pronouns and possessive adjectives (was he in Rome with his own wife or his friend's wife?) there is none with the corresponding words in Latin.

When a third person pronoun or possessive adjective in any form of indirect speech refers back to the subject of the main verb, the reflexives **sē** and **suus** must be used (cf. 17.1/2): **uxōrem rogāvit num cēnam sibi coxisset** (original **cēnamne mihi coxistī?**) *he asked his wife if she had cooked dinner for him* (original *have you cooked dinner for me?*).

Ambiguity is theoretically possible because a reflexive normally refers to the subject of the clause in which it occurs (9.1/4), as it does in: **Tiberius fēlīcem Priamum vocābat, quod superstes omnium suōrum exstitisset** *Tiberius used to call Priam happy on the grounds that he had outlived (had been the survivor of) all his own family.* Here, as elsewhere, the sense makes it obvious that **suōrum** refers to the subject of **exstitisset** (Priam), not to Tiberius (the **quod** clause is virtual indirect speech (29.1/2) and therefore comes under the same rules as normal indirect speech).

31.1/3 Periphrastic *fore ut* in indirect statement

The future infinitive passive (as **amātum īrī** *to be going to be loved*) is
rarely used (14.1/3). When the need for it arises in indirect statement
(e.g. in the reported form of **castra capientur** *the camp will be
captured*), Latin authors normally employ a periphrasis, **fore ut** +
subj., lit. [*it*] *to be going to be that* (for **fore**, the alternative future
infinitive of **sum**, see 14.1/3):

$$\left.\begin{array}{l}\textbf{Dīcit}\\\textbf{Dixit}\end{array}\right\}\quad\textbf{fore ut castra}\qquad\left\{\begin{array}{l}\textbf{capiantur}\\\textbf{caperentur}\end{array}\right.$$

$$He\left\{\begin{array}{l}says\\said\end{array}\right\}\quad that\ the\ camp\qquad\left\{\begin{array}{l}will\\would\end{array}\right\}\ be\ captured$$

This construction is sometimes used to replace a future infinitive
active in indirect statement. It is obligatory when a verb has no supine
and therefore no future active participle (or infinitive): **eī vīsus est
iuvenis dīcere, fore ut brevī convalesceret** *a young man seemed to be
saying to him that he would recover soon.*

31.1/4 Tense in indirect speech

The tense of the infinitive in the accusative and infinitive construction
depends wholly on the tense used in the original statement (17.1/2). In
indirect commands and petitions, in indirect questions, and in
subordinate clauses in all forms of indirect speech, a temporal
adjustment according to the rules governing sequence of tenses
(23.1/3) is made if the main verb is in a historic tense:

> **Dēsilīte, mīlitēs, nisi vultis aquilam hostibus prōdere.** *Jump down,
> soldiers, if you do not want to give up the standard to the enemy.*
> **Mīlitibus imperāvit ut dēsilīrent, nisi vellent aquilam hostibus
> prōdere.** *He gave the order to the soldiers that they should jump
> down, if they did not want to, etc.*

There are two consistent exceptions:

(*a*) A historic tense of the subjunctive (but *not* of the indicative) in a
subordinate clause must be retained in primary sequence:

> **Mīlēsia quaedam mulier, cum essem in Asiā, reī capitālis damnāta
> est.** *When I was in Asia, a certain Milesian woman was
> condemned on a capital charge.*

Teneō memoriā Mīlēsiam quandam mulierem, cum essem in Asiā, reī capitālis esse damnātam. *I remember (hold in memory) that when I was in Asia, a certain Milesian woman was condemned on a capital charge.*

(*b*) The reported version of two types of conditional sentences (see below), which, in fact, obey the rule given in (*a*).

31.1/5 Economy of introductory verbs in indirect speech

The distinctive nature of each construction used in indirect speech allows Latin authors, in the course of reporting a single speech, to switch from one type to another without any verb which would be appropriate to introduce the second:

Responsum ex decrētō est optāre pācem Rhodiōs: sī bellum esset nē quid ab Rhodiīs spērāret aut peteret rex. *In accordance with a decree a reply was made that the Rhodians desired peace; the king was told not to hope for or to ask for anything from the Rhodians if there were war (lit. the king should not hope, etc.).*

Here **optāre pācem Rhodiōs** is accusative and infinitive (representing an original statement) after **responsum est. Nē . . . spērāret aut peteret** is an indirect command; the original would have been either an imperative (*do not hope, O king . . .*) or a jussive subjunctive (*let the king not hope . . .*). Because, however, the indirect speech has already started, no introductory word meaning *they ordered* is required. When a positive indirect command or petition occurs in such a position, the introductory **ut** is omitted (English can use a similar construction):

Cicerō ad haec ūnum modo respondet: nōn esse consuētūdinem populī Rōmānī accipere ab hoste armātō condiciōnem: sī ab armīs discēdere velint, sē adiūtōre ūtantur lēgātōsque ad Caesarem mittant. *To this (these things) Cicero made only one reply, that it was not the practice of the Roman people to accept terms from an armed enemy; if they were willing to leave their arms, they should use his help (him as helper) and send envoys to Caesar (the passage is in the vivid present).*

Latin can even dispense with any introductory verb:

> **Consulis alterīus nōmen invīsum cīvitātī fuit: nimium Tarquiniōs regnō assuesse, nescīre eōs prīvātōs vīvere.** *The name of the other consul was hateful to the state; [it was thought] that the Tarquins had become too accustomed to royal power, that they did not know how to live as private citizens.*

31.1/6 Rhetorical questions in indirect speech

Often in the course of a formal speech a speaker asks questions purely for rhetorical effect; he does not expect them to be answered. In indirect speech these questions are treated as statements and put into the accusative and infinitive, although the appropriate introductory word (*why, who, when,* etc.) is retained:

> **Indignitāte Rōmānī accendēbantur: iam alterum exercitum victōrem in urbem reditūrum: sibi ultrō per contumēliās hostem insultāre; quandō autem sē, sī tum nōn essent, parēs hostibus fore?** *The Romans were fired with a sense of outrage; [they reflected that] the second victorious army was now about to return to the city; the enemy, of its own accord, was mocking and insulting them (mocking them through insults), but when were they going to be equal to the enemy if they were not then?*

The original rhetorical question here would be: **Quandō autem, sī nunc nōn sumus, parēs hostibus erimus?** *When will we be equal to the enemy if we are not now?*

31.1/7 Conditional sentences in indirect statement

Because Latin does not have an infinitive for each tense and because all finite verbs in indirect speech must in any case be in the subjunctive, some of the distinctions made in conditional sentences disappear when reported. The following table gives the indirect versions of all the conditional sentences of the table in 22.1/2 and should be used in conjunction with it. Each original sentence is reported after **dīcit** *he says* and after **dixit** *he said* to give its form after a primary tense and its form after a historic tense.

		CATEGORY 1	CATEGORY 2
		FUTURE	
(i)	Dīcit	tē, sī id dīcās, errātūrum esse.	tē, sī id dīcās, errātūrum esse.
	He says	*that if you were to say that you would be wrong.*	*that if you say that you will be wrong.*
(ii)	Dixit	tē, sī id dīcerēs, errātūrum esse.	tē, sī id dīcerēs, errātūrum esse.
	He said	*that if you were to say that you would be wrong.*	*that if you said that you would be wrong.*
		PRESENT	
(iii)	Dīcit	tē, sī id dīcerēs, errātūrum fuisse.	tē, sī id dīcās, errāre.
	He says	*that if you were (now) saying that you would be wrong*	*that if you are saying that you are wrong.*
(iv)	Dixit	tē, sī id dīcerēs, errātūrum fuisse.	tē, sī id dīcerēs, errāre.
	He said	*that if you were saying that you would be wrong.*	*that if you were saying that you were wrong.*
		PAST	
(v)	Dīcit	tē, sī id dixissēs, errātūrum fuisse.	tē, sī id dixerīs, errāre.
	He says	*that if you had said that you would have been wrong.*	*that if you said (or used to say) that you were wrong.*
(vi)	Dixit	tē, sī id dixissēs, errātūrum fuisse.	tē, sī id dixissēs, errāvisse.
	He said	*that if you had said that you would have been wrong.*	*that if you had said (or had been saying) that you were wrong.*

The table will not seem so intimidating if it is remembered that:

(*a*) In converting the main verb of a category 2 sentence, the normal rule (17.1/2) applies, i.e. that its tense must be reflected in the infinitive with which it is replaced.

(*b*) In converting the main verb of a category 1 sentence, the potential nature of the subjunctive is conveyed by the future infinitive (**errātūrus esse** *to be going to be wrong*) for the present subjunctive, and by the future-in-the-past infinitive (**errātūrus fuisse** *to have been going to be wrong*) for the imperfect and pluperfect subjunctives (cf. the composite future-in-the-past subjunctive, 23.1/3); the tenses of **esse** and **fuisse** obey the rule referred to above.

(c) In determining the tense of the subjunctive required in the **sī** clause, sequence of tenses (23.1/3) is everywhere observed except in category 1 (iii) and (v) where the imperfect subjunctive **dīcerēs** and the pluperfect **dixissēs** are used after the present indicative **dīcit** (cf. 31.1/4).

(d) In category 2 (v) and (vi) both **dixerīs** (perf. subj.) and **dixissēs** stand for either **dīcēbās** or **dixistī**. In both cases **errāvisse** stands for either **errābās** or **errāvistī**.

Notes

1 In conditional sentences of the category 2 type, the nature of the verbs used can have an effect on the tense of the **sī/nisi** clause. In all the permutations of the above example, the act of saying and the state of being in error are taken as occurring at the same time; the first simultaneously entails the second. However, in other cases the conditional clause may express something which clearly precedes the main clause, although this is often not made plain by the tenses used in English. Such sentences can have a future reference (5.1/3): **sī incolās armāverimus** (fut. perf.) **Hannibalem superābimus** *if we arm* (lit. *shall have armed*) *the inhabitants we shall conquer Hannibal.* In indirect speech this becomes:

> **Dīcit nōs sī incolās armāverīmus** (perf. subj.) **Hannibalem superātūrōs esse.** *He says that if we arm the inhabitants we shall conquer Hannibal.*
>
> **Dixit nōs sī incolās armāvissēmus Hannibalem superātūrōs esse.** *He said that if we armed the inhabitants we would conquer Hannibal.*

2 Category 2(iv) may also mean *he said that if you are saying that you are wrong* in a context where the original statement refers to a past state which has continued into the present. The same applies *mutatis mutandis* to category 2(ii).

31.2 Latin reading

1 Quo cruciatu animi Caesarem putamus vitam acturum fuisse si divinasset fore ut in eo senatu, quem maiore ex parte ipse cooptasset, ante ipsius Pompeii simulacrum trucidatus ita iaceret ut ad eius corpus non modo non amicorum, sed ne servorum quidem quisquam accederet?

2 Dictator, cum iam in manibus videret victoriam esse, litteras ad senatum misit: deum immortalium benignitate, suis consiliis, patientia militum, Veios iam fore in potestate populi Romani: quid de praeda faciendum censerent?

An unabashed temple-robber

3 Dionysius, de quo ante dixi, cum fanum Proserpinae Locris expilavisset, navigabat Syracusas, isque cum secundissimo vento cursum teneret, ridens 'videtisne' inquit 'amici, quam bona a dis immortalibus navigatio sacrilegis detur?' idque homo acutus cum bene planeque percepisset, in eadem sententia perseverabat: qui 5 cum ad Peloponnesum classem appulisset et in fanum venisset Iovis Olympii, aureum ei detraxit amiculum grandi pondere, quo Iovem ornarat e manubiis Karthaginiensium tyrannus Gelo, atque in eo etiam cavillatus est aestate grave esse aureum amiculum, hieme frigidum, eique laneum pallium iniecit, cum id esse ad omne anni 10 tempus aptum diceret. idemque Aesculapii Epidauri barbam auream demi iussit: neque enim convenire barbatum esse filium, cum in omnibus fanis pater imberbis esset. etiam mensas argenteas de omnibus delubris iussit auferri, in quibus cum more veteris Graeciae inscriptum esset BONORUM DEORUM, uti se corum 15 bonitate velle dicebat. idem Victoriolas aureas et pateras coronasque, quae simulacrorum porrectis manibus sustinebantur, sine dubitatione tollebat eaque se accipere, non auferre dicebat: esse enim stultitiam, a quibus bona precaremur, ab iis porrigentibus et dantibus nolle sumere. 20

The Helvetii appeal to Caesar

4 The Helvetii, a Gallic tribe living in what is now western Switzerland, decided, because of population pressure, to make a mass migration to a more favourable part of Gaul (58 BC). Their plans were seen by Caesar as contrary to Roman interests and he halted their advance at the river Arar (modern Saône). They then made a cautious approach to him about a peaceful solution to their problem.

Helvetii repentino eius adventu commoti cum id quod ipsi diebus viginti aegerrime confecerant, ut flumen transirent, illum uno die fecisse intellegerent, legatos ad eum mittunt: cuius legationis

Divico princeps fuit, qui bello Cassiano dux Helvetiorum fuerat. is
ita cum Caesare egit: si pacem populus Romanus cum Helvetiis   {
faceret, in eam partem ituros atque ibi futuros Helvetios ubi eos
Caesar constituisset atque esse voluisset: sin bello persequi
perseveraret, reminisceretur et veteris incommodi populi Romani
et pristinae virtutis Helvetiorum. quod improviso unum pagum
adortus esset, cum ii qui flumen transissent suis auxilium ferre non 1(
possent, ne ob eam rem aut suae magnopere virtuti tribueret aut
ipsos despiceret. se ita a patribus maioribusque suis didicisse, ut
magis virtute contenderent quam dolo aut insidiis niterentur. quare
ne committeret ut is locus ubi constitissent ex calamitate populi
Romani et internecione exercitus nomen caperet aut memoriam 1!
proderet.

*As well as translating the above passage, reconstruct (and translate)
Divico's original words (i.e. put the passage from* **sī pācem** . . . *into
direct speech).*

Notes

1 **quō cruciātū** abl. of manner (28.1/2*j*); **actūrum fuisse sī divīnasset**
would be **ēgisset sī divīnasset** in direct speech; **fore . . . iacēret** is used
instead of the acc. and inf. **sē iacitūrum esse.**

3 *l.*2 **cum** *when*; **secundissimō ventō** abl. of instrument (7.1/4). *l.*5 **quī**
an example of the way Latin often uses the relative to join a clause
with what precedes (see note on 17.3) – translate *he. l.*7 **eī** dat. of
disadvantage *from him* (28.1/1*e*); **grandī pondere** abl. of description
(6.1/3). *l.*8 **in eō** *about it. l.*10 **iniciō** takes an acc. and dat. (28.1/1*a*).
*l.*12 **neque enim** *for . . . not. l.*13 **pater** the father of Aesculapius was
Apollo, who was always represented as a beardless young man.
*l.*15 **BONORUM DEORUM** possessive gen. [*Property*] *of the
Beneficent Gods;* **ūtī** <**ūtor.** *l.*19 **bona** *blessings* (lit. *good things*); the
word is also to be understood with **porrigentibus et dantibus** and
sūmere.

4 *ll.*1f. **ut . . . transīrent** is a noun clause in apposition to **quod** but it
takes the form it has because of **confēcerant** (26.1/2*e*), *what they
themselves had . . . accomplished,* [*namely*] *that they crossed the river*
(i.e. *the crossing of the river*). *l.*4 **bellō Cassiānō** *the war against
Cassius* Divico had defeated a Roman army commanded by
Cassius (107 BC) and it is to this that he alludes in his speech with

the phrase **veteris incommodī**. *l.*8 **reminiscerētur** indirect positive command with **ut** omitted (31.1/5); translate *he should remember* (what Divico actually said was **reminiscere . . .!** *remember . . .!*). *ll.*11f. **nē . . . tribueret . . . despiceret** (and **nē committeret** in *l.*14) indirect negative commands (original: **nōlī . . . tribuere . . . despicere**).

31.3 Extra reading

The vanity of human wishes

Decimus Iūnius Iuvenālis (in English Juvenal), a younger contemporary of Martial, was born about AD 60 and lived on into the next century. A hard and poverty-stricken life seems to have prompted him to write satire, and his success in this genre is reflected in his popularity in the Middle Ages and later. The following passage is from his tenth satire, which was imitated by no less an author than Dr Johnson (*Let observation with extensive view/Survey mankind from China to Peru . . .*).

> Omnibus in terris, quae sunt a Gadibus usque
> Auroram et Gangen, pauci dinoscere possunt
> vera bona atque illis multum diversa, remota
> erroris nebula. quid enim ratione timemus
> aut cupimus? quid tam dextro pede concipis, ut te   5
> conatus non paeniteat votique peracti?
> evertere domos totas optantibus ipsis
> di faciles. nocitura toga, nocitura petuntur
> militia: torrens dicendi copia multis
> et sua mortifera est facundia, viribus ille   10
> confisus periit admirandisque lacertis,
> sed plures nimia congesta pecunia cura
> strangulat et cuncta exsuperans patrimonia census
> quanto delphinis ballaena Britannica maior.
> temporibus diris igitur iussuque Neronis   15
> Longinum et magnos Senecae praedivitis hortos
> clausit et egregias Lateranorum obsidet aedes
> tota cohors: rarus venit in cenacula miles.

Notes

Scan lines 3, 4, 8, 9, 10, 12 to discover the quantity of final **a**'s (the metre is the hexameter). *l.*1 **Gādēs** (modern Cadiz), which was beyond the Straits of Gibraltar, was at the western limits of the Roman World. *l.*2 **Gangēn**, acc. of **Gangēs** (25.1/4*e*), is symbolic of the furthest East. *ll.*3f. **illīs** dat. with **dīversa**, *things very* (**multum**) *contrary to them*, i.e. *their opposites*; scansion indicates **nebulā** (abl.) and, as the punctuation shows **remota erroris nebula** go together, we must have **remōtā** (fem. abl. s.) going with it; **ratiōne** abl. of instrument (7.1/4) *through* [*the exercise of*] *reason. l.*5 **dextrō pede** the superstitious Roman always stepped over a threshold with his right foot and hence this phrase came to mean *auspiciously. l.*6 **cōnātūs** and **vōtī peractī** gen. with **paeniteat** (20.1/2*b*); **peractī** must be translated by an abstract noun (12.1/2) – Juvenal is envisaging a very Roman way of going about anything, viz of first making a vow to a god that if the desired object were achieved the god would receive a dedication or offering. *l.*7 metre indicates **ēvertēre** (= **ēvertērunt** 4.1/6 note 1); **optantibus ipsīs** lit. *their masters desiring it*; in colloquial Latin (not the language Juvenal normally uses) **ipse** was used to mean *master* (cf. Irish use of *himself*). *l.*9 **multīs** dat. with **mortifera** (*l.*10) *fatal to many. ll.*10f. **sua** refers to **multīs** and so should be translated *their*; **confīsus** (compound of **fīdō** 25.1/5*e*) governs **vīribus** and **lacertīs**; the reference is to Milo (**ille** *that famous man, that man of old*), an overconfident Greek athlete who karate-chopped the fork of an oak-tree. The split tree immediately sprang back and secured Milo, who was subsequently devoured by wolves. *l.*12 we must tell from the sense that we have **cūrā** (abl.). *l.*14 **quantō** does not here have a preceding **tantō** (30.1/1 note 1). *l.*15 **igitur** *so, consequently* introduces examples of people whose vast wealth incurred the envy of Nero and was confiscated by him. *l.*18 **tōta cohors** the house of the Laterani was so huge that a whole cohort was required to take possession of it; **mīles** the army enforced the emperor's wishes but he rarely had occasion to take action against the poor who lived in garrets (**cēnācula**).

SUGGESTIONS FOR FURTHER STUDY

Editions of Latin texts with notes and a vocabulary

The Student's Catullus, Daniel H. Garrison, Routledge.
Vergil, *Aeneid Book I* edited by H. Gould and J. Whiteley, Duckworth.
Vergil, *Aeneid Book IV* edited by H. Gould and J. Whiteley, Duckworth.
H. Gould and J. Whiteley, *Selections from five Roman Authors*, Duckworth (contains passages from Nepos, Caesar, Sallust, Livy and Cicero).
Bilingual editions of these authors (and of nearly every other Latin writer) exist in the series *The Loeb Classical Library*, published by Harvard University Press. A number of other elementary editions are available from the Bristol Classical Press (a division of Duckworth, 61 Frith Street, London W1V 5TA, England) and from Bolchazy-Carducci Publishers (1000 Brown Street, Wauconda, Illinois 60603, USA; *internet address* http://bolchazy.com).

Works of reference

D. A. Kidd, *Latin–English, English–Latin Dictionary*, Collins (a small dictionary but good value for its price).
C. T. Lewis, *Elementary Latin Dictionary,* Oxford UP.
The Oxford Latin Dictionary, Oxford UP. (the largest Latin–English dictionary available).

B. H. Kennedy, *The Revised Latin Primer*, Longman (an elementary grammar).

E. C. Woodcock, *A New Latin Syntax*, Duckworth (an advanced treatment of Latin syntax).

L. R. Palmer, *The Latin Language*, Duckworth (a full account of Latin and of its history).

D. R. Dudley, *Roman Society*, Pelican.

Oxford Companion to Classical Literature, Oxford UP.

Oxford Classical Dictionary, Oxford UP.

Betty Radice, *Who's Who in the Ancient World*, Penguin.

H. J. Rose, *Handbook of Greek Mythology*, Routledge (an account of the mythological background used by all Latin poets).

P. Grimal, *Dictionary of Classical Mythology,* Penguin (an alphabetical arrangement of the basic information contained in the previous title).

Appendix 1

Regular Verbs – Finite Forms

ACTIVE

	First Conjugation stem in **a**	**Second Conjugation** stem in **e**	**Third Conjugation** stem in consonant	**Fourth Conjugation** stem in **i**
Present Indicative				
s. 1	amō *I love, am loving, do love*	moneō *I warn, am warning, do warn*	regō *I rule, am ruling, do rule*	audiō *I hear, am hearing, do hear*
2	amās	monēs	regis	audīs
3	amat	monet	regit	audit
pl.1	amāmus	monēmus	regimus	audīmus
2	amātis	monētis	regitis	audītis
3	amant	monent	regunt	audiunt
Present Subjunctive				
s. 1	amem	moneam	regam	audiam
2	amēs	moneās	regās	audiās
3	amet	moneat	regat	audiat
pl.1	amēmus	moneāmus	regāmus	audiāmus
2	amētis	moneātis	regātis	audiātis
3	ament	moneant	regant	audiant
Imperative				
s.	amā *love!*	monē *warn!*	rege *rule!*	audī *hear!*
pl.	amāte	monēte	regite	audīte

Imperfect Indicative

	amā-	monē-	regē-	audiē-
s. 1	amābam *I was loving, used to love*	monēbam *I was warning, used to warn*	regēbam *I was ruling, used to rule*	audiēbam *I was hearing, used to hear*
2	amābās	monēbās	regēbās	audiēbās
3	amābat	monēbat	regēbat	audiēbat
pl. 1	amābāmus	monēbāmus	regēbāmus	audiēbāmus
2	amābātis	monēbātis	regēbātis	audiēbātis
3	amābant	monēbant	regēbant	audiēbant

Imperfect Subjunctive

	amā-	monē-	regere-	audī-
s. 1	amārem	monērem	regerem	audīrem
2	amārēs	monērēs	regerēs	audīrēs
3	amāret	monēret	regeret	audīret
pl. 1	amārēmus	monērēmus	regerēmus	audīrēmus
2	amārētis	monērētis	regerētis	audīrētis
3	amārent	monērent	regerent	audīrent

Future Indicative

	amā-	monē-	reg-	audi-
s. 1	amābō *I shall love, shall be loving*	monēbō *I shall warn, shall be warning*	regam *I shall rule, shall be ruling*	audiam *I shall hear, shall be hearing*
2	amābis	monēbis	regēs	audiēs
3	amābit	monēbit	reget	audiet
pl. 1	amābimus	monēbimus	regēmus	audiēmus
2	amābitis	monēbitis	regētis	audiētis
3	amābunt	monēbunt	regent	audient

Regular Verbs – Finite Forms

ACTIVE

	First Conjugation stem in **a**	Second Conjugation stem in **e**	Third Conjugation stem in consonant	Fourth Conjugation stem in **i**
Perfect Indicative				
s. 1	amāvī *I loved, have loved*	monuī *I warned, have warned*	rexī *I ruled, have ruled*	audīvī *I heard, have heard*
2	amāvistī	monuistī	rexistī	audīvistī
3	amāvit	monuit	rexit	audīvit
pl. 1	amāvimus	monuimus	reximus	audīvimus
2	amāvistis	monuistis	rexistis	audīvistis
3	amāvērunt	monuērunt	rexērunt	audīvērunt
Perfect Subjunctive				
s. 1	amāverim	monuerim	rexerim	audīverim
2	amāverīs	monuerīs	rexerīs	audīverīs
3	amāverit	monuerit	rexerit	audīverit
pl. 1	amāverīmus	monuerīmus	rexerīmus	audīverīmus
2	amāverītis	monuerītis	rexerītis	audīverītis
3	amāverint	monuerint	rexerint	audīverint
Pluperfect Indicative				
s. 1	amāveram *I had loved*	monueram *I had warned*	rexeram *I had ruled*	audīveram *I had heard*
2	amāverās	monuerās	rexerās	audīverās
3	amāverat	monuerat	rexerat	audīverat
pl. 1	amāverāmus	monuerāmus	rexerāmus	audīverāmus
2	amāverātis	monuerātis	rexerātis	audīverātis
3	amāverant	monuerant	rexerant	audīverant

Pluperfect Subjunctive

	amo	moneo	rego	audio
s. 1	amāvissem	monuissem	rexissem	audīvissem
2	amāvissēs	monuissēs	rexissēs	audīvissēs
3	amāvisset	monuisset	rexisset	audīvisset
pl. 1	amāvissēmus	monuissēmus	rexissēmus	audīvissēmus
2	amāvissētis	monuissētis	rexissētis	audīvissētis
3	amāvissent	monuissent	rexissent	audīvissent

Future Perfect

	amo	moneo	rego	audio
s. 1	amāverō *I shall have loved*	monuerō *I shall have warned*	rexerō *I shall have ruled*	audīverō *I shall have heard*
2	amāveris	monueris	rexeris	audīveris
3	amāverit	monuerit	rexerit	audīverit
pl. 1	amāverimus	monuerimus	rexerimus	audīverimus
2	amāveritis	monueritis	rexeritis	audīveritis
3	amāverint	monuerint	rexerint	audīverint

Regular Verbs – Finite Forms

PASSIVE

	First Conjugation stem in **a**	Second Conjugation stem in **e**	Third Conjugation stem in consonant	Fourth Conjugation stem in **i**
Present Indicative				
s. 1	amor *I am loved, am being loved*	moneor *I am warned, am being warned*	regor *I am ruled, am being ruled*	audior *I am heard, am being heard*
2	amāris	monēris	regeris	audīris
3	amātur	monētur	regitur	audītur
pl. 1	amāmur	monēmur	regimur	audīmur
2	amāminī	monēminī	regiminī	audīminī
3	amantur	monentur	reguntur	audiuntur
Present Subjunctive				
s. 1	amer	monear	regar	audiar
2	amēris	moneāris	regāris	audiāris
3	amētur	moneātur	regātur	audiātur
pl. 1	amēmur	moneāmur	regāmur	audiāmur
2	amēminī	moneāminī	regāminī	audiāminī
3	amentur	moneantur	regantur	audiantur
Imperative				
s.	amāre *be loved!*	monēre *be warned!*	regere *be ruled!*	audīre *be heard!*
pl.	amāminī	monēminī	regiminī	audīminī

Imperfect Indicative

	amābar *I was being loved, used to be loved*	monēbar *I was being warned, used to be warned*	regēbar *I was being ruled, used to be ruled*	audiēbar *I was being heard, used to be heard*
s. 1	amābar	monēbar	regēbar	audiēbar
2	amābāris	monēbāris	regēbāris	audiēbāris
3	amābātur	monēbātur	regēbātur	audiēbātur
pl. 1	amābāmur	monēbāmur	regēbāmur	audiēbāmur
2	amābāminī	monēbāminī	regēbāminī	audiēbāminī
3	amābantur	monēbantur	regēbantur	audiēbantur

Imperfect Subjunctive

	amārer	monērer	regerer	audīrer
s. 1	amārer	monērer	regerer	audīrer
2	amārēris	monērēris	regerēris	audīrēris
3	amārētur	monērētur	regerētur	audīrētur
pl. 1	amārēmur	monērēmur	regerēmur	audīrēmur
2	amārēminī	monērēminī	regerēminī	audīrēminī
3	amārentur	monērentur	regerentur	audīrentur

Future Indicative

	amābor *I shall be loved*	monēbor *I shall be warned*	regar *I shall be ruled*	audiar *I shall be heard*
s. 1	amābor	monēbor	regar	audiar
2	amāberis	monēberis	regēris	audiēris
3	amābitur	monēbitur	regētur	audiētur
pl. 1	amābimur	monēbimur	regēmur	audiēmur
2	amābiminī	monēbiminī	regēminī	audiēminī
3	amābuntur	monēbuntur	regentur	audientur

For all second person singular forms given above, except in the imperative, there is a less common alternative with **-re** for **-ris**.

Regular Verbs – Finite Forms

PASSIVE

In the paradigms set out below only the masculine forms of the participle and gerundive are given. If the word, whether expressed or understood, with which they agree, is feminine or neuter, they must be changed to the appropriate feminine or neuter form.

	First Conjugation stem in **a**	**Second Conjugation** stem in **e**	**Third Conjugation** stem in consonant	**Fourth Conjugation** stem in **i**
			Perfect Indicative	
s. 1	amātus sum *I was loved, have been loved*	monitus sum *I was warned, have been warned*	rectus sum *I was ruled, have been ruled*	audītus sum *I was heard, have been heard*
2	amātus es	monitus es	rectus es	audītus es
3	amātus est	monitus est	rectus est	audītus est
pl.1	amātī sumus	monitī sumus	rectī sumus	audītī sumus
2	amātī estis	monitī estis	rectī estis	audītī estis
3	amātī sunt	monitī sunt	rectī sunt	audītī sunt
			Perfect Subjunctive	
s. 1	amātus sim	monitus sim	rectus sim	audītus sim
2	amātus sīs	monitus sīs	rectus sīs	audītus sīs
3	amātus sit	monitus sit	rectus sit	audītus sit
pl.1	amātī sīmus	monitī sīmus	rectī sīmus	audītī sīmus
2	amātī sītis	monitī sītis	rectī sītis	audītī sītis
3	amātī sint	monitī sint	rectī sint	audītī sint

Pluperfect Indicative

s. 1	amātus eram *I had been loved*	monitus eram *I had been warned*	rēctus eram *I had been ruled*	audītus eram *I had been heard*
2	amātus erās	monitus erās	rēctus erās	audītus erās
3	amātus erat	monitus erat	rēctus erat	audītus erat
pl. 1	amātī erāmus	monitī erāmus	rēctī erāmus	audītī erāmus
2	amātī erātis	monitī erātis	rēctī erātis	audītī erātis
3	amātī erant	monitī erant	rēctī erant	audītī erant

Pluperfect Subjunctive

s. 1	amātus essem	monitus essem	rēctus essem	audītus essem
2	amātus essēs	monitus essēs	rēctus essēs	audītus essēs
3	amātus esset	monitus esset	rēctus esset	audītus esset
pl. 1	amātī essēmus	monitī essēmus	rēctī essēmus	audītī essēmus
2	amātī essētis	monitī essētis	rēctī essētis	audītī essētis
3	amātī essent	monitī essent	rēctī essent	audītī essent

Future Perfect

s. 1	amātus erō *I shall have been loved*	monitus erō *I shall have been warned*	rēctus erō *I shall have been ruled*	audītus erō *I shall have been heard*
2	amātus eris	monitus eris	rēctus eris	audītus eris
3	amātus erit	monitus erit	rēctus erit	audītus erit
pl. 1	amātī erimus	monitī erimus	rēctī erimus	audītī erimus
2	amātī eritis	monitī eritis	rēctī eritis	audītī eritis
3	amātī erunt	monitī erunt	rēctī erunt	audītī erunt

Regular Verbs – Non-Finite Forms

Infinitives

	First Conjugation stem in a	Second Conjugation stem in e	Third Conjugation stem in consonant	Fourth Conjugation stem in i
Active				
Future	amātūrus esse *to be going to love*	monitūrus esse *to be going to warn*	rectūrus esse *to be going to rule*	auditūrus esse *to be going to hear*
Present	amāre *to love*	monēre *to warn*	regere *to rule*	audīre *to hear*
Perfect	amāvisse *to have loved*	monuisse *to have warned*	rexisse *to have ruled*	audīvisse *to have heard*
Passive				
Future	amātum īrī *to be going to be loved*	monitum īrī *to be going to be warned*	rectum īrī *to be going to be ruled*	audītum īrī *to be going to be heard*
Present	amārī *to be loved*	monērī *to be warned*	regī *to be ruled*	audīrī *to be heard*
Perfect	amātus esse *to have been loved*	monitus esse *to have been warned*	rectus esse *to have been ruled*	audītus esse *to have been heard*

Participles

	First Conjugation stem in a	Second Conjugation stem in e	Third Conjugation stem in consonant	Fourth Conjugation stem in i
Active				
Future	amātūrus *about to love, going to love*	monitūrus *about to warn, going to warn*	rectūrus *about to rule, going to rule*	auditūrus *about to hear, going to hear*
Present	amans *loving*	monens *warning*	regens *ruling*	audiens *hearing*
Passive				
Perfect	amātus *having been loved*	monitus *having been warned*	rectus *having been ruled*	audītus *having been heard*

Gerund

| amandum | monendum | regendum | audiendum |

Gerundive

| amandus | monendus | regendus | audiendus |

Supine (in -um)

| amātum | monitum | rectum | audītum |

N.B.

1 The following are first and second declension adjectives: future active and perfect passive participles, gerundive.
2 The present active participle is a third declension adjective (-ns, -ntis).
3 Where a participle forms part of an infinitive it must agree with the subject of that infinitive.
4 The gerund is a neuter noun of the second declension.
5 The supine in -ū is formed by replacing the -um of the above supines with -ū.

Appendix 2

Mixed Conjugation

Capiō *take*

Only the tenses and forms made from the present stem are given below. The other tenses and forms (made from the stem of the perfect or of the supine) are not irregular.

	ACTIVE		PASSIVE	
	Indicative	**Subjunctive**	**Indicative**	**Subjunctive**

Present

	Indicative	**Subjunctive**	**Indicative**	**Subjunctive**
s. 1	capiō *I take, am taking, do take*	capiam	capior *I am taken, am being taken*	capiar
2	capis	capiās	caperis	capiāris
3	capit	capiat	capitur	capiātur
pl.1	capimus	capiāmus	capimur	capiāmur
2	capitis	capiātis	capiminī	capiāminī
3	capiunt	capiant	capiuntur	capiantur

Imperfect

s. 1	capiēbam *I was taking, used to take*	caperem	capiēbar *I was being taken, used to be taken*	caperer
2	capiēbās	caperēs	capiēbāris	caperēris
3	capiēbat	caperet	capiēbātur	caperētur
pl.1	capiēbāmus	caperēmus	capiēbāmur	caperēmur
2	capiēbātis	caperētis	capiēbāminī	caperēminī
3	capiēbant	caperent	capiēbantur	caperentur

Future

s. 1	capiam *I shall take*		capiar *I shall be taken*
2	capiēs		capiēris
3	capiet		capiētur
pl.1	capiēmus		capiēmur
2	capiētis		capiēminī
3	capient		capientur

Imperative

s.	cape *take!*	capere *be taken!*
pl.	capite	capiminī

Infinitives

Present   capere *to take*   capī *to be taken*

Participle

Present   capiens *taking*

Gerund and Gerundive
capiendum   capiendus

Appendix 3

Deponent Verbs

	Cōnor *try*		Patior *suffer*	
	Indicative	**Subjunctive**	**Indicative**	**Subjunctive**
			Present	
s. 1	cōnor *I try, am trying, do try*	cōner	patior *I suffer, am suffering, do suffer*	patiar
2	cōnāris	cōnēris	pateris	patiāris
3	cōnātur	cōnētur	patitur	patiātur
pl.1	cōnāmur	cōnēmur	patimur	patiāmur
2	cōnāminī	cōnēminī	patiminī	patiāminī
3	cōnantur	cōnentur	patiuntur	patiantur
			Imperfect	
s. 1	cōnābar *I was trying, used to try*	cōnārer	patiēbar *I was suffering, used to suffer*	paterer
2	cōnābāris	cōnārēris	patiēbāris	paterēris
3	cōnābātur	cōnārētur	patiēbātur	paterētur
pl.1	cōnābāmur	cōnārēmur	patiēbāmur	paterēmur
2	cōnābāminī	cōnārēminī	patiēbāminī	paterēminī
3	cōnābantur	cōnārentur	patiēbantur	paterentur
			Future	
s. 1	cōnābor *I shall try*		patiar	
2	cōnāberis		patiēris	
3	cōnābitur		patiētur	
pl.1	cōnābimur		patiēmur	
2	cōnābiminī		patiēminī	
3	cōnābuntur		patientur	
			Perfect	
	cōnātus sum *I tried, have tried*	cōnātus sim	passus sum *I suffered, have suffered*	passus sim
	etc.	etc.	etc.	etc.

Pluperfect

cōnātus eram *I*   cōnātus essem   passus eram *I had*   passus essem
  had tried   *suffered*
etc.   etc.   etc.   etc.

Future Perfect

cōnātus erō *I*   passus erō *I shall have*
  shall have tried   *suffered*
etc.   etc.

Imperative

s.   cōnāre *try!*   patere *suffer!*
pl.   cōnāminī   patiminī

Infinitives

Future   cōnātūrus esse   passūrus esse *to be*
          to be going to try   *going to suffer*
Present   cōnārī *to try*   patī *to suffer*
Perfect   cōnātus esse *to*   passus esse *to have*
          have tried   *suffered*

Participles

Future   cōnātūrus *about to*   passūrus *about to*
          try, going to try   *suffer, going to suffer*
Present   cōnans *trying*   patiens *suffering*
Perfect   cōnātus *having tried*   passus *having suffered*

Gerund

cōnandum   patiendum

Gerundive

cōnandus   patiendus

Supine (in -um)

cōnātum   passum

Appendix 4

Irregular verbs

Sum *I am*

	Indicative	Subjunctive	Indicative	Subjunctive
	Present		**Perfect**	
s. 1	sum *I am*	sim	fuī *I have been, was*	fuerim
2	es	sīs	fuistī	fuerīs
3	est	sit	fuit	fuerit
pl.1	sumus	sīmus	fuimus	fuerīmus
2	estis	sītis	fuistis	fuerītis
3	sunt	sint	fuērunt	fuerint

	Imperfect		**Pluperfect**	
s. 1	eram *I was*	essem	fueram *I had been*	fuissem
2	erās	essēs	fuerās	fuissēs
3	erat	esset	fuerat	fuisset
pl.1	erāmus	essēmus	fuerāmus	fuissēmus
2	erātis	essētis	fuerātis	fuissētis
3	erant	essent	fuerant	fuissent

	Future		**Future Perfect**	
s. 1	erō *I shall be*		fuerō *I shall have been*	
2	eris		fueris	
3	erit		fuerit	
pl.1	erimus		fuerimus	
2	eritis		fueritis	
3	erunt		fuerint	

Imperative

s.	es *be!*
pl.	este

Infinitives

Future	futūrus esse *or* fore *to be*
	going to be
Present	esse *to be*
Perfect	fuisse *to have been*

Participles

Future futūrus *about to be, going to be*

Present	*none*
Perfect	*none*

Sum has no gerund or supine. For the other imperative see 21.1/1 note 3. There is an alternative imperfect subjunctive: **forem, forēs, foret**, etc.

Irregular Verbs

Possum (15.1/1), **fīō** (15.1/3), **volō** (15.1/5), **nōlō** (15.1/5), **mālō** (15.1/5), **eō** (15.1/6). The tenses of these verbs formed from the perfect stem are not listed below; they are regular except for **eō** (15.1/6a).

Indicative

		possum	fīō	volō	nōlō	mālō	eō
Present	s. 1	possum *I am able*	fīō *I am made, become*	volō *I wish, want*	nōlō *I do not wish*	mālō *I prefer*	eō *I go*
	2	potes	fīs	vīs	nōn vīs	māvīs	īs
	3	potest	fit	vult	nōn vult	māvult	it
	pl. 1	possumus	—	volumus	nōlumus	mālumus	īmus
	2	potestis	—	vultis	nōn vultis	māvultis	ītis
	3	possunt	fīunt	volunt	nōlunt	mālunt	eunt
Future	s. 1	poterō *I shall be able*	fīam *I shall be made, shall become*	volam *I shall wish, shall want*	nōlam *I shall not wish*	mālam *I shall prefer*	ībō *I shall go*
	2	poteris	fīēs	volēs	nōlēs	mālēs	ībis
	3	poterit	fīet	volet	nōlet	mālet	ībit
	pl. 1	poterimus	fīēmus	volēmus	nōlēmus	mālēmus	ībimus
	2	poteritis	fīētis	volētis	nōlētis	mālētis	ībitis
	3	poterunt	fīent	volent	nōlent	mālent	ībunt

Imperfect

		poteram *I was able*	fiēbam *I was being made, was becoming*	volēbam *I was wishing, was wanting*	nōlēbam *I was not wishing*	mālēbam *I was preferring*	ībam *I was*
s.	*1*	poteram	fiēbam	volēbam	nōlēbam	mālēbam	ībam
	2	poterās	fiēbās	volēbās	nōlēbās	mālēbās	ībās
	3	poterat	fiēbat	volēbat	nōlēbat	mālēbat	ībat
pl.	*1*	poterāmus	fiēbāmus	volēbāmus	nōlēbāmus	mālēbāmus	ībāmus
	2	poterātis	fiēbātis	volēbātis	nōlēbātis	mālēbātis	ībātis
	3	poterant	fiēbant	volēbant	nōlēbant	mālēbant	ībant

Subjunctive

Present

s.	*1*	possim	fiam	velim	nōlim	mālim	eam
	2	possīs	fiās	velīs	nōlīs	mālīs	eās
	3	possit	fiat	velit	nōlit	māiit	eat
pl.	*1*	possīmus	fiāmus	velīmus	nōlīmus	mālīmus	eāmus
	2	possītis	fiātis	velītis	nōlītis	mālītis	eātis
	3	possint	fiant	velint	nōlint	mālint	eant

Imperfect

s.	*1*	possem	fierem	vellem	nollem	mallem	īrem
	2	possēs	fierēs	vellēs	nollēs	mallēs	īrēs
	3	posset	fieret	vellet	nollet	mallet	īret
pl.	*1*	possēmus	fierēmus	vellēmus	nollēmus	mallēmus	īrēmus
	2	possētis	fierētis	vellētis	nollētis	mallētis	īrētis
	3	possent	fierent	vellent	nollent	mallent	īrent

Imperative

s.					nōlī *be unwilling!*		ī *go!*
pl.					nōlīte		īte

Participles

Present			volens *willing*	nōlens *unwilling*		iēns, euntis *going*
Future						itūrus *about to go, going to go*

Infinitives

Present	posse *to be able*	fierī *to be made*	velle *to wish*	nolle *not to wish*	malle *to prefer*	īre *to go*
Future						itūrus esse *to be going to go*
Perfect	potuisse *to have been able*		voluisse *to have wished*	nōluisse *not to have wished*	māluisse *to have preferred*	isse (īvisse) *to have gone*

These verbs have no other forms except for **eō**, which has supines **itum**, **itū**, and a gerund **eundum** (on the passive forms of **eō** see 15.1/6b).

Transitive compounds of **eō** have a perfect participle passive in **-itus**, e.g. **praeteritus** *having been passed* (**praetereō** *go by, pass*), and a gerundive in **-eundus**, e.g. **adeundus** *to be approached* (**adeō** *approach*).

Appendix 5

Classification of verbs with irregular principal parts

The principal parts of all third conjugation verbs must be learnt as they cannot be predicted from the present stem. A few verbs of the first and fourth conjugations also have irregular principal parts, together with a somewhat larger number from the second conjugation. Taking all such verbs, we can classify perfect stems into five groups:

(*a*) The present stem is used without change: **bibī (bibō)**, **vertī (vertō)**.

(*b*) The vowel of the present stem is lengthened: **iūvī (iuvō)**, **vīdī (videō**; here, as elsewhere with second conjugation verbs, the **e** of the present stem is dropped), **lēgī (legō)**. Sometimes an **m** or **n** is dropped: **vīcī (vincō)**, **rūpī (rumpō)**. Other verbs substitute **ē** for short **a**: **fēcī (faciō)**, **ēgī (agō)**.

(*c*) A large number of verbs add **s** to the present stem: **carpsī (carpō)**, **mansī (maneō)**. Where this **s** is preceded by **c** or **g**, the two combine to form **x**: **dīxī (dīcō)**, **rēxī (regō)**. In the majority of cases, however, a greater change is involved: **mīsī (mittō)**, **gessī (gerō)**, **vāsī (vādō)**.

(*d*) An added **u** (regular in the second conjugation) or **v** (regular in the first and fourth conjugations) occurs in conjugations where we do not expect them: **vetuī (vetō, -āre)**, **aperuī (aperiō, -īre)**, **dēlēvī (dēleō, -ēre)**. Sometimes the present stem is considerably modified: **nōvī (nōscō)**, **crēvī (cernō)**. In a few third conjugation verbs, **īv** is added: **petīvī (petō)**.

(*e*) A few verbs repeat their initial syllable (reduplication): **cucurrī (currō)**, **poposcī (poscō)**. In some cases there is a change of vowel: **tetigī (tangō**; for the loss of **n** compare **vīcī** and **rūpī** above). An initial **s** followed by a consonant is not repeated: **stetī (stō)**.

All the above types of perfect stem occur in the third conjugation; some of them occur in each of the other conjugations.

The supine stem of all verbs with regular principal parts ends in **t** (**amātum**, **monit-um, audīt-um**). With other verbs we have either **t** or **s**: **dat-um (dō)**, **rīs-um (rīdeō)**, **cess-um (cēdō)**. As in (*c*) above, the combination *c/g* + **s** results in **x**: **fix-um (fīgō)**. No rules can be given for the distribution of these two types. In both, the final consonant of the present stem is often lost: **mōt-um (moveō)**, **lūs-um (lūdō)**.

Appendix 6

Numerals

Cardinals

1	I	ūnus	20	XX	vīgintī
2	II	duo	30	XXX	trīgintā
3	III	trēs	40	XL	quadrāgintā
4	IIII or IV	quattuor	50	L	quinquāgintā
5	V	quinque	60	LX	sexāgintā
6	VI	sex	70	LXX	septuāgintā
7	VII	septem	80	LXXX	octōgintā
8	VIII	octo	90	XC	nōnāgintā
9	IX	novem	100	C	centum
10	X	decem	200	CC	ducentī
11	XI	undecim	300	CCC	trecentī
12	XII	duodecim	400	CCCC	quadringentī
13	XIII	tredecim	500	IƆ or D	quingentī
14	XIV	quattuordecim	600	IƆC	sescentī
15	XV	quindecim	700	IƆCC	septingentī
16	XVI	sēdecim	800	IƆCCC	octingentī
17	XVII	septendecim	900	IƆCCCC	nongentī
18	XVIII	duodēvīgintī	1,000	CIƆ or M	mille
19	XIX	undēvīgintī	10,000	CCIƆƆ	decem mīlia

Ordinals	Numeral Adverbs	Distributives
1 prīmus (prior), *first*	semel, *once*	singulī, *one each*
2 secundus (alter), *second*	bis, *twice*	bīnī, *two each*
3 tertius	ter	ternī, *or* trīnī
4 quartus	quater	quaternī
5 quintus	quinquiēs	quīnī
6 sextus	sexiēs	sēnī
7 septimus	septiēs	septēnī
8 octāvus	octiēs	octōnī
9 nōnus	noviēs	novēnī
10 decimus	deciēs	dēnī
11 undecimus	undeciēs	undēnī
12 duodecimus	duodeciēs	duodēnī
13 tertius decimus	terdeciēs	ternī dēnī
20 vīcensimus	vīciēs	vīcēnī
100 centensimus	centiēs	centēnī

Numeral adverbs ending in **-ēs** have an alternative form in **-ens**. All the above numerals ending in **-us** and **-ī** (except **vīgintī** and its compounds) are first and second declension adjectives.

KEY TO LATIN
READING EXERCISES

Explanations and more literal interpretations are given in round brackets. Some words which have no specific equivalent in the Latin original but which must be supplied in English are enclosed in square brackets. In each of units 3–5 a more difficult sentence has been analysed. Translations from Latin authors are as literal as possible and not to be taken as models of English style or as reflecting that of the original. References have been given for longer prose passages and for extracts from poetry of more than one line. In these references Roman numerals refer to books (e.g. of the *Aeneid*), Arabic to chapters in prose works, and in poetry to poems and/or lines.

1.2

(1) Where are the sailors? (2) The sailors are in the tavern. (3) The girls are not in the taverns. (4) Where is Rome? (5) Rome is in Italy. (6) The water of life. (7) The island of the farmers. (8) To (*or* for) the inhabitants of Spain and Italy. (9) Of the victories of Rome. (10) In the taverns of the sailors.

Note that most common nouns (see Noun *in* Glossary of grammatical terms) *in the above may also be taken in an indefinite sense (i.e. with a/an for a singular noun and no article for a plural). We would then have:*

(1) Where are there sailors? (2) There are sailors in a tavern. (3) There are no girls in taverns. (4) & (5) *do not contain common nouns.* (6) Water of life. (7) An island of farmers. (8) To (*or* for) inhabitants of Spain and Italy. (9) Of victories of Rome. (10) In taverns of sailors.

A broader context would be necessary for a definite choice. In some cases a combination of the two versions gives a third possibility, e.g. (2) There are sailors in the tavern.

2.2

(1) At first he/she was asking for (*or* used to ask for) the friendship of the inhabitants. (2) You used not to warn (*or* were not warning) the women of Gaul and now they are walking on the streets. (3) I used always to love (*or* was always loving) Italy and I love [it] now. (4) We used to fight (*or* were fighting) in the island of Sicily but the inhabitants denied [their] friendship. (5) Why do you overcome (*or* are you overcoming) the farmers of Greece? (6) You were hoping for (*or* used to hope for) the friendship of the girls, O sailors, but you do not obtain [it]. (7) The women of Greece were with the farmers of Italy but they used to refuse [their] friendship and always ask for money. (8) We are telling a story about Greece to the woman (*or* are telling the woman a story about Greece). (9) The farmer does not point out the road to the poet. (10) They walk on the streets of Rome and always listen to the poets. (11) You are walking with the sailors of Gaul, O women. (12) We used to warn the sailors in the tavern but they used always to fight. (13) When the women of Greece were living in Italy, I was fighting with the farmers of Spain. (14) The poets often stir up the farmers when they tell stories about the women of Gaul.

As mentioned in connection with 1.2/2, there can be ambiguity in isolated sentences as to whether common nouns should be translated with the definite or indefinite article; from here on, only the possibility with the definite article will normally be given. Another ambiguity is whether the imperfect should be translated into English by the past continuous (I was doing) *or the past habitual* (I used to do), *although even in isolated sentences (such as 12) a choice can sometimes be made. In the context of (4)* denied *is the idiomatic translation of the imperfect* **negābant***. In (4) and (7) we supply* their, *as Latin often does not require an equivalent of such words (4.1/4 and 9.1/5). In (3) we must understand the object of* **amō** (*in English* it, *i.e. Italy*); *in such cases Latin can use a pronoun (here* **eam** *8.1/2) but generally does not if there is no ambiguity.*

3.2

Possible ambiguities in the use of the imperfect are not indicated from here on.

(1) Are the boys walking with [their] schoolmaster in the forum? (2) Both Brutus and Cassius were sitting in the Senate-house and listening to the words of Pompey. (3) I was fighting in Gaul with the Gauls but you were sailing either to Greece or to Asia. (4) Why do you not give gifts either to the sons or to the daughters of Cassius? (5) Today I am walking not only in front of the temples but also across the forum. (6) I used to walk on the Appian Way and look at the inscriptions on (of) the tombs. (7) The souls of the dead live amid darkness under the earth. (8) I am going across the river because [my] enemies are [all] over (through) the fields. (9) O gods and goddesses, are you abandoning the Romans when they are fighting against the Carthaginians? (10) I was at the house of friends and was telling a story about the beginning of Rome to the boys (*or* was telling the boys a story about . . .). (11) On account of the danger the women are standing in front of the temples of the gods and giving gifts. (12) In the works of Vergil we read about the destruction of Troy. (13) In the sky we see stars around the moon. (14) Not even before the temple [are there] flames on the altar! (15) Tongilianus has a nose; I know, I don't deny [it]; but these days Tongilianus has nothing except a nose (Martial XII, 88).

Analysis of sentence 9 (according to the steps given in 2.2)

O di deaeque, Romanos relinquitis ubi contra Poenos pugnant?

(*a*) **Ō** + the vocative is used in addresses (1.1/3*b*); hence **dī** must be voc. pl. not nom. pl.; **deaeque** = **deae** + **-que**; **deaeque** is followed by a comma, which indicates that the preceding words form a sense unit; **-que** *and* joins elements of equal grammatical weight, and so **deae** should be the same case as **dī**; **Rōmānōs** acc. pl. of **Rōmānus** *a Roman*; **relinquitis** 2nd pl. pres. ind. act. of **relinquō** *leave, abandon*; its basic meaning is *you are leaving/abandoning*; **ubi** could be the conjunction *when* (introducing an adverbial clause) or the interrogative adverb *where . . .?*; **contrā** *against* prep. + acc. (3.1/4); Latin prepositions precede the word they govern, and, as **Poenōs** (acc. pl. of **Poenus** *Carthaginian*) immediately follows, we can take the two words together as *against the Carthaginians*; **pugnant** 3rd pl. pres. ind. act. of **pugnō** *fight*; it therefore means *they were fighting* (we supply *they* because there is no nominative plural that can act as subject).

(*b*) The finite verbs are **relinquitis** and **pugnant**; we have two clauses.

(*c*) We have already used the punctuation after **deaeque** to analyse the first words, which must mean *O gods and goddesses*; **relinquitis** is not preceded by a subordinating conjunction and so must be the main verb; **ubi** can only mean *where . . .?* if it is followed by a main verb and therefore here must mean *when*.

(*d*) The question mark indicates that we must change our first interpretation of **relinquitis** to *are you leaving/abandoning . . .?*; **Rōmānōs** can only be its direct object: *are you leaving/abandoning the Romans . . .?* The remaining words fit together as a subordinate clause *when they are fighting against the Carthaginians*, and the whole means: *O gods and goddesses, are you abandoning the Romans when they are fighting against the Carthaginians? Abandon* seems more apposite than *leave* in this context.

4.2

(1) The lofty horse stood inside the walls of Troy and poured [out] men. (2) When shall I leave Asia and see [my] native land again? (3) O fair girls, there are bad sailors in your city (*or* the bad sailors are in your city) and they are walking through all the streets. (4) My son saw ancient buildings when he was in Egypt. (5) Why, O Fortune, are you blind? Often you give wealth not to good but to bad men. (6) The road to Corinth is long but you will find there many beautiful statues. (7) O friends, when will you come to the Roman forum and see the monuments of ancient Rome? (8) Our poets sat under the shade of the cypress and did not work. (9) You have come to dinner without food, O friends. I have only fruit and wine. (10) Few reach (arrive at) the stars through difficulties (difficult things). (11) Once ignorant of troubles (bad things), we are now miserable because the tax collector has come to [our] town (*or* is coming depending on whether we have **vēnit** or **venit**; there would be no ambiguity in speech). (12) I shall go to Greece also and buy learned slaves. (13) In Italy even small boys used to drink wine. (14) You will see large cypresses near the temple of Diana. (15) When you were drinking a lot of wine (much wine) in the farmer's garden, you said stupid things. (16) You did not tell the truth (say true things), O Brutus. You were not in the Senate-house today. (17) Our Caecilianus does not dine without a boar, Titus. Caecilianus has a nice guest (Martial VII, 59).

Analysis of sentence 15 (according to the steps given in 2.2)

Ubi in horto agricolae multum vinum bibebas, stulta dixisti.

(*a*) **Ubi** can only be the conjunction as there is no question mark at the end of the sentence; **in** (prep.) may be followed by either acc. or abl. (3.1/4); **hortō** by itself can be either dat. s. or abl. s., but, as prepositions immediately precede the word they govern, it must be governed by **in** and so be abl.; the two words therefore mean *in the garden*; **agricolae** either gen. s. or dat. s. or nom. pl. of **agricola** *farmer* (voc. pl. is ruled out because of the punctuation); **multum** either acc. m. s. or nom. n. s. or acc. n. s. of **multus** *much* (voc. n. s. is ruled out because of the punctuation); **vīnum** either nom. s. or acc. s. of **vīnum** *wine* (voc. s. is ruled out because of the punctuation); **bibēbās**, 2nd s. impf. ind. act. of **bibō** *drink*, means *you used to drink* or *you were drinking*; **stulta** either nom. f. s. or abl. f. s. (in which case it would be pronounced **stultā**) or nom. n. pl. or acc. n. pl. of **stultus** *stupid* (voc. f. s. and voc. n. pl. are ruled out because of the punctuation); **dixistī**, 2nd s. perf. ind. act. of **dīcō**, means *you said* or *you have said*.

(*b*) The finite verbs are **bibēbās** and **dixistī**; we have two clauses.

(*c*) The comma after **bibēbās** indicates that it divides the two clauses.

(*d*) As **bibēbās** is not 3rd s., **vīnum** cannot be its subject; therefore **vīnum** must be acc. The subject of **bibēbās**, *you*, can only be m. or f., and so **multum** cannot be nom. n. s.; it can, however, agree with **vīnum**. As we do not have a verb which takes an indirect object, **agricolae** must be gen. s. (it cannot be nom. pl. because the verb is singular); as genitives normally follow the word they qualify, it should be taken with **hortō**. **dīcō** *say* is a transitive verb and we would expect to have an object after **dixistī**; **stulta** fits perfectly and so must be acc. n. pl. The meaning is *you said/have said stupid things* (**stulta** is being used as a noun, 4.1/3).

(*e*) **Ubi** as a conjunction means *when* and introduces an adverbial (subordinate) clause; this means that the other clause **stulta dixistī** must be the main clause (it has, in any case, no conjunction to lead us to suppose otherwise). The meaning of the **ubi** clause is either *when you were drinking much wine in the farmer's garden* or *when you used to drink* etc.; with either we must interpret **dixistī** as *you said* (not *you* *have said*) but the first is correct here because with the second we would expect an imperfect tense (*you used to say*) in the main clause. The sentence therefore means: *When you were drinking much wine in the farmer's garden, you said stupid things.*

5.2

(1) Because the Greeks had destroyed Troy, the Trojans wandered for many years. (2) After they found the gold, they mounted their horses and hurried to the wood. (3) When they saw our [men], the Gauls ran inside the walls of the town. (4) As soon as they took up a position on dry land, our [men] attacked the town. (5) He (*or* she) lived in Greece for many years since the Carthaginians had come to Italy with elephants. (6) We shall expect your daughter in autumn when she leaves (will have left) Rome. (7) If I fall (shall have fallen) from the wall, you will be punished tomorrow, O Davus. (8) Cassius was often angry if I had said harsh things (*or* whenever I said, etc.). (9) When you conquered both Gauls and Germans, your glory was great. (10) For ten years we waged war with the Carthaginians and did not conquer [them]. (11) Before I saw your letter, I was hesitant to live in Greece for a long time. (12) Although many weapons of the Spaniards appeared, they ran to battle. (13) He sighed and wept when he saw the blood-stained weapons of [his] friend. (14) I shall not come before I buy (shall have bought) the books of Vergil. (15) Yesterday, as bad slaves are accustomed [to do], the friends of Davus sat in the tavern for many hours and drank much wine.

Analysis of sentence 15 (according to the steps given in 2.2)

Heri, ut servi mali solent, amici Davi in taberna multas horas sederunt et vinum multum biberunt.

(*a*) **Heri** adv. *yesterday*; **ut** conj. *as, when* (with indicative); **servī** either gen. s. or nom. pl. of **servus** *slave* (voc. pl. is ruled out because of the punctuation); **malī** either gen. m. s. or gen. n. s. or nom. m. pl. of **malus** *bad* (voc. m. pl. is ruled out because of the punctuation); **solent** 3rd pl. pres. ind. act. of **soleō** *be accustomed*; its basic meaning is *they are accustomed*; **amīcī** gen. s. or nom. pl. of **amīcus** *friend* (voc. pl. is ruled out because of the punctuation); **Davī** can only be the gen. s. of **Davus** because it is a proper noun; **in** (prep.) may be followed by either the acc. or the abl. (3.1/4); **taberna** could be either nom. s. or abl. s. of

taberna (voc. s. is ruled out because of the punctuation); but, as prepositions immediately precede the word they govern, it must be governed by **in** and so be abl. (i.e. **tabernā**); the two words therefore mean *in the tavern*; **multās** acc. f. pl. of **multus** *many*; **hōrās** acc. pl. of **hōra** *hour*; **sēdērunt** 3rd pl. perf. ind. act. of **sedeō** *sit*; its basic meaning is *they sat/have sat*; **et** conj. *and*; **vīnum** either nom. s. or acc. s. of **vīnum** *wine* (voc. s. is ruled out by the punctuation); **multum** either acc. m. s. or nom. n. s. or acc. n. s. of **multus** *much* (voc. n. s. is ruled out by the punctuation); **bibērunt**, 3rd pl. perf. ind. act. of **bibō** *drink*, means *they drank/have drunk*.

(*b*) The finite verbs are **solent, sēdērunt** and **bibērunt**; we have three clauses.

(*c*) Commas enclose **ut . . . solent**; as **ut** is a subordinating conjunction and **solent** is a finite verb, it is reasonable to suppose that these words form one subordinate clause and that **heri** is to be taken with the subsequent words. The only other conjunction is **et**, which joins elements of equal grammatical weight; **sēdērunt** and **bibērunt** must therefore be main verbs.

(*d*) **Malī** is an adjective following a noun with which it can agree. Taken together the words mean either *of the bad slave* or *the bad slaves* (nom.); each in itself makes satisfactory sense but, as we have no other word in the clause for a genitive to attach itself to, the second interpretation is the correct one. This makes the phrase the subject of **solent**, and the clause means *as/when bad slaves are accustomed*. What is true for **servī** is also true for **amīcī**; it must be nom. pl. and subject of **sēdērunt**. **Davī** (gen.) follows **amīcī** and so goes with it: *the friends of Davus sat/have sat in the tavern*. The Latin **sedeō** and the English *sit* are not followed by a direct object (i.e. are intransitive), and therefore **multās hōrās** (which naturally go together) must be some other type of accusative. The meaning of **hōra** suggests a temporal phrase; an accusative to express time how long, *for many hours,* is appropriate to the context. **Vīnum multum** (which naturally go together and are singular) can only be the object of **bibērunt** (pl.); the meaning is *they drank/have drunk much wine*.

(*e*) We have one subordinate clause and two main clauses. **Heri** *yesterday* suggests that **sēdērunt** and **bibērunt** must be taken as *sat* and *drank*, not *have sat* and *have drunk*. As the main verbs are perfect and the verb of the **ut** clause is present, **ut** here must mean *as*, not *when*. The overall meaning is: *Yesterday, as bad slaves are accustomed* [i.e. *to do*], *the friends of Davus sat in the tavern for many hours and drank much wine.*

6.2

(1) It is [characteristic] of barbarians to paint their bodies. (2) The queen of the Britons, a woman of great bravery, used to fight with the Romans. (3) The Romans used not to sail in winter because they feared (used to fear) storms. (4) 'You are a many-headed monster (monster of many heads)', said Horace. (5) Cicero was a guest who did not eat much but was very amusing (a guest of not much food but of much jest). (6) The law takes notice of (sees) an angry man; an angry man does not take notice of the law. (7) It is [the mark] of a fool to persist in error. (8) It is [the mark] of good men to put up with grief. (9) There was a great temple of Jupiter on the Capitol and there the Romans used to sacrifice to the king of the gods. (10) After we finished the journey, we entered a shrine of Venus and gave thanks for [our] safety. (11) Since I was in Sicily with [my] father last year, I do not know the names of the consuls. (12) If the Gauls destroy (will have destroyed) our town, we shall wait in Italy for the leader of the Romans with [his] soldiers. (13) Poor wandering sweet soul, guest and companion of the body, to what places will you now depart, pale, stiff, naked, and not jest (give jokes) as you are accustomed [to do]?

7.2

(1) Juvenal, the Roman poet, used to long for a healthy mind in a healthy body. (2) Divine nature gave men fields, human skill built cities. (3) The people of Rome, the chief of cities, thought Horace a great poet. (4) The enemy began to climb the rampart with a ladder. (5) Because a lion had devoured Davus, I made a virtue of necessity and bought a new slave. (6) The Romans, since they did not have wives, kidnapped the girls of the Sabines. (7) After he conducted (made) successful battles, he took several cities of the enemy by force. (8) Since the Gauls will probably come, they have fortified the city with a rampart and ditch. (9) Our [men] took [their] arms quickly and climbed the rampart. (10) He hurried to Gaul with five legions by the nearest road. (11) True art lies hidden (it is art to hide art, *i.e. really*

great works of art are so skilfully made that we do not easily comprehend the art that went into them). (12) It was night and sleep held living things through all the earth (all lands). (13) Because they were in great danger, the Roman citizens freed their slaves and made catapults from [their] wives' hair. (14) The consul destroyed the town and sold the inhabitants' possessions for much money. (15) Baths, wine, sex harm our bodies, but baths, wine, sex make life [worthwhile].

8.2

(1) He was the first to bring (he first led) four elephants to Rome. (2) I also have farms and a house. (3) When the inhabitants carried everything from the fields into the city and were inside the walls, Gracchus moved camp to Cumae. (4) With these forces Hannibal remained at Carthage and waited for the Romans. (5) Large forces of Greeks assembled at Athens and sailed to Rhodes. (6) Although the Germans were quiet, Caesar advanced to their boundaries. (7) If I am at home, my mind is out of doors, but if I am out of doors, my mind is at home. (8) You did many things badly at Rome and on military service. (9) If you come with me from Rome to Brundisium, we will cross to Greece by ship. (10) He sacrificed a bull to Neptune, a bull to you, fair Apollo (*Aeneid III*, 119 adapted). (11) Trojan Aeneas sent us to your threshold (*Aeneid VII*, 221). (12) O Meliboeus, a god has created (made) this leisure for us, for I will always regard him as a god (he will always be a god for me), a tender lamb from my flocks will often stain his altar (*Eclogue I*, 6–8). (13) At some future time you will receive this man in the sky, laden with the spoils of the East (*Aeneid I*, 289). (14) You also, Caieta, nurse of Aeneas (Aenean nurse), gave, [when] dying, eternal fame to our shores (*Aeneid VII*, 1f.).

9.2

From this exercise onwards, possessive adjectives (my, his, *etc.*) *are not marked as insertions even though there is no corresponding word in the Latin.*

(1) Arms are of little value abroad unless there is wisdom at home. (2) After he conquered the enemy, Caesar sent a letter to the senate about himself, 'I came, I saw, I conquered.' (3) At dawn (first light) the

cavalry put to flight a large band of Carthaginians. (4) The leader of the Romans made an attack on the enemy with all his forces and many were killed (with the slaughter of many). (5) Cato killed himself with his own hand. (6) After the death of Clitus, Alexander with difficulty kept his hands from himself (*i.e. refrained from suicide*). (7) Demetrius had entrusted his sons to Gnidius, his guest-friend, with a large quantity of gold. (8) As Seneca the philosopher said, anger is a brief madness and has no control over itself (is with no control of itself). (9) In wine [there is] truth. (10) Equals [congregate] with equals. (11) Happy in the timeliness of his death. (12) Envy is blind. (13) Fortune favours (helps) the bold. (14) Art is long, life is short (*i.e. it takes a long time to acquire an art or skill*). (15) Stolen waters are sweet. (16) Nature's prescriptions (natural things) are not disgraceful. (17) O life, long to the man [who is] miserable, short to the man [who is] happy (*i.e. time passes slowly when we are miserable but quickly when we are happy*). (18) Mortal acts never deceive the gods. (19) Either the man is insane or he writes verses (*i.e. is a poet*). (20) The weeping of an heir is laughter behind the mask. (21) Against a lucky man [even] a god has little power (scarcely has strength). (22) I only count serene hours (I do not count hours unless serene. *There is a pun on* **serēnus** *which can mean* sunny *or* happy; *a sundial only functions in sunny weather and it is only then that we can enjoy ourselves out of doors*). (23) A learned man always has wealth in himself. (24) Where they create a wilderness they call it peace. (25) Many [are] the relatives of the fortunate. (26) [You must say] only fair things about the dead (nothing about the dead if [it is] not good).

10.2

(1) Those who race across the sea change the heavens, not their intellect. (2) Each is the maker of his own fortune. (3) Never has nature said one thing, wisdom another. (4) The same person who inflicts (causes) the wound of love heals it. (5) He who fears his very self (**sē** *is himself* **reflexive**, **ipsum** *is himself* **emphatic**) suffers constant tortures (there are constant tortures for him who . . .). (6) A sick man who makes his doctor his heir does himself a bad turn (does badly with himself). (7) What is food for some is poison for others. (8) Even a single hair (one hair) has its own shadow. (9) Disaster easily finds whomever it is seeking. (10) A man who suffers (makes) a shipwreck

for a second time blames Neptune wrongly (*i.e. he should have taken Neptune's hint on the first occasion*). (11) Love is not cured by herbs (is curable by no herbs). (12) Thais has black teeth, Laecania white. What is the reason? The latter has false (bought) teeth, the former her own (Martial V, 43). (13) You, the same person, are difficult, obliging, charming, unpleasant: I can live neither with you nor without you (Martial XII, 46). (14) When the togaed crowd shouts so loud a 'Bravo!' at you (for you), it is not you, Pomponius, but your dinner that is eloquent (not you [but] your dinner is eloquent. *Pomponius gave dinner to his audience to gain their favour*) (Martial VI, 48). (15) The little book which you are reciting is mine, O Fidentinus, but when you recite badly it begins to be yours (Martial I, 38).

11.2

(1) I saw 273 soldiers; 1000 sailors; 8000 sailors. (2) By 3000 Romans; concerning 641 Gauls; 100 Greek women. (3) Petilius, [who was] not going to cause any delay, was inciting the soldiers with fierce words. (4) Soon [it will be] night, [get] into the business (*i.e. the work you must do*). (5) The quarrels of lovers are the renewal of love. (6) You fall into Scylla [while] desiring to avoid Charybdis. (7) Roused [to action] by this letter, Caesar enlisted two legions in Gaul. (8) Jupiter from on high smiles at the perjuries of lovers. (9) A host of doctors is certain death to the sick (of the sick). (10) I fear Greeks even bearing gifts. (11) On that matter scholars contend and the dispute is still undecided (under, i.e. before, the judge). (12) In a short time we shall capture the citadel either abandoned by the enemy or with the enemy themselves. (13) One world is not enough for the youth of Pella (*Alexander the Great*). (14) Who will guard the guards themselves? (15) The safety of the state is the highest law. (16) You will dine well, my Fabullus, at my house within a few days if the gods are favourable to you, if you bring with you a good, large dinner, not without a fair girl and wine and wit and all manner of laughter (Catullus, poem 13, 1–5). (17) Leisure is troublesome for you, Catullus: in leisure you run riot and become too excited. Leisure has in past times (previously) destroyed both kings and prosperous cities (Catullus, poem 51, 13–16). (18) Sparrow, my girl's darling, with whom she is accustomed to play, whom she is accustomed to hold in her bosom, to whom, [when] seeking [it], she is accustomed to give the tip of her finger and provoke sharp bites . . .

I wish I could play with you just as she (herself) [does] and ease the sad cares of my mind! (Catullus, poem 2, 1–4, 9–10)

12.2

(1) When one dog barks, another immediately barks as well (**et**). (2) In the third year six letters written by Cicero reached (came to) the senate. (3) A change of land does not change character. (4) [When] recalled to defend his native land, Hannibal waged war against Publius Scipio. (5) There is great merit (praise) in doing (giving) a favour. (6) The capture of others did not frighten him. (7) Having left his city and companions and fleet (city and companions and fleet having been left), Aeneas seeks the sceptre and seat of Palatine Evander (*i.e. has gone to see king Evander on the Palatine hill*) (*Aeneid IX,* 8–9). (8) They raise a sign of the capture of the city (*i.e. that the city has been captured*) from the wall. (9) They gather herbs fearsome to mention, not only to eat. (10) When the arrival of the enemy had been announced, Hannibal moved camp. (11) The violation of guests, the killing of envoys, the damage to shrines have caused this (so) great desolation. (12) The consul came into the city in triumph (triumphing) [with] Cluilius, the leader of the Volscians, bound and walking in front of his chariot. (13) Looking back, Horatius saw the three Curiatii coming at long intervals. (14) After divorcing the sister of Octavian (sister of Octavianus having been divorced), Antonius (Mark Antony) married Cleopatra. (15) Fearing (*i.e. because he feared*) barbers' knives, Dionysius used to singe his hair with a live coal. (16) However, swift moons restore the losses caused by the heavens; when we have descended to where father Aeneas, to where rich Tullus and Ancus [have gone], we are dust and a shade . . . When once you have died and Minos has delivered (made) an august judgement on you, neither your [noble] birth, Torquatus, nor your eloquence, nor your piety will bring you back (Horace, *Odes IV*, 7, 13–16, 21–24). (17) Whom you, Melpomene, have once looked upon with favourable eye at his birth (being born), him neither toil at the Isthmian Games will make famous as a boxer, nor will a swift horse bring him as winner in Greek chariot, nor will the business of war display him on the Capitol as a leader decorated with Delian leaves (*i.e. laurel*) because he has crushed the haughty threats of kings: but the waters which flow past fertile Tibur and the thick leaves of woods

(*i.e. topics suitable for a lyric poet*) will make him famous in Aeolian song (Horace, *Odes IV*, 3, 1–12).

13.2

(1) He sent envoys to seek peace. (2) When he was in Rome, he used never to go away a foot from his wife. (3) Caesar put individual legates in charge of each legion (single legates in charge of single legions) so that each man would have them as witnesses of his valour. (4) You were questor 14 years ago. (5) To murder a man brigands get up during the night. (6) He brought out the slaves whom he had captured in foraging a few days previously. (7) Why don't I send my little books to you, Pontilianus? Lest you send me yours, Pontilianus (Martial VII, 3). (8) They launched a raft 200 feet long, 50 feet wide, into the river. (9) So that he would not completely remove fear of his return and so that he might delay help from the barbarians (the barbarians' help), he broke up the last section of the bridge. (10) Caesar pitched camp three miles from their camp. (11) The centurions fell fighting bravely so that they would not lose the military glory (glory of the military thing) which they had won. (12) The soldiers erected a rampart 80 feet high. (13) These men in turn are again in arms after a year, those remain at home. (14) After doing these things (these things having been done) he left Labienus on the mainland with 3 legions and 2000 horsemen to defend the harbours and attend to the supply of provisions (the provision thing). He himself, with 5 legions and the same number of horsemen as (which) he was leaving on the mainland, set sail (unmoored his ships) towards the west. And, after sailing with (having been carried forward by) a gentle south-west wind, he did not keep to (hold) his course when the breeze dropped (wind having been interrupted) about midnight and, carried a long distance (**longē**) by the tide, at dawn (first light) he saw he had left Britain behind (saw Britain left behind) on his left. Then, when the tide changed (tide having been changed), by [using] oars he tried hard to reach (he strove with oars so that he might reach) that part of the island where disembarkation was easy . . . Caesar landed his army and captured a site suitable for a camp; when he learned from prisoners where the enemy forces had taken up a position, he left 10 cohorts and 300 horsemen on the coast to guard the ships and marched in the direction of the enemy (*this sentence must be restructured for an*

idiomatic translation; the literal meaning of the Latin is: Caesar, army having been landed and a place suitable for a camp having been captured, when he learnt from prisoners in what place the forces of the enemy had settled, 10 cohorts and 300 horsemen having been left by the sea so that they might guard the ships, marched towards the enemy) (Caesar, *de Bello Gallico V*, 8 & 9 adapted).

14.2

(1) They tried to transfer part of their forces. (2) He who chases two hares captures neither. (3) Two kings were appointed each year at Carthage, just as [were two] consuls at Rome (as consuls at Rome, so 2 kings . . .). (4) Mountains are in labour, an absurd mouse will be born (*i.e. after a lot of fuss a trivial result will be achieved*). (5) Times change and we change with them (in them; *the English* change *can be transitive:* you have changed your clothes; *or intransitive:* my, how you've changed. **Mūtō** *in the active can only be transitive, but in the passive can have either a passive sense or an intransitive one, the latter use being somewhat similar to deponent verbs; if* **mūtor** *is not followed by an agent or instrument it is normally translated by* I change). (6) He whom the gods love dies young. (7) You chase happy men, Death, you flee from the miserable. (8) At the moment of our birth (being born) we die and our end follows from our beginning (*i.e. the time of our death is fixed at birth – an astrological belief*). (9) Light troubles speak, huge ones are dumb. (10) Some races increase, others diminish (*what was said about* **mūtō** *applies to* **minuō**). (11) Neither love nor a cough can be hidden (is hidden). (12) Fortune, when she flatters, comes to trap [us]. (13) A donkey is recognised by its ears. (14) The envoys threw themselves at Caesar's feet and, speaking humbly, asked for peace in tears (weeping). (15) Women come to look; they come to be looked at themselves (**ipsae** *shows that the subject is feminine and to bring this out we must supply* women *not simply* they). (16) Cinna is said to write little verses against me. He whose poems no one reads does not write (Martial III, 9). (17) He who believes Acerra smells of yesterday's wine is mistaken: Acerra always drinks up to daylight (Martial I, 28). (18) A certain man, dearest Julius, is bursting with envy because Rome reads me, he is bursting with envy. He is bursting with envy because in every crowd I am always pointed out (I am shown with a finger), he is bursting with envy. He is bursting with

envy because both emperors gave me 'the right of [three] children', he is bursting with envy. He is bursting with envy because I have (there is to me 8.1/5) a pleasant country estate near the city and a small house in the city, he is bursting with envy. He is bursting with envy because friends find me pleasant (I am pleasant to friends), because [I am] a frequent guest, he is bursting with envy. He is bursting with envy because I am loved and approved of; let whoever is bursting with envy burst! (Martial IX, 97).

15.2

(1) No one can escape either death or love (neither death nor love can anyone escape). (2) Whom she wishes to destroy, Fortune makes stupid. (3) Profit cannot be made without another's loss. (4) Wisdom without eloquence is of little benefit to states (benefits states little). (5) The Romans who had survived the slaughters fled into the citadel. (6) I went away before dawn (light) so that those men would not see me. (7) The fates lead [him who is] willing; they drag [him who is] unwilling (*i.e. it is useless to fight against one's destiny*). (8) Now the waves are carrying the women (*we must translate so to bring out the gender*) from the reef to the shore (land). (9) Maecenas goes to play, I to bed (to sleep). (10) A poet is born, not made. (11) Everything was (all things were) sea, and the sea had no shores (shores also were lacking to the sea). (12) It is foolish to wish to take vengeance on a neighbour with arson (fire). (13) He who goes on to say what (the things which) he wants, will hear what he doesn't want. (14) While I lived with you, while a light breeze carried me, this boat of mine (this my boat) ran through quiet waters. (15) I shall go to announce to Alcumena what my master has ordered. (16) He not only took part in all transactions but was in charge [of them]. (17) [A statue of] Mercury is not made from [just] any sort of wood (*i.e. you can't make a silk purse out of a sow's ear*). (18) *F.* I don't want to be Caesar, to walk among the Britons, to put up with Scythian hoar-frosts. *H.* I don't want to be Florus, to walk around the bars, lurk around the bistros (**taberna** inn, **popīna** eating-house *were both associated with low life*), to put up with gorged mosquitoes. (19) When he died (he having died) the supreme command (the sum total of authority) reverted to no one person. (20) No one can walk 700 miles in three days. (21) Your beard is white, your hair is black. You cannot dye your beard –

this is the reason – and you can [dye] your hair, Olus (Martial IV, 36). (22) I don't like you, Sabidius, and I cannot say why; I can say only this, I don't like you (Martial I, 32).

15.3

He himself, comforting his sick love with hollow tortoise-shell (*i.e. lyre*), used to sing of you, sweet wife, of you by himself (with himself) on the lonely shore, of you when day was coming, of you when it was departing. After entering (having entered) even the jaws of Taenarus, Dis's lofty portal, and the grove gloomy with black fear, he approached both the Shades and their fearsome king and hearts not knowing [how] to soften through human prayers. But stirred by the song from the deepest seats of Erebus the insubstantial shades began to move and the images of those lacking the light [of day], as numerous as the thousands of birds [which] hide themselves in the leaves when it is evening or winter rain drives [them] from the mountains, mothers and men and the bodies of mighty heroes [that have] finished with life, boys and unmarried girls, and young men put on funeral pyres before the faces of their parents, whom the black mud and ugly reed of the Cocytus and the unlovely swamp with its sluggish water bind in a circle (**circum** round about) and the Styx, with its nine intervening streams (poured nine times in between) encloses. Indeed the abodes themselves (*i.e. the houses of the dead*) and Death's inmost region and the Furies with blue snakes intertwined in their hair were stunned, and Cerberus held agape his three mouths (gaping held his three mouths) and the revolving wheel of Ixion stopped in the wind (Vergil, *Georgics IV*, 464–484).

16.2

(1) They position their chariots in such a way that they have a ready retreat to their own men. (2) When Alexander the Great had come to the tomb of Achilles, he said, 'O fortunate youth, since you have found in Homer a herald of your valour!' (have found Homer a herald . . .). (3) A miser does nothing right except when he dies. (4) They sent guards round all the gates so that no one might go out from the city. (5) That man has lived well who was able to die when he wished. (6) The water which is carried [down] by the River Nile is so muddy and turbid that it causes many different diseases. (7) Caesar

built forts and in them (there) placed catapults so that, when he had drawn up his line of battle, the enemy fighting on (from) the sides could not surround his men. (8) Who [is] so depraved that he hesitates to prefer Seneca to Nero? (9) Tarquinius used to love Servius in such a way that he was commonly considered Servius's son (son of him; *here to avoid ambiguity we would substitute the proper name*). (10) So great a storm arose that the ships were unable to keep to (hold) their course. (11) The suitable nature of the place, the ignorance and weariness of the enemy, [and] the valour of our soldiers and their experience in other battles had the result (it was effected by the suitable . . .) that they did not withstand even one attack of our men and immediately fled (turned their backs). (12) No one is so wild that he cannot become gentle. (13) Verres destroyed Sicily to such extent that it cannot be restored. (14) Whenever the cohort made an attack, the enemy used to flee. (15) Since solitude and life without friends are full of traps and fear, reason itself warns [us] to make friends (procure friendships). (16) Although Socrates could have easily been rescued (was able to be rescued) from prison, he refused (was unwilling). (17) It is your business (your thing is being done), when a neighbour's wall (the nearest wall) is on fire. (18) That man seems to me to be equal to a god, that man, if it is right, [seems to me] to surpass the gods who, sitting opposite, looks at you again and again and hears you laughing sweetly, [something] which snatches every sense (all senses) from unhappy me; for as soon as I have seen you, Lesbia, no voice remains in my mouth (for me in the mouth), but my tongue is numb, a fine flame runs under my limbs, my ears ring with their own sound, my eyes are covered with double night (Catullus, poem 51).

16.3

And now, returning, he had escaped all dangers, and Eurydice, given back [to him], was coming to the upper breezes (*i.e. the upper world*), following behind – for Proserpine had laid down (given) this condition – when a sudden madness seized the unwary lover, pardonable indeed, if the Shades knew [how] to pardon; he stopped and, already under the light itself, forgetful, alas! and with mind overcome, looked back at his Eurydice. Then all his labour was wasted and the compact of the cruel tyrant was broken and three times a crash was heard in the infernal swamps. She said, 'What terrible madness (what so great madness; **quis** *is repeated for emphasis*) has destroyed both unhappy me and you, Orpheus? See, again the cruel fates call me back and sleep hides my swimming eyes. And now farewell; I am borne [back] surrounded by thick night (huge night) and, alas no longer yours, stretching out my weak hands to you.' She spoke and suddenly fled from his eyes in the opposite direction like smoke mixed with (into) the thin breezes, nor did she see him thereafter as he clutched vainly at the shadows wishing to say many things (clutching vainly at the shadows and wishing . . .); nor did the ferryman of Orcus allow [him] to cross again the swamp that stood in his way (Vergil, *Georgics IV*, 485–503).

17.2

(1) I marvel, wall, that you have not fallen in ruins since you hold up the tedious writings (boring things) of so many authors. (2) Wicked Chloe inscribed on the tombs of her seven husbands that she made/did [it] (*the play on the two meanings of* **faciō** *is impossible to reproduce*). What could be more naïve? (Martial IX, 15). (3) You say that the hare is not cooked and you ask for whips. You prefer, Rufus, to carve the cook rather than the hare (Martial III, 94). (4) Though your [toga] is dirty, Attalus, whoever says that it is like snow (you have a snowy toga) tells the truth (**tamen** however *need not be translated here*) (Martial IV, 34). (5) Aemilius eats his lettuces, eggs and mackerel at the baths and says he is not dining at home (Martial XII, 19). (6) Aristotle says that small creatures are born that live one day. (7) They, fearing punishments and tortures [at the hands] of the Gauls whose fields they had plundered, said that they wished to remain with him. (8) *A.* Where does that woman live? *B.* Here. *A.* Where do they say she is from? *B.* [From] Samos. (9) When Caesar was making enquiries about the character and customs of the Nervii, he discovered as follows: merchants could not approach them (there was no approach to them for merchants); they allowed no wine or other things pertaining to luxury to be imported because they thought that these things weaken character (that minds become weak through these things); they were fierce men and of great courage, and they found fault with the rest of the Belgians who had surrendered themselves to the Roman people and had discarded their ancestral valour; they asserted that they would send no envoys nor accept any peace terms.

(10) When Publius Scipio Nasica had come to [the house of] the poet Ennius and a maid had told him that Ennius was not at home, he felt that the woman had spoken on her master's orders (order) and that he was inside. A few days later, when Ennius had come to [the house of] Scipio and was asking for him from the door, Nasica shouted that he was not at home. Then Ennius said, 'What? Don't I recognise your voice?' At this point Nasica [said,] 'You are a shameless person. When I was asking for you, I believed your maid that you were not at home. Don't you believe me in person (lit. myself)?'

17.3

Did you attempt to bring your wicked and sacrilegious hands against that temple of Apollo, so ancient, sacred and holy? If in childhood you had not been trained in these pursuits and studies so that you might learn and get to know what has (those things which have) been committed to writing, were you not even later able, when you came to those very places, to learn that which has been transmitted orally and in writing (handed down to memory and writing)? That Latona after long wandering and flight fled to Delos and there gave birth to Apollo and Diana; from this belief among men that island is considered sacred to (of) those gods: and the strength of this belief both is and always has been so great that not even the Persians, when they had declared war on all Greece, gods and men, and had put in their fleet of a thousand ships in number at Delos, attempted either to desecrate or to touch anything. Did you dare to ravage this shrine? Was any greed [ever] so great that it would destroy such great religious feeling? (Cicero, *in Verrem II*, 1, 18).

18.2

(1) In order to win quickly you must for a long time prepare for war. (2) War must be neither feared nor provoked. (3) Cato always used to say, 'Carthage must be destroyed', when he gave (was making) a speech in the Senate house. (4) He used to come to the senate for the purpose of dissembling. (5) There is no point in arguing about taste (about tastes it is not to be argued). (6) To love and to be wise is scarcely allowed [even] to a god. (7) Night hurries on, Aeneas, we waste the hours in weeping. (8) O pupils, the things which you have said are correct, with the necessary exceptions and changes (things-to-

be-excepted having been excepted and things-to-be-changed having been changed). (9) We must deliberate often, we must make a decision once (*as the Latin does not specify who should deliberate and make a decision we may translate either by* we *or* you). (10) Youth must be overcome by reason, not by violence. (11) Moderation must be applied in jesting. (12) No opportunity for taking precautions should be lost. (13) Almost every day Indutiomarus used to range with all his cavalry in front of the camp, sometimes in order to get to know the camp's layout, sometimes for the purpose of holding a parley or causing alarm (frightening). (14) *The following is a literal translation*: Everything had to be done by Caesar at the one time: the flag (*i.e. the sign that the soldiers should assemble*) had to be displayed, the signal had to be given on the trumpet, soldiers had to be recalled from their work; those who had set out from the camp for the purpose of seeking [material for] a rampart had to be summoned, the line of battle had to be drawn up, the soldiers had to be encouraged. A large part of which things the shortness of time and the enemy's attack was hindering . . . Caesar, necessary things having been ordered, ran down to encourage the soldiers and came upon the tenth legion. Having encouraged the soldiers with a short speech, he gave the signal for joining battle. And having set out to the other part as well for the purpose of encouraging, he ran into fighting men. So great was the shortness of time and so prepared was the mind of the enemy for fighting that time was lacking not only for attaching decorations but also for putting on helmets and taking covers off shields. Into what part each man came from his work and what standards he saw first, at these he took up a position (**constitit** <**consistō**) so that he might not lose time for fighting in seeking his own men. *The following is in normal English. This translation is given by way of example to show how much we must sometimes change what is in the Latin, even to the extent of adding words (as* Romans *in the penultimate sentence) in order to express its meaning clearly.* Caesar had to do everything at once: display the flag, give the trumpet signal, recall soldiers from their work, summon those who had left the camp to look for material for a rampart, draw up the line of battle, and encourage the troops. Lack of time and the enemy's attack hindered much of this . . . Caesar gave orders for what was necessary, ran down to encourage the troops and came upon the tenth legion. After encouraging the soldiers with a short address he gave the signal to commence battle. He then left to encourage the other flank but ran into men already fighting. Time was so short and the enemy were so mentally prepared for fighting that the Romans were unable not only to attach their decorations but also to put on their helmets and take the covers from their shields. As each man came from his work to a particular place, he took up a position with the first standards he saw so that he would not lose fighting-time in looking for his own men (Caesar, *de Bello Gallico II*, 20–21 adapted).

18.3

The Greek leaders have returned, the altars smoke, barbarian (*i.e. Trojan*) plunder is being placed at [the altars of] ancestral gods. Wives bring grateful presents for the safety of their husbands; the men sing of Troy that they have conquered. Impartial old men and timid girls marvel; a wife hangs on the words (from the mouth) of her husband as he tells (husband relating) his story. And one person (someone) drawing up a table (table having been placed) illustrates (shows) the fierce battles and depicts all Troy with a little wine. Here the Simois used to go, here is the Sigean land, here the lofty palace of old Priam had stood . . . For others it has been destroyed, for me alone Troy remains, which the victorious colonist (*i.e. present inhabitant*) ploughs with captive ox. Already there is a crop where Troy was, and the fertile ground, to be cut with a sickle, grows rank with Phrygian blood. The half-buried bones of men are struck by the curved ploughs. Grass covers the ruined houses (Ovid, *Heroides I*, 25–34, 51–56).

19.2

(1) Silver is of less value (cheaper) than gold, gold [is of less value] than good qualities. (2) The race of the Suebi is by far the greatest and most warlike of all the Germans. (3) I see and approve what is better (better things), I follow what is worse (worse things). (4) Human beings do more from habit than from reason. (5) Philosophy, not that type (that one) concerning nature, which was older, but this type (this one), in which the life and character of men are discussed (it is discussed about the life and character . . .) is said to have been started (been discovered) by Socrates. (6) What is harder than stone, what softer than water? (7) The later day is the pupil of the earlier. (8) The

Upper Gods look on mortal affairs (things) with just eyes. (9) From the older ox the younger one learns to plough. (10) They burnt all the grain so that, with the hope of return removed (hope of return having been removed), they might be more prepared to undergo all dangers (for all dangers going-to-be-undergone 18.1/2c). (11) The good opinion of men is more secure than money. (12) The Haedui informed Caesar that, after their fields had been laid waste (fields having been laid waste), they did not easily keep the enemy's violence from their towns. (13) Among the German communities it was the greatest commendation to ravage their boundaries as widely as possible and to have wildernesses around them (boundaries having been ravaged as widely as possible to have . . .). (14) They left their baggage in Italy and boarded the ships unencumbered so that a greater number could be embarked. (15) All the best things are very rare (each best thing is . . .). (16) Verres sent [a message] to King Antiochus to ask for the most beautiful vases that he had seen. (17) The sun is many times greater and larger than the entire earth. (18) Caesar was informed by a letter of Labienus that all the Belgians were conspiring against the Roman people. (19) Isocrates is of too great a talent to be compared with Lysias (of greater talent than that he might be compared . . .). (20) Corruption of the best is the worst [form of corruption]. (21) I have completed a monument more lasting than bronze and loftier than the royal structure of the Pyramids, which neither devouring rain nor the raging North Wind could destroy or the countless succession of years and the flight of time (Horace, *Odes III*, 30, 1–5).

19.3

My native place is Sulmo, very rich in cold waters, which is ninety miles from the city. I was born here, and indeed so that you may know the time (**tempora** *plural for singular*), when both consuls fell by the same fate. And I was not the first child; I was born after the birth of my brother (brother having been born) who had come into the world twelve months before. The same morning star was present at the birthdays of both; one day was celebrated with two cakes. From the start, at a young age, our education began (we were educated), and through the care of our father we went to men in (of) the city famous for their ability. From a young age my brother was inclined to oratory, born for the powerful weapons of the wordy forum. But [when] still (**iam**) a boy the rites of the celestials used to delight me and the Muse used to draw me secretly to her work. Often my father said, 'Why do you attempt a useless pursuit? Homer himself left no wealth.' I had been influenced by his words and, abandoning the whole of Helicon, attempted to write words freed from metre (**modīs** *plural for singular*). Of its own accord song came in suitable rhythms, and what I was trying to write was verse (Ovid, *Tristia IV*, 10, 3–26 with omissions).

20.2

(1) A young person should be modest. (2) What does it matter to you? (3) No one should be greedy, least [of all] an old man. (4) A fall harms the exalted much more easily. (5) A woman who marries many men does not please many men. (6) It is the characteristic of foolish men to see the faults of others, [but] to forget their own. (7) Folly should be warned, not punished. (8) Mighty undertakings must have small beginnings (there must be very small beginnings of very great things). (9) It is better to trust virtue than fortune (it is better trusted to virtue than to fortune). (10) Those men need skill to cover their shameful deeds with oratory. (11) No wickedness lacks an example. (12) After a long fight (when it had been fought for a long time) our men gained possession of the baggage and the camp. (13) He who is allowed to do wrong, does wrong less. (14) It does not concern us at all (it concerns us nothing) to tell these things again or in another way. (15) Whoever spares the evil harms the good. (16) The Almighty heard and turned his eyes to the royal walls and the lovers forgetful of (having forgotten) their better reputation (Vergil, *Aeneid IV*, 220–1). (17) Wars must be undertaken for the purpose of living without harm in peace (on account of that reason [i.e.] that it may be lived, etc.). (18) A reputation in trouble is not easily helped (it is not easily helped to a struggling reputation; **succurrō** *takes the dative*). (19) Each must use his own judgement. (20) Even hares jump on a dead lion. (21) Thus is the way to the stars (thus it is gone to the stars), you who are born of gods and who will beget gods (born from gods and going to beget gods). (22) Egnatius, because he has white teeth, smiles everywhere. If he goes (it is gone) to a defendant's bench (*i.e. in a law court*), when the speaker is arousing tears (weeping), that fellow smiles; if there is mourning at the pyre of a dutiful son, when a bereft mother bewails her only boy, that fellow smiles. Whatever it is, wherever he is,

whatever he is doing, he smiles: he has this disease, neither refined, in my opinion – as I think – nor polite (Catullus, poem 39, 1–8). (23) He hears different voices and enjoys the conversation of the gods. (24) Because Cassandra was not believed, Troy fell. (25) An emperor must die in harness (standing). (26) There is nothing more harmful to health than much wine.

21.2

(1) Go to the ant, you sluggard, and consider its ways and learn wisdom. (2) Trust your boat to the winds, do not trust your heart to girls. (3) It is not, believe me, the mark of a wise man to say, 'I shall live.' Tomorrow's life is too late. Live today! (Martial I, 15, 11–12). (4) You demand that I give you my little books, Tucca. I won't, because you want to sell, not read, [them] (Martial VII, 77). (5) It is a universal law which orders that we be born and die. (6) 'Away, o stay (be) away, uninitiated men,' the prophetess screams, 'and withdraw from the whole grove; and you, enter upon the road and snatch your sword from its sheath. Now you need courage, Aeneas, now [you need] a stout heart.' (Vergil, *Aeneid VI*, 258–261). (7) Go, chase Italy on the winds, seek a kingdom over the waves. (8) He embraces the woman's waist (the middle of the woman). (9) Varro ordered the Gaditani to make ten warships; he also had several made at Hispalis. (10) Ambiorix arrived among the Nervii and encouraged [them] not to lose the opportunity of freeing themselves for ever and of taking vengeance on the Romans. (11) Caesar retreated and ordered his men not to hurl weapons at the enemy. (12) An enormous pine is shaken more often by the winds, and lofty towers come down with a heavier fall, and thunderbolts strike the tops of mountains (Horace, *Odes II*, 10, 9–12). (13) Carried through many peoples and through many seas, I come, brother, for these unhappy offerings so that I may present you with the last gift due to the dead and vainly address the dumb ash. Since fortune has taken you yourself from me, alas unhappy brother undeservedly snatched from me, now, however, as it is (**intereā** in the present situation), receive these things which, by the ancient custom of our fathers, are presented for offerings by way of sad gift, wet with a brother's many tears, and forever, brother, hail and farewell (Catullus, poem 101). (14) He allowed Galba to station the legion in these places in order to pass the winter if he thought there was need.

(15) Nor, however, was Indutiomarus able to persuade any German community to cross the Rhine. (16) You, Fortune, I follow. From now I spurn treaties (let treaties be at a distance); these I have trusted enough; war must [now] be taken (used) as the judge (Lucan I, 226f.). (17) Hail, Caesar, those who are about to die salute you.

22.2

(1) Let justice be done, let the sky fall (*i.e. even if the consequences are disastrous*)! (2) An overseer should be first to rise and last to go to bed (should rise first and go to sleep last). (3) If you had stayed silent, you would have remained a philosopher (*i.e. if you had kept your mouth shut we wouldn't have known how silly you are*). (4) May you perish [as] the last of your family (*i.e. die in the knowledge that with you your family becomes extinct*)! (5) You would quickly break a bow if you were to have it always strung (stretched). (6) Let a trial be made on a worthless body. (7) If I were to say that this road is not rough, I would be lying. (8) Love conquers everything; let us too yield to love. (9) May they perish who have anticipated what we say (have said our things before us)! (10) I wish the Roman people had one neck! (11) Let him who does not want to become lazy [fall in] love. (12) Whenever any large vase or bigger work of art was found they used to carry [it] off happily. (13) Let him who has done a favour be silent; let him who has received it tell. (14) What evil would you desire for a miser except 'May he live for a long time'? (15) You would make many trials (try many things) before you find a good man. (16) Paula wants to marry me, I don't want to marry Paula: she is an old woman. I would be willing if she were older (more an old woman *i.e. closer to death when Martial, as her husband, would inherit her property*) (Martial X, 8). (17) Lycoris has disposed of all the girl friends whom she had, Fabianus. I wish she would become friendly with my wife! (a friend to my wife) (Martial IV, 24). (18) A friend has made a small mistake (has erred a little) and if you were not to pardon it (which if you were not to pardon), you would be thought ungracious. (19) Let us drink, we must die. (20) One must not cry 'Success!' before victory (sing '**triumphe**', *the ritual cry shouted during triumphal processions*). (21) I would not have done it if it had not been necessary. (22) In vain would you demand youth back when you have come (it has been come) to old age. (23) If Pompey were a private [citizen] at this time, he would

still have to be chosen (was still to-be-chosen) for so great a war. (24) We would have lost memory itself together with our voice if it were as much in our power to forget as to be silent. (25) It is useful that there are gods and, as it is useful, let us consider that there are; let incense and unmixed wine be given on ancient altars (Ovid, *Ars Amatoria I*, 637f.). (26) If a good man were to have the (this) power of being able by snapping his fingers to insert his name into the wills of wealthy people, he would not use this power (if a good man were to have this power [i.e.] that he could insert etc.). (27) No one dances when sober, unless he chances to be mad (perhaps is mad). (28) God said, 'Let there be light', and there was light ('Let light be made', and light was made).

22.3

Of all these by far the most civilised are those who dwell in Kent—a district which is entirely maritime (which district is all maritime)—and do not differ much from Gallic custom. Most [who are] further from the coast do not sow grain but live on milk and flesh and are clothed in skins. All the Britons dye themselves with woad, which produces a blue colour, and this makes their appearance more terrifying in battle (because of this they are more terrifying in appearance in battle); they have long hair and every part of their body is shaved except their head and upper lip (they are with long hair and with every part of their body shaved, etc.). Groups of ten and twelve have wives in common, and particularly brothers with brothers and fathers with sons (lit. parents with children *but naturally only males are meant*); but the offspring born of these [wives] are considered the children of those men to whom each girl was first taken as a bride (Caesar, *de Bello Gallico V*, 14).

23.2

(1) Let us see what follows (those things which follow), firstly, whether the world is governed by provident gods (by the providence of the gods), then, whether the gods look after human affairs. (2) What is it, Catiline? Surely you do not hesitate, on my orders (me ordering), to do what (that which) you were already doing of your own will? (3) Surely you see that even drops of moisture falling on rocks perforate the rocks in a long period [of time]? (Lucretius IV, 1286f.). (4) He sleeps well who does not realise (feel) how badly he sleeps. (5) If the

gods had wished me to continue my life, they would have preserved my home (this home for me) (Vergil, *Aeneid II*, 641f.). (6) When his friends asked him how they should inter him, the philosopher Diogenes ordered that he be thrown out unburied. Then his friends [said,] 'For the birds and wild beasts?' 'No indeed,' he said, 'but put a stick beside me so that I can drive them away.' 'How will you be able as you will not be conscious (have feeling)?' 'How then will the mangling of wild beasts bother me if I am not conscious?' (be a bother to me feeling nothing) (Cicero, *Tusculan Disputations I*, 104 adapted). (7) If all the Athenians took delight in tyrannical laws, surely these laws would not on that account be considered just? (8) I am not particularly keen to want to please you, Caesar, nor to know whether you are black or white (a white or black man) (Catullus, poem 93). (9) When Socrates was asked (Socrates, when it was asked of him) whether he thought Archelaus, the king of the Macedonians, happy, said, 'I don't know as I have never talked with him.' 'You cannot know this otherwise?' 'By no means.' (in no way) 'So you cannot say whether even the great king of the Persians is happy?' (say even about the great king of the Persians whether he is happy) 'No, since I don't know if he is a good man or not.' 'Really? Do you think that a happy life depends on that?' 'My opinion is (I think thus) that the good are happy, the wicked are miserable.' 'So Archelaus is miserable?' 'Certainly, if he is unjust.' (Cicero, *Tusculan Disputations V*, 35 adapted). (10) When his friends asked whether (to friends asking whether) he wanted to be taken to his country if anything happened [to him] Anaxagoras said, 'It is not necessary as the distance to the underworld is the same everywhere.' (everywhere there is the same amount of road to . . .). (11) I haven't known for a long time how you are as you write nothing; and I haven't written anything to you (within) these two months. Because you were not with my brother Quintus, I didn't know where I should send a letter or to whom I should give it. I want to know how you are and where you will spend the winter (Cicero, *ad Familiares VII*, 9). (12) Whoever you are, come out here! Why do you beguile me, peerless boy, and where do you go, [though] sought? Certainly it is not my beauty nor my age which you might be fleeing from, and nymphs have loved me too. You give me vague hope (promise me I-know-not-what hope) with your friendly face, and when I have stretched out my arms to you, you stretch out [yours] of your own accord; when I have smiled you smile [at me]; your tears too have I often noticed when I was crying; you also return signs with a nod. I am you! (I am that person of yours). I have felt it and my image does not deceive me. I burn with love of myself, I both provoke and endure flames [of passion]! What am I to do? Am I to be asked or am I to ask? What then shall I ask? Already grief saps my strength and not much of my life remains (nor is much time of my life left), and I am destroyed at an early age (in first age). Nor is death painful for me as in it I shall lay aside my griefs (for me going to lay aside griefs in death). My wish is that this one, the object of my love (who is loved), should live longer (should be more lasting)! As it is (**nunc**) we two will die united in one soul (Ovid, *Metamorphoses III*, 454–73 with omissions).

24.2

They were making their way (**ībant**), hidden under the lonely night, through the darkness (shade) and through the vacant home of Dis (Pluto) and his empty kingdom, as [on] a journey in forests under the scant light of the uncertain moon (through the uncertain moon under its scant light) when Jupiter has hidden the sky with shade, and black night has taken colour from the world. In front of the entrance itself and in the first [part of the] jaws of the Underworld Grief and avenging Cares have placed their beds, and pale Diseases and gloomy Old Age dwell . . . From here is the road which leads to the waters of Tartarean Acheron. Here the murky stream boils with mud in a huge quagmire (with mud and a huge quagmire) and spews out all its sand into Cocytus. A dread ferryman guards these waters and streams, Charon with his terrible filth; a mass of (very much) unkempt grey hair lies on his chin, his eyes stand [out] with fire, a dirty cloak hangs down by a knot from his shoulders. He himself pushes his boat with a pole and attends to the sails and carries over the bodies (*i.e. the shades of the dead, not their actual bodies of flesh and bone*) in his dark skiff; [he is] already rather old but the old age of a god is hardy and robust. Here to the banks a whole crowd was coming in a rush (having been poured forth was rushing), mothers and men and the bodies of mighty heroes [that have] finished with life, boys and unmarried girls, and young men put on funeral pyres before the faces of their parents, as numerous as the leaves [which] fall and drop in woods at the first cold of autumn, or as numerous as the birds [that] flock to land from the deep sea when the cold [part of the] year puts them to flight across the sea and sends them to sunny lands. They were standing, begging to cross the passage first, and were holding out their hands through love of the further bank. But the sullen sailor takes now these, now those, but others he drives far away and wards them off from the sand (wards off others having been driven far away) (Vergil, *Aeneid VI*, 268–275, 295–316).

Scansion

ī-bānt | ōbscū- | rī sō- | lā sūb | nōc-tě pěr | ūm-brăm

pēr-quě dŏ- | mōs Dī- | tīs vă-cŭ- | ās ět ĭ- | nā-nĭ-ă | rēg-nă

quā-lě pěr | īn-cēr- | tām lū | nām sūb | lū-cě mă- | līg-nā

ēst ĭ-těr | īn sīl- | vīs ŭ-bĭ | caē-lūm | cōn-dĭ-dĭt | ūm-brā

Iūp-pĭ-těr | ēt rē- | būs nōx | āb-stŭ-lĭt | ā-tră cŏ- | lō-rěm

The way in which Vergil uses metre for special effects can be clearly seen in the first line where the spondees (– –) of the first four feet help convey the gloom of the scene.

24.3

Burning inwardly with strong anger, in my bitterness I speak to my mind (*i.e. address myself*); created out of matter, ashes of the earth, I am like a leaf with which the winds play. Whereas it is proper for a wise man to place his foundations on rock, I, in my folly, am like a flowing river, never staying on the same course. I am carried [along] like a ship without a sailor, as a wandering bird is carried along the paths of the air; chains do not keep me nor does a key; I seek men like myself, and I am joined to rogues. For me a serious heart (seriousness of the heart) is [too] serious a matter; a joke is pleasant and sweeter than honeycombs; whatever Venus orders is pleasant toil; she (*lit.* who) never dwells in faint hearts. I go on the broad way after the manner of youth; I am entangled in vices, forgetful of virtue; greedy for pleasure more than for salvation I, dead in soul, look after (**cūram gerō**) the [needs of the] flesh.

25.2

(1) Who would know [of] Hector if Troy had been fortunate? (2) You, Roman, remember [how] to govern peoples with your rule – these will be your skills – and to impose the custom of peace, to spare the submissive and subdue the proud (Vergil, *Aeneid VI*, 851–3). (3) I hate and love. Perhaps you ask why I am doing this. I do not know but I feel it happening and I am in torture (Catullus, poem 85). (4) Mirrors were invented so that man might know himself (man himself might know himself). (5) Many brave men lived before Agamemnon but all, unwept and unknown, are pressed by a long night because they lack a sacred bard (Horace, *Odes IV*, 9, 25–28). (6) Romulus, raising his weapons towards the sky, said, 'Jupiter, bidden by your omens I have laid the first foundations for the city here on the Palatine.' (7) Having spoken thus he twisted a huge spear with mighty strength. (8) He sees Aeneas laying the foundations of citadels and restoring buildings. (9) Perhaps it will be pleasing at some future time to remember even these things. (10) A woman either loves or hates: there is no third [possibility]. (11) If I cannot bend the Upper Gods, I shall move Acheron. (12) You, Tityrus, at ease in the shade, teach the woods to echo [the name of] fair Amaryllis (Vergil, *Eclogue I*, 4f.). (13) Together with me in the woods you will imitate Pan in singing. (14) When he was augur, he dared to say that those things which are done for the safety of the state are done with the best [of] omens. (15) He says that nothing is superior to, nothing better than, an unmarried life. (16) I would not dare to defend faulty morals. (17) Who could know the heavens except by heaven's gift, and discover god except [he] who is himself part of the gods? (Manilius II, 115f.). (18) A dog does not eat the flesh of a dog.

25.3

Night was beginning – for indeed it is a pleasure to remember—when, full of love, I was going out from my father's door. I did not delay; throwing aside fear together with my clothes I started to move my pliant arms in the clear sea. The water was shining with the image of the reflected moon and there was the brightness of day in the silent night. With my arms below each shoulder already tired I manfully raised myself high on the surface of the water. When at a distance I saw a light, I said, 'In it is my flame; those shores hold my goddess.'

And suddenly strength returned to my weary arms and the water seemed more yielding than it had been. You received me with an embrace and gave (joined) happy kisses, kisses, great gods! worth seeking (worthy to be sought) across the sea (Ovid, *Heroides 18*, 55–102 with omissions).

Scansion

nōx ĕ-răt | īn-cĭ-pĭ- |ēns‖ nā- | mqu(e) ēst mĕ-mĭ- | nīs-sĕ vŏ- | lūp-tās

   cūm fŏ-rĭ- | būs pă-trĭ- | īs‖ ĕ-grĕ-dĭ- | ē-băr ă- | māns

nēc mŏ-ră | dē-pŏ-sĭ- | tō‖ pă-rĭ- | tēr cūm | vēs-tĕ tĭ- | mō-rĕ

   iāc-tā- | bām lĭ-quĭ- | dō‖ brāc-chĭ-ă | lēn-tă mă- | rī

ūn-dă rĕ- | pēr-cūs- | saē‖ ră-dĭ- | ā-băt ĭ- | mā-gĭ-nĕ | lū-naē

   ēt nĭ-tŏr | īn tă-cĭ- |tā‖ nōc-tĕ dĭ- | ūr-nŭs ĕ- | răt

26.2

(1) With impartial foot pale death strikes [the doors of] the huts of the poor and the towers of the rich. O fortunate Sestius, the brief sum of life forbids us to enter upon long hope (Horace, *Odes I*, 4, 13–15). (2) Age does not prevent [us] from maintaining the pursuit of literature up to the last period of old age. (3) Add [the fact] that you cannot be with yourself for an hour. (4) Begin, small boy, to recognise your mother with a smile. (5) I understood that you were afraid that your earlier letters had not been delivered to me. (6) [The fact] that I breathe and please, if [indeed] I please, is due to you (is yours). (7) I am afraid that I may not be able to recover the jewels I have lent. (8) It must not be doubted that expediency can never conflict with morality. (9) They are indignant that you have the shapes of human beings. Indeed, they even say, heaven help me, that it is a sin that a plebeian be made consul. (10) There was no one at all of the soldiers in the fort who was not wounded. (11) It happens that an image seems to do this during sleep. (12) The soldiers were then with difficulty restrained from bursting into the town and were incensed over the matter (bore that matter with displeasure) because it seemed that Trebonius was responsible for their not capturing the town (it was due to T. that they did not capture the town). (13) But the appearance of the whole affair was changeable, uncertain, horrible and pitiful.

Scattered from their own men, some yielded, others pressed on; they kept to neither standards nor ranks; wherever danger overtook each person, there he resisted and repelled [the enemy]; arms, weapons, horses, men, friend and foe (enemies and citizens) were mixed together; nothing was done by plan or command; chance ruled everything (Sallust, *Jugurtha* 51). (14) It is a habit of mankind not to want the same person to excel in too many things. (15) In this flight Fabius, a certain Paelignian from the lowest ranks of (from) Curio's army, caught up with the front column of fugitives and kept asking (was asking) for Varus, calling him by name in a loud voice so that he might appear to be one of his soldiers and to want to give some warning and say something. When Varus, having been called several times, looked and stopped and asked who he was or what he wanted, he went for Varus's exposed arm with his sword and almost killed him. Varus avoided this danger by raising his shield against the other's attempt. Fabius was surrounded by the nearest soldiers and killed (Caesar, *de Bello Civili II*, 35). (16) Unfortunate poverty contains nothing harsher (has nothing harsher in itself) than that it makes people absurd (Juvenal III, 152f.). (17) In every disaster the most miserable kind of misfortune is to have been fortunate. (18) It is ridiculous that a man who does not know how to rule himself should rule others.

26.3

When the earth had opened up because of some heavy rain (rains), Gyges went down into the hole (that hole) and noticed, as stories tell, a bronze horse in whose sides there were doors. When he opened them he saw the body of a dead man of unusual size with (and) a golden ring on his finger. When he took it off, he put it on himself, [and] then, as he was the royal shepherd, he returned to the shepherds' council. There, whenever he turned the bezel of the ring towards his palm, he was seen by no one; he, however, saw everything. Likewise, he appeared (was seen) again whenever he turned the ring [back] to its place. And so, by using this opportunity afforded by the ring, he killed his master, the king, and removed those he considered to be in his way; and in these crimes no one was able to see him. In this way, through the help of the ring, he suddenly became king of Lydia (Cicero, *de Officiis III*, 38).

27.2

(1) The gardens of Caesar (*possessive genitive*); Andromache [wife] of Hector (*possessive genitive*); the flight of Pompey (*subjective genitive*); praise of just deeds (lit. things done rightly; *objective genitive*); the books of Plato (*possessive genitive*); the art of writing (*appositional genitive*). (2) With minds aroused (aroused with respect to mind) by these words, both brave Achates and father Aeneas had already been burning for a long time to break out from the cloud (**animum** *accusative of respect*) (Vergil, *Aeneid I*, 579–581). (3) Say in what lands flowers come up (are born) inscribed with the names of kings (*or* with the names of kings inscribed on them), and keep Phyllis for yourself (*i.e. if you can*; **rēgum** *possessive genitive*; **nōmina** *accusative of respect*) (Vergil, *Eclogue* III, 106f.). (4) He will teach the birds of the air the languages and emotions of men (**hominum** *possessive genitive*; **doceō** *takes the accusative of the person or creature taught and the accusative for what is taught*). (5) I used to wonder, Amaryllis, why you sadly called on the gods (**quid** *adverbial accusative,* in respect of what, why). (6) I am free and belong to a free state (and of a free state —*possessive genitive used as a predicate*). (7) It is the duty of a general to conquer no less by wisdom than by the sword (**imperātōris** *genitive of characteristic*). (8) The authority of Commius was regarded highly in these parts (**Commiī** *possessive genitive*; **magnī** *genitive of value*). (9) What a woman you have as a wife! (**mulieris** *partitive genitive, here used humorously with* **quid** *for* **quālem mulierem** *what sort of woman— see* 30.1/1 note 1). (10) Time neither for taking counsel nor for arming (taking arms) was given to the Germans (*the gerundive construction* **consiliī habendī** *and the gerund* **capiendī** *are broader uses of the possessive genitive in the sense of* associated with, suitable for). (11) There was a general opinion that Lucius Crassus had not come into contact with more learning than what he had been able [to grasp] in the first training of childhood, but that Marcus Antonius had been wholly lacking in, and ignorant of, all education (**L. Crassum** *and* **M. Antōnium** *subjects in accusative and infinitive constructions*; **doctrīnae** *partitive genitive*; **omnis ērudītiōnis** *objective genitive after* **expertem** *and* **ignārum**). (12) Titus Roscius is considered a veteran and noble gladiator with very many victories (**plūrimārum palmārum** *descriptive genitive*). (13) There is always something new from Africa (**novī**

partitive genitive). (14) At the top of his chest a pliant band of twisted gold goes around his neck (**obtortī aurī** *attributive genitive as it gives the material from which the* **circulus** *is made*) (Vergil, *Aeneid V*, 558f.). (15) I offer my guests and friends hope in order that they may think that they will live a safer life under (through) my protection (**vītam** *cognate accusative*). (16) O fortunate Rome that came to life when I was consul (O fortunate Rome born when . . . ; **Rōmam** *accusative of exclamation*). (17) Catiline used to remind one of his poverty, another of his greed (**admoneō** *takes the accusative and genitive*). (18) A man just and tenacious of his purpose neither the passion of citizens ordering what is wrong (wrong things) nor the face of a threatening tyrant shakes in his firm mind (**prōpositī** *objective genitive after* **tenācem**; **cīvium** *and* **tyrannī** *possessive genitives*) (Horace, *Odes III*, 3, 1–4). (19) Religion was able to urge such great evil (so much of evils; **malōrum** *partitive genitive*). (20) I am a man; I consider nothing human foreign to me (**hūmānī** *partitive genitive*).

27.3

It is sweet, when the winds are stirring up the waters on the mighty sea, to watch from land the great toil of another; not because it is a pleasing joy that someone is in trouble, but because it is sweet to perceive what ills you yourself are free from. It is also sweet to behold the mighty contests of war drawn up over the plains without any share in danger yourself. But nothing is sweeter than to dwell in (occupy) lofty, calm positions, well fortified by the learning of the wise, from where you can look down on others and see them straying everywhere and seeking life's road in their wandering, struggling in talent, contending in noble birth, striving night and day with surpassing effort to come to the height of power and to control the world. O the unhappy minds of men, O blind hearts! In what darkness of life and in what great dangers is passed this life, such as it is! (Lucretius II, 1–16).

28.2

(1) Throw yourselves into the (that) pursuit in which you are [engaged] so that you can be both an honour to yourselves, and a benefit to your friends, and an advantage to the state (**vōbīs, amīcīs** *and* **reī pūblicae** *are datives of advantage;* **honōrī, ūtilitātī** *and*

ēmolumentō *are predicative datives*). (2) The conquering cause was pleasing to the gods but the conquered to Cato (**placeō** *takes the dative*). (3) Already bent old age will be coming with silent foot (**tacitō pede** *could be regarded either as an instrumental ablative or, better, as an ablative of manner*). (4) We are not able to hear the signal for retreat (**receptuī** *dative of purpose – the signal is given in order to tell the soldiers to retreat*). (5) You must despair of harmony while your mother-in-law is alive (**tibi** *dative of agent;* **salvā socrū** *ablative absolute without participle*). (6) Do what you like since your fists are stronger (you are stronger with respect to your fists; **pugnīs** *on this interpretation is ablative of respect; it could also be ablative of cause, in which case the meaning would be* you are stronger because of your fists; **tibi** *is dative after* **licet** *– 20.1/2c*). (7) I am a barbarian here because I am not understood by anyone (**ūllī** *dative of agent*). (8) No one can take clothes from a naked man (**nūdō** *dative of disadvantage*). (9) Quintus Fabius held an assembly to elect censors (**censōribus creandīs** *dative of purpose*). (10) One must not nourish [creatures] which have hooked claws (**uncīs unguibus** *ablative of description, lit.* are with hooked claws). (11) For many Quintia is beautiful. For me she is fair, tall, upright; I admit that she has these individual [qualities] (*lit.* that these individual things [are] thus; **multīs** *and* **mihi** *are datives of reference and could be translated* in the opinion of many, in my opinion) (Catullus, poem 86, 1f.). (12) If we could live without a wife, we would all be free of this nuisance (**eā molestiā** *ablative after* **careō** *– 20.1/1*). (13) When I give a sign with my toga, then, mark me, raise a shout on all sides, attack the mob and scatter everything with your swords (**togā** *instrumental ablative;* **mihi** *ethic dative;* **clāmōre sublātō** *ablative absolute;* **ferrō** *instrumental ablative*). (14) When he finished, a tearful cry was immediately raised by the (that) crowd that was at the meeting-place, and they stretched their hands towards the Senate house begging that [the senators] return their children, brothers [and] relatives to them. Fear and necessity had caused women also to mingle with the crowd of men in the forum (**sibi** *indirect object after* **redderent**; **turbae** *indirect object after* **immiscuerat**, *lit.* had mixed women also into the crowd). (15) After my departure he removed fear from the good, hope from the impudent [and] servitude from the state (**bonīs** *and* **cīvitātī** *are datives of advantage because both benefited, but* **audācibus** *is dative of disadvantage because the impudent did not, lit.* he drove away fear for the good, hope for the impudent, etc.). (16) On the same day envoys sent by the enemy came to Caesar about peace. Caesar doubled the number of hostages for them which he had previously ordered and commanded that they be taken to the continent (**eōdem diē** *ablative of time when;* **hīs** *dative of disadvantage*). (17) It is a disaster for many when a good man dies (**calamitāte** *ablative of attendant circumstances, lit.* with disaster for many a good man dies). (18) He had scarcely said these things when by chance twin doves came flying from the sky to under the very face of the hero and sat on the verdant ground (**caelō** *ablative of place from which;* **solō** *ablative of place where*) (Vergil, *Aeneid VI*, 190–192). (19) Son, what great (*lit.* so great) grief arouses ungovernable anger? Why do you rage? Or where has your care for me gone? Will you not first see where you left your father Anchises, weary with age, and whether your wife Creusa and your boy Ascanius survive? (**tibi** *dative of reference;* **aetāte** *ablative of cause*) (*Aeneid II*, 594–598). (20) Dare, my friend (guest), to despise wealth, and make yourself also worthy of the god, and come not harshly to a poor home (*lit.* to needy circumstances; **rēbus egēnīs** *can be taken as a dative of motion towards with* **venī** *or as a dative with the adjective* **asper**, *i.e.* harsh towards; *Vergil frequently has such ambiguities;* **deō** *abl. with* **dignus**) (*Aeneid VIII*, 364f.). (21) What fortune, O son of a goddess, pursues you through such great dangers? What force drives you to [these] wild shores? Are you that Aeneas whom kindly Venus bore to Dardanian Anchises by the water of Phrygian Simois? (**deā** *ablative of origin;* **immānibus ōrīs** *dative of motion towards;* **Dardaniō Anchīsae** *dative of advantage*) (*Aeneid I*, 615–618). (22) Mossy fountains and grass softer than sleep, ward off the summer heat from the herd; already the parched summer is coming, already buds are swelling on the sluggish branch (**somnō** *ablative of comparison;* **pecorī** *dative of advantage*) (*Eclogue VII*, 45, 47f.).

Scansion

```
  5      dēs-pē- | rān-dă tĭ- | bī ‖ sāl- |vā cōn- |cōr-dĭ-ă| sōc-rū

 21  l.1  quīs tē | nā-tĕ dĕ- | ā ‖ pēr| tān-tă pĕ- | rī-cŭ-lă | cā-sŭs

 22  l.2  sōl-stĭ-tĭ- | ūm pĕ-cŏ- | rī ‖ dē- | fēn-dĭ-tĕ |iăm vĕ-nĭt | aēs-tās
```

28.3

Servius Galba came to (had) this end after living through five emperors over seventy-three years in prosperity (prosperous fortune), and [being] happier in others' rule than in his own. In his family there was ancient nobility and great wealth. His was a mediocre character, rather without faults than possessed of (with) virtues. He neither neglected nor pushed his reputation (neither neglectful nor a pusher of his reputation). Not greedy for the money of others, he was sparing of his own and miserly with that of the state. He was tolerant, without [giving cause for] blame, of friends and freedmen when he fell in with good ones; whenever they were bad, he was imperceptive to a fault. But the distinction of his origins and the anxiety of the times acted as a screen (were for a screen *predicative dative*), with the result that what was laziness was called wisdom. In the prime of life (when his life was flourishing) he achieved military distinction (prospered in respect of military praise) in Germany. As proconsul he governed Africa with moderation, [and], already old, Nearer Spain with equal justice; he seemed greater than a private citizen when he was one, and was by the consent of all capable of rule—if he had not ruled (*a condensed way of saying* and would have continued to be so considered if he had not ruled) (Tacitus, *Histories I*, 49).

29.2

(1) Because it was built last, the city is called Neapolis (Naples). (2) Themistocles used to walk at night saying that he was not able to sleep. (3) It so happens that they are present because they are doing their duty, but they are silent because they are avoiding danger. (4) While you are fortunate, you will count (i.e. have) many friends. (5) And while these things were being done in a completely different region, Saturnian Juno sent Iris from heaven to bold Turnus. He then, by chance, was sitting in the grove of his ancestor Pilumnus in a sacred valley (Vergil, *Aeneid IX*, 1–4). (6) He who grieves before it is necessary grieves more than is necessary. (7) Finally, he broke out into crimes and iniquities after he had set aside shame and fear [and] started to use his own talent exclusively. (8) If ever you are called as a witness in a doubtful and uncertain case, although a Phalaris orders you to be false and, after bringing up his bull, dictates perjuries,

believe that it is the greatest wrong to prefer life to honour and, on account of life, to lose the reasons for living (Juvenal, *Satire VIII*, 80–4). (9) Thinking this a by no means suitable place for disembarking, he waited at anchor till the ninth hour for the remaining ships to assemble there. (10) Let them hate provided they fear. (11) Although that year it had been stirred up by many different risings, the people did not elect more than three tribunes. (12) Even if the deceitful woman has sworn both by her eyes and her Juno and her Venus, she will show no faith (there will be no faith in [her]); Jupiter laughs at the false vows of lovers and orders the winds to bear them off unkept. How I would like to rest for long nights with you and to stay awake with you for long days, faithless one and undeservedly requiting me with hostility; faithless one, but, although faithless, nevertheless dear ([Tibullus] III, 6, 47–50, 53–56). (13) He arrived at the camp of the enemy before the Germans were able to get an inkling of what was happening. (14) Hasdrubal, the leader of the Carthaginians, held himself at a distance from the enemy until, at his earnest and lengthy entreaty (for him entreating much and for a long time), four thousand infantry and five hundred cavalry were sent from Africa as (*lit.* for) reinforcements. (15) Although they were abandoned by their leader and by fortune, our men nevertheless placed all hope of safety in their courage. (16) As long as Galatea possessed me, I had (there was for me) neither hope of liberty nor care for my savings. Although many a victim went from my folds and [many a] rich cheese was pressed for the thankless city, my right hand used never to return home heavy with money (Vergil, *Eclogue I*, 31–35). (17) The bravest of all these are the Belgians because they are furthest away from the civilisation and refinement of the Province.

Scansion

5   *l*.1   āt-qu(e) ĕ-ă | dī-vēr- | sā ‖ pĕ-nĭ- | tūs dūm | pār-tĕ gĕ- | rūn-tŭr

    l.4   Pī-lūm- | nī Tūr- | nūs ‖ sāc- | rā-tā | vāl-lĕ sĕ- | dē-băt

16   *l*.3   quām-vīs | mūl-tă mĕ- | īs ‖ ē- | xī-rēt | vīc-tĭ-mă | saēp-tīs

29.3

(*a*) What slender youth bathed in liquid scents courts you, Pyrrha, amid many a rose under a pleasant grotto? For whom do you, simple in your elegance, tie back your golden hair? Alas, how often will he lament your [lack of] faith and changed gods and, unaccustomed [to do so], will marvel at seas rough with black winds, [he] who now credulously enjoys you, all gold (golden you), who, ignorant of the deceitful breeze, hopes [you to be] always free; always lovable. Unhappy [are they] to whom you shine untried; a sacred wall makes known with votive tablet that I have hung up my dripping clothes to the god who rules the sea (ruling over the sea) (Horace, *Odes I*, 5). (*b*) Do not ask, it is wrong to know, what end the gods have apportioned for me [and] what for you, Leuconoe, and do not make trial of Babylonian numbers. How better [it is] to endure whatever will be, whether Jupiter has assigned [us] many winters or [he has assigned as our] last [the one] which now breaks the Tyrrhenian sea on the opposing rocks; be wise, strain your wine, and within a short space cut back far-reaching (long) hope. While we are talking envious time will have fled; pluck the day, trusting the next as little as possible (Horace, *Odes I*, 11).

30.2

(1) He used to prefer to be, [rather] than seem, good. (2) A Phrygian hero fell for every spear the maiden hurled (how many spears the maiden hurled, so many Phrygian heroes fell). (3) In that year it happened by chance that the enemy made a move in Samnium every time that (as often as) the dictator went away from his army. (4) He sent scouts to choose a suitable place for a camp. (5) The more of recent and ancient history (things) I consider, the more I perceive in all affairs a mockery of things human (Tacitus, *Annals III*, 18). (6) Nothing is so strong that there is no danger to it even from [something] weak. (7) Nothing is so great or so remarkable that all do not gradually cease to marvel at it (Lucretius II, 1028f.). (8) A man dies as often as he loses loved ones (people that are his own). (9) There is nothing which is more becoming than resolution. (10) The more the Parthians drink, the thirstier they are. (11) [As] what an artist I die! (12) The more skilful a gambler, the worse he is (by how much a gambler is better in his skill, by so much . . .). (13) If my control over prosperity had matched my noble birth and rank (if there had been [to me] so much control of prosperous things, how much there was noble birth and rank to me), I would have come to this city as a friend

rather than as a captive; and you would not have disdained to receive me, descended from (born of) famous ancestors and ruling vast peoples, with a treaty for peace. My present condition is splendid for you as it is degrading for me. I had horses, men, arms, wealth; what marvel if I lost these unwillingly? For if you wish to rule over all, does it follow that all accept slavery? If I had been surrendered at the beginning and were being dragged [here], neither my fortune nor your name (glory) would have become well known, and oblivion would follow my punishment; but on the other hand, if you preserve me unharmed, I will be an everlasting example of your mercy (Tacitus, *Annals XII*, 37). (14) The brightness of the sun is greater (brighter) than [that] of any heavenly body, since it shines so far and wide in the vast universe. (15) A judge passes judgement as much about himself as about the guilty party. (16) They were cutting down trees bigger than a soldier could carry. (17) A person who obeys with propriety gives the appearance of being (seems to be) worthy of giving orders in the future. (18) It is very stupid to tear out one's hair when grieving (in grief) as though sorrow were eased by baldness. (19) He learned that the condition of the state was much different from what he had hoped (the state being much otherwise than he had hoped). (20) I wish there were the same law for a husband as there is for a wife! (21) A beggar [when] dead beside the Acheron is assessed at the same (equal) rating as that man [who is] very rich.

30.3

Near the Cimmerians there is a cave with long recess, a hollow mountain, the home and sanctuary of sluggish Sleep, to which Phoebus rising, or in middle course, or setting, is never able to reach with his rays. Fogs mixed with darkness and a dusk of uncertain light are breathed from the ground. There the watchful bird of crested beak does not call forth the Dawn with his crowing (songs), nor do restless dogs or a goose, more keen-scented than dogs, break the silence with their noise. No wild beast, no domestic animals, no branches moved by a breeze or the cries of human tongue make a sound. Dumb quiet dwells [there]. Nevertheless, from the deepest part of the rock a stream of the water of Lethe comes out, [and] along it (along which) the ripple, falling with a murmur, invites sleep with rustling pebbles. Before the cave's entrance, fertile poppies flower, and countless plants, from whose sap damp night takes sleep and scatters it over the dark earth. There is no door in the whole house lest it should creak with turned pin; there is no guard on the threshold. But in the middle of the cave there is a lofty couch of ebony, filled with down, of one colour, veiled with a dark coverlet, on which the god himself lies, his limbs relaxed in drowsiness. Everywhere around him, imitating different shapes, as many empty dreams lie as the harvest [bears] ears of corn, the forest bears leaves, [or] the shore [grains of] sand [that have been] tossed up (Ovid, *Metamorphoses XI*, 592–615).

Scansion

*l.*18   nūl-lă dŏ- | mō tō-| tā ||cūs- |tōs īn| lī-mĭ-nĕ| nūl-lŭs

31.2

(1) Under what mental torture do we imagine that Caesar would have spent his life if he had foreseen that he [was going to be] savagely killed in front of the statue of Pompey himself, in that senate which, for the greater part, he had chosen himself, [and] was going to lie [there] under such conditions (in such a way) that no one, not only of his friends but not even of his slaves, went up to his body? (Cicero, *de Divinatione II*, 23 adapted). (2) The dictator, when he saw that victory was now in his hands, sent a letter to the senate [saying] that, through the bounty of the immortal gods, through his own plans [and] through the patience of the soldiers, Veii would now be in the power of the Roman people; what did they consider should be done about the booty? (Livy V, 20 adapted). (3) After (when) he had plundered the shrine of Proserpine at Locri, Dionysius, whom I mentioned before, was sailing to Syracuse, and, when he was holding to his course on a very favourable wind, he said with a laugh (laughing), 'Do you see, my friends, how good a voyage the immortal gods give (is given by the gods) to temple-robbers?' And when the sharp fellow had well and truly (plainly) grasped this, he persisted in the same opinion. When he put his fleet in at the Peloponnese and came to the temple of Olympian Jupiter, he took from the god (him) the gold mantle of great weight with which the tyrant Gelo had adorned [the statue of] Jupiter from the spoils of the Carthaginians. He even made a joke about it [saying] that a gold mantle is heavy in summer [but] cold in winter; and he put a woollen cloak on the god (him) as he said that

this was suitable for every time of the year. The same person ordered that the gold beard of Aesculapius at Epidaurus be removed, for, [he asserted], it was not fitting that a son should be bearded when his father, in all his temples, had no beard. He even ordered that silver tables be removed from all shrines; since, according to the custom of old Greece, there was inscribed on them '[Property] of the Beneficent Gods', he used to say that he wished to take advantage of their beneficence. The same person used, without hesitation, to take the little gold figures of victory and the bowls and garlands which were held in the outstretched hands of statues, and used to say that he was accepting, not removing, them, as it was folly to be unwilling to take [blessings] from those [beings] from whom we pray for blessings when they proffered and gave [them] (Cicero, *de Natura Deorum III*, 83–84). (4) The Helvetii [were] alarmed by his sudden arrival [and] because they realised that he had done in one day what (that which) they themselves had, with extreme difficulty, accomplished in twenty, [namely] the crossing of the river, sent envoys to him. The head of this deputation was Divico, who had been leader of the Helvetii in the war against Cassius (Cassian war). He treated with Caesar as follows: if the Roman people were to make peace with the Helvetii, they would go and stay in that region (go to that region and be there) where Caesar placed them and wanted them to be; but if he persisted in pursuing [them] with war, he should remember both the former reversal suffered by (of) the Roman people and the traditional courage of the Helvetii. Because he had, without warning, attacked one community when the men who had crossed the river were unable to bring help to their fellow tribesmen (their own men), he should not, on that account, either impute too much (greatly) to his own merit or despise them (themselves). The lessons they had learnt from their fathers and ancestors had had the result (they had learnt from . . . in such a way) that they fought with courage rather than relied upon trickery and ambush. Consequently he should not be the cause of that place where they had stopped taking its name from a disaster for the Roman people and the destruction of an army, or of its handing down the memory [of such] (he should not bring it about that that place . . . should take its name from . . . or hand down the memory . . .) (Caesar, *de Bello Gallico I*, 13). Divico's original words: Si pacem populus Romanus nobiscum faciet, in eam partem ibimus atque ibi

erimus ubi nos constitueris atque esse volueris; sin bello persequi
perseverabis, reminiscere et veteris incommodi populi Romani et
nostrae pristinae virtutis. quod improviso unum pagum adortus es,
cum ii qui flumen transierant suis auxilium ferre non possent, noli ob
hanc rem aut tuae magnopere virtuti tribuere aut nos despicere. ita a
patribus   maioribusque   nostris   didicimus   ut   magis   virtute
contendamus quam dolo aut insidiis nitamur. quare noli committere
ut hic locus ubi constitimus ex calamitate populi Romani et
internecione exercitus nomen capiat aut memoriam prodat. *In
reporting Divico's words Caesar says* **ipsōs despiceret** *because* **sē
despiceret** *would be (at any rate theoretically) ambiguous;* **sē** *could
refer to the subject of* **despiceret** (despise himself) *or to the speaker and
the Helvetii* (despise them, *see 31.1/2). To achieve absolute clarity
Caesar uses* **ipsōs** *(and thereby makes* **sē** *unnecessary) which, because of
its ending, can only refer to the Helvetii.* The original words of Divico
would have been **nōs despicere**, *not* **nōs ipsōs despicere.** *The English
version of this is:* If the Roman people make peace with us, we will go
and stay in that region where you place (will have placed) us and want
(will have wanted) us to be; but if you persist in pursuing us with war,
remember both the former reversal suffered by the Roman people and
our traditional courage. Because you, without warning, attacked one
community when the men who had crossed the river were unable to
bring help to their fellow tribesmen, do not, on that account, either
impute too much to your own merit or despise us. The lessons we have
learnt from our fathers and ancestors have had the result that we fight
with courage rather than rely on trickery and ambush. Consequently
do not be the cause of this place where we have stopped taking its
name from a disaster for the Roman people and the destruction of an
army, or of its handing down the memory of such.

31.3

In all the lands which lie (are) from Cadiz to the East and the Ganges
few are able to distinguish real advantages and their opposites (things
very contrary to them) when the cloud of error has been removed. For
what do we fear or desire through [the exercise of] reason? What do
you begin so auspiciously that you do not regret your attempt and the
fulfilment of your vow? The compliant gods have overturned whole
families at their masters' desire. Things that will bring harm (things

going to harm) are sought in civilian life and on military service; fatal to many are a flowing abundance of speech (speaking) and their own eloquence; that man [of old] perished through confidence in (confident in) his strength and his remarkable shoulders. But more are strangled by money accumulated with excessive care and by property surpassing all [other] patrimonies by as much as a British whale is greater than dolphins (**strangulat** *has been translated by a passive*). Consequently, in the reign of terror (dreadful times) and at Nero's order, a whole cohort shut off Longinus and the vast gardens of wealthy Seneca and besieged (**obsidet** *is vivid present*) the splendid house of the Laterani; [but] a soldier rarely comes to garrets (Juvenal X, 1–18).

Scansion

*l.*3   vē-ră bŏ- | n(a) āt-qu(e) īl-|līs || mūl-|tūm dī-|vēr-să rĕ-|mō-tā

*l.*4   ēr-rō-|rīs nĕ-bŭ-|lā||quĭd ĕ-|nīm ră-tĭ-|ō-nĕ tĭ-|mē-mŭs

*l.*8   dī fă-cĭ-|lēs||nŏ-cĭ-|tū-ră tŏ-|gā|| nŏ-cĭ-|tū-ră pĕ-|tūn-tŭr

*l.*9   mī-lĭ-tĭ-|ā tōr-|rēns|| dī-|cēn-dī| cō-pĭ-ă| mūl-tīs

*l.*10 ēt sŭ-ă| mōr-tĭ-fĕ-|r(a) ēst|| fā-|cūn-dĭ-ă| vī-rĭ-bŭs| īl-lĕ

*l.*12 sēd plū- | rēs nĭ-mĭ-|ā|| cōn-|gēs-tă pĕ-|cū-nĭ-ă| cū-rā

VOCABULARY

More words have been included in the vocabulary than occur in the reading exercices in order to increase its usefulness and to give a fuller listing of common Latin words. In using it the following should be noted:

(a) The abbreviations are explained on p. xxvi.

(b) The accent is only given on the few words where the law of the penultimate (p. xvii) does not apply.

(c) If a word is given with three terminations (**bonus, -a, -um, fortis, -is, -e**) it should be taken as an adjective. Otherwise adjectives are marked as such.

(d) Where a verb is given in the first person singular and the present infinitive only, it should be taken as having a regular perfect and supine. Note that a few verbs ending in **-iō** belong to the first conjugation (e.g. **nuntiō, -āre**), as does one verb ending in **-eō (creō, -āre)**. Where alternative forms of a verb exist, these are given in brackets (e.g. **lavō**).

(e) A verb is marked as transitive (tr.) or intransitive (intr.), or sometimes both, according to the way in which it is used, which will not necessarily be the same as its English equivalent. This information is not given when it is stated that a verb is followed by a case other than the accusative (e.g. **ūtor**); such verbs are by definition intransitive.

(f) In most cases, the last syllable of the stem (as well as the genitive ending) is given with nouns of the third declension e.g. **fortitūdō, -dinis** (stem **fortitūdin-**), **impcrātor, -ōris** (stem **imperātōr-**). With irregular nouns the genitive is given in its entirety.

ā or **ab** (prep. + abl.) *by; from; since*

abdō, -ere, abdidī, abditum (tr.) *hide* (tr.,), *conceal*

abeō (ab + eō, -īre; intr.) *go away*

abhinc (adv.) *ago* (13.1/6*b*)

abiciō, -ere, abiēcī, abiectum (tr.) *throw away*

abigō, -ere, abēgī, abactum (tr.) *drive away*

aboleō, -ēre, abolēvī, abolitum (tr.) *destroy*

abscēdō, -ere, abscessī, abscessum (intr.) *go away*

absens, -entis (adj.) *absent*

absistō, -ere, abstitī (no sup.; intr.) *retire, withdraw*

absolvō, -ere, absolvī, absolūtum (tr.) *free, acquit*

abstinens, -entis (adj.) *temperate; continent*

abstineō, -ēre, abstinuī, abstentum (tr.) *restrain*

abstulī (perf. of **auferō**)

absum (ab + sum) abesse, āfuī (no sup.; intr.) *be distant, be away*

absurdus, -a, -um *ridiculous*

abundō, -āre (+ gen. or abl.) *be rich in*

ac (conj.) *and* (3.1/5)

accēdō, -ere, accessī, accessum (intr.) *go up, approach*

accendō, -ere, accendī, accensum (tr.) *set fire to, kindle*

accidit (impersonal use) *it happens*

accidō, -ere, accidī (no sup.; intr.) *fall down; happen*

accipiō, -ere, accēpī, acceptum (tr.) *take; receive, accept; learn*

accommodō, -āre (tr.) *fix, attach*

accumbō, -ere, accubuī, accubitum (intr.) *lie down (at table)*

accūsō, -āre (tr.) *accuse*

ācer, ācris, ācre *keen, fierce*

acerbus, -a, -um *unpleasant, bitter*

Acerra, -ae *male cognomen*
acervus, -ī (m) *pile, heap*
Achāicus, -a, -um *Greek*
Achātēs, -ae *hero in Vergil's Aeneid*
Acherōn, -ontis (m) *river of the Underworld*
Achillēs, -is *hero in Homer's Iliad*
aciēs, -ēī (f) *line of battle*
ācriter (adv.) *fiercely*
actum, -ī (n) *act, deed*
actus, -a, -um (perf. pple. of agō)
acus, -ūs (f) *needle*
acūtus, -a, -um *sharp, pointed; keen-witted*
ad (prep. + acc.) *to, towards; near*
addō, -ere, addidī, additum (tr.) *add*
addūcō, -ere, adduxī, adductum (tr.) *take*
ademptus (perf. pple. of adimō)
adeō (ad + eō, -īre; intr., tr.) *approach; reach*
adeō (adv.) *so, to such an extent*
adfuī (perf. of adsum)
adhibeō, -ēre (tr.) *apply, use*
adhūc (adv.) *still, as yet*
adiciō, -ere, adiēcī, adiectum (tr.) *throw towards; add*
adimō, -ere, adēmī, ademptum (tr.) *remove, take away, snatch; sap (strength)*
aditus, -ūs (m) *approach*
adiungō, -ere, adiunxī, adiunctum (tr.) *join, attach*
adiūtor, -ōris (m) *helper, supporter*
administrō, -āre (tr.) *perform, carry out; manage, govern*
admīror, -ārī (tr.) *marvel (at), wonder (at)*
admoneō, -ēre (tr.) *remind*
admoveō, -ēre, admōvī, admōtum (tr.) *move near, bring up*
adnuō, -ere, adnuī, adnūtum (intr.) *nod*
adorior, -īrī, adortus sum (tr.) *attack*
adōrō, -āre (tr.) *worship*
adsum (ad + sum; intr.) *be present*
adulescens, -entis (adj.) *young*
adulescens, -entis (m or f) *young person*
adulescentia, -ae (f) *(the period of) youth*

adūrō, -ere, adussī, adustum (tr.) *singe*
adveniō, -īre, advēnī, adventum (intr.) *come, arrive*
adventus, -ūs (m) *arrival*
adversus (adv.) *opposite*
adversus (prep. + acc.) *against*
aedēs, -is (f) *temple;* (pl.) *house*
aedificium, -ī (n) *building*
aedificō, -āre (tr.) *build*
aedīlis, -is (m) *a lower-ranking magistrate, aedile*
aeger, aegra, aegrum *sick*
aegrē (adv.) *scarcely, with difficulty*
aegrōtō, -āre (intr.) *be sick*
Aegyptus, -ī (f) *Egypt*
Aemilius, -ī *male nomen*
Aenēās, -ae (25.1/4e) *hero of Vergil's Aeneid*
Aenēis, -idos (f) *Vergil's epic poem, the Aeneid*
Aenēius, -a, -um (adj. of Aenēās)
aēneus (4 syllables), -a, -um *(made of) bronze*
Aeolius, -a, -um *Aeolian*
Aeolus, -ī *god of the winds*
aequō, -āre (tr.) *make level; equalize*
aequor, -oris (n) *smooth surface; sea;* (pl.) *waters*
aequus, -a, -um *level; equal; just*
āēr (2 syllables), āēris (3 syllables; m) *air, atmosphere*
āerius (4 syllables) -a, -um *of or belonging to the air*
aes, aeris (n) *bronze, copper; money*
Aesculāpius, -ī *god of medicine*
aestās, -tātis (f) *summer*
aestimō, -āre (tr.) *assess, put a value on, value*
aestuō, -āre (intr.) *boil, seethe; burn* (intr.)
aestus, -ūs (m) *tide*
aetās, -tātis (f) *age, life; time*
aeternus, -a, -um *eternal, everlasting*
Aetōlus, -a, -um (adj. of Aetōlia, a region in north-western Greece) *Aetolian*
aevum, -ī (n) *age; lifetime*
afferō (ad + ferō), afferre, attulī, allātum (tr.) *bring*
Āfrica, -ae (f) *Africa*

Āfricus, -a, -um *African; south-western*

Agamemnōn, -onis (25.1/4e) *hero in Homer's Iliad*

ager, agrī (m) *field*

agger, -eris (m) *rampart*

aggredior, -ī, aggressus sum (tr.) *approach; attack; undertake*

agitātor, -ōris (m) *person who drives animals*

agitō, -āre (tr.) *set in motion, shake, stir*

agmen, -minis (n) *column (of soldiers)*

agnus, -ī (m) *lamb*

agō, -ere, ēgī, actum (tr., intr.) *do, manage; drive; spend (one's life); (+ cum) treat with, deal with*

agrestis, -is, -e *rural; wild; coarse*

agricola, -ae (m) *farmer*

aiō (defective verb; tr.) *say, affirm* (25.1/5a, i)

ait (3rd s. pres. ind. act. of **aiō**)

Albānus, -a, -um (adj. of **Alba (Longa)** old town near Rome) *Alban*

albus, -a, -um *white*

Alcumēna, -ae *woman's name (character from Greek mythology)*

āleātor, -ōris (m) *gambler*

āles, ālitis (m) *bird*

aliās (adv.) *at another time*

aliās . . . aliās *at one time . . . at another time*

aliēnus, -a, -um *of or belonging to others; foreign; strange*

aliquandō (adv.) *once, formerly; at some future time; sometimes*

aliquis (-quī), aliqua, aliquid (-quod) (pron. and adj.) *someone, something; some* (10.1/1j)

aliquot (indecl. adj.) *several, some*

aliter (adv.) *otherwise*

alius, -a, -ud (pron. and adj.) *other* (10.1/1c)

alligō, -āre (tr.) *bind, enclose*

alloquor, -ī, allocūtus sum (tr.) *address, speak to*

almus, -a, -um *kindly*

alō, -ere, aluī, altum (tr.) *nourish, feed*

Alpēs, -ium (f. pl.) *the Alps*

altāria, -ium (n. pl.) *altar*

alter, altera, alterum *other of two* (10.1/1d)

altitūdō, -dinis (f) *height; depth*

altum, -ī (n) *a high position (in the sky); the open sea*

altus, -a, -um *high, lofty; deep*

amābilis, -is, -e *lovable; pleasant*

amans, -antis (m) *lover*

amāritūdō, -dinis (f) *bitterness*

amārus, -a, -um *bitter*

Amaryllis, -idis (-idos) *Greek female name*

ambigō, -ere (n. o. p.; intr., tr.) *dispute, call into question*

ambiguus, -a, -um *doubtful; changeable; ambiguous*

Ambiorix, -igis *Gallic chief*

ambitiō, -ōnis (f) *canvassing for votes; ambition*

ambo, -ae, -ō (pl. adj.) *both*

ambulō, -āre (intr.) *walk*

āmens, -entis (adj.) *mad, insane*

āmentia, -ae (f) *madness*

amīca, -ae (f) *(female) friend*

amīcitia, -ae (f) *friendship*

amictus, -ūs (m) *cloak*

amiculum, -ī (n) *mantle*

amīcus, -a, -um *friendly*

amīcus, -ī (m) *friend*

āmittō, -ere, āmīsī, āmissum (tr.) *lose*

amnis, -is (m) *river*

amō, -āre (tr., intr.) *love, like*

amor, -ōris (m) *love, affection*

amplector, -ī, amplexus sum (tr.) *embrace, hug*

amplexus, -ūs (m) *act of embracing, embrace*

amplius (adv.) *further, any more*

amplus, -a, -um *large*

an, anne (conj.) *or* (introducing a second clause in direct and indirect questions 23.1/1f; see also 23.1/3 note 3)

Anaxagorās, -ae (25.1/4e) *Greek philosopher*

Anchīsēs, -ae (25.1/4e) *father of Aeneas*

ancilla, -ae (f) *female servant, maid*

ancora, -ae (f) *anchor*

Ancus, -ī *fourth king of Rome*
Andromachē, -ēs *wife of Hector in Homer's Iliad*
angō, -ere, anxī, anctum (tr.) *choke*
anguis, -is (m) *snake*
angustia, -ae (f) *narrow space*
anima, -ae (f) *soul, spirit: life; heart* (as centre of emotions)
animadvertō, -ere, animadvertī, animadversum (tr.) *become aware of, notice*
animal, -ālis (n) *living being, animal*
animus, -ī (m) *mind, intellect; courage; soul*
annōn = **an nōn** (23.1/1*f*)
annus, -ī (m) *year*
anser, -eris (m) *goose*
ante (prep. + acc. and adv.) *before* (13.1/6*a*)
ante . . . quam (see **antequam**)
anteā (adv.) *before, previously*
antequam (conj.) *before* (29.1/3*b*,i)
Antiochus, -ī *a Greek king*
antīquus, -a, -um *ancient*
Antōnius, -ī *male nomen*
antrum, -ī (n) *cave*
ānulus, -ī (m) *ring*
anus, -ūs (f) *old woman*
aper, aprī (m) *wild boar*
aperiō, -īre, aperuī, apertum (tr.) *open*
apertus, -a, -um *open; uncovered, exposed; having been opened* (perf. pple. of **aperiō**)
apis, -is (f) *bee*
Apollō, Apollinis *Apollo* (9.3)
appāreō, -ēre (intr.) *appear, be visible*
apparō, -āre (tr.) *prepare*
appellō, -āre (tr.) *name; call (out to)*
appellō, -ere, appulī, appulsum (tr.) *bring to land in, put in* (of ships)
appetō, -ere, appetīvī (-iī), appetītum (tr.) *approach; seek; be greedy for; attack*
Appia (see **via**)
applicō, -āre (tr.) *cause to go, drive*
appropinquō, -āre (intr.) *approach*
appulī (perf. of **appellō, -ere**)
aprīcus, -a, -um *sunny*
aptō, -āre (tr.) *fit on; prepare; adapt*
aptus, -a, -um *suitable*

apud (prep. + acc.) *at, near, with; at the house of; in the works of; in*
aqua, -ae (f) *water*
aquila, -ae (f) *eagle; the standard of a legion*
Aquilō, -ōnis (m) *the North Wind*
āra, -ae (f) *altar*
Arar, -aris (m) *river in Gaul, the modern Saône*
arātrum, -ī (n) *plough*
arbitrium, -ī (n) *judgement, verdict*
arbitror, -ārī (tr., intr.) *consider, think, judge*
arbor, -oris (f) *tree*
Arcadia, -ae (f) *rural area in Greece celebrated for its peaceful life-style*
arceō, -ēre, arcuī (no sup.; tr.) *ward off, keep away*
accessō, -ere, accessīvī (-iī), accessītum (tr.) *send for, summon*
Archelāus, -ī *a Macedonian king*
arcus, -ūs (m) *bow* (for shooting arrows)
ardeō, -ēre, arsī (no sup.; intr.) *burn* (intr.); *be keen*
ardor, -ōris (m) *burning; fire; enthusiasm; excitement, passion*
arduus, -a, -um *tall, lofty; difficult*
argenteus, -a, -um *made of silver*
argentum, -ī (n) *silver; money*
Argī, -ōrum (m. pl.) *Greek city of Argos*
Argolicus, -a, -um *Argive; Greek*
argūmentum, -ī (n) *proof, argument*
arguō, -ere, arguī, argūtum (tr.) *prove; bring a charge against*
āridus, -a, -um *dry;* (neut. s.) *dry land*
Ariovistus, -ī *German leader*
arista, -ae (f) *ear of corn, grain*
Aristotelēs, -is *celebrated Greek philosopher, Aristotle*
arma, -ōrum (n. pl.) *arms, weapons*
armātus, -a, -um *armed*
armō, -āre (tr.) *equip with weapons, arm; fortify*
arō, -āre (tr.) *plough*
arrectus, -a, -um (perf. pple. of **arrigō**)
arrīdeō, -ēre, arrīsī, arrīsum (intr.) *smile*

arrigō, -ere, arrexī, arrectum
(tr.) *arouse, excite*
ars, artis (f) *art, skill, ability;* (pl.)
pursuits
artifcx, -ficis (m) *artist*
artificium, -ī (n) *skill*
artus, -ūs (m) *limb*
arx, arcis (f) *citadel*
Ascanius, -ī *another name of Iulus,
son of Aeneas*
ascendō, -ere, ascendī, ascensum
(tr.) *climb*
Asia, -ae (f) *that part of Asia known
to the Romans; Asia Minor*
asinus, -ī (m) *donkey*
aspectus, -ūs (m) *act of seeing;
appearance*
asper, aspera, asperum *rough, harsh*
aspergō, -ere, aspersī, aspersum
(tr.) *sprinkle, splash*
aspiciō, -ere, aspexī, aspectum
(tr.) *look at, look on, see*
assentior, -īrī, assensus sum
(intr.) *agree*
assiduus, -a, -um *constant*
assuescō, -ere, assuēvī, assuētum (intr.;
for pronunciation see p. xiii)
become accustomed; (perf.) *be
accustomed*
assurgō, -ere, assurrexī, assurrectum
(intr.) *rise, stand up*
ast (conj.) *but*
astrum, -ī (n) *star*
at (conj.) *but, but on the other hand*
āter, ātra, ātrum *black*
Athēnae, -ārum (f. pl.) *Athens*
Athēniensis, -is (m or f) *an Athenian*
Atlanticus, -a, -um *of or connected
with Mt. Atlas in north-west Africa;
Atlantic*
atque (conj.) *and* (3.1/5)
ātrium, -ī (n) *open central room in a
Roman house*
atrox, -ōcis (adj.) *savage, cruel*
Attalus, -ī *male cognomen*
Attica, -ae (f) *region in central
eastern Greece*
attingō, -ere, attigī, attactum
(tr.) *touch, lay hands on; come
into contact with; take up* (an
activity)
attulī (perf. of **afferō**)
auctor, -ōris (m) *maker, writer*

auctōritās, -tātis (f) *influence, power,
authority*
audācia, -ae (f) *boldness, audacity*
audax, -ācis (adj.) *bold; impudent*
audeō, -ēre, ausus sum (tr.,
intr.) *dare; be bold* (25.1/5e)
audiō, -īre (tr.) *hear, listen to*
auferō, auferre, abstulī, ablātum
(tr.) *take away, remove, carry off*
augeō, -ēre, auxī, auctum
(tr.) *increase* (tr.)
augescō, -ere, auxī (no sup.;
intr.) *increase* (intr.)
augur, -uris (m) *official interpreter of
auspices and auguries, augur*
augurium, -ī (n) *art of interpreting the
will of the gods through birds; sign*
Augustus, -a, -um (adj. of **Augustus**)
Augustan; **mensis Augustus** *month
of August*
Augustus, -ī *title granted Octavius
Caesar, the first Roman emperor*
aura, -ae (f) *breeze*
aureus, -a, -um *golden*
aurum, -ī (n) *gold*
auris, -is (f) *ear*
Aurōra, -ae (f) *(goddess of the)
dawn; the East*
ausim (alternative 1st s. pres. subj.
act. of **audeō** (25.1/5e))
auspicium, -ī (n) *divination from
observing birds,* (pl.) *portents, omens*
aut (conj.) *or* (3.1/5)
aut . . . aut *either . . . or* (3.1/5)
autem (conj., normally 2nd word) *on
the other hand, however*
autumnus, -ī (m) *autumn*
auxilium, -ī (n) *help*
avāritia, -ae (f) *greed, avarice*
avārus, -a, -um *greedy for money,
miserly*
avē, avēte (imp.) *hail, hello; goodbye*
(21.1/1 note 2)
Avernus, -a, -um *infernal, belonging to
the Underworld*
Avernus, -ī (m) *the Underworld*
āvertō, -ere, āvertī, āversum (tr.) *turn
aside* (tr.)*, avert*
avidus, -a, -um *greedy; eager*
avis, -is (f) *bird; omen*

Babylōn, -ōnis (f) *city on the
Euphrates in Mesopotamia*

Babylōnius, -a, -um (adj. of **Babylōn**) *Babylonian*
Bacchus, -ī *god of wine* (9.3)
bacillum, -ī (n) *stick, staff*
Baiae, -ārum (f. pl.) *holiday resort near Naples*
ballaena, -ae (f) *whale*
balneum, -ī (n) *public baths*
barba, -ae (f) *beard*
barbarus, -a, -um *barbarian* (adj.)
barbarus, -ī (m) *barbarian, i.e. neither Greek nor Roman*
barbātus, -a, -um *bearded*
Barca, -ae *Carthaginian general*
beātus, -a, -um *happy, prosperous*
Belgae, -ārum, (m. pl.) *inhabitants of north-eastern Gaul*
bellicōsus, -a, -um *warlike*
bellicus, -a, -um *warlike, military*
bellum, -ī (n) *war*
bellus, -a, -um *nice*
bēlua, -ae (f) *monster*
bene (adv.) *well* (17.1/3)
beneficium, -ī (n) *kindness, favour; help*
benevolentia, -ae (f) *friendship, good will*
benignitās, -tātis (f) *kindness, bounty*
bestiola, -ae (f) *small creature*
bibō, -ere, bibī (no sup.; tr.) *drink*
bīduum, -ī (n) *period of two days*
bīnī, -ae, -a *two each, two* (12.1/4c)
bis (adv.) *twice*
blandior, -īrī (intr.) *flatter*
blandulus, -a, -um (diminutive of **blandus**)
blandus, -a, -um *charming, sweet*
bona, -ōrum (n. pl.) *goods, possessions*
bonitās, -tātis (f) *kindness, beneficence*
bonus, -a, -um *good; kind, beneficent; virtuous; advantageous, beneficial*
bōs, bovis (m) *bull, ox;* (f) *cow*
bracchium, -ī (n) *(human) arm*
brevī (tempore) *in a short time*
brevis, -is, -e *short*
brevitās, -tātis (f) *shortness; conciseness*
Britannia, -ae (f) *Britain*
Britannicus, -a, -um *British*
Britannus, -ī (m) *Briton*
Brundisium, -ī (n) *town in south-*

eastern Italy (modern Brindisi)
Brūtus, -ī *male cognomen*

cachinnus, -ī (m) *laugh, laughter*
cadō, -ere, cecidī, cāsum (intr.) *fall; set* (of the sun)
cadus, -ī (m) *jar*
Caeciliānus, -ī *male cognomen*
caecus, -a, -um *blind*
caedēs, -is (f) *slaughter, massacre; execution*
caedō, -ere, cedīdī, caesum (tr.) *beat, kill; cut down*
caelebs, caelibis (adj.) *unmarried*
caelestis, -is, -e *celestial, divine*
caelicola, -ae (m or f) *an inhabitant of the sky, god, goddess*
caelum, -ī (n) *sky, heavens*
caenum, -ī (n) *mud, filth*
caeruleus, -a, -um *blue*
Caesar, -aris *cognomen of Gaius Iulius Caesar, which subsequently became the normal designation of an emperor*
caesus, -a, -um (perf. pple. of **caedō**)
Caiēta, -ae *nurse of Aeneas after whom a port near Rome was named*
calamitās, -tātis (f) *misfortune, disaster*
calefaciō, -ere (compound of **faciō**; tr.) *make warm* (15.1/3 note 2)
calidus, -a, -um *hot*
cālīgō, -āre (n. o. p.; intr.) *be dark, dim, gloomy*
cālīgō, -ginis (f) *darkness*
calliditās, -tātis (f) *craftiness, cunning*
calvitium, -ī (n) *baldness*
campus, -ī (m) *open space, plain*
candēla, -ae (f) *candle, taper*
candens, -entis (adj.) *red-hot*
candidus, -a, -um *white, fair*
candor, -ōris (m) *brightness*
canīnus, -a, -um (adj. of **canis**)
canis, -is (m or f) *dog*
cānitiēs, -ēī (f) *grey hair*
canō, -ere, cecinī, cantum (intr., tr.) *sing*
Cantium, -ī (n) *Kent*
cantus, -ūs (m) *song*
cānus, -a, -um *white*
capax, -ācis (adj.) *capable, competent*
capillus, -ī (m) *hair*
capiō, -ere, cēpī, captum (tr.) *take; capture; reach (a harbour, etc.)*

capitālis, -is, -e *entailing the death penalty, capital*
Capitōlium, -ī (n) *the Capitol*
captīvus, -ī (m) *captive*
captō, -āre (tr.) *seek to trap*
captus, -a, -um (perf. pple. of capiō)
caput, capitis (n) *head*
carbō, -ōnis (m) *charcoal; a piece of charcoal, a coal*
cardō, -dinis (m) *one of the two pins on which a door is hinged*
careō, -ēre (+ abl.) *lack, be free of*
carmen, -minis (n) *song; poem; poetry*
carō, carnis (f) *flesh*
carpō, -ere, carpsī, carptum (tr.) *pluck*
cārus, -a, -um *dear*
cāseus, -ī (m) *cheese*
Cassandra, -ae *daughter of Priam*
Cassiānus, -a, -um (adj. of Cassius)
Cassius, -ī *male nomen*
castellum, -ī (n) *fort*
castra, -ōrum (n. pl.) *military camp*
castus, -a, -um *chaste*
cāsus, -ūs (m) *fall; chance, fortune; event; accident; misfortune; danger*
cathedra, -ae (f) *arm-chair*
Catilīna, -ae *male cognomen*
Catō, -ōnis *male cognomen*
Catullus, -ī *Roman poet (c.87–54 BC)*
causā (abl. with preceding gen.) *for the sake of, by reason of*
causa, -ae (f) *reason; cause*
cautus, -a, -um *careful, wary*
caveō, -ēre, cāvī, cautum (+ acc. or dat.) *beware (of); take precautions, take care*
cavillor, -ārī (intr.) *jest, make a joke*
cavus, -a, -um *hollow*
cedidī (perf. of cadō)
cecīdī (perf. of caedō)
cēdō, -ere, cessī, cessum (intr.) *yield*
cedrus, -ī (f) *cedar*
celebrātus, -a, -um *famous, well-known*
celebrō, -āre (tr.) *observe (a day), celebrate*
celer, celeris, celere *swift* (9.1/1 note 2)
celeritās, -tātis (f) *speed*
celeriter (adv.) *quickly*
cēlō, -āre (tr.) *hide* (tr.)
celsus, -a, -um *high, lofty*

cēna, -ae (f) *dinner*
cēnāculum, -ī (n) *garret, attic*
cēnō, -āre (intr., tr.) *dine (on)*
censeō, -ēre, censuī, censum (tr.) *consider; vote; assess*
censor, -ōris (m) *Roman magistrate, censor*
census, -ūs (m) *property, wealth; assessment, rating*
centum (indecl. adj.) *hundred*
centuriō, -ōnis (m) *centurion (officer in command of 100 soldiers)*
cēpī (perf. of capiō)
Cerberus, -ī *three-headed dog which guarded the entrance to the Underworld*
cernō, -ere, crēvī, crētum (tr.) *discern, see, perceive*
certāmcn, -minis (n) *fight, contest*
certē (adv.) *certainly*
certō (adv.) *certainly*
certō, -āre (intr.) *contend, fight, struggle*
certus, -a, -um *fixed, certain, sure; having definite knowledge*
cervix, -īcis (f) *neck*
cessī (perf. of cēdō)
cessō, -āre (intr.) *delay; do nothing*
cēterus, -a, -um *the rest of; (pl.) the others, the rest*
ceu (conj.) *as, in the same way as*
Charōn, -ōnis (m) *ferryman of the Underworld*
Charybdis, -is (f) *whirlpool mentioned in Homer's Odyssey*
cibus, -ī (m) *food*
cicer, -eris (n) *chick-pea*
Cicerō, -ōnis *celebrated Roman statesman and author (106–43 BC)*
cieō, -ēre, cīvī, citum (tr.) *stir up*
Cimmeriī, -ōrum (m. pl.) *mythical people supposed to live in the furthest north*
cingō, -ere, cinxī, cinctum (tr.) *surround*
cinis, cineris (m or f) *ash*
Cinna, -ae *male cognomen*
circā (adv.) *about*
circā (prep. + acc.) *about; in the neighbourhood of*
Circē (-a), -ēs (-ae) (25.1/4e) *witch in Homer's Odyssey*
circiter (adv.) *about*

circulus, -ī (m)   circle; band
circum (adv.)   round about
circum (prep. + acc.)   around
circumdō, -are, circumdedī,
    circumdatum (tr.)   surround
circumfundō, -ere, circumfūdī,
    circumfūsum (tr.)   pour around
circumveniō, -īre, circumvēnī,
    circumventum (tr.)   go around,
    circumvent; surround
cista, -ae (f)   chest
citerior, -ior, -ius   nearer
cito (adv.)   quickly
citō, -āre (tr.)   set in motion; call; cite
citrā (prep. + acc.)   on the nearer side
    of
citus, -a, -um   fast, rapid
cīvis, -is (m or f)   citizen
cīvitās, -tātis (f)   community; state
clādēs, -is (f)   disaster
clāmo, -āre (intr., tr.)   shout, make a
    noise
clāmor, -ōris (m)   shout, cry
clangor, -ōris (m)   noise, blast
clāritās, -tātis (f)   brightness,
    distinction
clārō, -āre (tr.)   make famous
clārus, -a, -um   bright; distinguished,
    famous
classis, -is (f)   fleet
claudō, -ere, clausī, clausum (tr.)   shut
    (off)
claudus, -a, -um   lame
clausī   (perf. of claudō)
clāvis, -is (f)   key
clēmentia, -ae (f)   mercy
Cleopatra, -ae   queen of Egypt
clipeus, -ī (m)   shield
cloāca, -ae (f)   sewer, (underground)
    drain
Clōdius, -ī   male nomen
Cluilius, -ī   male cognomen
coctus, -a, -um   (perf. pple. of coquō)
cocus, -ī (m)   cook
Cōcȳtus, -ī (m)   river of the
    Underworld
coepī (2 syllables),   (perf. of incipiō)
coeptum (2 syllables), -ī (n)
    undertaking, scheme
coerceō (4 syllables), -ēre (tr.)   confine,
    restrict
cōgitō, -āre (tr.)   think
cognātus, -ī (m)   (male) relative

cognōmen, -minis (n)   name (6.3)
cognōscō, -ere, cognōvī, cognitum
    (tr.)   get to know, learn; recognize;
    (perf.) know, (25.1/5b)
cōgō, -ere, coēgī (3 syllables)
    coactum (tr.)   gather together; force
cohors, -ortis (f)   cohort (unit in
    Roman army)
cohortor, -ārī (tr.)   encourage, urge
collis, -is (m)   hill
collocō, -āre (tr.)   place, arrange;
    station
colloquium, -ī (n)   conversation
colloquor, -ī, collocūtus sum (intr.,
    tr.)   talk with; hold a parley
collūceō, -ēre, colluxī (no sup.;
    intr.)   shine, give light
collum, -ī (n)   neck
colō, -ere, coluī, cultum (tr.)   till;
    worship
colōnus, -ī (m)   settler, colonist
color, -ōris (m)   colour
columba, -ae (f)   dove
coma, -ae (f)   hair; foliage
combūrō, -ere, combussī, combustum
    (tr.)   burn (tr.)
comes, comitis (m or f)   companion
comitium, -ī (n)   meeting-place; (pl.)
    elections
commendō, -āre (tr.)   entrust
commisceō, -ēre, commiscuī,
    commixtum (tr.)   mix, mingle
committō, -ere, commīsī, commissum
    (tr.)   join (battle); entrust; bring it
    about (that)
Commius, -ī   male nomen
commodum, -ī (n)   benefit, advantage
commoror, -ārī (intr.)   stay, remain
commoveō, -ēre, commōvī, commōtum
    (tr.)   stir, alarm, agitate; disturb,
    rouse to action
commūnis, -is, -e   belonging to several
    people, held in common; public
commūtō, -āre (tr.)   change (tr.)
comparō, -āre (tr.)   match with, put in
    the same class as, compare with;
    procure
comperiō, -īre, comperī, compertum
    (tr.)   find out, discover
compescō, -ere, compescuī (no sup.;
    tr.)   restrain
complector, -ī, complexus sum
    (tr.)   embrace

complūrēs, -ēs, -a (pl. adj.) *several, many*

compos, -otis (adj.) *in control of*

comprimō, -ere, compressī, compressum (tr.) *check*

cōnātus, -ūs (m) *effort, attempt*

concēdō, -ere, concessī, concessum (intr., tr.) *submit; overlook, pardon; grant, allow*

concidō, -ere, concidī (no sup.; intr.) *fall*

concīdō, -ere, concīdī, concīsum (tr.) *cut up; kill, slaughter*

conciliō, -āre (tr.) *obtain, procure*

concilium, -ī (n) *assembly; council*

concipiō, -ere, concēpī, conceptum (tr.) *conceive; undertake, begin*

concitō, -āre (tr.) *stir up, arouse*

conclāmō, -āre (tr., intr.) *shout, scream*

concordia, -ae (f) *harmony*

concors, -rdis (adj.) *harmonious, united*

concurrō, -ere, concurrī, concursum (intr.) *assemble; engage in battle, charge*

concursus, -ūs (m) *crowd*

condemnō, -āre (tr.) *condemn*

condiciō, -ōnis (f) *arrangement; terms*

condidī (perf. of **condō**)

condō, -ere, condidī, conditum (tr.) *hide; found, establish*

conferō, conferre, contulī, collātum (tr.) *bring together, compare*

conficiō, -ere, confēcī, confectum (tr.) *do, perform; complete, finish, accomplish*

confidentia, -ae (f) *self assurance; audacity*

confīdō, -ere, confīsus sum (+ dat.) *be confident in* (25.1/5e)

confirmō, -āre (tr.) *assert*

confīsus, -a, -um (perf. pple. of **confīdō**)

confiteor, -ērī, confessus sum (tr.) *admit*

confugiō, -ere, confūgī (no sup.; intr.) *flee (for refuge)*

congerō, -ere, congessī, congestum (tr.) *gather, accumulate*

congestus, -a, -um (perf. ppl. of **congerō**)

coniciō, -ere, coniēcī, coniectum (tr.) *throw, hurl*

coniugium (4 syllables), **-ī** (n) *marriage*

coniunx (2 syllables), **-ugis** (m or f) *spouse*

coniūrātiō (5 syllables), **-ōnis** (f) *conspiracy*

coniūrō (3 syllables), **-āre** (intr.) *conspire*

cōnor, -ārī (tr.) *try, attempt*

conscendō, -ere, conscendī, conscensum (tr., intr.) *climb up, mount; board (a ship)*

conscrībō, -ere, conscripsī, conscriptum (tr.) *write, compose; enrol, enlist*

consensus, -ūs (m) *agreement, consent*

consequor, -ī, consecūtus sum (tr.) *follow; catch up with; achieve*

conservō, -āre (tr.) *preserve, look after*

consīderō, -āre (tr.) *contemplate on, consider*

consīdō, -ere, consēdī (no sup.; intr.) *take up a position, settle*

consilium, -ī (n) *plan; ability to plan; wisdom*

consistō, -ere, constitī (no sup.; intr.) *stop (intr.); take up a position*

conspiciō, -ere, conspexī, conspectum (tr.) *see, notice*

constantia, -ae (f) *resolution*

constitī (perf. of **consistō** or **constō**)

constituō, -ere, constituī, constitūtum (tr.) *set up, erect; locate, place*

constō, -āre, constitī (no sup.; intr.) *stand together, take up a position; remain constant*

consuescō, -ere, consuēvī, consuētum (intr., tr.; for pronunciation see p. xiii) *become accustomed (to); (perf.) be in the habit of* (25.1/5b)

consuētūdō, -dinis (f; for pronunciation see p. xiii) *habit, custom, practice*

consul, -ulis (m) *consul, highest Roman magistrate*

consulō, -ere, consuluī, consultum (tr., intr.) *consult; (+ dat.) take thought for, look after*

consūmō, -ere, consumpsī, consumptum (tr.) *destroy; eat, devour*

contemnō, -ere, contempsī,

contemptum (tr.)   *despise, disregard*
contendō, -ere, contendī, contentum
(tr., intr.)   *strive, contend, fight;*
conflict; go quickly, march
contentus, -a, -um   *satisfied, content*
continens, -entis (f)   *mainland,*
continent
continentia, -ae (f)   *restraint, self-*
control
contineō, -ēre, continuī, contentum
(tr.)   *restrain, tie down; hold, govern*
contingō, -ere, contigī, contactum
(tr.)   *touch*
contorqueō, -ēre, contorsī, contortum
(tr.)   *twist; hurl*
contrā (adv.)   *on the opposite side*
contrā (prep. + acc.)   *opposing;*
against
contrādīcō, -ere, contrādixī,
contrādictum (intr.)   *speak against,*
oppose
contrōversia, -ae (f)   *dispute*
contudī   (perf. of contundō)
contumēlia, -ae (f)   *insult, affront*
contundō, -ere, contudī, contūsum
(tr.)   *crush, subdue*
contus, -ī (m)   *pole*
convalescō, -ere, convaluī (no sup.;
intr.)   *get well, recover*
convenienter (adv., + dat.)   *in*
accordance with
conveniō, -īre, convēnī, conventum
(intr.)   *come together, assemble*
convenit (impersonal use)   *it befits, it*
is fitting; it is agreed (20.1/2c)
convertō, -ere, convertī, conversum
(tr.)   *turn upside down, turn*
convīcium, -ī (n)   *angry noise, clamour,*
cry
convincō, -ere, convīcī, convictum
(tr.)   *find guilty, convict*
convīva, -ae (m)   *guest at a meal*
convīvium, -ī (n)   *banquet*
cooptō, -āre (tr.)   *choose*
coorior, -īrī, coortus sum (intr.)   *arise*
cōpia, -ae (f)   *abundance;* (pl.)
supplies, provisions; forces, troops
(see also novae cōpiae)
coquō, -ere, coxī, coctum (tr.)   *cook*
cor, cordis (n)   *heart*
Corinthus, -ī (f)   *city in southern*
Greece, Corinth

cornū, -ūs (n)   *horn*
corōna, -ae (f)   *wreath, garland, crown*
corpus, -poris (n)   *body*
corrumpō, -ere, corrūpī, corruptum
(tr.)   *harm*
corruptiō, -ōnis (f)   *act of bribing or*
seducing, corruption
cottīdiē (adv.)   *daily, every day*
coxī   (perf. of coquō)
crās (adv.)   *tomorrow*
crastinus, -a, -um   *belonging to*
tomorrow, tomorrow's
crātēr, -ēris (-ēros) (m;
25.1/4e)   *mixing bowl*
crēdō, -ere, crēdidī, crēditum   (+ dat.)
believe (20.1/1); (+ dat. of person
and acc. of thing) *entrust*
crēdulus, -a, -um   *credulous;* (+ dat.)
trusting (in)
creō, -āre (tr.)   *create; appoint, elect;*
(pass.) *be born*
crepitō, -āre (intr.)   *rattle, rustle*
crepusculum, -ī (n)   *twilight, dusk*
crescō, -ere, crēvī, crētum (intr.)   *grow*
Creūsa, -ae   *first wife of Aeneas*
crīmen, -minis (n)   *accusation, charge*
crīnis, -is (m)   *hair*
cristātus, -a, -um   *having a comb,*
crested
cruciātus, -ūs (m)   *torture*
crūdēlis, -is, -e   *cruel*
crūdus, -a, -um   *uncooked, raw; hardy,*
vigorous
cruentus, -a, -um   *blood-stained*
cubīle, -is (n)   *bed*
cubō, -āre, cubuī, cubitum (intr.)   *lie*
down, go to bed
cucurrī   (perf. of currō)
culex, -licis (m)   *gnat (mosquito?)*
culmen, -minis (n)   *summit, peak*
culpa, -ae (f)   *guilt, fault*
culter, cultrī (m)   *knife*
cultus, -ūs (m)   *cultivation; training;*
state of living in a civilized way,
civilization
cum (conj.)   *when; since; whenever;*
although (16.1/3)
cum (prep. + abl.)   *together with, with*
cumba, -ae (f)   *boat, skiff*
cunctor, -ārī (intr.)   *delay, loiter*
cunctus, -a, -um   *all*
cupiditās, -tātis (f)   *desire, greed*

cupīdō, -dinis (m or f) *strong desire;*
  lust
cupidus, -a, -um *anxious, eager;*
  (+ gen.) *desirous of, eager for*
cupiō, -ere, cupīvī (-iī), cupītum
  (tr.) *desire*
cupressus, -ī (f) *cypress*
cūr . . .? (interr. adv.) *why . . .?*
cūra, -ae (f) *care; worry*
Cūria, -ae (f) *Senate-house*
Cūriātius, -ī *male nomen*
Cūriō, -ōnis *male cognomen*
cūriōsus, -a, -um *careful, painstaking,*
  meticulous
cūrō, -āre (tr.) *take care of, attend to;*
  undertake, arrange; see to it (that)
currō, -ere, cucurrī, cursum
  (intr.) *run; travel quickly, race*
currus, -ūs (m) *chariot*
cursūra, -ae (f) *(the action of)*
  running
cursus, -ūs (m) *course; passage,*
  journey
curvō, -āre (tr.) *bend, make curved*
curvus, -a, -um *bent, curved*
custōdia, -ae (f) *custody,*
  imprisonment; prison
custōdiō, -īre (tr.) *keep watch over,*
  guard
custōs, custōdis (m) *guard, custodian*
cutis, -is (f) *skin*

damnō, -āre (tr.) *condemn*
damnum, -ī (n) *loss*
Danaī, -ōrum (m. pl.) *another name*
  for the Greeks in epic poetry
Daphnis, -idis *male character in*
  pastoral poetry
Dardanius, -a, -um *descended from*
  Dardanus, a son of Jupiter;
  Dardanian
Dārius, -ī *Persian king*
datus, -a, -um (perf. pple. of **dō**)
Dāvus, -ī (m) *common slave's name*
dē (prep. + abl.) *down from; about,*
  concerning
dea, -ae (f) *goddess* (3.1/3)
dēbellō, -āre (tr.) *subdue*
dēbeō, -ēre (tr.) *owe; (+ inf.) be*
  obliged to (ought, should, must, etc.)
dēbilitō, -āre (tr.) *weaken*
dēcēdō, -ere, dēcessī, dēcessum
  (intr.) *depart*

decem (indecl. adj.) *ten*
dēcernō, -ere, dēcrēvī, dēcrētum (tr.,
  intr.) *decree*
decet, -ēre, decuit (no sup.; + acc.) *it*
  becomes, befits (20.1/2a)
dēcidō, -ere, dēcidī (no sup.; intr.) *fall*
  down, go down, descend
decimus, -a, -um *tenth*
dēcrētum, -ī (n) *decision, decree*
dēcurrō, -ere, dē(cu)currī, dēcursum
  (intr.) *run down*
decus, -coris (n) *honour, glory*
dēdecet, -ēre, dēdecuit (no sup.;
  + acc.) *it does not become, does not*
  befit (20.1/2a)
dēdecus, -coris (n) *disgrace,*
  dishonour; (pl.) iniquities
dedī (perf. of **dō**)
dēdignor, -ārī (tr.) *scorn, disdain*
dēdō, -ere, dēdidī, dēditum (tr.) *give*
  up, surrender (tr.)
dēdūcō, -ere, dēduxī, dēductum
  (tr.) *lead away; escort; take as a*
  bride
dēfatīgātiō, -ōnis (f) *weariness*
dēfendō, -ere, dēfendī, dēfensum
  (tr.) *defend; ward off*
dēferō, dēferre, dētulī, dēlātum
  (tr.) *convey, take; denounce*
dēformis, -is, -e *ugly*
dēfungor, -ī, dēfunctus sum
  (+ abl.) *be finished with*
dēgō, -ere (n. o. p.; tr.) *spend (time,*
  etc.)
deinde (adv.) *afterwards, next, then*
dēlātus, -a, -um (perf. pple. of **dēferō**)
dēlectō, -āre (tr.) *please; (pass.*
  + abl.) *take delight in*
dēleō, -ēre, dēlēvī, dēlētum
  (tr.) *destroy*
dēlīberō, -āre (intr., tr.) *consider*
  carefully, deliberate
dēliciae, -ārum (f. pl.) *darling*
dēligō, -ere, dēlēgī, dēlectum
  (tr.) *choose*
dēlinquō, -ere, dēlīquī, dēlictum
  (intr.) *do wrong, err*
Dēlius, -a, -um (adj. of
  Dēlus) *Delian*
delphīnus, -ī (m) *dolphin*
dēlūbrum, -ī (n) *temple, shrine*
Dēlus (-os), -ī (f) *Delos (island in the*
  Aegean)

dēmānō, -āre (intr.)   *flow down*
dēmens, -entis (adj.)   *mad*
dēmentia, -ae (f)   *madness*
dēmittō, -ere, dēmīsī, dēmissum
  (tr.)   *send down, let go, lose;* (pass.)
  come down
dēmō, -ere, dempsī, demptum
  (tr.)   *take away, remove*
dēmonstrō, -āre (tr.)   *point out*
Dēmosthenēs, -is   *famous Greek orator*
dēnī, -ae, -a   *ten each; ten* (12.1/4c)
dens, -entis (m)   *tooth*
densus, -a, -um   *thick*
dēpellō, -ere, dēpulī, dēpulsum
  (tr.)   *drive away, remove*
dēpendeō, -ēre, dēpendī (no sup.;
  intr.)   *hang down*
dēpōnō, -ere, dēposuī, dēpositum
  (tr.)   *put down, take down; take off*
dēpopulor, -ārī (tr.)   *ravage, lay waste*
dēprehendō, -ere, dēprehendī,
  dēprehensum (tr.)   *catch, seize*
dēpulī (perf. of **dēpellō**)
descendō, -ere, descendī, descensum
  (intr.)   *go down, descend*
descensus, -ūs (m)   *descent*
dēserō, -ere, dēseruī, dēsertum
  (tr.)   *abandon*
dēsīderium, -ī (n)   *desire, longing; need*
dēsīderō, -āre (tr.)   *desire, long for*
dēsidiōsus, -a, -um   *idle, lazy*
dēsiliō, -īre, dēsiluī (no sup.; intr.)
  jump down
dēsinō, -ere, dēsīvī (-iī), dēsitum (tr.,
  intr.)   *cease; stop* (tr., intr.)
dēsistō, -ere, destitī (no sup.; tr.,
  intr.)   *leave off, cease; stop* (tr.,
  intr.)
dēspērō, -āre (intr., tr.)   *despair (of),*
  give up hope
despiciō, -ere, despexī, despectum
  (tr.)   *look down on; despise, disdain*
dēsum (dē + sum; + dat.)   *be lacking,*
  fail
dēterior, -ior, -ius   *worse, inferior*
dētestor, -ārī (tr.)   *feel abhorrence for,*
  loathe
dētrahō, -ere, dētraxī, dētractum
  (tr.)   *take away; take off, remove*
deus, -ī (m)   *god* (3.1/3b)
dēveniō, -īre, dēvēnī, dēventum
  (intr.)   *come (by chance)*
dēvorō, -āre (tr.)   *devour*

dext(e)ra (manus)   *right hand*
dexter, dext(e)ra, dext(e)rum   *on the*
  right-hand side, right
Diāna, -ae   *Diana* (9.3)
dīcō, -ere, dixī, dictum (tr.)   *say,*
  speak, mention
dictātor, -ōris (m)   *chief magistrate*
  appointed in an emergency, dictator
dictō, -āre (tr.)   *prescribe, dictate*
dictum, -ī (n)   *what is said;* (pl.) *words*
dictus, -a, -um   (perf. pple. of **dīcō**)
didicī (perf. of **discō**)
diēs, -ēī (m)   *day*
differō, differre, distulī, dīlātum (intr.,
  tr.)   *be different, differ; postpone*
difficilis, -is, -e   *difficult*
difficultās, -tātis (f)   *difficulty*
digitus, -ī (m)   *finger*
dignus, -a, -um (+ abl.)   *worthy (of)*
dīligō, -ere, dīlexī, dīlectum (tr.)   *love*
dīmicō, -āre (intr.)   *fight*
dīmidium, -ī (n)   *half*
dīmittō, -ere, dīmīsī, dīmissum
  (tr.)   *send away; let go, let escape;*
  lose
dīnoscō, -ere (n. o. p.; tr.)   *tell apart,*
  distinguish
Diogenēs, -is   *Greek philosopher*
Dionȳsius, -ī   *notorious Greek tyrant*
  of Syracuse
dīruō, -ere, dīruī, dīrutum (tr.)   *pull*
  down, destroy
dīrus, -a, -um   *dreadful, fearful*
dīs   (dat. or abl. pl. of **deus** (3.1/3b))
Dīs, Dītis   *another name of Pluto* (9.3)
dīs, dītis (adj.)   *rich* (9.1/2)
discēdō, -ere, discessī, discessum
  (intr.)   *go away, leave; split open,*
  open up
discessus, -ūs (m)   *departure*
disciplīna, -ae (f)   *training; study;*
  pursuit
discipulus, -ī (m)   *pupil*
discō, -ere, didicī (no sup.; tr.)   *learn*
discrīmen, -minis (n)   *dividing-line;*
  distinction; decision; crisis
disertus, -a, -um   *eloquent*
dispergō, -ere, dispersī, dispersum
  (tr.)   *scatter, disperse* (tr.)
disputō, -āre (intr., tr.)   *debate,*
  discuss; argue
dissimilis, -is, -e   *dissimilar*
dissimilitūdō, -dinis (f)   *difference*

dissimulō, -āre (tr.)   *conceal one's thoughts, dissemble*
distineō, -ēre, distinuī, distentum (tr.)   *keep apart*
distō, -āre (n. o. p.; intr.)   *be distant*
diū (adv.)   *for a long time*
diurnus, -a, -um   *belonging to day*
diūtissimē (adv.)   (supl. of **diū**) *for a very long time*
diūtius (adv.)   (compar. of **diū** (19.1/2 note 1))   *for a longer time*
diuturnus, -a, -um   *long-lasting*
dīversus, -a, -um   *(turned) in the opposite direction; different, contrary*
dīves, dīvitis (adj.)   *rich* (9.1/2)
Divico (nom.)   *leader of the Helvetii*
dīvidō, -ere, dīvīsī, dīvīsum (tr.)   *divide*
dīvīnō, -āre (tr.)   *foresee*
dīvīnus, -a, -um   *divine*
dīvitiae, -ārum (f. pl.)   *riches*
dīvus, -ī (m)   *god*
dixī (perf. of **dīcō**)
dō, dare, dedī, datum (tr.)   *give*
doceō, -ēre, docuī, doctum (tr.)   *teach*
doctrīna, -ae (f)   *education, learning*
doctus, -a, -um   *learned*
documentum, -ī (n)   *example, evidence*
doleō, -ēre (intr.)   *grieve, be sorry; be sore*
dolor, -ōris (m)   *pain; grief*
dolus, -ī (m)   *trick, deceit*
dominātus, -ūs (m)   *rule, control*
dominus, -ī (m)   *master; ruler*
domitor, -ōris (m)   *tamer*
domō, -āre, domuī, domitum (tr.)   *tame*
domus, -ūs (f)   *house, home* (9.1/3 note 3)
dōnec (conj.)   *until; while, as long as* (29.1/3b,ii)
dōnō, -āre (tr.)   *present; give*
dōnum, -ī (n)   *gift*
dormiō, -īre (intr.)   *sleep*
dōs, dōtis (f)   *dowry*
dubitātiō, -ōnis (f)   *hesitation*
dubitō, -āre (intr., tr.)   *doubt, be hesitant*
dubius, -a, -um   *uncertain, doubtful*
ducentī, -ae, -a   *two hundred*
dūcō, -ere, duxī, ductum (tr.)   *lead, bring; consider; marry* (with man as subject); *prolong, continue* (tr.); *draw out, waste (time)*

dulcis, -is, -e   *sweet, pleasant*
dum (conj.)   *until; while, as long as; provided that* (29.1/3b, iii)
dummodo (conj.)   *provided that* (29.1/3b, iii)
duo, duae, duo   *two* (11.1/5b)
duodēnī, -ae, -a   *twelve each; twelve* (12.1/4c)
duplicō, -āre (tr.)   *double*
dūrē (adv.)   *harshly; hardly*
dūrus, -a, -um   *hard, tough*
dux, ducis (m)   *leader*
duxī (perf. of **dūcō**)

ē or **ex** (prep. + abl.)   *out of, from*
eadem (nom. f.s. of **īdem**)
ebenus, -ī (m)   *ebony (wood)*
ēbrius, -a, -um   *drunk*
ecce (interj.)   *behold! look!*
edax, -ācis (adj.)   *devouring, destructive*
ēdictum, -ī (n)   *proclamation*
ēditus, -a, -um   *high, lofty*
ēdō, -ere, ēdidī, ēditum (tr.)   *bring forth, give birth to*
edō, -esse, ēdī, ēsum (tr.)   *eat* (25.1/5d)
ēducō, -āre (tr.)   *rear, train*
ēdūcō, -ere, ēduxī, ēductum (tr.)   *take out; rescue*
efferō, efferre, extulī, ēlātum (tr.)   *carry out; take away for cremation*
efficiō, -ere, effēcī, effectum (tr.)   *cause; produce; see to it that*
effugiō, -ere, effūgī (no sup.; tr., intr.)   *escape*
effundō, -ere, effūdī, effūsum (tr.)   *pour out; waste*
egēnus, -a, -um   *needy, deprived*
egeō, -ēre, eguī (no sup.; + gen. or abl.)   *lack, want*
egestās, -tātis (f)   *poverty*
ēgī (perf. of **agō**)
Egnātius, -ī   *male nomen*
ego (pron.)   *I* (8.1/1)
ēgredior, -ī, ēgressus sum (intr., tr.)   *go out; leave; disembark*
ēgregius, -a, -um   *outstanding, splendid*
ēgressus, -ūs (m)   *disembarkation*
ēiciō, -ere, ēiēcī, ēiectum (tr.)   *throw out, toss up*
ēlectrum, -ī (n)   *an alloy of gold and silver*

ēlegans, -antis (adj.) *refined*
ēlegantia, -ae (f) *refinement, elegance*
elementum, -ī (n) *elemental substance* (in 24.3 *earth* is meant)
elephantus, -ī (m) *elephant*
ēloquentia, -ae (f) *eloquence*
ēloquium, -ī (n) *oratory*
ēmensus, -a, -um (perf. pple. of ēmētior)
ēmergō, -ere, ēmersī, ēmersum (intr.) *come up (to), come (to)*
ēmētior, -īrī, ēmensus sum (tr.) *measure out; live through*
ēmīror, -ārī (tr.) *marvel at*
emō, -ere, ēmī, emptum (tr.) *buy*
ēmolumentum, -ī (n) *advantage, benefit*
emptor, -ōris (m) *buyer*
ēn (interj.) *behold! see!*
enim (conj., normally 2nd word) *for* (introducing a reason); *for instance, of course*
Ennius, -ī *early Roman poet*
eō (abl. neut. s of is) *for this reason*
eō (adv.) *to there, to that point*
eō, īre, iī (īvī), itum (intr.) *go* (15.1/6 and p. 294)
Epicūrēus, -ī (m) *follower of the Greek philosopher Epicurus*
Epidaurus, -ī (f) *city in southern Greece*
Ēpīrus, -ī (f) *region in north-western Greece*
epistula, -ae (f) *letter, epistle*
eques, equitis (m) *horseman*
equidem (adv.) *indeed*
equitātus, -ūs (m) *cavalry*
equus, -ī (m) *horse*
ērādīcō, -āre (tr.) *destroy*
eram (impf. of sum)
Erebus, -ī (m) *another name of the Underworld*
ergō (conj.) *therefore, well*
ērigō, -ere, ērexī, ērectum (tr.) *raise up*
Eriphȳla, -ae *female character in Greek mythology*
ēripiō, -ere, ēripuī, ēreptum (tr.) *seize, snatch*
erō (fut. of sum)
errō, -āre (intr.) *wander; err, be wrong*
error, -ōris (m) *wandering; error*

ēructō, -āre (tr.) *disgorge, spew up*
ērudītiō, -ōnis (f) *culture, education*
ērumpō, -ere, ērūpī, ēruptum (tr.) *break out from*
erus, -ī (m) *master*
este (2nd pl. imp. of sum)
ēsum (sup. of edō, ēsse)
et (conj. and adv.) *and; even, too* (3.1/5)
et ... et *both ... and* (3.1/5)
etiam (adv.; 3 syllables) *even, also* (3.1/5)
etiamsī (conj.) *even if* (29.1/4a)
Etruscī, -ōrum (m. pl.) *inhabitants of Etruria in the north-west of Italy, Etruscans*
etsī (conj.) *even if* (29.1/4a)
Euander, -drī *king in Vergil's Aeneid, Evander*
Eumenides, -um (f. pl.) *the Furies*
Eurōpa, -ae (f) *Europe*
Eurydicē, -ēs *wife of Orpheus*
ēvādō, -ere, ēvāsī, ēvāsum (intr., tr.) *get clear (of), escape*
ēvellō, -ere, ēvelli (ēvulsī), ēvulsum (tr.) *tear out*
ēveniō, -īre, ēvēnī, ēventum (intr.) *happen, come about*
ēvenit (impersonal use) *it happens*
ēventus, -ūs (m) *outcome, issue*
ēvertō, -ere, ēvertī, ēversum (tr.) *overturn, upset*
ēvocō, -āre (tr.) *call forth*
ex (see ē)
excēdō, -ere, excessī, excessum (intr., tr.) *go out, withdraw (from)*
excellō, -ere (n. o. p.; intr.) *be superior, excel*
excelsus, -a, -um *lofty, high; exalted*
excidium, -ī (n) *destruction*
exciō, -īre (tr.) *draw out, rouse*
excipiō, -ere, excēpī, exceptum (tr.) *set aside, exclude, except; capture; receive*
excitō, -āre (tr.) *stir up, arouse*
exclāmō, -āre (intr., tr.) *shout*
excolō, -ere, excoluī, excultum (tr.) *improve, develop, educate*
excruciō, -āre (tr.) *torture*
excubō, -āre, excubuī, excubitum (intr.) *spend the night in the open*
exēgī (perf. of exigō)
exemplar, -āris (n) *pattern, example*

exemplum, -ī (n)   *specimen, example*
exeō (compound of eō, īre; intr.)   *come out, go out*
exerceō, -ēre (tr.);   *train, exercise* (tr.); *keep busy, occupy*
exercitātiō, -ōnis (f)   *experience*
exercitus, -ūs (m)   *army*
exhālō, -āre (tr.)   *breathe out*
exigō, -ere, exēgī, exactum (tr.)   *execute, complete; demand*
exiguitās, -tātis (f)   *shortness*
exiguus, -a, -um   *small; small in amount, a little*
existimō, -āre (tr.)   *value; suppose, think*
exitium, -ī (n)   *destruction, death*
exitus, -ūs (m)   *end; death*
exorior, -īrī, exortus sum (intr.)   *arise, appear; become*
expediō, -īre (tr.)   *extricate; solve (a problem); prepare for use*
expedit (impersonal use)   *it is expedient, profitable* (20.1/2c)
expedītus, -a, -um   *free, ready; unencumbered; light-armed*
experīmentum, -ī (n)   *trial, experiment*
experior, -īrī, expertus sum (tr.)   *try*
expers, -rtis (adj., + gen.)   *destitute of, lacking in*
expetō, -ere, expetīvī (-iī), expetītum (tr.)   *ask for, request; seek after*
expīlō, -āre (tr.)   *rob, plunder*
explōrātor, -ōris (m)   *scout, spy*
expōnō, -ere, exposuī, expositum (tr.)   *disembark, land*
expectō, -āre (tr., intr.)   *expect, wait (for)*
exstinguō, -ere, exstinxī, exstinctum (tr.)   *quench; destroy*
exstō, -āre, exstitī (no sup.; intr.)   *exist, be*
exstruō, -ere, exstruxī, exstructum (tr.)   *erect*
exsultō, -āre, exsultāvī (no sup.; intr.)   *spring up; run riot*
exsuperō, -āre (tr.)   *surpass*
extemplō (adv.)   *at once, on the spot, immediately*
extrā (prep. + acc.)   *beyond, outside; without*
extrūdō, -ere, extrūsī, extrūsum (tr.)   *push out*

extulī   (perf. of **efferō**)
exuō, -ere, exuī, exūtum (tr.)   *put off, take off*

faber, fabrī (m)   *blacksmith; maker*
Fabiānus, -ī   *male cognomen*
Fabius, -ī   *male nomen*
Fabricius, -ī   *male nomen*
fābula, -ae (f)   *story; drama, play*
Fabullus, -ī   *male cognomen*
faciēs, -ēī (f)   *appearance, aspect*
facile (adv.)   *easily*
facilis, -is, -e   *easy; compliant, indulgent, obliging*
facinus, -noris (n)   *crime*
faciō, -ere, fēcī, factum (tr.)   *make, cause, do*
factiō, -ōnis (f)   *party, faction*
factum, -ī (n)   *deed*
factus, -a, -um   (perf. pple. of **faciō**)
fācundia, -ae (f)   *eloquence*
fallax, -ācis (adj.)   *deceitful, treacherous*
fallō, -ere, fefellī, falsum (tr.)   *deceive, trick, beguile;* (pass.) *be mistaken*
falsus, -a, -um   *untrue, wrong; false*
falx, falcis (f)   *sickle*
fāma, -ae (f)   *fame; reputation*
familia, -ae (f)   *family; household (i.e. family, slaves, and dependants)*
fānum, -ī (n)   *shrine, temple*
fās (indecl. noun)   *(what is) right; divine law* (25.1/4d)
fateor, -ērī, fassus sum (tr.)   *confess*
fatīgō, -āre (tr.)   *tire, make weary*
fātum, -ī (n)   *fate, divine will; death*
fātus, -a, -um   (perf. pple. of **for**)
faucēs, -ium (f. pl.)   *jaws; entrance*
faveō, -ēre, fāvī, fautum (+ dat.)   *favour*
favus, -ī (m)   *honeycomb*
fēcī   (perf. of **faciō**)
fēcundus, -a, -um   *fertile*
fefellī   (perf. of **fallō**)
fēlīcitās, -tātis (f)   *good fortune; aptness*
fēlix, -īcis (adj.)   *lucky, fortunate, happy*
fēmina, -ae (f)   *woman, female*
fera, -ae (f)   *wild animal*
feriō, -īre (n. o. p.; tr.)   *strike* (15.1/4)

ferō, ferre, tulī, lātum (tr., intr.)   *carry (off), bear; endure, suffer; lead* (intr. of a road); *say, tell; propose* (a law) (15.1/4)
ferōciter (adv.)   *fiercely*
ferox, -ōcis (adj.)   *fierce*
ferrūgineus, -a, -um   *rust-coloured, dark*
ferrum, -ī (n)   *iron; sword(s)*
fertilis, -is, -e   *fertile*
ferus, -a, -um   *wild, rough; fierce*
fessus, -a, -um   *weary*
fēteō, -ēre (n. o. p.; intr.)   *have an offensive smell, smell* (intr.)
fidēlis, -is, -e   *faithful; trustworthy*
Fīdentīnus, -ī   *male cognomen*
fidēs, -eī (f)   *faith, trust; honesty; protection*
fīdō, -ere, fīsus sum (+ dat.)   *trust* (25.1/5e)
fīgō, -ere, fīxī, fīxum (tr.)   *fix*
fīlia, -ae (f)   *daughter*
fīlius, -ī (m)   *son*
findō, -ere, fidī, fissum (tr.)   *cleave*
fingō, -ere, finxī, fictum (tr.)   *make, devise; invent, fabricate*
fīniō, -īre (tr.)   *finish*
fīnis, -is (m)   *end, limit;* (pl.) *boundaries*
fīnitimus, -a, -um   *neighbouring*
fīō, fierī, factus sum (intr.)   *be made, become* (15.1/3 and p. 294)
firmus, -a, -um   *strong, stout*
fit (impersonal use)   *it happens*
fīxī   (perf. of **fīgō**)
flagellum, -ī (n)   *whip*
flāgitium, -ī (n)   *shameful act, outrage*
flāmen, -minis (n)   *wind, breeze*
flamma, -ae (f)   *flame; passion*
flāvus, -a, -um   *yellow, golden*
flēbilis, -is, -e   *tearful*
flectō, -ere, flexī, flexum (tr.)   *bend* (tr.)
fleō, -ēre, flēvī, flētum (intr., tr.)   *weep; lament*
flētus, -ūs (m)   *(act of) weeping*
flexilis, -is, -e   *pliant, flexible*
flōreō, -ēre, flōruī (no sup.; intr.)   *flower, bloom; prosper, thrive, flourish*
Flōrus, -ī   *male cognomen*
flōs, flōris (m)   *flower*

fluctus, -ūs (m)   *wave*
flūmen, -minis (n)   *river*
fluō, -ere, fluxī, fluxum (intr.)   *flow*
fluvius, -ī (m)   *river*
focus, -ī (m)   *hearth; altar*
fodiō, -ere, fōdī, fossum (tr.)   *dig*
foedus, -a, -um   *fearful, horrible*
foedus, -deris (n)   *agreement, treaty, compact*
folium, -ī (n)   *leaf*
fons, fontis (m)   *fountain, spring*
for, fārī, fātus sum (intr., tr.)   *speak* (25.1/5a,i)
forās (adv.)   *(to) outside* (with verbs of motion)
fore   (alternative fut. inf. of **sum**)
forent   = **essent**
forīs (adv.)   *outside, out of doors, abroad*
foris, -is (f.; usually pl.)   *door, entrance*
forma, -ae (f)   *appearance; shape; beauty*
formīca, -ae (f)   *ant*
formīdō, -dinis (f)   *fear*
formīdulōsus, -a, -um   *fearsome*
formōsus, -a, -um   *beautiful*
fors, fortis (f)   *chance, luck*
forsan (adv.)   *perhaps*
forsitan (23.1/3 note 3)   *it is possible that, possibly*
fortasse (adv.)   *perhaps*
forte (adv.)   *by chance, perhaps*
fortis, -is, -e   *strong, powerful; brave*
fortiter (adv.)   *bravely, manfully*
fortitūdō, -dinis (f)   *bravery*
fortūna, -ae (f)   *fortune; good fortune, luck; success; rank*
fortūnātus, -a, -um   *fortunate, lucky*
forum, -ī (n)   *public square in the centre of a town*
fossa, -ae (f)   *ditch*
foveō, -ēre, fōvī, fōtum (tr.)   *cherish*
fragilis, -is, -e   *brittle*
fragor, -ōris (m)   *crash*
frangō, -ere, frēgī, fractum (tr.)   *break* (tr.)
frāter, frātris (m)   *brother*
frāternus, -a, -um   *of a brother, fraternal*
fremō, -ere, fremuī, fremitum (intr.)   *bellow*

frequens, -entis (adj.) *frequent*
frequenter (adv.) *often*
frētus, -a, -um (+ abl.) *relying on*
frīgidus, -a, -um *cold, chilly*
frīgus, -oris (n) *coldness, chill*
frons, frondis (f) *leaf, foliage*
fructus, -ūs (m) *fruit, crop; profit, advantage*
frūmentārius, -a, -um *connected with corn or food*
frūmentum, -ī (n) *grain, corn*
fruor, -ī, fructus sum (+ abl.) *enjoy*
frustrā (adv.) *in vain, to no purpose*
fūdī (perf. of **fundō, -ere**)
fuga, -ae (f) *flight; exile*
fugiō, -ere, fūgī (no sup.; intr., tr.) *flee (from)*
fugō, -āre (tr.) *put to flight, rout*
fuī (perf. of **sum**)
fulciō, -īre, fulsī, fultum (tr.) *prop*
fulgeō, -ēre, fulsī (no sup.; intr.) *shine*
fulgur, -uris (n) *flash of lightning, thunderbolt*
fūmō, -āre, fūmāvī (no sup.; intr.) *emit smoke, smoke*
fūmus, -ī (m) *smoke*
fundāmentum, -ī (n) *foundation*
fundō, -āre (tr.) *lay the foundations of*
fundō, -ere, fūdī, fūsum (tr.) *pour, pour out*
fundus, -ī (m) *farm*
fungor, -ī, functus sum (+ abl.) *perform, discharge* (an office)
fūr, fūris (m) *thief*
furō, -ere (n. o. p.; intr.) *behave madly, rage*
furor, -ōris (m) *madness*
furtim (adv.) *secretly*
furtīvus, -a, -um *stolen*
fustis, -is (m) *stick*
futūrus, -a, -um *going to be* (fut. pple. of **sum**)

Gādēs, -ium (f. pl.) *modern Cadiz in south-western Spain*
Gādītānī, -ōrum (m. pl.) *inhabitants of Gades (Cadiz)*
Galatēa, -ae *female name*
Galba, -ae *male cognomen*
galea, -ae (f) *helmet*
Gallia, -ae (f) *Gaul*

Gallicus, -a, -um *Gallic*
Gallus, -ī (m) *inhabitant of Gaul*
Gangēs, -is (m) *river Ganges in eastern India*
gaudeō, -ēre, gāvīsus sum (intr.) *rejoice* (25.1/5e)
gaudium, -ī (n) *joy*
gelidus, -a, -um *cold*
Gelō, -ōnis *Greek tyrant of Syracuse*
geminus, -a, -um *twin; double*
gemma, -ae (f) *bud*
gemō, -ere, gemuī, gemitum (intr., tr.) *groan; lament*
genitus, -a, -um (perf. pple. of **gignō**)
genius, -ī (m) *guardian spirit of a family or an individual*
gens, gentis (f) *race, people; family*
genū, -ūs (n) *knee*
genuī (perf. of **gignō**)
genus, -neris (n) *birth, origin; race; class; type*
Germānia, -ae (f) *Germany; name of two Roman provinces*
Germānus, -ī (m) *inhabitant of Germany, German*
gerō, -ere, gessī, gestum (tr.) *carry, bring, bear; wage, do*
gessī (perf. of **gerō**)
gestiō, -īre, gestīvī (-iī) (no sup.; intr.) *become elated, excited*
gestus, -a, -um (perf. pple. of **gerō**)
gignō, -ere, genuī, genitum (tr.) *produce, give birth to*
gladiātor, -ōris (m) *gladiator*
gladius, -ī (m), and **gladium, -ī** (n) *sword*
glomeror, -ārī (intr.) *collect in a group, flock together*
glōria, -ae (f) *glory*
gracilis, -is, -e *slender*
gradior, -ī, gressus sum (intr.) *step, walk*
Graeca, -ae (f) *Greek woman*
Graecia, -ae (f) *Greece*
Graecus, -ī (m) *inhabitant of Greece, Greek*
grammaticus, -ī (m) *scholar*
grandis, -is, -e *great; loud; large*
grātēs agō (+ dat.) *give thanks to, thank*
grātiā (abl. with preceding gen.) *for the sake of, by reason of*

grātia, -ae (f)   *favour, goodwill; charm*
grātiās agō (+ dat.)   *give thanks to, thank*
grātulātiō, -ōnis (f)   *(act of) rejoicing*
grātus, -a, -um   *pleasing; pleasant, charming; grateful*
gravis, -is, -e   *heavy; earnest, serious; painful*
gravitās, -tātis (f)   *heaviness; seriousness, sobriety*
graviter (adv.)   *gravely; with displeasure*
gurges, -gitis (m)   *waters (of a river), stream; sea*
gustus, -ūs (m)   *taste, flavour*
gutta, -ae (f)   *drop*
Gȳgēs, -is   *shepherd who became king of Lydia*

habeō, -ēre (tr.)   *have; hold; contain; consider;* (pass.) *be considered;* (with reflex.) *be in such a way, be*
habētō (s. fut. imp. act. of **habeō** (21.1/1 note 3))
habitō, -āre (intr., tr.)   *dwell, live; inhabit*
Haeduī, -ōrum (m. pl.)   *a tribe of Gauls*
haedus, -ī (m)   *young goat*
haereō, -ēre, haesī, haesum (+ dat.)   *stick; cling to*
Hannibal, -alis   *Carthaginian general*
harēna, -ae (f)   *sand, grain of sand; arena*
harundō, -dinis (f)   *reed*
haruspicium, -ī (n)   *method of divination from the entrails of sacrificed animals*
Hasdrubal, -alis   *Carthaginian general*
hasta, -ae (f)   *spear*
hastile, -is (n)   *spear (shaft)*
haud (adv.)   *no, not* (for **haud sciō an** see 23.1/3 note 3)
hauriō, -īre, hausī, haustum (tr.)   *drain*
Hector, -oris   *Trojan hero in Homer's Iliad*
heia (exclam.)   *hey!*
Helicōn, -ōnis (m)   *mountain in Greece sacred to Apollo and the Muses*
Helvētiī, -ōrum (m. pl.)   *Celtic tribe living in western Switzerland*

herba, -ae (f)   *plant, herb; grass*
hērēs, -ēdis (m or f)   *heir*
heri (adv.)   *yesterday*
hērōs, hērōos (m)   *hero (25.1/4e)*
hesternus, -a, -um   *of yesterday*
heu (interj.)   *alas!*
hiātus, -ūs (m)   *gap, hole*
hīberna (castra)   *winter quarters*
Hibernia, -ae (f)   *Ireland*
hībernus, -a, -um   *of winter, wintry*
hīc (adv.)   *here*
hic, haec, hoc (pron. and adj.)   *this near me (8.1/2)*
hiemō, -āre (intr.)   *pass the winter*
hiems, hiemis (f)   *winter*
hinc (adv.)   *from here, hence, henceforth*
Hispalis, -is (f)   *ancient city on the site of the modern Seville*
Hispānia, -ae (f)   *Spain*
Hispānus, -ī (m)   *inhabitant of Spain, Spaniard*
hodiē (adv.)   *today*
Homērus, -ī   *Homer, the most famous Greek poet and author of the Iliad and Odyssey*
homō, hominis (m)   *human being*
honestās, -tātis (f)   *quality of being honourable; morality*
honestus, -a, -um   *honourable*
honor, -ōris (m)   *honour; high public office*
hōra, -ae (f)   *hour*
Horātius, -ī   *the Roman poet Horace (65–8 BC)*
horreō, -ēre, horruī (no sup.; intr., tr.)   *shudder, shiver; tremble at; bristle*
horribilis, -is, -e   *terrifying*
hortor, -ārī (tr.)   *urge, encourage*
hortus, -ī (m)   *garden*
hospes, -pitis (m or f)   *host; guest*
hostis, -is (m)   *enemy*
hūc (adv.)   *(to) here* (with verbs of motion)
hūmānitās, -tātis (f)   *human nature; culture, refinement*
hūmānus, -a, -um   *human; civilized*
humilis, -is, -e   *low*
humus, -ī (f)   *ground*

iaceō, -ēre (intr.)   *lie, be recumbent*

iaciō, -ere, iēcī, iactum (tr.)　*throw;*
　lay, build
iactō, -āre (tr.)　*toss, throw*
iam (one syllable, adv.)　*already, now*
iamdūdum (adv.)　*already for a long*
　time
iānua, -ae (f)　*door*
ībant　(3rd pl. impf. ind. act. of eō)
ibi (adv.)　*there, in that place*
ibidem (adv.)　*in the same place*
idcircō (adv.)　*on that account,*
　therefore; for this reason
īdem, eadem, idem (pron. and
　adj.)　*the same* (10.1/1a)
identidem (adv.)　*again and again*
ideō (adv.)　*for this reason*
idōneus, -a, -um　*suitable*
iēcī　(perf. of iaciō)
igitur (adv.)　*therefore*
ignārus, -a, -um (+ gen.)　*ignorant of,*
　unacquainted with; imperceptive
ignāvus, -a, -um　*faint-hearted,*
　cowardly; lazy
ignis, -is (m)　*fire; heavenly body;*
　passion
ignōrō, -āre (tr.)　*be ignorant of, not*
　know
ignoscō, -ere, ignōvī, ignōtum (+ acc.
　of thing and dat. of person)　*forgive*
ignōtus, -a, -um　*unknown*
iī　(m. nom. pl. of is (8.1/2) or 1st s.
　perf. ind. act. of eō)
Īlium, -ī (n)　*another name of Troy*
illacrimābilis, -is, -e　*unwept for*
ille, illa, illud (pron. and adj.)　*that*
　(over there; 8.1/2)
illīc (adv.)　*there*
illínc (adv.)　*from there*
illūc (adv.)　*(to) there* (with verbs of
　motion)
illustris, -is, -e　*bright, shining*
imāgō, -ginis (f)　*image, reflection*
imber, imbris (m)　*rain*
imberbis, -is, -e　*beardless*
imbuō, -ere, imbuī, imbūtum
　(tr.)　*stain*
imitor, -ārī (tr.)　*copy, imitate*
immānis, -is, -e　*savage, wild; huge*
immemor, -oris (adj. + gen.)　*forgetful*
　(of)
immensus, -a, -um　*boundless, vast*
immisceō, -ēre, immiscuī, immixtum
　(tr.)　*mix* (tr.), *cause to mingle*

immītis, -is, -e　*cruel*
immittō, -ere, immīsī, immissum
　(tr.)　*cause to go, send*
immortālis, -is, -e　*immortal*
impedīmentum, -ī (n)　*obstacle,*
　hindrance; (pl.) *baggage*
impediō, -īre (tr.)　*obstruct, impede,*
　prevent
impellō, -ere, impulī, impulsum
　(tr.)　*drive, force*
imperātor, -ōris (m)　*general;*
　commander; emperor
imperitō, -āre (+ dat.)　*rule over*
imperium, -ī (n)　*authority; rule,*
　command; empire
imperō, -āre (+ acc. of thing and dat.
　of person)　*order, rule*
impetrō, -āre (tr.)　*obtain by request*
impetus, -ūs (m)　*attack*
impiger, impigra, impigrum　*swift*
impius, -a, -um　*wicked*
implectō, -ere, implexī, implexum
　(tr.)　*intertwine*
impleō, -ēre, implēvī, implētum
　(tr.)　*fill*
implicō, -āre (tr.)　*entwine, entangle*
implōrō, -āre (tr.)　*entreat, beseech*
impōnō, -ere, imposuī, impositum
　(tr.)　*place on; impose; embark* (tr.)
impotens, -entis (+ gen.)　*with no*
　control (over); raging
improbē (adv.)　*wrongly*
improbō, -āre (tr.)　*blame*
improbus, -a, -um　*wicked; shameless*
imprōvīsō (adv.)　*without warning*
imprūdens, -entis (adj.)　*ignorant;*
　incautious
impudens, -entis (adj.)　*shameless*
impudentia, -ae (f)　*shamelessness*
impūrus, -a, -um　*dirty; morally*
　impure, vile
īmus　(1st pl. pres. ind. act. of eō)
īmus, -a, -um　*lowest, deepest* (21.1/3)
in (prep.)　(+ acc.) *to, into; against;*
　(+ abl.) *in, on*
inamābilis, -is, -e　*unlovely*
inānis, -is, -e　*empty*
incautus, -a, -um　*unwary*
incēdō, -ere, incessī (no sup.;
　intr.)　*go, march*
incendium, -ī (n)　*fire*
incendō, -ere, incendī, incensum
　(tr.)　*kindle, burn* (tr.)

incertus, -a, -um　*not fixed, uncertain*
incidō, -ere, incidī, incāsum (intr.)　*fall into; fall in with; occur*
incipiō, incipere, coepī (2 syllables), **coeptum** (2 syllables) (intr., tr.)　*begin* (25.1/5*a*,ii)
incitō, -āre (tr.)　*provoke*
inclārescō, -ere, inclāruī (no sup.; intr.)　*become well known, famous*
incohō, -āre (tr.)　*begin, initiate, enter upon*
incola, -ae (m or f)　*inhabitant, colonist*
incolō, -ere, incoluī (no sup.; tr.)　*inhabit, dwell in*
incolumis, -is, -e　*safe, unharmed*
incomitātus, -a, -um　*unaccompanied*
incommodum, -ī (n)　*reversal, disaster*
increpō, -āre, increpuī, increpitum (tr.)　*upbraid*
incultus, -a, -um　*unkempt*
incumbō, -ere, incubuī (no sup.; intr.)　*throw oneself into; apply oneself to*
incūriōsus, -a, -um (+ gen.)　*indifferent to, not interested in*
incursus, -ūs (m)　*attack*
incūsō, -āre (tr.)　*find fault with, reproach*
inde (adv.)　*thence, from there*
indicō, -āre (tr.)　*make known, declare*
indīcō, -ere, indixī, indictum (tr.)　*declare, proclaim*
indigeō, -ēre, indiguī (no sup.; + gen. or abl.)　*lack, be in need of*
indignē (adv.)　*undeservedly; unworthily*
indignitās, -tātis (f)　*unworthy treatment; sense of outrage*
indignor, -ārī (tr.)　*take offence (at), be indignant (at)*
indignus, -a, -um (+ abl.)　*unworthy (of)*
indolēs, -is (f)　*innate character, nature*
indomitus, -a, -um　*untamed; ungovernable*
indulgeō, -ēre, indulsi, indultum (+ dat.)　*indulge*
induō, -ere, induī, indūtum (tr.)　*put on*
Indutiomarus, -ī　*a leader of the Gauls*
ineō (compound of **eō, īre**; tr.)　*go to, enter*

ineptus, -a, -um　*foolish, stupid*
infēlix, -līcis (adj.)　*unhapppy, unlucky*
inferī, -ōrum (m. pl.)　*the dead and the gods of the Underworld*
inferiae, -ārum (f. pl.)　*offerings to the dead*
inferior, -ior, -ius　*lower*
inferō, inferre, intulī, illātum (tr.)　*bring in, import*
inferus, -a, -um　*lower*
inficiō, -ere, infēcī, infectum (tr.)　*dye*
infimus, -a, -um　*lowest*
infinītus, -a, -um　*indefinite; without limits*
infirmitās, -tātis (f)　*weakness*
informis, -is, -e　*ugly; degrading*
infortūnium, -ī (n)　*trouble, misfortune*
infrā (adv.)　*below, underneath*
infrā (prep. + acc.)　*below; inferior to*
ingenium, -ī (n)　*talent; character*
ingens, -entis (adj.)　*huge*
ingrātus, -a, -um　*ungrateful, thankless*
ingredior, -ī, ingressus sum (tr., intr.)　*go (into)*
inhiō, -āre (intr.)　*gape*
inhūmānitās, -tātis (f)　*want of human feeling; cruelty*
inhumātus, -a, -um　*unburied*
iniciō, -ere, iniēcī, iniectum (tr.)　*throw in; instil; put on*
inimīcus, -a, -um　*unfriendly, hostile*
inimīcus, -ī (m)　*(personal) enemy*
initium, -ī (n)　*beginning*
iniūria, -ae (f)　*unjust treatment, harm*
iniussū (25.1/4*d*)　*without the order (of)*
iniustus, -a, -um　*unjust*
innumerābilis, -is, -e　*countless*
innumerus, -a, -um　*countless*
innuptus, -a, -um　*unmarried*
inopia, -ae (f)　*shortage, lack; poverty*
inops, inopis (adj.)　*poor, needy*
inquam (defective verb; tr.)　*say* (25.1/5*a*,i)
inquit　(3rd s. pres. or perf. ind. act. of **inquam**)
insānia, -ae (f)　*madness*
insāniō, -īre (intr.)　*be mad*
insānus, -a, -um　*mad*
inscientia, -ae (f)　*ignorance*
inscītus, -a, -um　*strange*
inscrībō, -ere, inscripsi, inscriptum (tr.)　*write, inscribe*

insequor, -ī, insecūtus sum (intr.,
tr.)   *press on; pursue, chase*
inserō, -ere, inseruī, insertum (tr.)   *put
in, insert*
insidiae, -ārum (f. pl.)   *ambush*
insigne, -is (n)   *(military) decoration*
insignis, -is, -e   *famous*
insolens, -entis (adj.)   *unaccustomed*
inspiciō, -ere, inspexī, inspectum
(tr.)   *examine*
instituō, -ere, instituī, institūtum
(tr.)   *train*
institūtiō, -ōnis (f)   *training,
instruction*
instō, -āre, institī (no sup.; intr.,
tr.)   *stand on; threaten*
instruō, -ere, instruxī, instructum
(tr.)   *build; draw up; organize,
arrange*
insuāvis, -is, -e (for pronunciation see
p. xiii)   *disagreeable, ungracious*
insula, -ae (f)   *island*
insultō, -āre (+ dat.)   *jump on; mock,
insult*
insum (in + sum; intr.)   *be in*
integer, -gra, -grum   *whole, complete;
not wounded, fresh*
integrātiō, -ōnis (f)   *renewal*
intellegō, -ere, intellexī, intellectum
(tr.)   *understand; realize*
intellexī   (perf. of intellegō)
intemptātus, -a, -um   *untried, untested*
inter (prep. + acc.)   *among, between*
intereā (adv.)   *meanwhile, in the
present situation*
interēmī   (perf. of interimō)
intereō (compound of eō, īre;
intr.)   *die, perish*
interest (compound of sum; impersonal
use)   *it concerns* (20.1/2d)
interfector, -ōris (m)   *murderer*
interficiō, -ere, interfēcī, interfectum
(tr.)   *kill*
interfuī   (perf. of intersum)
interfūsus, -a, -um   *poured between*
interim (adv.)   *meanwhile*
interimō, -ere, interēmī, interemptum
(tr.)   *kill*
interior, -ior, -ius   *interior, inner;
internal, inward; further from the
coast*
intermittō, -ere, intermīsī, intermissum
(tr.)   *interrupt*

interneciō, -ōnis (f)   *destruction*
intersum (inter + sum; + dat.)   *be
among, be between, take part in*
intervallum, -ī (n)   *interval*
intimus, -a, -um   *most remote, inmost*
intrā (prep. + acc.)   *inside, within*
intrō, -āre (tr., intr.)   *enter*
intus (adv.)   *inside*
inultus, -a, -um   *unavenged*
inūsitātus, -a, -um   *unusual*
inūtilis, -is, -e   *useless*
invādō, -ere, invāsī, invāsum (tr.,
intr.)   *attack; enter upon*
invalidus, -a, -um   *weak*
inveniō, -īre, invēnī, inventum
(tr.)   *find; discover*
invertō, -ere, invertī, inversum
(tr.)   *invert, turn*
investīgō, -āre (tr.)   *track down, search
out*
invicem (adv.)   *in turn*
invideō, -ēre, invīdī, invīsum (+ dat. of
person)   *envy* (20.1/1)
invidia, -ae (f)   *envy*
invidus, -a, -um   *ill-disposed, envious*
invīsus, -a, -um   *hateful, unpopular*
invītō, -āre (tr.)   *attract, invite*
invītus, -a, -um   *unwilling*
iocor, -ārī (intr.)   *jest, joke*
iocus, -ī (m)   *joke, jest* (25.1/4b)
ipse, ipsa, ipsum (pron. and adj.)   *self*
(10.1/1b)
īra, -ae (f)   *anger*
īrascor, -ī, (n. o. p.; + dat.)   *be angry
(with)*
īrātus, -a, -um   *angry*
īre (pres. inf. act. of eō)
Īris, -is (-idis)   *goddess of the rainbow
who also acted as a divine messenger*
irrīdeō, -ēre, irrīsī, irrīsum
(tr.)   *laugh at, mock*
irritus, -a, -um   *useless, ineffective*
irrumpō, -ere, irrūpī, irruptum (tr.,
intr.)   *burst into; interrupt, disturb*
is, ea, id (pron. and adj.)   *this* or *that*
(8.1/2)
Isocratēs, -is   *Greek orator*
iste, ista, istud (pron. and adj.)   *that
near you* (8.1/2)
Isthmius, -a, -um   *of the Isthmian
Games*
it (3rd s. pres. ind. act. of eō)
ita (adv.)   *thus; to such an extent, so*

Italia, -ae (f)   *Italy*

item (adv.)   *likewise, as well*

iter, itineris (n)   *road, journey*

iterum (adv.)   *again, for a second time*

ītur (3rd s. pres. ind. pass. of eō)

itūrus, -a, -um (fut. pple. of eō)

iubeō, -ēre, iussī, iussum (tr.)   *command, order*

iūcundus, -a, -um   *pleasant, charming*

iūdex, -dicis (m)   *judge*

iūdicium, -ī (n)   *court of law; trial; judgement, verdict; considered opinion*

iūdicō, -āre (tr., intr.)   *judge; give judgement*

iugulō, -āre (tr.)   *slaughter, kill, murder*

iugum, -ī (n)   *yoke* (for chariot, plough, etc.)

Iūlius, -ī   *male nomen*

Iūlus (3 syllables), **-ī**   *son of Aeneas*

iūmentum, -ī (n)   *beast of burden*

iungō, -ere, iunxī, iunctum (tr.)   *join, attach*

Iūnō, Iūnōnis   *Juno* (9.3)

iunxī (perf. of iungō)

Iuppiter, Iovis   *Jupiter* (9.3)

iūre (adv.)   *according to the law, rightly*

iūrō, -āre (intr., tr.)   *swear (on oath)*

iūs, iūris (n)   *law, right, privilege*

iussī (perf. of iubeō)

iussū (25.1/4*d*)   *by command (of)*

iussus, -a, -um (perf. pple. of iubeō)

iustitia, -ae (f)   *justice*

iustus, -a, -um   *lawful, just: impartial; correct*

iuvat (impersonal use)   *it pleases* (20.1/2*a*)

iuvenis, -is (m)   *young man*

iuventūs, -tūtis (f)   *(period of) youth*

iuvō, -āre, iūvī, iūtum (tr.)   *help*

iuxtā (prep. + acc.)   *next to, beside*

Ixīonius, -a, -um (adj. of **Ixīon**, a character in Greek mythology) *belonging to Ixion*

Karthāginiensis, -is (m)   *a Carthaginian*

Karthāgō, -inis (f)   *Carthage, city in northern Africa*

L. (abbreviation for **Lūcius**)

Labiēnus, -ī   *cognomen of Caesar's second in command*

lābor, -ī, lapsus sum (intr.)   *fall; flow*

labor, -ōris (m)   *labour, toil, task*

labōrō, -āre (intr.)   *labour, toil; be troubled, be in difficulty*

labrum, -ī (n)   *lip*

lac, lactis (n)   *milk; sap*

lacertus, -ī (m) (1)   *mackerel*

lacertus, -ī (m) (2)   *(upper) arm*

lacessō, -ere, lacessīvī (-iī), lacessītum (tr.)   *provoke, challenge*

lacrima, -ae (f)   *tear*

lacrimō, -āre (intr.)   *cry, weep*

lactūca, -ae (f)   *lettuce*

Laecānia, -ae   *Greek female name*

laedō, -ere, laesī, laesum (tr.)   *hurt*

Laelius, -ī   *male nomen*

laetitia, -ae (f)   *happiness*

laetus, -a, um   *happy*

laevus, -a, -um   *on the left-hand side, left*

lampas, -padis (f; 25.1/4*e*)   *torch*

lāneus, -a, -um   *made of wool, woollen*

languor, -ōris (m)   *lassitude, drowsiness*

laniātus, -ūs (m)   *(act of) mangling*

lapillus, -ī (m)   *small stone, pebble*

lapis, -pidis (m)   *stone, rock*

lapsus, -a, -um (perf. pple. of **labor**)

Lar, Laris (m)   *household god* (9.3)

lassus, -a, -um   *weary*

lātē (adv.)   *broadly; over a wide area*

Laterānus, -ī   *male cognomen*

latitō, -āre (intr.)   *lurk*

Lātōna, -ae   *mother of Apollo and Diana*

lātrō, -āre (intr.)   *bark*

latrō, -ōnis (m)   *brigand, thief*

lātus, -a, -um   *broad*

latus, -teris (n)   *side, flank*

laudō, -āre (tr.)   *praise*

laus, laudis (f)   *praise, renown, glory*

Lāvīnius, -a, -um (adj. of **Lāvīnium**, a town in Italy founded by Aeneas) *Lavinian*

lavō, -āre (-ere), lāvī, lautum (lavātum, lōtum; tr., intr.)   *wash*

lēgātiō, -ōnis (f)   *embassy, deputation*

lēgātus, -ī (m)   *army officer, legate; ambassador, envoy*

legiō, -ōnis (f)   *largest unit in Roman army, legion*

legō, -ere, lēgī, lectum (tr.)   *read; collect, gather*

lēnis, -is, -e   *gentle, mild*

lentus, -a, -um   *leisurely, unhurried, at ease; shuggish, slow; pliant*

leō, -ōnis (m) *lion*
lepōs, -pōris (m) *charm, grace*
lepus, -poris (m) *hare*
Lesbia, -ae *pseudonym of the woman addressed by Catullus in his poetry*
Lēthē, -ēs (f) *river of the Underworld which caused forgetfulness in those who drank its water*
lētum, -ī (n) *death*
Leuconoē, -ēs *female name*
levis, -is, -e (1) *not heavy, light*
lēvis, -is, -e (2) *smooth*
leviter (adv.) *lightly; superficially*
levō, -āre (tr.) *lift; ease*
lex, lēgis (f) *law; condition*
libellus, -ī (m) *little book*
līber, lībera, līberum *free*
liber, librī (m) *book*
līberī, -ōrum (m. pl.) *children*
līberō, -āre (tr.) *free, set free*
lībertās, -tātis (f) *freedom*
lībertus, -ī (m) *freedman*
libet, -ēre, libuit (libitum est) (+ dat.) *it is pleasing* (20.1/2c)
lībum, -ī (n) *cake*
licet (conj.) *although* (29.1/4b)
licet, -ēre, licuit (licitum est) (+dat) *it is allowed* (20.1/2c)
lignum, -ī (n) *wood*
līmen, -minis (n) *threshold*
līmōsus, -a, -um *muddy*
līmus, -ī (m) *mud*
lingua, -ae (f) *tongue; language*
linquō, -ere, līquī (no sup.; tr.) *leave, abandon*
liquidus, -a, -um *liquid, molten; clear, limpid*
liquō, -āre (tr.) *make clear, strain* (wine, etc.)
līs, lītis (f) *lawsuit, dispute*
littera, -ae (f) *letter of the alphabet;* (pl.) *epistle* (8.1/4); *literature*
lītus, -toris (n) *shore*
locō, -āre (tr.) *place, station; lend*
Locrī, -ōrum (m. pl.) *Greek city in southern Italy*
locuplēs, -lētis (adj.) *wealthy, rich*
locus, -ī (m) *place* (25.1/4b)
locūtus, -a, -um (perf. pple. of **loquor**)
longē (adv.) *a long way, far*
Longīnus, -ī *male cognomen*
longus, -a, -um *long; tall*
loquax, -ācis (adj.) *talkative*

loquor, -ī, locūtus sum (intr., tr.) *speak, talk*
lōrīca, -ae (f) *corselet*
Lūcifer, -erī (m) *the morning star*
lucrum, -ī (n) *profit*
luctor, -ārī (intr.) *struggle*
luctus, -ūs (m) *grief*
lūcus, -ī (m) *grove*
lūdibrium, -ī (n) *mockery, derision*
lūdō, -ere, lūsī, lūsum (intr.) *play*
lūdus, -ī (m) *game, sport; school;* (pl.) *public games*
lūgeō, -ēre, luxī, luctum (intr., tr.) *mourn*
lūmen, -minis (n) *light; eye*
lūna, -ae (f) *moon*
luō, -ere, luī (no sup.; tr.) *atone, suffer*
lux, lūcis (f) *light*
luxuria, -ae (f) *indulgence, luxury*
luxuriō, -āre (intr.) *grow rank*
Lycōris, -idis *Greek female name*
Lȳdia, -ae (f) *country in Asia Minor*
Lȳsiās, -ae (25.1/4e) *Greek orator*

M. (abbreviation for **Marcus**)
Macedonēs, -um (m. pl.) *inhabitants of Macedonia*
mactō, -āre (tr.) *sacrifice*
Maecēnās, -ātis *patron of Vergil and Horace*
Maeonidēs, -ae *another name of Homer*
maereō, -ēre (n. o. p.; intr., tr.) *grieve (for)*
maeror, -ōris (m) *grief*
maestus, -a, -um *unhappy, sad*
magis (adv.) *more*
magister, -trī (m) *schoolmaster*
magistrātus, -ūs (m) *office of a magistrate, public office*
magnanimus, -a, -um *brave, mighty*
magnificus, -a, -um *magnificent, splendid*
magnitūdō, -dinis (f) *size*
magnopere (adv.) *greatly*
magnus, -a, -um *great, large, important*
maiestās, -tātis (f) *dignity*
maior, -ior, -ius *greater, older*
maiōrēs, -um (m. pl.) *ancestors*
male (adv.) *badly*
maleficium, -ī (n) *injury; crime*
malignē (adv.) *poorly, badly*

malignus, -a, -um   *scanty, poor; mean*
mālō, malle, māluī (no sup.; tr.)   *prefer* (15.1/5 and p. 294)
malus, -a, -um   *bad, evil*
mandō, -āre (tr.)   *entrust, commit*
maneō, -ēre, mansī, mansum (intr.)   *stay, remain; abide by*
mānēs, -ium (m. pl.)   *shades of the dead*
mānō, -āre, mānāvī (no sup.; intr.)   *be wet, drip*
mansī (perf. of **maneō**)
mansuescō, -ere, mansuēvī, mansuētum (intr.; for pronunciation see p. xiii)   *grow tender, soften*
manubiae, -ārum (f. pl.)   *booty*
manus, -ūs (f)   *hand; band of men*
mare, maris (n)   *sea*
maritimus, -a, -um   *by the sea, maritime*
marītus, -ī (m)   *husband*
Mars, Martis   *god of war* (9.3)
māter, mātris (f)   mother
māteria, -ae (f)   *material; matter*
mātrōna, -ae (f)   *married woman, matron*
māvīs (2nd s. pres. ind. act. of **mālō**)
maximē (adv.)   *most*
maximus, -a, -um   *greatest*
mēcum   = cum + mē
medicābilis, -is, -e   *curable*
medicus, -ī (m)   *doctor*
medius, -a, -um   *middle* (21.1/3); *mediocre, middling*
Meliboeus, -ī   *shepherd in Vergil's Eclogues*
melior, -ior, -ius   *better*
Melpomenē, -ēs   *one of the nine Muses*
membrum, -ī (n)   *part of the human body; limb*
mementō (s. imp. of **meminī**)
meminī, meminisse (+ acc. or gen.)   *remember* (25.1/5a,ii)
memor, -oris (adj. + gen.)   *mindful of, remembering*
memorābilis, -is, -e   *memorable*
memoria, -ae (f)   *memory*
mendīcus, -ī (m)   *beggar*
mendōsus, -a, -um   *faulty*
mens, mentis (f)   *mind*
mensa, -ae (f)   *table*
mensis, -is (m)   *month*
mentiō, -ōnis (f)   *mention, reference*

mentior, -īrī (intr.)   *tell a lie, lie*
mentum, -ī (n)   *chin*
mercātor, -ōris (m)   *merchant*
Mercurius, -ī   *Mercury* (9.3)
mereō, -ēre (tr.)   *deserve; have a claim to*
merīdiēs, -ēī (m)   *midday*
meritō (adv.)   *deservedly*
merum, -ī (n)   *unmixed wine*
merus, -a, -um   *pure, undiluted*
messis, -is (f)   *harvest*
metuō, -ere, metuī, metūtum (tr.)   *fear; be afraid of*
metus, -ūs (m)   *fear; anxiety*
meus, -a, -um   *my*
migrō, -āre (intr.)   *move position, leave*
mīles, -litis (m)   *soldier*
Mīlēsius, -a, -um (adj. of **Mīlētus**, Greek city in Asia Minor)   *Milesian*
mīlia, -ium (n. pl.)   *thousands* (11.1/5e)
mīlitāris, -is, -e   *military*
mīlitia, -ae (f)   *military service*
mille (indecl. adj.)   *thousand*
Milō, -ōnis (m)   *male cognomen; famous Greek athlete*
mina, -ae (f)   *Greek unit of currency*
minae, -ārum (f. pl.)   *threats*
Minerva, -ae   *Minerva* (9.3)
minimē (adv.)   *least of all; no*
minimus, -a, -um   *smallest*
minister, -trī (m)   *servant*
ministrō, -āre (+ dat.)   *attend to*
minor, -ārī (+acc. of thing and dat. of person)   *threaten* (20.1/1)
minor, -or, -us   *smaller; younger*
Mīnōs, -ōis   *an Underworld judge*
minuō, -ere, minuī, minūtum (tr.)   *lessen; reduce; cease; (pass.) grow smaller, diminish*
minus (adv.)   *to a smaller degree, less*
minus, -nōris (n)   *a smaller amount, less*
mīrābilis, -is, -e   *remarkable, wonderful*
mīrificus, -a, -um   *wonderful, remarkable*
mīror, -ārī (intr., tr.)   *marvel (at)*
mīrus, -a, um   *extraordinary, remarkable, marvellous*
misceō, -ēre, miscuī, mixtum (tr.)   *mix*
miscuī (perf. of **misceō**)
miser, misera, miserum   *unhappy*
miserābilis, -is, -e   *pitiful*
miseret, -ēre, miseruit (no

sup.; + acc.)   *it moves to pity* (20.1/2*b*)
miseria, -ae (f)   *unhappiness, distress*
mīsī   (perf. of mittō)
mītescō, -ere (n.o.p.; intr.)   *become gentle*
mītis, -is, -e   *mild, kind, gentle*
mittō, -ere, mīsī, missum (tr.)   *send*
mixtus, -a, -um   (perf. pple. of misceō)
moderātē (adv.)   *with moderation*
moderātiō, -ōnis (f)   *restraint, moderation; control (over)*
modestē (adv.)   *in a restrained manner, with propriety*
modo (adv.)   *only*
modo (conj.)   *provided that* (29.1/3*b*, iii)
modus, -ī (m)   *size, limit; method, way; metre*
moenia, -ium (n. pl.)   *walls*
mōlēs, -is (f)   *effort, exertion*
molestia, -ae (f)   *nuisance, trouble*
molestus, -a, -um   *troublesome*
mollis, -is, -e   *soft, yielding*
moneō, -ēre (tr., intr.)   *advise, warn*
mons, montis (m)   *mountain*
monstrō, -āre (tr.)   *show, point out*
monumentum, -ī (n)   *monument*
mora, -ae (f)   *delay*
morbus, -ī (m)   *sickness, disease*
mordeō, -ēre, momordī, morsum (tr.)   *bite*
morior, -ī, mortuus sum (intr.)   *die*
moror, -ārī (tr., intr.)   *delay*
mors, mortis (f)   *death*
morsus, -ūs (m)   *bite*
mortālis, -is, -e   *mortal, of or concerning human beings*
mortifer, -fera, -ferum   *bringing death, fatal*
mortuus, -a, -um   *dead* (perf. pple. of morior)
mortuus, -ī (m)   *dead man*
mōs, mōris (m)   *custom; (pl.) habits, character*
mōtus, -ūs (m)   *movement; rising rebellion*
moveō, -ēre, mōvī, mōtum (tr.)   *move* (tr.), *set in motion, provoke*
mox (adv.)   *soon*
mulier, -eris (f)   *woman; wife*
multitūdō, -dinis (f)   *great number, crowd, mob*
multum (adv.)   *much*

multus, -a, -um   *much, many a;* (pl.) *many*
munditia, -ae (f)   *elegance*
mundus, -ī (m)   *the world, the earth; the universe*
mūnīmentum, -ī (n)   *fortification*
mūniō, -īre (tr.)   *fortify*
mūnitiō, -ōnis (f)   *fortification*
mūnus, -neris (n)   *something given as a duty; gift*
mūraena, -ae (f)   *type of eel*
murmur, -uris (n)   *murmur*
mūrus, -ī (m)   *wall*
mūs, mūris (m)   *mouse*
muscōsus, -a, -um   *covered with moss, mossy*
mūtō, -āre (tr.)   *change* (tr.)
mūtus, -a, -um   *dumb, saying nothing*
myrtus, -ī (f)   *myrtle*

nactus   (perf. pple. of nanciscor)
nam or namque (conj.)   *for* (introducing a reason)
nanciscor, -ī, nactus sum (tr.)   *obtain*
narrō, -āre (tr.)   *narrate, tell, say*
nascor, -ī, nātus sum (intr.)   *be born; grow*
Nāsīca, -ae   *male cognomen*
nāsus, -ī (m)   *nose*
nāta, -ae (f)   *daughter*
nātālis, -is (m)   *birthday:* (pl.) *parentage, origins*
nātiō, -ōnis (f)   *tribe, race*
natō, -āre (intr.)   *swim*
nātū (25.1/4*d*)   *by birth*
nātūra, -ae (f)   *nature; quality, character*
nātūrālis, -is, -e   *natural*
nātus, -a, -um (perf. pple. of nascor)
nātus, -ī (m)   *son;* (pl.) *children*
naufragium, -ī (n)   *shipwreck*
nausea, -ae (f)   *sea-sickness; nausea*
nauta, -ae *(m)*   *sailor*
nāvigātiō, -ōnis (f)   *voyage*
nāvigō, -āre (intr.)   *sail, journey by sea*
nāvis longa   *warship*
nāvis, -is (f)   *ship*
nāvita, -ae (m)   *sailor*
nē (conj. + subj.)   *lest, (so) that … not* (13.1/5, 21.1/2. 26.1/2)
-ne (interr.) (used to introduce a question (3.1/8 and 23.1/3))
nē (neg. adv. with certain uses of subj.

22.1/1) *not*

nē ... quidem *not even* (3.1/5)

Neāpolis, -is (f) *Naples*

nebula, -ae (f) *fog, cloud*

nec (conj.) *nor, and ... not* (3.1/6)

nec ... nec *neither... nor* (3.1/6)

necessārius, -a, -um *essential, necessary*

necessārius, -ī (m) *person with whom one is closely associated, friend*

necesse est (impersonal use) *it is necessary*

necessitās, -tātis (f) *necessity*

necne (conj.) *or not* (in direct alternative questions 23.1/3 note 5)

necō, -āre (tr.) *kill*

nefārius, -a, -um *evil, wicked*

nefās (indecl. noun) *wickedness, wrong, sin* (25.1/4*d*)

neglegō, -ere, neglexī, neglectum (tr.) *neglect*

negō, -āre (tr.) *deny, refuse; say ... not*

negōtium, -ī (n) *business, work, transaction; trouble*

nēmō, -minis (m or f) *no one* (25.1/4*d*)

nemus, -moris (n) *wood, grove*

Neptūnus, -ī *Neptune* (9.3)

nēquāquam (adv.) *by no means*

neque (= nec) *nor, and ... not* (3.1/6)

nequeō (defective verb; intr.) *be unable* (25.1/5*a*, i)

nēquior, -ior, -ius *worse*

nēquīquam (adv.) *in vain, to no effect*

Nerō, -ōnis *Roman emperor* AD *54–68*

Nervīī, -ōrum (m. pl.) *tribe in north-eastern Gaul*

nesciō, -īre (tr.) *not know* (for **nesciō an** see 23.1/3 note 3)

nescioquis (-quī), -quae, -quid (-quod) (pron. and adj.) *I-know-not-who/what, someone; some; vague*

nescius, -a, -um, *not knowing (how); ignorant (of)*

neu (conj.; on pronunciation see p.xv) *nor* (in purpose clauses and indirect commands)

neuter, neutra, neutrum (pron. and adj.; on pronunciation see p. xv) *neither of two*

nēve = neu

niger, nigra, nigrum *black*

nihil, nīl (indecl. noun) *nothing*

Nīlus, -ī (m) *the river Nile*

nimis (adv.) *excessively, too much; particularly*

nimis (indecl. noun; + gen.) *excess (of; 27.1/4k)*

nimium (adv.) *excessively, too*

nimius, -a, -um *excessive*

ningit, -ere, ninxit (no sup.; impers.) *it is snowing*

nisi (conj.) *unless, if not, except*

niteō, -ēre, nituī (no sup.; intr.) *shine*

nītor, -ī, nixus (nīsus) sum (+ abl.) *lean on, rely on; strive*

nitor, -ōris (m) *brightness*

niveus, -a, -um *white as snow; cold as snow*

nōbilis, -is, -e *famous; noble*

nōbilitās, -tātis (f) *nobility in rank or birth*

nōbiscum = cum + nōbīs

nocens, -entis (adj.) *harmful*

noceō, -ēre (+ dat.) *harm, injure*

noctū (adv.) *at night*

nōdus, -ī (m) *knot*

nōlō, nolle, nōluī (no sup.; intr., tr.) *not want, be unwilling* (see 15.1/5 and p. 294)

nōmen, -minis (n) *name, family name*

nōminō, -āre (tr.) *name, call*

nōn (adv.) *no, not*

nōn modo ... sed etiam *not only ... but also*

nōn sōlum ... sed etiam *not only ... but also*

nōnāgintā (indecl. adj.) *ninety*

nōngentī, -ae, -a *nine hundred*

nōnne (interr. adv. 23.1/1*e* (see also 23.1/3))

nōnnumquam (adv.) *not never, i.e. sometimes*

nōnus, -a, -um *ninth*

nōs (pron.) *we* (8.1/1)

noscō, -ere, nōvī, nōtum (tr.) *get to know; (perf.) know* (25.1/5*b*)

noster, nostra, nostrum *our*

notō, -āre (tr.) *mark, make note of; notice*

nōtus, -a, -um (perf. pple. of **noscō**)

novae cōpiae (f. pl.) *reinforcements*

novem (indecl. adj.) *nine*

nōvī (perf. of **noscō**)

noviēs (adv.)   *nine times*
novō, -āre (tr.)   *renew, restore*
novus, -a, -um   *new, strange*
nox, noctis (f)   *night*
nūbēs, -is (f)   *cloud*
nūbilum, -ī (n)   *cloud*
nūbō, -ere, nupsī, nuptum (+dat.)
   marry (with woman as subject)
nūdulus, -a, -um   (diminutive of
   nūdus)
nūdus, -a, -um   *naked*
nullus, -a, -um (pron. and adj.)   *none,
   no one* (10.1/1e)
num   (interr. adv. 23.1/1d; conj.
   introducing indirect questions 23.1/3)
nūmen, -minis (n)   *divinity, divine being
   of either sex*
numerō, -āre (tr.)   *count*
numerus, -ī (m)   *number; rhythm*
numquam (adv.)   *never*
nunc (adv.)   *now; as it is*
nuntiō, -āre (tr.)   *announce, report*
nuntius, -ī (m)   *messenger; message*
nusquam (adv.)   *nowhere*
nūtriō, -īre (tr.)   *nourish, feed*
nūtrix, -trīcis (f)   *nurse*
nūtus, -ūs (m)   *nod*
nympha, -ae (f)   *nymph; wife*

ō   (interj. preceding a vocative or
   exclamation)
ob (prep. + acc.)   *because of*
obiciō, -ere, obiēcī, obiectum (tr.)   *put
   in the way*
oblīviō, -ōnis (f)   *state of forgetting,
   oblivion*
oblīviscor, -ī, oblītus sum (+ acc. or
   gen.)   *forget*
obscēnus, -a, -um   *loathsome, filthy*
obscūrus, -a, -um   *dark; hidden from
   sight*
observō, -āre (tr.)   *observe, note,
   perceive; adhere to, keep to*
obses, -sidis (m or f)   *hostage*
obsideō, -ēre, obsēdī, obsessum (tr.)
   besiege
obsidiō, -ōnis (f)   *siege*
obstō, -āre, obstitī, obstātum (+dat.)
   be in the way of
obsum (ob + sum; + dat.)   *be a trouble
   to, bother*
obtemperātiō, -ōnis (f)   *obedience*
obtentus, -ūs (m)   *veil, screen*

obtestor, -ārī (tr.)   *entreat, implore*
obtortus, -a, -um   *twisted*
obtulī   (perf. of offerō)
occāsiō, -ōnis (f)   *opportunity*
occāsus, -ūs (m)   *setting*
occidō, -ere, occidī, occāsum
   (intr.)   *die*
occīdō, -ere, occīdī, occīsum (tr.)   *kill*
occulō, -ere, occuluī, occultum
   (tr.)   *hide*
occupō, -āre (tr.)   *take hold of, occupy,
   seize*
occurrō, -ere, oc(cu)currī, occursum
   (+dat.)   *run into, meet*
Ōceanus, -ī (m)   *sea which the ancients
   envisaged as surrounding Europe,
   Africa, and Asia*
ocelus, -ī (m)   *(little) eye*
Octāviānus, -ī   *one of the names of the
   Emperor Augustus*
octāvus, -a, -um   *eighth*
octingentī, -ae, -a   *eight hundred*
octo (indecl. adj.)   *eight*
octōgintā (indecl. adj.)   *eighty*
oculus, -ī (m)   *eye*
ōdī, ōdisse, ōsum (tr.)   *hate*
   (25.1/5a,ii)
odium, -ī (n)   *hatred*
odor, -ōris (m)   *smell, fragrance, scent*
offerō, offerre, obtulī, oblātum (tr.)
   bring, provide
officium, -ī (n)   *duty; employment,
   office*
ōlim (adv.)   *once, at some time in the
   past; at some future time*
Ōlus, -ī   *male praenomen*
Olympius, -a, -um   (adj. of Olympia
   place in southern Greece)   *Olympian*
ōmen, -minis (n)   *sign indicative of the
   future, omen*
omnīnō (adv.)   *completely*
omnipotens, -entis (adj.)   *almighty*
omnis, -is, -e   *all, every*
onus, oneris (n)   *load, burden*
onustus, -a, -um   *laden*
opācus, -a, -um   *shaded, dark*
operiō, -īre, operuī, opertum
   (tr.)   *cover*
opēs (pl. of ops)
opīniō, -ōnis (f)   *belief, opinion*
opīnor, -ārī (tr.)   *consider, suppose,
   think*
oportet, -ēre, oportuit (no sup.; + acc.)

it behoves (20.1/2*a*)

opperior, -īrī, oppertus sum (intr., tr.)
wait (for)

oppidum, -ī (n)   *town*

opportūnitās, -tātis (f)   *opportuneness, timeliness; opportunity*

oppositus, -a, -um   *situated opposite, facing; opposing*

oppugnō, -āre (tr.)   *attack*

ops, opis (f; 25.1/4*d*)   *aid;* (pl.) *resources, wealth; power*

optimus, -a, -um   *best*

optō, -āre (tr.)   *desire*

opulentus, -a, -um   *wealthy*

opus, operis (n)   *work; need* (20.1/2*f*); *work of art*

ōra, -ae (f)   *edge; shore*

ōrātiō, -ōnis (f)   *speech, oration; oratory*

ōrātor, -ōris (m)   *speaker*

orbis, -is (m)   *circle; wheel; world*

orbus, -a, -um   *bereaved, bereft*

Orcus, -ī (m)   *another name of the Underworld*

ordō, -dinis (m)   *line, row; line of soldiers, rank*

Oriens, -entis (m)   *the East*

orīgō, -ginis (f)   *beginning; source*

orior, -īrī, ortus sum (intr.)   *arise; be born*

ornāmentum, -ī (n)   *ornament;* (pl.) *jewels*

ornō, -āre (tr.)   *adorn, decorate*

ōrō, -āre (tr.)   *beg*

Orpheus, -eī   *legendary singer*

ortus, -a, -um   (perf. pple. of **orior**)

ōs, ōris (n)   *mouth; face; beak*

os, ossis (n)   *bone*

osculum, -ī (n)   *kiss*

ostendō, -ere, ostendī, ostentum (-sum) (tr.)   *show*

ostium, -ī (n)   *door, entrance, portal*

ostrea, -ae (f)   *oyster*

ōsus, -a, -um   (perf. pple. of **ōdī**)

ōtium, -ī (n)   *leisure*

Ovidius, -ī   *the Roman poet Ovid (43 BC–AD 17)*

ovīle, -is (n)   *sheepfold*

ōvum, -ī (n)   *egg*

P.   (abbreviation for **Publius**)

pābulātiō, -ōnis (f)   *foraging*

Paelignus, -a, -um   (adj. of **Paelignī**, a people of central Italy) *Paelignian*

paenitet, -ēre, paenituit (no sup.; + acc.)   *it repents* (20.1/2*b*)

pāgus, -ī (m)   *community (of people)*

pāla, -ae (f)   *bezel (of a ring)*

Palātīnus, -a, -um   (adj. of **Palātium**)

Palātium, -ī (n)   *the Palatine hill at Rome*

Palinūrus, -ī   *helmsman of Aeneas*

pallens, -entis (adj.)   *pale, wan*

pallidus, -a, -um   *pale*

pallium, -ī (n)   *cloak*

palma, -ae (f)   *palm (of the hand); palm-tree; victory*

palmes, -mitis (m)   *branch of a grape vine*

pālor, -ārī (intr.)   *wander, stray*

palūs, -ūdis (f)   *swamp*

Pān, Pānos   *pastoral god*

pandō, -ere, pandī, passum (tr.)   *open, spread* (tr.)

pangō, -ere, pepigī (pēgī), pactum (tr.)   *fix, make*

pānis, -is (m)   *bread*

papāver, -veris (n)   *poppy*

papȳrus, -ī (f)   *ancient equivalent of paper, papyrus*

pūr, paris (adj.)   *like, equal; same; similar*

parātus, -a, -um   *prepared, ready*

parcō, -ere, peperci, parsum (+dat.)   *spare*

parcus, -a, -um   *thrifty, sparing*

parens, -entis (m or f)   *parent, ancestor*

pāreō, -ēre (+ dat.)   *obey*

pariēs, -ietis (m)   *wall*

pariō, -ere, peperī, partum (tr.)   *bring forth, give birth to; acquire*

Paris, -idis   *son of Priam*

pariter (adv.)   *together*

parō, -āre (tr.)   *prepare; obtain*

pars, partis (f)   *part, section; share; side; region*

Parthī, -ōrum (m. pl.)   *inhabitants of Parthia (approximately modern Iran), Parthians*

partim (adv.)   *partly*

parturiō, -īre, parturīvī (no sup.; intr.)   *be in labour (of child birth)*

partus, -a, -um   (perf. pple. of **pariō**)

parum (adv.)   *insufficiently, too little, scarcely*

parum (indecl. noun; + gen.)
insufficiency (of; 27.1/4k)
parvus, -a, -um *small*
pascō, -ere, pāvī, pastum (tr., intr.)
feed
passer, -eris (m) *sparrow*
passim (adv.) *in every direction,
everywhere*
passus, -a, -um (perf. pple. of **patior**
and **pandō**)
passus, -ūs (m) *step, pace*
pastor, -ōris (m) *shepherd*
patefaciō, -ere, patefēcī, patefactum (tr.)
open up; make visible
pater, patris (m) *father*
patera, -ae (f) *bowl*
patiens, -entis (adj.) *tolerant; hardy*
patientia, -ae (f) *endurance, patience*
patior, -ī, passus sum (tr.) *suffer, allow;
endure*
patria, -ae (f) *native land; native
place*
patrimōnium, -ī (n) *family estate,
patrimony*
patrius, -a, -um *native, ancestral;
belonging to one's father*
paucī, -ae, -a (pl.) *few*
Paula, -ae *female name*
paulātim (adv.) *gradually*
paulum (adv.) *a little; to a small extent*
pauper, -peris (adj.) *poor*
pauperiēs, -ēī (f) *poverty*
paupertās, -tātis (f) *poverty*
paveō, -ēre (n.o.p.; intr., tr.) *fear*
pavor, -ōris (m) *fear, terror*
pax, pācis (f) *peace*
peccō, -āre (intr.) *do wrong*
pectus, -toris (n) *chest, heart*
pecūlium, -ī (n) *savings (of a slave)*
pecūnia, -ae (f) *money*
pecus, -coris (n) *livestock; herd*
pecus, -udis (f) *an individual domestic
animal*
pedes, -ditis (m) *foot-soldier*
peior, -ior, -ius *worse*
pelagus, -ī (n) *sea*
Pellaeus, -a, -um (adj. of **Pella**, a town
in Macedonia) *Pellaean*
pellis, -is (f) *skin of an animal, hide*
pellō, -ere, pepulī, pulsum (tr.) *drive*
Peloponnēsus, -ī (f) *southern area of
Greece, Peloponnese*
Penātēs, -ium *household gods* (9.3)

pendeō, -ēre, pependī (no sup.; intr.)
hang (intr.); *depend on, follow from*
pendō, -ere, pependī, pensum (tr.)
weigh (tr.)
penetrālia, -ium (n. pl.) *inner shrine,
sanctuary*
penitus (adv.) *deeply; completely*
peperī (perf. of **pariō**)
per (prep. + acc.) *through; during; by
means of; around*
peractus, -a, -um *finished,
accomplished, fulfilled*
percipiō, -ere, percēpī, perceptum (tr.)
perceive, notice; grasp
percommodē (adv.) *very opportunely*
percussiō, -ōnis (f) *act of striking or
snapping*
percutiō, -ere, percussī, percussum (tr.)
strike
perditus, -a, -um *depraved*
perdō, -ere, perdidī, perditum (tr.) *lose;
destroy; waste*
perennis, -is, -e *lasting, enduring*
pereō (compound of **eō, īre**; intr.)
disappear, perish, die
perfectus, -a, -um *complete, entire*
perficiō, -ere, perfēcī, perfectum
(tr.) *bring to a conclusion; bring it
about, achieve*
perfidus, -a, -um *faithless, treacherous*
perfugiō, -ere, perfūgi (no sup.; intr.)
take refuge; escape (intr.)
perfundō, -ere, perfūdī, perfūsum (tr.)
pour over, drench
Pergama, -ōrum (n. pl.) *(the citadel
of) Troy*
pergō, -ere, perrexī, perrectum
(intr.) *proceed, go on (to do
something)*
perīclum, -ī (n) (another form of
perīculum)
perīculum, -ī (n) *danger*
periī (perf. of **pereō**)
perīrātus, -a, -um *very angry, furious*
perītus, -a, -um (+ gen.) *experienced
(in)*
periūrium (4 syllables), **-ī** (n) *false
oath, perjury*
permaneō, -ēre, permansī, permansum
(intr.) *continue, remain*
permisceō, -ēre, permiscuī, permixtum
(tr.) *bring together, mix up*
permittō, -ere, permīsī, permissum

(+acc. of thing and dat. of person) *allow*

perpetuus, -a -um *continuous; continual* (**in perpetuum** *forever*)

perrāro (adv.) *very rarely*

Persae, -ārum (m. pl.) *inhabitants of Persia, Persians*

persequor, -ī, persecūtus sum (tr.) *pursue*

persevērō, -āre (intr.) *persist*

persōna, -ae (f) *mask; character in a play; particular individual*

persuādeō, -ēre, persuāsī, persuāsum (+ dat.; for pronunciation see p. xiii) *persuade*

pertineō, -ēre, pertinuī (no sup.; intr.) (+ **ad**) *be related to, concern, pertain to*

pertundō, -ere, pertudī, pertūsum (tr.) *bore through, perforate*

perturbō, -āre (tr.) *disturb, trouble*

perveniō, -īre, pervēnī, perventum (intr.) *arrive, come*

pervigilō, -āre (intr.) *stay awake*

pēs, pedis (m) *foot; measure of length*

pessimus, -a, -um *worst*

petō, -ere, petīvī (-iī), petītum (tr.) *seek, look for; ask, make a request* (**ā/ab** + abl. for person asked)

petra, -ae (f) *rock*

Phalaris, -idis *notorious Greek tyrant of Agrigentum in Sicily*

philosophia, -ae (f) *philosophy*

philosophus, -ī (m) *philosopher*

Phoebus, -ī *another name of Apollo, especially in his capacity as sun god*

Phrygius, -a, -um (adj. of **Phrygia**, country of Asia Minor whose most famous city was Troy) *Phrygian*

Phyllis, -idis (-idos) *Greek female name*

pietās, -tātis (f) *sense of duty towards whom it is due* (gods, parents, etc.), *piety*

piger, pigra, pigrum *sluggish; lazy*

piget, -ēre, piguit (no sup.; + acc.) *it vexes* (20.1/2*b*)

Pīlumnus, -ī *ancestor of Turnus*

pingō, -ere, pinxī, pictum (tr.) *paint; depict*

pinguis, -is, -e *fat, rich in fat; fertile*

pīnus, -ūs (f) *pine-tree*

piscis, -is (m) *fish*

pius, -a, -um *showing* **pietās**, *pious, good*

placeō, -ēre, placuī (or **placitus sum** 25.1/5*e*) (+dat.) *please, be pleasing to, delight*

placidus, -a, -um *favourable; quiet, peaceful*

plācō, -āre (tr.) *conciliate, appease*

Plancus, -ī *male cognomen*

plānē (adv.) *clearly, plainly*

plangō, -ere, planxī, planctum (tr., intr.) *smite; beat one's breast in mourning; mourn*

plānus, -a, -um *even, flat;* (of speech) *clear*

Platō, -ōnis *celebrated Greek philosopher*

plaudō, -ere, plausī, plausum (intr., tr.) *clap one's hands; applaud*

plēbeius, -a, -um (adj. of **plebs**) *plebeian*

plebs, plēbis (f) or **plēbēs, plēbeī** (f) *the common people*

plēnus, -a, -um (+gen.) *full (of)*

plērusque, plēraque, plērumque (pron. and adj.) *the greater number of*

pluit, -ere, pluit (no sup.; impers.) *it is raining*

plūma, -ae (f) *feather, down*

plūmeus, -a, -um *filled with feathers or down*

plūrimus, -a, -um *most, very many*

plūs (adv.) *to a higher degree, more*

plūs, plūris (n.; 19.1/1 note 1) *more*

Plūtō, -ōnis *god who ruled over the Underworld* (9.3)

poena (2 syllables), **-ae** (f) *punishment*

poenās dō *pay the penalty, be punished*

Poenus (2 syllables), **-ī** (m) *inhabitant of Carthage, Carthaginian*

poēta (3 syllables), **-ae** (m) *poet*

polliceor, -ērī (tr.) *promise*

Pompeiānus, -a, -um *belonging to Pompey*

Pompeius, -ī *the Roman statesman Pompey*

Pompōnius, -ī *male nomen*

pōmum, -ī (n) *fruit*

pondus, -deris (n) *weight, quantity*

pōne (adv.) *behind*

pōnō, -ere, posuī, positum (tr.) *place, put; pitch (camp); lay aside*

pons, pontis (m) *bridge*

Pontiliānus, -ī   *male cognomen*
pontus, -ī (m)   *sea*
popīna, -ae (f)   *low eating-house*
populāris, -is, -e   *likely to win support; popular, winning*
populor, -ārī (tr.)   *ravage*
populus, -ī (m)   *people*
porrigō, -ere, porrexī, porrectum (tr.)   *stretch out* (tr.); *offer, proffer; launch*
porta, -ae (f)   *door*
portitor, -ōris (m)   *ferryman*
portō, -āre (tr.)   *carry*
portus, -ūs (m)   *harbour*
poscō, -ere, poposcī (no sup.; tr.)   *demand*
positus, -a, -um   (perf. pple. of pōnō)
possessiō, -ōnis (f)   *occupation*
possum, posse, potuī (no sup.; intr.)   *be able* (15.1/1)
post (adv. and prep. + acc)   *after* (13.1/6a)
post ... quam   (see postquam)
posteā (adv.)   *afterwards, later*
posteā ... quam   (see posteāquam)
posteāquam (conj.)   *after* (29.1/3a)
posterior, -ior, -ius   *coming after, later*
posterus, -a, -um   *future, later, next*
postquam (conj.)   *after* (29.1/3a)
postrēmō (adv.)   *finally, at last*
postrēmus, -a, -um   *latest, last*
postrīdiē (adv.)   *on the next day*
postulō, -āre (tr.)   *claim*
posuī   (perf. of pōnō)
pote (indecl. adj.)   *able, possible*
potens, -entis (adj.)   *powerful;* (+ gen.) *ruling*
potentia, -ae (f)   *ability, power*
potestās, -tātis (f)   *control, command, power*
potior, -īrī, potītus sum (+ gen. or abl.)   *acquire, be master of*
potissimum (adv.)   *especially*
potius (adv.)   *rather*
pōtor, -ōris (m)   *drinker*
potuī   (perf. of possum)
praecipitō, -āre (intr., tr.)   *fall headlong, come down quickly; hurl down*
praecō, -ōnis (m)   *herald*
praeda, -ae (f)   *booty, plunder*
praedīves, -vitis (adj.)   *very wealthy*
praefectus, -ī (m)   *commander*

praeferō, praeferre, praetulī, praelātum (tr.)   *exhibit, display; prefer*
praeficiō, -ere, praefēcī, praefectum (+ acc. and dat.)   *set in command of*
praefluō, -ere (n.o.p.; tr.)   *flow past*
praefuī   (perf. of praesum)
praemittō, -ere, praemīsī, praemissum (tr.)   *send ahead*
praemium, -ī (n)   *reward*
praemūniō, -īre (tr.)   *fortify*
praenōmen, -minis (n)   *male first name* (6.3)
praesens, -entis (adj.)   *being present; immediate; now existing*
praesidium, -ī (n)   *guard, garrison; fort; protection*
praestituō, -ere, praestituī, praestitūtum (tr.)   *arrange, fix (a time)*
praestō, -āre, praestitī, praestitum (-ātum) (tr., intr.)   *produce, render;* (+ dat.) *be superior to; surpass*
praesum (prae + sum; + dat.)   *be in command of*
praeter (prep. + acc.)   *except; beyond*
praetereā (adv.)   *thereafter; in addition, as well as; moreover*
praeteritus, -a, -um   *past, former, earlier*
praetōrium, -ī (n)   *(army) headquarters*
prātum, -ī (n)   *meadow*
prāvus, -a, -um   *crooked; faulty; wrong; bad, wicked*
precēs, -um (f. pl.)   *prayers*
precor, -ārī (tr.)   *pray for, pray to*
prehendō, -ere, prehendī, prehensum (tr.)   *grasp*
premō, -ere, pressī, pressum (tr.)   *press*
prensō, -āre (tr.)   *try to grasp, clutch at*
pretium, -ī (n)   *value, worth; reward*
Priamus, -ī   *Priam, the last king of Troy*
prīdiē (adv.)   *on the previous day*
prīmō (adv.)   *at first*
prīmum (adv.)   *in the first place* (cum prīmum   *as soon as*)
prīmus, -a, -um   *first*
princeps, -cipis (m)   *chief, chief man, head; emperor*
principium, -ī (n)   *beginning, origin*

prior, -ior, -ius   *earlier, former;*
  superior, better
priscus, -a, -um   *ancient*
pristinus, -a, -um   *former, previous;*
  traditional
prius (adv.)   *earlier, previously*
prius ... quam   (see **priusquam**)
priusquam (conj.)   *before* (29.1/3*b*)
prīvātus, -ī (m)   *private person, person*
  without public office
prō (prep. + abl.)   *before; on behalf of*
probō, -āre (tr.)   *approve of*
probrum, -ī (n)   *disgrace; disgraceful*
  conduct
prōcēdō, -ere, prōcessī, prōcessum
  (intr.)   *go forward, advance; set out*
procul (adv.)   *at a distance, far off,*
  away
prōcurrō, -ere, prō(cu)currī, prōcursum
  (intr.)   *run out, run ahead*
prōdō, -ere, prōdidī, prōditum (tr.)
  give rise to, produce; give up; betray;
  hand down, transmit
prōdūcō, -ere, prōduxī, prōductum (tr.)
  bring out
proelium (3 syllables), **-ī** (n)   *battle*
profānus, -a, -um   *not in religious use;*
  uninitiated
proficiscor, -ī, profectus sum (intr.)   *set*
  out
profugus, -ī (m)   *fugitive, exile*
prōgeniēs, -ēī (f)   *offspring*
prōgredior, -ī, prōgressus sum (intr.)
  advance
prohibeō, -ēre (tr.)   *ward off, prevent;*
  hinder, restrain
prōiciō, -ere, prōiēcī, prōiectum (tr.)
  throw out, throw away; give up,
  discard
prōmissus, -a, -um   *(allowed to grow)*
  long
prōmittō, -ere, prōmīsī, prōmissum (tr.)
  promise
prōmō, -ere, prompsī, promptum (tr.)
  bring out; produce
prope (adv.)   *near, nearly, almost*
prope (prep. + acc.)   *near*
properō, -āre (intr.)   *hurry*
propinquus, -ī (m)   *relative, kinsman*
prōpōnō, -ere, prōposuī, prōpositum (tr.)
  set before; offer; expose to view,
  display
prōpositum, -ī (n)   *intention, purpose*

proprius, -a, -um   *belonging to oneself;*
  private; characteristic (of), proper (for)
propter (prep. + acc.)   *on account of*
propereā (adv.)   *for this reason*
  (29.1/2)
prōpulsō, -āre (tr.)   *drive back, repel*
prōrumpō, -ere, prōrūpī, prōruptum
  (intr.)   *break out (into an action)*
prōsequor, -ī, prōsecūtus sum (tr.)
  follow; pursue
Prōserpina, -ae   *wife of Pluto,*
  Proserpine
prosper, prospera, prosperum
  prosperous
prosperē (adv.)   *successfully*
prōsum (prō + sum; + dat.)   *be of*
  benefit to, help (15.1/2)
prōtegō, -ere, prōtexī, prōtectum (tr.)
  protect
prōtinus (adv.)   *from the start*
prōvehō, -ere, prōvexī, prōvectum (tr.)
  carry forward
prōvidentia, -ae (f)   *providence*
prōvideō, -ēre, prōvīdī, prōvīsum
  (tr., + dat.)   *provide for, attend to*
prōvincia, -ae (f)   *province*
prōvocō -āre (tr.)   *challenge, provoke*
proximus, -a, -um   *nearest; last (in*
  time)
prūdens, -entis (adj.)   *wise, prudent*
prūdenter (adv.)   *prudently*
prūdentia, -ae (f)   *foresight*
pruīna, -ae (f)   *hoar-frost*
pūblicānus, -ī, (m)   *tax collector*
pūblicus, -a, -um   *belonging to the*
  state; public
pudet, -ēre, puduit (puditum est) (+acc.)
  it shames (20.1/2*b*)
pudor, -ōris (m)   *(feeling of) shame;*
  modesty; honour
puella, -ae (f)   *girl; sweetheart*
puer, puerī (m)   *boy; male slave*
puerīlis, -is, -e   *of or belonging to*
  childhood
pueritia, -ae (f)   *childhood*
pugil, -lis (m)   *boxer*
pūgiō, -ōnis (m)   *dagger*
pugna, -ae (f)   *fight, battle*
pugnō, -āre (intr.)   *fight*
pugnus, -ī (m)   *fist*
pulcher, pulchra, pulchrum   *beautiful,*
  handsome
pulchrē (adv.)   *beautifully*

pulchritūdō, -dinis (f) *beauty*
pullus, -a, -um *dark*
pulsō, -āre (tr.) *strike, knock*
pulvis, -veris (m) *dust*
pūmex, -micis (m) *(pumice) rock*
pūniō, -īre (tr.) *punish*
pūrus, -a, -um *clean, unsoiled, pure*
putō, -āre (tr.) *think; consider,*
  imagine
pȳramis, -idis (f) *pyramid*
Pyrrha, -ae *female name*

quadrāgintā (indecl. adj.) *forty*
quadringentī, -ae, -a *four hundred*
quaerō, -ere, quaesīvī (-iī) quaesītum
  (tr.) *seek, look for; ask* (a question)
  make enquiries (**ā/ab**+abl. for person
  asked)
quaestor, -ōris (m) *a Roman official*
quālis, -is, -e *what kind of? of what*
  sort (30.1/1)
quam (adv. and conj.) *as, than, etc.*
  (30.1/1 note 4)
quam (interr. and exclam. adv.) *how*
quam (used as relative pr., adj.,
  etc.) fem. acc. s. of **qui, quis**
  (10.1/1*f-i*))
quamquam (conj.) *although* (29.1/4*b*)
quamvīs (conj.) *although* (29.1/4*b*)
quandō (adv.) (when preceded by **sī**,
  etc.) *ever*
quandō...? (interr. adv.) *when...?*
quandōquidem (conj.) *since, because*
  (29.1/2)
quantus, -a, -um *how much/great*
  (30.1/1)
quārē...? (interr. adv.) *why...?*
quartus, -a, -um *fourth*
quasi (conj. and adv.) *as if, as though*
  (30.1/1 note 6)
quater (adv.) *four times*
quatiō, -ere, (no perf.), **quassum**
  (tr.) *shake*
quattuor (indecl. adj.) *four*
quattuordecim (indecl. adj.) *fourteen*
-que (conj.) *and* (3.1/5)
queō (defective verb; intr.) *be able*
  (25.1/5*a*,i)
quercus, -ūs (f) *oak*
queror, -ī, questus sum (intr.,
  tr.) *complain (about)*
quī (quis), quae (qua), quod, quid
  (relative, interrogative, and indefinite

pronoun and adjective (10.1/1 *f-i*))
quia (conj.) *because* (29.1/2)
quīcumque, quaecumque, quodcumque
  whoever, whatever (10.1/1*j*)
quīdam, quaedam, quiddam, quoddam
  (pron. and adj.) *a certain*
  (person/thing) (10.1/1*j*)
quidem (adv.) *indeed, even*
quidquam (see **quisquam**)
quidquid (see **quisquis**)
quiēs, quiētis (f) *rest, quiet, sleep*
quiēscō, -ere, quiēvī, quiētum (intr.)
  be quiet
quīn (conj. and adv.) *but that, that not,*
  etc; *further, indeed* (26.1/2*b, c, f*)
quingentī, -ae, -a *five hundred*
quīnquāgintā (indecl. adj.) *fifty*
quīnque (indecl. adj.) *five*
Quīntia, -ae *female name*
quīntus, -a, -um *fifth*
Quīntus, -ī *male praenomen*
quippe (adv. giving a causal sense to an
  adjectival clause (30.1/2*d*))
quisquam, quidquam (quicquam) (pron.
  and adj.) *any(one) at all* (10.1/1*j*)
quisque, quaeque, quidque, quodque
  (pron. and adj.) *each* (10.1/1*j*)
quisquis, quidquid (generalizing rel.
  pron. and adj.) *whoever, whatever*
quīvīs, quaevīs, quidvīs, quodvīs, (pron.
  and adj.) *anyone, anything; any*
quō (interr. adv.) *(to) where* (with
  verbs of motion)
quoad (conj.) *until; while, as long as*
  (29.1/3*b*,ii)
quod (conj.) *because* (29.1/2)
quōminus (conj. + subj.) *so that ...*
  not (26.1/2*c*)
quōmodo (interr. adv.) *how*
quōnam (interr. adv.) *to what place,*
  where
quondam (adv.) *once, formerly*
quoniam (conj.; 3 syllables) *since*
  (29.1/2)
quoque (adv.) *also, too*
quot (indecl. adj.) *how many* (30.1/1)
quotannīs (adv.) *every year*
quotiens (conj.) *as often as, whenever*
  (30.1/1)
quotiens (interr. and exclam. adv.)
  how often
quotienscumque (conj.) *whenever, every*
  time that

radiō, -āre (intr.) *shine*
radius, -ī (m) *ray (of light)*
rādō, -ere, rāsī, rāsum (tr.) *shave*
rāmus, -ī (m) *branch*
rapiō, -ere, rapuī, raptum (tr.) *seize, carry off*
raptor, -ōris (m) *robber*
rārus, -a, -um *rare, uncommon*
rāsus, -a, -um (perf. pple. of **rādō**)
ratiō, -ōnis (f) *reason, cause, explanation; method; the faculty of reason*
ratis, -is (f) *raft; boat*
recēdō, -ere, recessī, recessum (intr.) *go back; depart, go away*
recens, -entis (adj.) *fresh, recent*
receptus, -ūs (m) *retreat*
recessus, -ūs (m) *inner part, recess*
recipiō, -ere, recēpī, receptum (tr.) *take back, recover, accept, admit;* (with acc. pron. used reflexively) *retreat, return*
recitō, -āre (tr.) *recite*
rectē (adv.) *rightly*
rectus, -a, -um *straight; direct; right, proper*
reddō, -ere, reddidī, redditum (tr.) *give back; hand over, deliver; render, cause to be, cause, make*
redeō (compound of **eō, īre**; intr.) *go back, return*
reditiō, -ōnis (f) *return*
reditus, -ūs (m) *return*
referō, referre, rettulī, relātum (tr.) *bring back; report back*
rēfert, rēferre, rētulit (no sup.) *it concerns* (20.1/2d)
refugiō, -ere, refūgī (no sup.; intr., tr.) *flee back, flee; shun; recoil*
rēgālis, -is, -e *royal*
rēgia, -ae (f) *palace*
rēgīna, -ae (f) *queen*
regiō, -ōnis (f) *area, district, region*
rēgius, -a, -um *royal*
regnum, -ī (n) *kingdom; royal power*
regō, -ere, rexī, rectum (tr.) *rule, govern*
rēiciō, -ere, rēiēcī, rēiectum (tr.) *throw, hurl; reject*
relanguescō, -ere, relanguī (no sup.; intr.) *become weak*
relictus, -a, -um (perf. pple. of **relinquō**)

religiō, -ōnis (f) *feeling of religious awe; religious belief, religion*
religiōsus, -a, -um *holy*
religō, -āre (tr.) *tie back*
relinquō, -ere, relīquī, relictum (tr.) *leave* (tr.); *leave behind, abandon*
relīquī (perf. of **relinquō**)
reliquus, -a, -um *the rest of, the remaining,* (pl.) *the other*
remaneō, -ēre, remansī (no sup.; intr.) *remain, stay behind*
reminiscor, -ī (n.o.p.; + acc. or gen.) *remember*
remittō, -ere, remīsī, remissum (tr.) *send back, return*
removeō, -ēre, remōvī, remōtum (tr.) *set aside, take away, remove, get rid of*
rēmus, -ī (m) *oar*
renīdeō, -ēre (n.o.p.; intr.) *shine; smile*
renuntiō, -āre (tr.) *announce, declare*
reor, rērī, ratus sum (intr.) *think*
reparō, -āre (tr.) *restore, repair*
rependō, -ere, rependī, repensum (tr.) *repay, require*
repente (adv.) *suddenly*
repentīnus, -a, -um *sudden*
repercutiō, -ere, repercussī, repercussum (tr.) *reflect, mirror*
reperiō, -īre, repperī, repertum (tr.) *discover, find*
repetō, -ere, repetīvī (-iī) repetītum (tr.) *repeat; demand back*
rēpō, -ere, repsī (no sup.; intr.) *creep*
repperī (perf. of **reperiō**)
reprehendō, -ere, reprehendī reprehensum (tr.) *find fault with, blame*
reprehensiō, -ōnis (f) *blame, reprimand*
repudiō, -āre (tr.) *reject; divorce*
requiescō, -ere, requiēvī, requiētum (intr.) *lie in rest, rest*
requīrō, -ere, requīsīvī (-iī), requīsītum (tr.) *ask (a question)*
rēs, reī (f) *thing, matter, business* (11.1/1 note 2); (pl.) *the world; universe*
rescindō, -ere, rescidī, rescissum (tr.) *break up*
rescīscō, -ere, rescīvī (-iī), rescitum (tr.)

find out
resecō, -āre, resecuī, resectum (tr.)
cut back, prune
resistō, -ere, restitī (no sup.; intr.)
stop (intr.); (+dat) *resist*
resonō, -āre, resonāvī (no sup.; tr., intr.)
echo, resound
respiciō, -ere, respexī, respectum (intr.,
tr.) *look back (at)*
respondeō, -ēre, respondī, responsum
(intr.) *speak in answer, reply*
rēspūblica, reīpūblicae (f.; also written
as two words) *the body politic, the
state* (11.1/1 note 3)
restat (impersonal use) *it remains*
restitī (perf. of **resistō** and **restō**)
restituō, -ere, restituī, restitūtum (tr.)
restore, revive, bring back
restō, -āre, restitī (no sup.; intr.)
remain
retineō, -ēre, retinuī, retentum (tr.)
*check, restrain; hold fast; preserve;
retain*
retrō (adv.) *backwards*
reus, -ī (m) *defendant; guilty party*
revocō, -āre (tr.) *call back*
revolvō, -ere, revolvī, revolūtum (tr.)
roll back; go back over, consider
rex, rēgis (m) *king*
rexī (perf. of **regō**)
Rhēnus, -ī (m) *the river Rhine*
Rhodiī, -ōrum (m. pl.) *inhabitants of
Rhodes*
Rhodus, -ī (f) *Rhodes*
rīdeō, -ēre, rīsī, rīsum (intr., tr.) *laugh
(at); smile (at)*
rīdiculus, -a, -um *absurd*
rigidus, -a, -um *stiff, numb*
rīpa, -ae (f) *bank*
rīsī (perf. of **rīdeō**)
rīsus, -ūs (m) *laughter; smile*
rīvus, -ī (m) *stream, brook*
rogō, -āre (tr.) *ask* (a question; + acc.
of person and of thing asked for)
rogus, -ī (m) *funeral pyre*
Rōma, -ae (f) *Rome*
Rōmānus, -a, -um *Roman*
Rōmānus, -ī (m) *inhabitant of Rome,
Roman*
Rōmulus, -ī *legendary founder of
Rome*
rosa, -ae (f) *rose*
Roscius, -ī *male nomen*

rota, -ae (f) *wheel*
rotundus, -a, -um *round*
ruber, rubra, rubrum *red*
Rūfus, -ī *male cognomen*
ruīna, -ae (f) *fall, collapse;* (pl.)
ruins
ruīnōsus, -a, -um *ruined*
rumpō, -ere, rūpī, ruptum (tr., intr.)
break, burst (tr.); *rush*
ruō, -ere, ruī (no sup.; intr.) *rush,
hurry on; fall*
rūpī (perf. of **rumpō**)
ruptor, -ōris (m) *one who breaks,
breaker*
ruptus, -a, -um (perf. pple. of **rumpō**)
rursus (adv.) *again*
rūs, rūris (n) *country* (as opposed to
city); *land; country estate*
rusticus, -a, -um *connected with the
country or farming*
Rutulī, -ōrum (m. pl.) *one of the
Italian races who opposed Aeneas*

Sabidius, -ī *male nomen*
Sabīnī, -ōrum (m. pl.) *the Sabines*
sacer, sacra, sacrum *sacred*
sacerdōs, -dōtis (m or f) *priest;
priestess*
sacrātus, -a, -um *holy, sacred*
sacrificō, -āre (intr., tr.) *sacrifice*
sacrilegus, -a, -um *sacrilegious,
wicked*
sacrilegus, -ī (m) *temple-robber*
sacrum, -ī (n) *ceremony, rite*
saeculum, -ī (n) *lifetime, generation;
age*
saepe (adv.) *often*
saeptum, -ī (n) *paddock, fold*
sagax, -ācis (adj.) *keen-scented;
perceptive*
sagitta, -ae (f) *arrow*
sāl, salis (m) *salt; wit*
saltō, -āre (intr.) *dance*
salūs, -ūtis (f) *safety*
salūtō, -āre (tr.) *greet, salute*
salvē, salvēte (imp.) *hail! hello!*
salvus, -a, -um *safe, secure; alive*
Samnium, -ī (n) *region in central Italy*
Samus (-os), -ī (f) *Samos (island in
the Aegean)*
sanctus, -a, -um *sacred*
sanguis, -guinis (m) *blood*
sānitās (f) *health*

sānō, -āre (tr.)   *heal, cure*
sānus, -a, -um   *healthy; sane*
sapiens, -entis (adj.)   *wise*
sapientia, -ae (f)   *wisdom*
sapiō, -ere, sapīvī (-iī) (no sup.; intr.)
   be wise, be intelligent
satiō, -āre (tr.)   *satisfy*
satis (adv.)   *sufficiently, adequately,*
   enough
satis (indecl. noun, + gen.)   *a*
   sufficiency of (27.1/4k); *sufficient,*
   enough
satura, -ae (f)   *satire*
Sāturnia, -ae   *daughter of Saturn,*
   i.e. Juno (9.3)
Sāturnus, -ī   *Saturn* (9.3)
saucius, -a, -um   *wounded*
saxum, -ī (n)   *stone, rock; reef*
scālae, -ārum (f. pl.)   *ladder*
scelerātus, -a, -um   *wicked*
scelus, -eris (n)   *crime*
sceptrum, -ī (n)   *sceptre, royal staff*
scientia, -ae (f)   *knowledge*
scīlicet (adv.)   *doubtless, of course*
scindō, -ere, scicidī (scidī), scissum (tr.)
   divide, split (tr.); *carve*
sciō, -īre (tr.)   *know*
Scīpiō, -ōnis   *male cognomen*
scrībō, -ere, scripsī, scriptum (tr.)
   write; compose
scripsī (perf. of scrībō)
scriptor, -ōris (m)   *writer, author*
scriptus, -a, -um   (perf. pple. of
   scrībō)
scūtum, -ī (n)   *shield*
Scylla, -ae (f)   *sea-monster mentioned*
   in Homer's Odyssey
Scythicus, -a, -um   *Scythian*
   (Scythia was a remote land north of
   the Black Sea)
sē   (acc. or abl. of 3rd pers. reflex.
   pron. (9.1/4))
secō, -āre, secuī, sectum (tr.)   *cut*
secundus, -a, -um   *second, favourable,*
   successful
secūtus, -a, -um   (perf. pple. of
   sequor)
sed (conj.)   *but*
sedeō, -ēre, sēdī, sessum (intr.)   *sit*
sēdēs, -is (f)   *seat; dwelling place, home*
sedīle, -is (n)   *seat, bench*
seges, segetis (f)   *crop*
segnitia, -ae (f)   *laziness*

semel (adv.)   *once, a single time, just once*
sēmisepultus, -a, -um   *half-buried*
semper (adv.)   *always*
senātus, -ūs (m)   *permanent political*
   body at Rome, senate
Seneca, -ae   *Roman philosopher and*
   writer (c. AD 4–65)
senecta, -ae (f)   *old age*
senectūs, -tūtis (f)   *old age*
senex, senis (m)   *old man;* (as adj.) *old*
sēnī, -ae, -a   *six each; six* (12.1/4c)
senior, -ior, -ius   *older*
sensī   (perf. of sentiō)
sensus, -ūs (m)   *feeling, sense; emotion;*
   understanding
sententia, -ae (f)   *opinion; vote*
sentiō, -īre, sensī, sensum (tr., intr.)
   feel; get an inkling of; be conscious
sepeliō, -īre, sepelīvī (-iī), sepultum (tr.)
   bury
septem (indecl. adj.)   *seven*
septimus, -a, -um   *seventh*
septingentī, -ae, -a   *seven hundred*
septuāgintā (indecl. adj)   *seventy*
sepulchrum, -ī (n)   *tomb*
sepultus, -a, -um   (perf. pple. of sepeliō)
sequor, -ī, secūtus sum (tr.)   *follow,*
   accompany; chase
serēnus, -a, -um   *cloudless, clear;*
   cheerful
seriēs, -ēī (f)   *succession*
sērō (adv.)   *late, at a late time*
serō, -ere, seruī, sertum (tr.)   *join,*
   interweave
serō, -ere, sēvī, satum (tr.)   *plant, sow*
sērus, -a, -um   *late*
serviō, -īre (+ dat.)   *serve, be of use to*
servitūs, -tūtis (f)   *servitude, slavery*
Servius, -ī   *sixth king of Rome*
servō, -āre (tr.)   *watch over, guard;*
   preserve
servus, -ī (m)   *slave*
sescentī, -ae, -a   *six hundred*
Sestius, -ī   *male nomen*
seu (conj.)   *or if*
seu ... seu   *whether ... or*
sex (indecl. adj.)   *six*
sexāgintā (indecl. adj)   *sixty*
sextus, -a -um   *sixth*
sī (conj.)   *if* (22.1/2)
sibi   (dat. of 3rd pers. reflex. pron.
   (9.1/4))
sīc (adv.)   *so, thus; in such a way; to*

such an extent
Sicilia, -ae (f) *Sicily*
sīcut (conj.) *as, just as*
sīdus, -deris (n) *star*
Sīgēius (4 syllables), **-a, -um** (adj. of **Sīgēum** promontory near Troy)
signum, -ī (n) *sign, signal; military standard; statue*
silens, -entis (adj.) *silent*
silentium, -ī (n) *silence*
silva, -ae (f) *forest, wood*
similis, -is, -e *similar*
Simoīs, -oentis (m) *river near Troy*
simplex, -licis (adj.) *not elaborate, simple; naive*
simul (adv.) *at the same time; together*
simulac (conj.) *as soon as* (29.1/3a)
simulācrum, -ī (n) *image, ghost; statue*
sīn (conj.) *but if*
sine (prep. + abl.) *without*
singulī, -ae, -a *one each* (12.1/4c); *single, individual*
sinister, -tra, -trum *on the left-hand side, left*
sinō, -ere, sīvī, situm (tr.) *allow; let be*
sinus, -ūs (m) *fold; bosom; bay*
sitiō, -īre (n.o.p.; intr.) *be thirsty*
situs, -a, -um *dependent on*
situs, -ūs (m) *position; layout; structure*
sīve (another form of **seu**)
sōbrius, -a, -um *sober*
socius, -ī (m) *companion, ally*
Sōcratēs, -is *famous Greek philosopher*
socrus, -ūs (f) *mother-in-law*
sōl, sōlis (m) *sun*
soleō, -ēre, solitus sum (intr.) *be accustomed* (25.1/5e)
solidus, -a, -um *solid; firm, fixed*
sōlitūdō, -dinis (f) *solitude, wilderness*
sollicitūdō, -dinis (f) *anxiety, worry*
sollicitus, -a, -um *restless, uneasy*
sōlor, -ārī (tr.) *comfort*
solstitium, -ī (n) *summer solstice; summer heat*
sōlum (adv.) *only*
solum, -ī (n) *ground, soil, earth*
sōlus, -a, -um *alone; lonely* (10.1/1e)
solvō, -ere, solvī, solūtum (tr.) *loosen, untie, unmoor; free, release; relax*
somniō, -āre (intr.) *have a dream, dream*

somnium, -ī (n) *dream*
somnus, -ī (m) *sleep*
sonitus, -ūs (m) *sound, noise*
sonō, -āre, sonuī, sonitum (intr., tr.) *make a noise; utter (a sound)*
sonus, -ī (m) *sound, noise*
sophōs (interj.) *bravo!*
sopor, -ōris (m) *sleep*
sordidus, -a, -um *dirty*
soror, -ōris (f) *sister*
sors, sortis (f) *destiny, fate, condition*
spargō, -ere, sparsī, sparsum (tr.) *sprinkle, scatter*
spatium, -ī (n) *area, space; distance; (period of) time*
speciēs, -ēī (f) *appearance; beauty; pretext*
speciō, -ere, spexī, spectum (tr.) *observe, watch*
spectō, -āre (tr.) *watch, look at*
speculum, -ī (n) *mirror*
spēlunca, -ae (f) *cave*
spernō, -ere, sprēvī, sprētum (tr.) *despise, reject*
spērō, -āre (tr.) *hope (for)*
spēs, -eī (f) *hope*
spīculum, -ī (n) *spear*
spīrō, -āre (intr.) *breathe*
spissus, -a, -um *thick*
splendeō, -ēre (n.o.p.; intr.) *shine*
splendidus, -a, -um *august*
spolium, -ī (n) *spoils, plunder*
spondeō, -ēre, spopondī, sponsum (intr., tr.) *pledge, promise*
sponte (+ possessive adj. or noun in gen., 25.1/4d) *of my (your, etc.) own accord*
squālor, -ōris (m) *filth*
stagnum, -ī (n) *swamp*
statim (adv.) *immediately*
statua, -ae (f) *statue*
statuō, -ere, statuī, statūtum (tr.) *set up; erect; establish; decide*
status, -ūs (m) *physical condition; situation*
stella, -ae (f) *star*
sterilis, -is, -e *barren*
sternō, -ere, strāvī, strātum (tr.) *spread; scatter, pave; overthrow*
stetī (perf. of **stō**)
stimulus, -ī (m) *goad*
stirps, -pis (f) *offspring, child*
stō, -āre, stetī, statum (intr.) *stand, be*

standing

Stōicī, -ōrum (m. pl.)   *Greek philosophical sect, the Stoics*

stolidus, -a, -um *stupid*

strangulō, -āre (tr.)   *strangle*

strātus, -a, -um   (perf. pple. of **sternō**)

strepō, -ere, strepuī, strepitum (intr.)   *make a loud noise*

strīdor, -ōris (m)   *creaking sound*

struō, -ere, struxī, structum (tr.)   *build; arrange; contrive*

studeō, -ēre, studuī (no sup.; intr., tr.) (+ dat. or inf.) *devote oneself to; be keen to;* (+ acc.) *concentrate on, study*

studium, -ī (n)   *pursuit, activity*

stultē (adv.)   *stupidly*

stultitia, -ae (f)   *stupidity, folly*

stultus, -a, -um   *stupid, foolish*

stupeō, -ēre, stupuī (no sup.; intr.)   *be dumb*

Styx, Stygis (f)   *river of the Underworld*

suādeō, -ēre, suāsī, suāsum (+ acc. of thing and dat. of person; for pronunciation see p. xiii)   *advise, recommend* (20.1/1)

suāvis, -is, -e (for pronunciation see p. xiii)   *sweet, pleasant*

sub (prep.)   (+acc.) *up to;* (+abl.) *under; in front of*

subamārus, -a, -um   *slightly bitter, tart*

subeō (compound of **eō, īre**; intr., tr.)   *undergo, endure; approach*

subiectus, -a, -um   *submissive*

subigō, -ere, subēgī, subactum (tr.)   *propel, push; subdue*

subitō (adv.)   *suddenly*

subitus, -a, -um   *sudden*

sublātus, -a, -um   (perf. pple. of **tollō**)

sublīmis, -is, -e   *high, lofty*

submoveō, -ēre, submōvī, submōtum (tr.)   *remove, drive off*

subscrībō, -ere, subscripsī, subscriptum (intr., tr.)   *write underneath or after; add, append*

subsellium, -ī (n)   *bench* (in a law court)

subvectō, -āre (tr.)   *carry over*

subveniō, -īre, subvēnī, subventum (+ dat.)   *come to help, help*

succumbō, -ere, succubuī, succubitum (+ dat.)   *yield (to)*

succurrō, -ere, succurrī, succursum (+ dat.)   *help*

Suēbī, -ōrum (m. pl.; for pronunciation see p. xiii)   *German tribe*

sufficiō, -ere, suffēcī, suffectum (+dat.)   *be sufficient for, suffice*

suī   (gen. of 3rd pers. reflex. pron. (9.1/4); also from **suus**)

Sulmo, -ōnis (m)   *town near Rome*

sum, esse, fuī (no sup.; intr.)   *be, exist* (see p. 293)

summa, -ae (f)   *total, whole*

summus, -a, -um   *highest* (21.1/3); *greatest*

sūmō, -ere, sumpsī, sumptum (tr.)   *take, take up; consume, eat*

suntō   (3rd pl. fut. imp. of **sum** (21.1/1 note 3))

suopte (see note on 16.2,18)

super (adv.)   *over, above*

superbus, -a, -um   *proud*

superfuī   (perf. of **supersum**)

superī, -ōrum (m. pl.)   *the gods who live in the sky*

superior, -ior, -ius   *higher; upper; earlier*

superō, -āre (tr.; intr.)   *overcome; surpass; be left, survive*

superstes, -stitis (adj.)   *remaining, surviving*

supersum (**super + sum**; + dat)   *survive*

superus, -a, -um   *upper, on earth* (as opposed to the Underworld)

supplēmentum, -ī (n)   *reinforcements*

suppliciter (adv.)   *humbly*

supplicium, -ī (n)   *punishment*

suprā (adv.)   *above, on top*

suprā (prep. + acc.)   *on top of*

suprēmus, -a, -um   *highest; furthest, last*

surgō, -ere, surrexī, surrectum (intr.)   *rise; get up (from bed); arise*

suscipiō, -ere, suscēpī, susceptum (tr.)   *take up; undertake*

suspendō, -ere, suspendī, suspensum (tr.)   *hang, suspend*

suspīrō, -āre (intr.)   *sigh*

sustineō, -ēre, sustinuī (no sup.; tr.)   *hold (up), support; withstand*

sustulī   (perf. of **tollō**)

suus, -a, -um   (3rd pers. reflex. poss. adj. (9.1/5))

Syrācūsae, -ārum (f. pl.)   *Greek city in Sicily*

T.   (abbreviation for **Titus**)

taberna, -ae (f)   *tavern; hut*

tabula, -ae (f)   *board; (commemorative) tablet*

taceō, -ēre (intr., tr.)   *be silent (about)*

tacitus, -a, -um   *silent*

tactus, -a, -um   (perf. pple. of **tangō**)

taedet, -ēre, taeduit, taesum est (+ acc.)   *it wearies* (20.1/2*b*)

taedium, -ī (n)   *boredom; boring thing*

Taenarius, -a, -um   *Taenarian* (see note on *1*.4 of 15.3)

tālis, -is, -e   *such, of such a sort* (30.1/1)

tam (adv.)   *so, to such an extent* (30.1/1)

tamen (adv.)   *however, nevertheless, yet*

tametsī (conj.)   *even if* (29.1/4*a*)

tamquam (conj.)   *in the same way as, just as*

tandem (adv.)   *after some time, at length*

tangō, -ere, tetigī, tactum (tr.)   *touch*

tantum (adv.)   *only; exclusively*

tantundem (tantum + dem)   (see note on 23.2, 10)

tantus, -a, -um   *so great, so much, as much* (30.1/1)

tardō, -āre (tr., intr.)   *delay, hold up*

tardus, -a, -um   *slow, sluggish*

Tarentum, -ī (n)   *town in southern Italy*

Tarquinius, -ī   *nomen of a family which produced the fifth and the seventh kings of Rome*

Tartara, -ōrum (n. pl.)   *another name of the Underworld*

Tartareus, -a, -um   (adj. of **Tartara**)

taurus, -ī (m)   *bull*

tectum, -ī (n)   *roof; building, house*

tectus, -a, -um   (perf. pple. of **tegō**)

tēcum   = cum + tē

tegimentum, -ī (n)   *covering*

tegō, -ere, texī, tectum (tr.)   *cover, hide* (tr.)

tellūs, -ūris (f)   *land*

tēlum, -ī (n)   *spear, missile; weapon*

tempestās, -tātis (f)   *storm*

templum, -ī (n)   *temple; region, position*

temptō, -āre (tr.)   *attempt, try; make trial of*

tempus, -poris (n)   *time; period of time*

tenax, -ācis (adj.)   *holding fast, tenacious*

tendō, -ere, tetendī, tensum (tentum) (tr., intr.)   *extend, stretch out, bend; be inclined*

tenebrae, -ārum (f. pl.)   *darkness*

teneō, -ēre, tenuī, tentum (tr.)   *hold, hold to; occupy; keep; maintain; restrain; prevent*

tener, tenera, tenerum   *tender, delicate; young*

tensus, -a, -um   (perf. pple. of **tendō**)

tenuis, -is, -e   *thin, fine; insubstantial*

ter (adv.)   *three times*

tergum, -ī (n)   *back (of humans or animals); rear*

terra, -ae (f)   *land, earth*

terreō, -ēre (tr.)   *terrify, frighten*

terribilis, -is, -e   *frightening, terrible*

terrificus, -a, -um   *terrifying*

territō, -āre, territāvī (no sup.; tr.)   *frighten*

terror, -ōris (m)   *panic, fear*

tertius, -a, -um   *third*

testāmentum, -ī (n)   *will, testament*

testis, -is (m or f)   *witness*

testūdō, -dinis (f)   *tortoise (shell)*

tetigī   (perf. of **tangō**)

Teucrī, -ōrum (m. pl.)   *another name of the Trojans*

texī   (perf. of **tegō**)

Thāis, -idis, (-idos)   *Greek female name*

Thēbae, -ārum (f. pl.)   *city in Greece, Thebes*

Themistoclēs, -is   *Athenian statesman*

thermae, -ārum (f. pl.)   *(warm) baths*

Thessalia, -ae (f)   *Thessaly, region in north-eastern Greece*

Tibullus, -ī   *Roman poet   (c. 55–19 BC)*

Tībur, Tīburis (n)   *town near Rome on the River Anio*

timeō, -ēre, timuī (no sup.; tr., intr.)   *fear, be afraid (of)*

timidus, -a, -um   *fearful*

timor, -ōris (m)   *fear*

tingō, -ere, tinxī, tinctum (tr.)   *dye*

tintinō, -āre (n.o.p.; intr.) *make a ringing sound*

titulus, -ī (m) *inscription*

Tītyrus, -ī *herdsman in Vergil's Eclogues*

toga, -ae (f) *formal garment of a Roman man, toga, symbolic both of being Roman and of civilian life*

togātus, -a, -um *wearing a toga*

tolerō, -āre (tr.) *put up with, bear*

tollō, -ere, sustulī, sublātum (tr.) *raise; remove, take; eliminate*

tonat, -āre, tonuit (no sup.; impers.) *it is thundering*

tondeō, -ēre, totondī, tonsum (tr.) *cut the hair of*

Tongiliānus, -ī *male cognomen*

tonsor, -ōris (m) *barber*

tonsōrius, -a, -um *belonging to a barber*

tormentum, -ī (n) *catapult; torture; torment*

torpeō, -ēre (n.o.p.; intr.) *be numb*

Torquātus, -ī *male cognomen*

torqueō, -ēre, torsī, tortum (tr.) *twist; torture*

torrens, -entis (adj.) *flowing, rushing*

torridus, -a, -um *parched*

torsī (perf. of **torqueō**)

tortus, -a, -um (perf. pple. of **torqueō**)

torus, -ī (m) *couch, bed*

tot (indecl. adj.) *so many, as many* (30.1/1)

totidem (indecl. adj.; emphatic form of **tot**)

totiens (adv.) *so often* (30.1/1)

tōtus, -a, -um *all, the whole of, a whole* (10.1/1e)

trādō, -ere, trādidī, trāditum (tr.) *hand over, present*

trādūcō, -ere, trāduxī, trāductum (tr.) *cross over (tr.), transfer*

trahō, -ere, traxī, tractum (tr.) *draw; drag*

trāiciō, -ere, trāiēcī, trāiectum (tr., intr.) *cross*

trāmes, -mitis (m) *track; course*

tranquillus, -a, -um *calm*

trans (prep. + acc.) *across, over*

transeō (compound of **eō, īre**; tr., intr.) *cross, go over*

transfīgō, -ere, transfixī, transfixum (tr.) *pierce (through)*

transmittō, -ere, transmīsī, transmissum (tr., intr.) *travel across, cross*

traxī (perf. of **trahō**)

Trebōnius, -ī *male nomen*

trecentī, -ae, -a *three hundred*

tremō, -ere, tremuī (no sup.; intr., tr.) *tremble (at)*

trepidus, -a, -um *timid; anxious*

trēs, trēs, tria *three* (11.1/5)

tribūnus, -ī (m) *tribune (military officer or civilian magistrate)*

tribuō, -ere, tribuī, tribūtum (tr.) *grant, give, apportion; give credit, impute*

trīduum, -ī (n) *period of three days*

trīgintā (indecl. adj.) *thirty*

trilix, -īcis (adj.) *with triple thread*

tristis, -is, -e *sad; gloomy; sullen*

triumphō, -āre (intr.) *celebrate a triumph*

triumphus, -ī (m) *triumph; the cry* **triumphe!** *(success!)*

Troia (2 syllables), -ae (f) *Troy, city in north-western Asia Minor whose siege by the Greeks is the subject of Homer's Iliad*

Troiānus (3 syllables), -a, -um *Trojan*

Trōius (3 syllables), -a, -um *Trojan*

trucīdō, -āre (tr.) *kill savagely*

tū (pron.) *you* (sing.) (8.1/1)

tuba, -ae (f) *(straight) trumpet*

Tucca, -ae *male cognomen*

tueor, -ērī, tuitus sum (tr.) *see, observe*

Tullus, -ī *third king of Rome*

tum (adv.) *then, at that time; next*

tumidus, -a, -um *swollen; haughty*

tumulus, -ī (m) *burial mound, grave, tomb; hill*

tunc (another form of **tum**)

turba, -ae (f) *crowd, mob*

turbidus, -a, -um *disturbed, turbid, murky*

turbō, -āre (tr., intr) *stir up; riot*

turgeō, -ēre, tursī (no sup., intr.) *swell*

Turnus, -ī *leader of the Italian opposition to Aeneas*

turpis, -is, -e *disgraceful; ugly*

turris, -is (f) *tower*

tūs, tūris (n) *frankincense, incense*

tussis, -is (f) *cough*

tūtō (adv.) *safely*

tūtor, -ārī (tr.) *preserve, protect*

tūtus, -a, -um   *safe, secure*

tuus, -a, -um   *your* (with reference to one person)

tyrannicus, -a, -um   *tyrannical, despotic*

tyrannus, -ī (m)   *absolute ruler; tyrant*

Tyrius, -a, -um   (adj. of **Tyrus** *Tyre* a city on the east coast of the Mediterranean) *Tyrian*

Tyrrhēnum mare   *Tyrrhenian sea* (sea on the west coast of Italy)

ūber, ūberis (adj.)   *copious, rich*

ubi (conj.)   *when* (29.1/3*a*)

ubi...? (interr. adv.)   *where...?*

ubicumque (conj.) *wherever*

ulciscor, -ī, ultus sum (tr.)   *take vengeance on*

Ulixēs, -is   *Ulysses, hero of Homer's Odyssey*

ullus, -a, -um (pron. and adj.)   *any (one)* (10.1/1*e*)

ulmus, -ī (f)   *elm*

ulterior, -ior, -ius   *further, more distant*

ultimus, -a, -um   *furthest; last; final*

ultrā (prep. + acc.)   *beyond*

ultrix, -īcis (f. adj.)   *avenging*

ultrō (adv.)   *of one's own accord*

ultus, -a, -um   (perf. pple. of **ulciscor**)

umbra, -ae (f)   *shade, shadow; shade (soul) of someone dead, ghost*

umerus, -ī (m)   *shoulder*

ūmidus, -a, -um   *wet, moist, damp*

ūmor, -ōris (m)   *moisture*

umquam (adv.)   *at any time, ever*

ūnā (adv.)   *together*

uncus, -a, -um   *hooked*

unda, -ae (f)   *wave, ripple; water*

unde...? (interr. adv.)   *from where...?*

undecim (indecl. adj.)   *eleven*

undique (adv.)   *from everywhere; from all sides*

unguis, -is (m)   *nail (of finger or toe); claw, talon*

ūnicolor, -ōris (adj.)   *having one colour*

ūnicus, -a, -um   *sole, (one and) only; peerless*

ūniversus, -a, -um   *general, universal; entire*

ūnus, -a, -um   *one* (10.1/1*e*)

urbānus, -a, -um   *polite, refined*

urbs, urbis (f)   *city*

urgeō, -ēre, ursī (no sup.; tr.)   *press; court*

ūrō, -ere, ussī, ustum (tr.)   *burn* (tr.)

usquam (adv.)   *anywhere*

usque (adv.)   *right up (to), as far (as)*

usque (prep. + acc.)   *up to*

usquequāque (adv.)   *everywhere*

ut (conj. + ind.)   *when* (29.1/3*a*), *as* (30.1/1)

ut (conj. + subj.)   *so that, that* (purpose 13.1/5; result 16.1/1; indirect command, etc. 21.1/2; other noun clauses 26.1/2)

ut (exclamatory adv.)   *how*

uter, utra, utrum...?   *which of two...?* (10.1/1*d*)

uterque, utraque, utrumque   *each of two, either* (10.1/1*d*)

utī   (another form of **ut**)

ūtī (pres. inf. of **ūtor**)

ūtilis, -is, -e   *useful*

ūtilitās, -tātis (f)   *quality of being useful; benefit; expediency*

utinam   (adv. used to emphasize optative subjunctive (22.1/1*a*))

ūtor, -ī, ūsus sum (+ abl.)   *use, make use of; take advantage of*

utpote   (adv. giving a causal sense to an adjectival clause (30.1/2*d*)

utrum   (adv. introducing alternative questions (23.1/1*f*))

ūvidus, -a, -um   *wet, dripping*

uxor, -ōris (f)   *wife*

vacuus, -a, -um   *vacant, empty, free; destitute of, free of*

vādō, -ere, vāsī (no sup.; intr.)   *go*

vae (interj.)   *alas*

vāgīna, -ae (f)   *sheath, scabbard*

vagor, -ārī (intr.)   *wander, range*

vagus, -a, -um   *wandering*

valē, valēte (imp.)   *goodbye* (21.1/1 note 2)

valeō, -ēre (intr.)   *be in sound health, be well, be strong*

valētūdō, -dinis (f)   *health; good health*

validus, -a, -um   *strong*

vallis, -is (f)   *valley*

vallum, -ī (n)   *rampart*

vānus, -a, -um   *empty; useless, false*

vāpulō, -āre (intr.)   *be beaten* (25.1/5*f*)

varius, -a, -um   *various, different; changeable*

Varrō, -ōnis *male cognomen*
Vārus, -ī *male cognomen*
vās, vāsis and **vāsum, -i** (n) *vase*
vāsī (perf. of **vādō**)
vastitās, -tātis (f) *wilderness, desolation*
vastō, -āre (tr.) *ravage, lay waste*
vastus, -a, -um *huge*
vātēs, -is (m or f) *prophet(ess); poet*
-ve (conj.) *or* (3.1/5)
-ve ... -ve *either ... or* (3.1/5)
vehemens, -entis (adv.) *violent, strong*
vehō, -ere, vexī, vectum (tr.) *carry;* (pass.) *ride*
Veientēs, -ium (m. pl.) *the people of the city Veii, an early rival of Rome*
Veiī, -ōrum (m. pl.) *city to the north of Rome captured in 396 BC*
vel (conj.) *or* (3.1/5)
vel ... vel *either ... or* (3.1/5)
vēlāmen, -minis (n) *covering, coverlet*
velle (pres. inf. of **volō**)
vēlum, -ī (n) *sail*
velut (adv.) *as, like, in the same way as*
velutī (adv.) (another form of **velut**)
vendidī (perf. of **vendō**)
venditātor, -ōris (m) *a person who tries to push or promote something*
vendō, -ere, vendidī, venditum (tr.) *sell*
venēnum, -ī (n) *poison*
vēneō, vēnīre, vēniī, vēnitum (intr.) *be sold* (25.1/5f)
veniō, -īre, vēnī, ventum (intr.) *come*
venter, ventris (m) *stomach*
ventus, -ī (m) *wind*
vēnumdō, -are, vēnumdedī, vēnumdatum (tr.) *sell*
Venus, Veneris *goddess of love* (9.3)
vēr, vēris (n) *spring*
verbōsus, -a, -um *talkative, wordy*
verbum, -ī (n) *word*
verēcundus, -a, -um *seemly, modest*
vereor, -ērī (tr., intr.) *fear, be afraid (of)*
Vergilius, -ī (m) *the Roman poet Vergil (70–19 BC)*
vēritās, -tātis (f) *truth*
veritus (perf. pple. of **vereor**)
vērō (adv.) *indeed, in fact; in truth* (23.1/2)
Verrēs, -is *notorious Roman provincial governor*
versiculus, -ī (m) (deprecatory

diminutive of **versus**)
versor, -ārī (intr.) *keep active, be busy*
versus, -a, -um (perf. pple. of **vertō**)
versus, -ūs (m) *verse*
vertō, -ere, vertī, versum (tr.) *turn* (tr.)
vērus, -a, -um *true; real*
vescor, -ī (n.o.p.; + acc. or abl.) *feed on*
vesper (m; defective noun) *evening*
Vesta, -ae *the goddess Vesta* (9.3)
vester, vestra, vestrum *your* (with reference to more than one person)
vestibulum, -ī (n) *vestibule, entrance*
vestigium, -ī (n) *trace*
vestīmentum, -ī (n) *article of clothing;* (pl.) *clothes*
vestiō, -īre (tr.) *clothe, dress*
vestis, -is (f) *clothes*
vetō, -āre, vetuī, vetitum (tr.) *forbid*
vetus, -teris (adj.) *old; veteran; ancient; former*
vexī (perf. of **vehō**)
vexillum, -ī (n) *military standard, flag*
vexō, -āre (tr.) *damage, injure, plunder; disturb;* (pass.) *be in trouble*
via Appia *Appian Way, Roman road from Rome to southern Italy*
via, -ae (f) *road, street; journey*
vīcī (perf. of **vincō**)
vīcīnus, -a, -um *situated close by, neighbouring*
vīcīnus, -ī (m) *neighbour*
vicis (gen. 25.1/4d) *interchange, alternation*
victima, -ae (f) *animal offered for sacrifice, victim*
victor, -ōris (m) *victor, conqueror*
victōria, -ae (f) *victory*
Victōriola, -ae (f) *small statue of the goddess Victory*
victrix, -rīcis (f. adj.) *conquering, victorious*
victūrus, -a, -um (fut. pple. of **vincō** or **vīvō**)
victus, -a, -um (perf. pple. of **vincō**)
vidēlicet (adv.) *clearly, evidently*
videō, -ēre, vīdī, vīsum (tr.) *see, look at*
videor (pass. of **videō**) *be seen; seem*
vidētur (impersonal use) *it seems (good)* (20.1/2g)
vigeō, -ēre, viguī (no sup.; intr.) *thrive*
vigil, -ilis (adj.) *wakeful, watchful*

vīgintī (indecl. adj.)   *twenty*
vīlicus, -ī (m)   *overseer on a farm*
vīlis, -is, -e   *cheap, of a low value; worthless*
villa, -ae (f)   *country house*
vinciō, -īre, vinxī, vinctum (tr.)   *bind*
vincō, -ere, vīcī, vīctum (tr., intr.)   *conquer, defeat; win*
vinculum, -ī (n)   *bond, fastening; chain*
vindex, -dicis (m)   *defender, champion*
vīnum, -ī (n)   *wine*
violō, -āre (tr.)   *treat with indignity or violence, violate*
vir, virī (m)   *man; male; husband; hero*
vīrēs   (pl. of **vis**)
virgō, -ginis (f)   *girl, maiden*
viridis, -is, -e   *green; unripe; robust; fresh; young*
virtūs, -tūtis (f)   *virtue; courage, valour*
vīrus, -ī (n)   *poison*
vīs (f; irregular)   *force, violence, power,* (pl.) *strength* (7.1/1 note 3)
vīs   (2nd s. pres. ind. act. of **volō, velle**)
vīsō, -ere, vīsī (no sup.; tr.)   *visit*
vīsus, -a, -um   (perf. of **videō**)
vīta, -ae (f)   *life*
vitium, -ī (n)   *moral failing, fault, defect; vice*
vītō, -āre (tr.)   *avoid, shun*
vitrum, -ī (n)   *a blue dye made from leaves, woad*
vīvō, -ere, vixī, victum (intr.)   *live, be alive*
vīvus, -a, -um   *alive, living*
vix (adv.)   *scarcely; with difficulty*
vixī   (perf. of **vīvō**)
vōbiscum   = **cum + vōbīs**
vocō, -āre (tr.)   *call; summon*
volō, -āre (intr.)   *fly*
volō, velle, voluī (no sup.; tr., intr.)   *wish, want, be willing* (15.1/5 and p. 294)
Volscī, -ōrum (m. pl.)   *people of central Italy*
volucris, -is (f)   *bird*
voluntās, -tātis (f)   *choice, wish*
voluptās, -tātis (f)   *pleasure*
volvō, -ere, volvī, volūtum (tr.)   *roll, turn* (tr.)
vorāgō, -ginis (f)   *quagmire*
vōs (pron.)   *you* (pl.) (8.1/1)
vōtīvus, -a, -um   *offered in fulfilment of a vow, votive*

vōtum, -ī (n)   *vow, promise*
voveō, -ēre, vōvī, vōtum (tr.)   *make a vow, vow*
vox, vōcis (f)   *voice; noise* (of birds or animals)
Vulcānus, -ī   *Vulcan* (9.3)
vulgō (adv.)   *commonly*
vulgus, -i (n)   *the common people*
vulnerō, -āre (tr.)   *wound, hurt*
vulnus, -neris (n)   *wound, injury*
vult   (3rd s. pres. ind. act. of **volō, velle**)
vultus, -ūs (m)   *face, expression*

Xerxēs, -is   *Persian king who invaded Greece in 480 BC*

INDEX

For definitions of basic terms and concepts see the **Glossary of grammatical terms**.